The Allure of Nezahualcoyotl

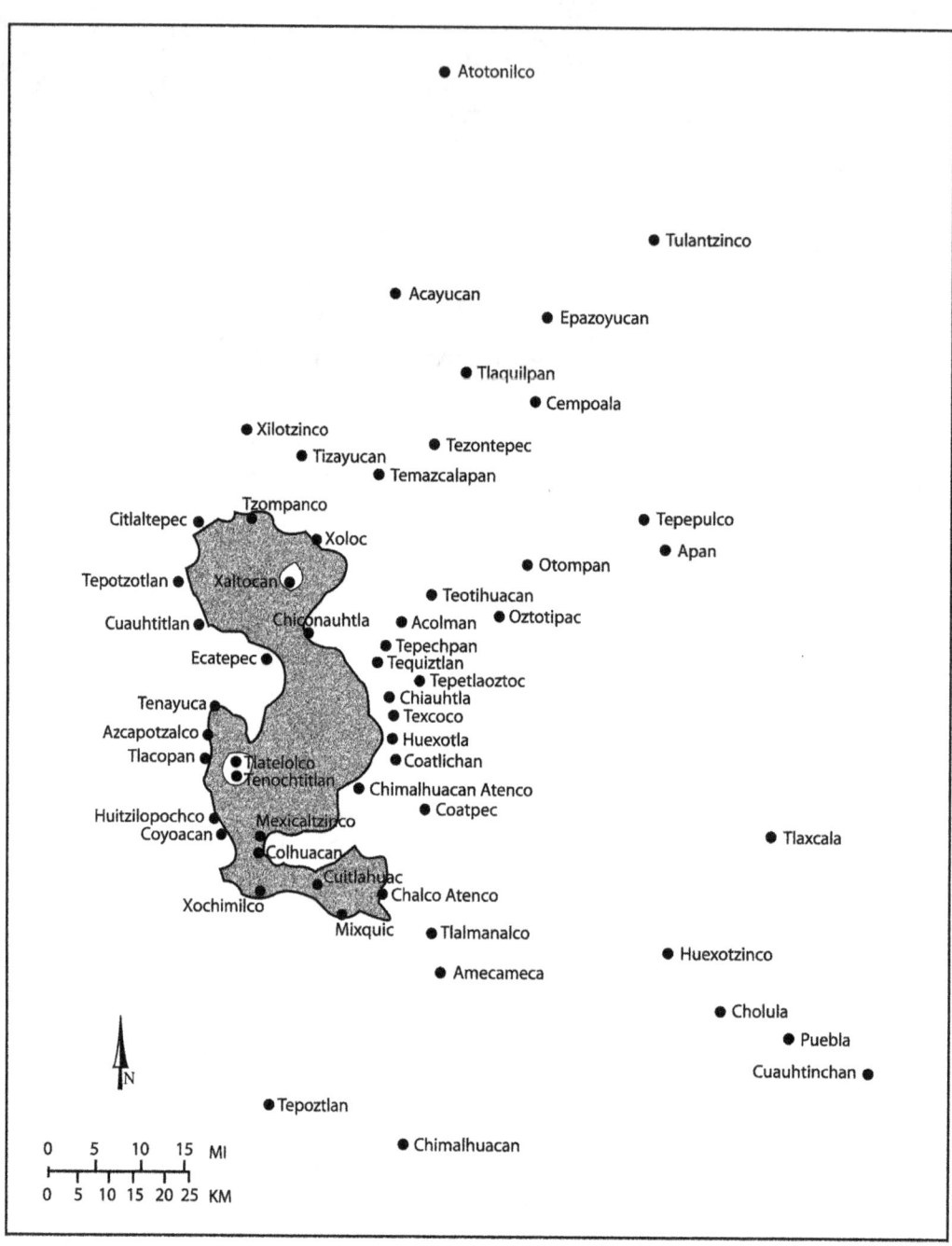

Map of central Mexico in the Aztec period.

The ALLURE of NEZAHUALCOYOTL

Pre-Hispanic History,
Religion, and
Nahua Poetics

Jongsoo Lee

UNIVERSITY OF NEW MEXICO PRESS   ALBUQUERQUE

© 2008 by the University of New Mexico Press
All rights reserved. Published 2008
Printed in the United States of America
First paperbound printing, 2015
Paperbound ISBN: 978-0-8263-4338-3

20 19 18 17 16 15   1 2 3 4 5 6

Library of Congress Cataloging-in-Publication Data

Lee, Jongsoo, 1964–
 The allure of Nezahualcoyotl : pre-Hispanic history, religion, and Nahua poetics / Jongsoo Lee.
  p. cm.
 Includes bibliographical references and index.
 ISBN 978-0-8263-4337-6 (cloth : alk. paper)
 1. Nezahualcóyotl, King of Texcoco, 1402–1472. 2. Aztecs—Kings and rulers—Biography. 3. Texcoco de Mora (Mexico)—Antiquities. 4. Nahuatl poetry—History and criticism. I. Title.
 F1219.75.N49L44 2008
 972'.018—dc22
                    2007048454

An earlier version of chapter 4 appeared as "Analyzing Nezahualcoyotl's Texcoco: Politics, Conquests, and Laws," *Estudios de Cultura Nahuatl* 37 (2006): 231–52. Reproduced by permission. An earlier version of chapter 5 appeared as "Nezahualcoyotl and the Notion of Individual Authorship in Nahuatl Poetry," *Confluencia* 20, no. 1 (2004): 73–86. Parts of chapters 6 and 7 were published in "A Re-Interpretation of Nahuatl Poetics: Rejecting the Image of Nezahualcoyotl as a Peaceful Poet," *Colonial Latin American Review* 12, no. 2 (2003): 232–49. Reproduced by permission. See www.informaworld.com. Part of chapter 8 appeared as "Westernization of Nahuatl Religion: Nezahualcoyotl's Unknown God," *Latin American Indian Literatures Journal* 19, no. 1 (2003): 19–48. Reproduced by permission. An earlier version of the epilogue appeared as "The Colonial Legacy in Cardenal's Poetry: Images of Quetzalcoatl, Nezahualcoyotl, and the Aztecs," *Hispania* 87, no. 1 (2004): 22–31. © 2004 The American Association of Teachers of Spanish and Portuguese, Inc. Reproduced by permission.

Book design and type composition by Melissa Tandysh
Composed in 11/13.5 Adobe Jenson Pro   Display type is Brioso Pro
Cover illustration: Nezahualcoyotl (1402–1472) in a warrior costume, *Códice Ixtlilxochitl* (1996:f. 106r). Reproduced with permission of the Bibliothèque nationale de France.

To Jiyoung and Gia

CONTENTS

List of Illustrations / ix

Acknowledgments / xi

Introduction / 1

Part One: The Sources / 17

CHAPTER ONE: The Sources, Colonial Ideology, and Texcoca Regionalism / 19

Part Two: Revising Pre-Hispanic History / 47

CHAPTER TWO: Founding the Texcoca Dynasty: Chichimec Xolotl and Toltec Topiltzin Quetzalcoatl / 49

CHAPTER THREE: Revisiting Pre-Hispanic Central Mexico: Texcoca Reality before Nezahualcoyotl / 73

CHAPTER FOUR: Reexamining Nezahualcoyotl's Texcoco: Politics, Government, and Legal System / 96

Part Three: Revising the Study of Nahua Poetics / 129

CHAPTER FIVE: Nezahualcoyotl and the Notion of Individual Authorship in Nahua Poetry / 131

CHAPTER SIX: A Reinterpretation of Nahua Poetics: Nahua Cosmogony, Nahua Songs, and Nezahualcoyotl / 151

CHAPTER SEVEN: A Reinterpretation of Nahua Poetic Themes: Ephemerality, War and Sacrifice, and Nezahualcoyotl / 173

Part Four: Revising the Study of Nahua Religion / 191

CHAPTER EIGHT: The Westernization of Nahua Religion: Nezahualcoyotl's Unknown God / 193

CHAPTER NINE: Conclusion / 229

EPILOGUE: Nezahualcoyotl and the Irony of Colonialism in Ernesto Cardenal's Poetry / 233

Notes / 241

Glossary / 254

References / 260

Index / 271

LIST OF ILLUSTRATIONS

FRONTISPIECE.	Map of central Mexico in the Aztec period	ii
FIG. 2.1.	Quinatzin as the first ruler of Texcoco and his reception of the two immigrant groups, Tlailotlaca and Chimalpaneca	51
FIG. 2.2.	Tlotzin's and Quinatzin's foundation of Texcoco	52
FIG. 2.3.	Quinatzin-Tlaltecatzin's founding of Texcoco	53
FIG. 2.4.	Three Chichimec leaders of the eastern Basin of Mexico	55
FIG. 2.5.	Xolotl's arrival at the Basin of Mexico	58
FIG. 2.6.	Xolotl's reception of the three Chichimec leaders	60
FIG. 2.7.	Xolotl's subject city-states	61
FIG. 2.8.	Tenacacaltzin's succession to Nopaltzin and his departure from Tenayuca	62
FIG. 2.9.	Chichimec leaders searching for the Colhua princess	68
FIG. 3.1.	Huetzin receives tribute from Yacanex and his subjects	77
FIG. 3.2.	Chichimec war between Huetzin and Yacanex	79
FIG. 3.3.	Tepanec-Acolhuacan war	80
FIG. 3.4.	Techotlalatzin's attack on Xaltocan	84
FIG. 3.5.	Acolman and its subject cities during Huehue Ixtlilxochitl's and Tezozomoc's reign	85
FIG. 3.6.	Preparation for the Tepanec-Acolhuacan war and the appointment of Nezahualcoyotl as the legitimate heir of Texcoco	88
FIG. 3.7.	Tezozomoc's distribution of Acolhuacan cities after the Tepanec-Acolhuacan war	89
FIG. 3.8.	Tlotzin's Toltecization near Coatlichan	92
FIG. 3.9.	Quinatzin's reception of the Tlailotlaca	93
FIG. 3.10.	Techotlalatzin's reception of the four immigrant groups	94

FIG. 4.1.	Nezahualcoyotl's birth in 1 Rabbit (1402)	98
FIG. 4.2.	A fifteen-year-old Mexica youth goes to the *calmecac* and *cuicacalli*	100
FIG. 4.3.	Itzcoatl's appointment of Nezahualcoyotl as the ruler of Texcoco	101
FIG. 4.4.	Nezahualcoyotl's reception of the craftsmen	104
FIG. 4.5.	Nezahualcoyotl's conquest of Cuauhtitlan with Moctezuma Ilhuicamina and his appointment of Cocopin as the ruler of Tepetlaoztoc	109
FIG. 4.6.	Nezahualcoyotl's conquest of Tulantzinco during the reign of Moctezuma Ilhuicamina	110
FIG. 4.7.	Nezahualcoyotl's arrival at Xicotepec	111
FIG. 4.8.	Nezahualcoyotl's conquest of Xicotepec	112
FIG. 4.9.	Nezahualcoyotl's and Nezahualpilli's court and their tributaries	114
FIG. 4.10.	Three types of adultery and punishments	121
FIG. 4.11.	Three types of robbery and punishments	122
FIG. 4.12.	Nobleman's misconduct and punishment	123
FIG. 4.13.	Mexica examples of misconduct	124
FIG. 4.14.	Mexica punishments for drinking, robbery, and adultery	125
FIG. 4.15.	Mexica allies and the way they begin warfare	126
FIG. 5.1.	Pictorial representation of Cuicatlan (Song Place)	137
FIG. 5.2.	Huehue Ixtlilxochitl's death	144
FIG. 6.1.	Mexica immigration with eight different ethnic groups	157
FIG. 6.2.	Separation of the Mexica from the eight ethnic groups	158
FIG. 6.3.	Huehuetl and its carved images	169
FIG. 8.1.	Nezahualcoyotl's construction of the temple dedicated to Huitzilopochtli	203
FIG. 8.2.	The primitive Templo Mayor in Tenochtitlan: Tlaloc with Huitzilopochtli	204
FIG. 8.3.	Huitzilopochtli's temple in Texcoco	207

ACKNOWLEDGMENTS

Several years ago I encountered beautiful, full-colored images on the wall in a hallway at Indiana University. At first, I thought they were Buddhist paintings of the type that I had been familiar with since I was a little boy, but later I discovered that they were actually excerpts from Aztec and Maya painted books. This incident sparked my curiosity and inspired me to pursue a research agenda focusing on the world of ancient Mexico. This book is the first major product of my research agenda.

There are numerous teachers and friends whom I wish to thank for their comments, suggestions, and encouragement during the process of writing this book. My deepest appreciation goes to Gordon Brotherston who introduced me to the painted books of Mesoamerica and who imparts his knowledge with great enthusiasm and generosity. I have been fortunate to get to know him as a teacher and person. I would like to give my special thanks to Joe Campbell who encouraged me to study Nahuatl and who taught me how to appreciate the language. His suggestions have been a tremendous help in the translations from Nahuatl that appear in this book. However, I am fully responsible for any errors. I thank my friends and colleagues for their support and encouragement. My sincere thanks go to Galen Brokaw who studied Nahuatl together with me and who has always challenged my ideas in productive ways. I appreciate him sharing his perspectives as a specialist in the colonial period and spending hours reading my manuscript. I also thank José Rabasa, Katherine Larson, Kate Myers, Karen and Robert Upchurch, and Eduardo de Douglas for their encouragement and friendship.

I am grateful for the Summer Junior Faculty Fellowships and Small Grants that the University of North Texas awarded me to work on this book. I am also grateful for the following institutions and publishers for allowing me to reproduce images: Museum of the American Indian Heye Foundation, Biblioteca Nacional de Antropología e Historia, Bibliothèque nationale de France, University of Utah Press, University of California Press, José Porrúa Turanzas, Fondo de Cultura Económica, and El Colegio Mexiquense. Initial versions of some of the chapters have been published as articles, as noted on the copyright page, even though they are significantly altered. I wish to thank the editors and publishers of these journals for their permission to reprint my work. My deep appreciation goes to the anonymous reviewers who gave my manuscript such a meticulous reading. Their comments were invaluable. I also thank Luther Wilson and Lisa Pacheco at the University of New Mexico Press for their encouragement and patience.

Finally, I deeply appreciate my parents, who inspired me to be a teacher and gave me endless support from overseas. I also thank my wife, Jiyoung, and my daughter, Gia, who have always supported me with their patience and love. I dedicate this book to them.

Introduction

Nezahualcoyotl, the poet-king of Texcoco (1402–1472), has been described as one of the most important pre-Hispanic figures in Nahua history. From the conquest to the present, he has been portrayed as a symbol of the Aztec civilization and culture in historical as well as literary texts: a great conqueror who built a powerful empire before the conquest; a prudent governor who established an efficient government and created a fair legal system; a patron of the arts who welcomed artists and poets in his city; a poet himself who composed philosophical songs; a sage-prophet who anticipated the destruction of the Aztec world and thus the arrival of the Spaniards; and a devoted religious king who rejected human sacrifice by intuiting an unknown, true god. By focusing on these images of Nezahualcoyotl, many chroniclers, historians, anthropologists, and literary critics have frequently presented him as a clear contrast to the Spanish images of the bloodthirsty Mexica who were mainly interested in conducting human sacrifice and conquering their neighbors. This study, however, argues that all these images of Nezahualcoyotl were invented by a European colonial ideology after the conquest. I demonstrate that Spanish friars who interpreted pre-Hispanic history from a Judeo-Christian perspective created this image of Nezahualcoyotl, and their chronicles have repeatedly served as reliable sources for most Nahua scholars who study this figure. Because of the diverse disciplines of the scholars who take up this topic, including anthropologists, historians, literary critics, philosophers, and those interested in religious studies, this distorted pre-Hispanic history and culture became popular and widely accepted in Nahua studies. By reexamining current images of Nezahualcoyotl, this project proposes to revise the version of pre-Hispanic Mexican history that Western scholarship has continuously "reproduced" for the last five centuries.

Indigenous Past, Judeo-Christian Interpretation, and Nezahualcoyotl

For the indigenous peoples, the conquest meant the brutal destruction of their world system under colonial exploitation, whereas for the Spanish colonizers, it meant the great inauguration of building a New World under Christianity. The Spaniards in the sixteenth century were fervent, religious men and considered the conquest of the Aztec empire as God's providence.[1] They considered themselves the true Christians, God's chosen people, who would facilitate the establishment of the Christian kingdom all over the world (Lafaye 1976:34–35). From the beginning of the colonization of Mexico, the Spanish colonizers used this biblical perspective to justify their military actions and to describe indigenous peoples and civilization. The first conquistadores in Mexico, such as Hernán Cortés (1993:238–40) and Bernal Díaz del Castillo (1992:44–45), represented Aztec society as a satanic world and the conquest of this satanic world as the sacred and obligatory mission of the Spaniards as good Christians.[2] This somewhat simplified description of the indigenous world appeared later in more sophisticated and detailed form, and with broader topics, in the chronicles of friars such as Fray Andrés de Olmos, Fray Toribio de Benavente (better known by his Nahuatl name Motolinia), Fray Bartolomé de Las Casas, Fray Diego Durán, and many others. The Spanish friars of the sixteenth century in New Spain actively engaged in examining and interpreting the indigenous world. They acquired a good command of native languages and were able to access indigenous sources such as oral traditions and pictorial scripts. The friar chroniclers provide richer and more reliable descriptions of Aztec society and thus are undoubtedly significant sources. They, however, selected, excluded, and even invented many aspects of pre-Hispanic indigenous society according to the ideological demands of their religious orders. The main purpose of friars' writing about indigenous society was not to record the past as it was, but to find a better way to evangelize the natives. Fray Bernardino de Sahagún (1997a:17) explained that a doctor should know his patients well enough to cure them, by which he meant that the better the friars understood the indigenous people, the easier they would be able to eradicate indigenous idolatry and convert the natives to Christianity.

The Franciscan religious order was the most dominant in sixteenth-century New Spain. The twelve famous Franciscan friars arrived in New Spain only three years after the conquest in 1524 (Ricard 1995:83–84; Baudot 1995:73).[3] The Franciscans in sixteenth-century New Spain tried to establish an ideal Indian church that would prepare for the arrival of the Messiah and construct the Christian millennial kingdom on earth. They believed that the earthly Christian kingdom would be realized upon the conversion of the Indians.[4] For this reason, they extensively studied indigenous origins and religion and argued that the Indians were one of the tribes that appeared in the Bible and had been controlled by Satan until the arrival of Christianity. On the other hand, the

Franciscans found laudable traditions and practices in indigenous society, such as their governing system and laws, and they tried to prove that the indigenous people were capable human beings and thus could assume a decisive role in the arrival of the millennium. In the chronicles of the Franciscans, the Aztecs appeared as civilized human beings, though ones whose barbarity (e.g., human sacrifice) tainted their advanced civilization, like the Roman pagans before the preaching of Christianity.

Unlike the Franciscans, some friars of other religious orders such as the Dominicans, Augustinians, and Jesuits maintained a diffusionist rather than a millennial approach, arguing that the New World had already been preached to by Saint Thomas, one of the apostles whom Jesus sent to evangelize the world.[5] These friars found several significant similarities between Christian and indigenous religious practices, such as the use of the cross, fasting, and self-sacrifice. Based on these similarities, they argued that the New World had already been preached to, even before the conquest, by a Christian missionary. As Jacques Lafaye (1976:153–54) demonstrates, Spanish friars focused on Quetzalcoatl as the most suitable candidate among the indigenous gods because in his numerous representations, this god bore a cross on his headgear, wore a conical bonnet like the papal tiara, and carried a curved stick shaped like a bishop's crosier. In addition, the religious practices attributed to him, such as rejection of human sacrifice, fasting, singing, and dancing, were also very similar to those of the Christian religion.[6] The Dominican friars in New Spain, such as Fray Diego Durán (1971:57–69), identified one of the main indigenous gods, Quetzalcoatl, with Saint Thomas.[7] Both the millennial approach of the Franciscans and the apostolic approach of other religious orders to indigenous origin and civilization were part of an ongoing and well-known discussion among Spanish friars and intellectuals during the sixteenth and seventeenth centuries.[8]

In the chronicles of the friars, Nezahualcoyotl and his city, Texcoco, began to appear respectively as a wise and prudent king and a cultural center of pre-Hispanic Mexico. The first Franciscan chroniclers, such as Olmos and Motolinia, focused on Nezahualcoyotl's religion and government. Olmos, whose works were collected in several later chronicles, such as those of Fray Gerónimo de Mendieta, Alonso de Zorita, and Fray Juan de Torquemada, briefly describes him as a religious skeptic who doubted indigenous gods and detested religious practices.[9] Motolinia (1971:321–22, 352–59) recorded in detail the rigid but fair practices of Nezahualcoyotl's legal system in Texcoco. By relying on these Franciscan chronicles, the Dominican Las Casas (1967, 2:383–84) also described Nezahualcoyotl as a strict legal practitioner and lawmaker. Motolinia (1971:322) compared him with the Bible's King David due to his strict legal practice. These first descriptions of Nezahualcoyotl by the Spanish friars provided only a fragmentary and selective view of Nezahualcoyotl's life. The reason they were interested in the Texcoca king, however, was evident. By presenting Nezahualcoyotl as a religious skeptic and prudent legal practitioner before the conquest, the friars wanted to demonstrate that the indigenous people, who doubted their own gods and maintained highly advanced institutions, would welcome the new religion and would be capable of accomplishing the friars' dream of establishing the Indian church founded on Christianity. In this context, Las Casas especially, who drew freely from Olmos's and Motolinia's works for his own books, is more noteworthy.[10] The indigenous histories discovered by Las Casas's Franciscan colleagues may have informed his argument about indigenous rationality in the famous debate with Juan Ginés de Sepúlveda at Valladolid in 1550. For Las Casas, presenting Nezahualcoyotl as a fair legal practitioner in the pre-Hispanic Americas could have served as a clear counterexample to the supporters of Sepúlveda who denied the rationality of the Indians.

Judeo-Christian Interpretation, Texcoca Regionalism, and Nezahualcoyotl

The fragmented information on Nezahualcoyotl became more elaborate and detailed in the works of native Texcoca chroniclers, such as Juan Bautista Pomar in the second half of the sixteenth century, and don Fernando de Alva Ixtlilxochitl in the first half of the seventeenth century. The works of these chroniclers have served as the main sources for later scholars who study pre-Hispanic Texcoco and Nezahualcoyotl. These Texcoca mestizo chroniclers began to record a regional history of their own city-state by actively taking advantage of the Judeo-Christian perception of indigenous history that their Spanish masters had previously applied to their chronicles. As Enrique Florescano (1994:125–27) argues, the chronicles of these mestizo writers are examples of "disindigenization," in which the writers "thought and judged Indians by the conquerors' value and followed European models of history by modifying indigenous oral and pictorial traditions." The Texcoca chroniclers Pomar and Alva Ixtlilxochitl provided the most poignant examples of disindigenization, and at the center of their history, Nezahualcoyotl appears as the most important figure, who espoused political and religious values similar to those of the colonizers even before their arrival in central Mexico.

Pomar wrote the *Relación geográfica de Texcoco* (1993) in response to the *Relaciones geográficas* questionnaire made by King Philip II. Pomar (1993: 174–75, 182) perpetuated the portrayal of Nezahualcoyotl as a religious skeptic and a prudent king who enforced a strict legal code, which the Franciscan chroniclers had briefly mentioned. He explained that even though Nezahualcoyotl conducted human sacrifice, he doubted indigenous gods and that Nezahualcoyotl left his religious ideas in his songs. At the end of the sixteenth century, another Texcoca chronicler, Alva Ixtlilxochitl, developed and elaborated on depictions of Nezahualcoyotl by combining the previous Franciscan chronicles and Pomar's chronicle with a theory of apostolic evangelization. Alva Ixtlilxochitl (1997, 1:531–32, 2:8–9) took advantage of the Quetzalcoatl–Saint Thomas myth, which Durán and other Spanish friars had initiated. He presented Quetzalcoatl as a white-bearded Christian saint who brought the symbol of the cross and came to teach natural laws and the practice of fasting to the Indians. In Alva Ixtlilxochitl's chronicles, Nezahualcoyotl appears as the true heir of "civilized" practices, such as law, an efficient government system, peaceful religion, and artistic acts, such as songs that the Christian apostle Quetzalcoatl had supposedly introduced to the New World. In this scheme, Alva Ixtlilxochitl tries to extend Nezahualcoyotl's apostolic role between Quetzalcoatl and the Virgin of Guadalupe, whose cult began to attract the Mexican Creoles in the middle of the seventeenth century. He suggested that Nezahualcoyotl had in some way prepared the way for the Virgin of Guadalupe because it was Nezahualcoyotl who first constructed the causeway toward Tepeyac, where the Virgin originally appeared (1997, 1:445).[11]

At the same time, Alva Ixtlilxochitl tried to make Nezahualcoyotl into a Texcoca analogue of King David, an image to which Motolinia had already alluded. If we compare the descriptions of Nezahualcoyotl in his chronicles with those of King David in the first chronicles of the Bible, both kings share strikingly similar features: both built a strong state with vast territory; they maintained an efficient government system; they were poets who composed seventy or more songs; they were very cautious about maintaining and practicing laws; and they were religious devotees who constructed temples. Thus, as Edmundo O'Gorman (1997:217) points out, Alva Ixtlilxochitl wrote an apologetic history of the Texcoca dynasty and in the center of this history, Nezahualcoyotl's role is most crucial.[12] With such an apologetic Texcoca history, Pomar (1993:136) and Alva Ixtlilxochitl (1997:405) began to distinguish their city, Texcoco, and the Texcoca from the Mexica of Tenochtitlan, who, according to these chroniclers, were the creators of human sacrifice and obligated neighboring city-states to follow their barbarous practice.

If Pomar and Alva Ixtlilxochitl tried to convert their regional ancestor into a Judeo-Christian precursor, the Spanish Franciscan friar Juan de Torquemada presented Nezahualcoyotl from a slightly different point of view. Torquemada repeated almost the same story of Nezahualcoyotl as Alva Ixtlilxochitl, because they seem to have used the same sources, and they claimed each other's chronicles as one of their sources. Like Alva Ixtlilxochitl, Torquemada (1975, 1:155–56, 164–69, 2:353–54) focuses on the advanced government system, legal practices, and artistic activities of Nezahualcoyotl, and he compares this king with King David. This Spanish chronicler, however, rejects the Quetzalcoatl–Saint Thomas myth as a fable and accepts the previous Franciscan view of the indigenous people. Following Franciscan friars such as Motolinia, Olmos, Mendieta, and Sahagún, whose chronicles Torquemada reproduces in his *Monarquía indiana*, he compares indigenous society to that of the Greeks or Romans, in which barbarism and civilization coexisted before the true religion, Christianity, arrived. Torquemada finds in Nezahualcoyotl's peaceful and civilized practices a clear example of the positive side of an indigenous civilization that would embrace Christianity, not like the militaristic, barbarous Mexica who represent the satanic side of indigenous civilization. For both Alva Ixtlilxochitl and Torquemada, Nezahualcoyotl played a significant political, religious, and cultural role that would facilitate the arrival of the true religion, just as King David had before the arrival of Jesus Christ in Israel.

Along with the Judeo-Christian interpretation of Texcoca political, cultural, and religious history, the two main chroniclers of Nezahualcoyotl, Alva Ixtlilxochitl and Torquemada, began to describe Texcoco as both the most politically powerful and the most culturally advanced center of all the city-states in central Mexico before the conquest. In the Texcoca histories of these chroniclers, the Texcoca dynasty originated from the most powerful Chichimec emperor, Xolotl, and played the leading role in the Basin of Mexico for approximately three centuries, from the fall of Tula in the second half of the twelfth century to the middle of the fourteenth century. According to Alva Ixtlilxochitl and Torquemada, the Chichimec leader, Xolotl, established himself in Tenayuca after the fall of the Toltec empire and governed an empire that extended far beyond the Basin of Mexico. Xolotl left this empire to his Texcoca descendants, but approximately four generations later, Nezahualcoyotl's father, Huehue Ixtlilxochitl, lost political control of the empire in the Tepanec-Acolhuacan war (1415–1418) against the rebellious Azcapotzalca ruler Tezozomoc. Nezahualcoyotl, however, recuperated the Texcoca empire fifteen years later by defeating Tezozomoc's son Maxtla with the support of his Chichimec allies. In the Texcoca histories of Alva Ixtlilxochitl and Torquemada, Nezahualcoyotl appears as the central figure because he rebuilt Texcoco, which replaced Tenochtitlan as the political center of the Basin of Mexico.

The Texcoca supremacy that Alva Ixtlilxochitl and Torquemada describe at the beginning of the seventeenth century is, however, exclusively based on a Texcoca interpretation of pre-Hispanic history. From the conquest to the first half of the seventeenth century when these chroniclers were writing, indigenous political units such as *altepeme* (city-states) or ethnic groups in central Mexico had maintained their own historical tradition and had attempted to use it to better their political status within colonial society. The subject towns took advantage of the conquest to cast off their imperial duties while the dominant towns such as Tenochtitlan and Texcoco lost their political power (Lockhart 1992:27). Under the colonial rule, previously dominant city-states competed equally for status with their previous subject cities. In this context, the Texcoca *tlacuiloque* (painter-scribes) began to aggrandize their history in the pictorial scripts in the middle of the sixteenth century, and later Texcoca chroniclers such as Alva Ixtlilxochitl based their works on these scripts. The Spanish friar Torquemada simply followed in his chronicle what the Texcoca historians provided. The contemporary chroniclers of other regions, such as don

Fernando Alvarado Tezozomoc and don Domingo Francisco de San Antón Muñón Chimalpahin Quauhtlehuanitzin, present a quite different history of pre-Hispanic central Mexico.

Creole Patriotism, Mexican Nationalism, and Nezahualcoyotl

The view of Nezahualcoyotl as a great conqueror, while simultaneously a symbol of all positive aspects of pre-Hispanic indigenous civilization, created by Spanish friars and later developed by Texcoca chroniclers, was widely accepted by Creole patriots and Mexican nationalists. From their emergence as a social group in colonial New Spain, the Creoles suffered Spanish imperial prejudice based on the theory of climatic determinism, according to which European men degenerated on American soil. Based solely on their birthplace, for example, Mexican Creoles were refused high political and religious posts in colonial society. As Enrique Florescano (1994) and David A. Brading (1985, 1991) explain, at the end of the seventeenth century, Mexican Creoles distinguished themselves from the Spaniards by trying to establish their unique identity through defending and promoting their native land and history against imperial prejudice and practice. They focused on the pre-Hispanic indigenous tradition and claimed it as a part of the glorious past of their homeland. As descendants of the conquistadores, however, Mexican Creoles had to find a way to harmoniously unite indigenous and Hispanic traditions, or at least to establish a certain connection between the two. To incorporate the indigenous past into a Creole history in Mexico, the Mexican Creoles took advantage of the sixteenth- and seventeenth-century chronicles of the friars and the native noble elites, both indigenous and mestizo, who viewed the pre-Hispanic period from a Judeo-Christian perspective. Mexican Creoles freely adapted Franciscan millennialism and the apostolic evangelization, depending on their political and religious needs. However, they usually tried to promote the pre-Hispanic indigenous world as highly advanced and civilized, intentionally connecting themselves to pre-Hispanic indigenous civilization. By doing so, Mexican Creoles were able to proudly say that their history was as old as, and at the same time as glorious as, that of their European counterparts.

The most significant chroniclers who provided Mexican Creoles with a theoretical background were the Franciscan friar Torquemada and the Texcoca mestizo chronicler Alva Ixtlilxochitl. Both chroniclers made a smooth transition from the pre-Hispanic period, through the conquest, to contemporary history. In the beginning of the seventeenth century, Torquemada elevated the pre-Hispanic indigenous past to the level of classical antiquity by arguing that the Christian evangelization redeemed the Indians from their paganism. In this process of the evangelization, it was not the conquistadores but rather the first Franciscans who truly introduced Christianity to the natives (Florescano 1994:187–88; Brading 1985:9). In this scheme, New Spain inherited, or at least did not need to reject, the entire indigenous past and at the same time was founded on the Christian tradition, which Creole intellectuals—most of whom were priests—more than welcomed. Naturally, Nezahualcoyotl, who allegedly practiced a cultural and religious system similar to that of the Christian tradition, appeared as the main focus of the Creole texts.

There were, however, many other Creoles who believed in the Quetzalcoatl–Saint Thomas myth and were therefore able to extend the Christian foundation of New Spain to the pre-Hispanic period, which Alva Ixtlilxochitl had previously argued for in the late sixteenth century by depicting Nezahualcoyotl as the heir of Quetzalcoatl. The Creoles of the second half of the seventeenth century were developing another important Christian symbol, the Virgin of Guadalupe, and attempted to elaborate this Marian cult using apostolic evangelization theory. They began to present the pre-Hispanic apostle Quetzalcoatl as a precursor of the Virgin of Guadalupe, whom the Indian Juan Diego encountered in Tepeyac.[13] Alva Ixtlilxochitl's work presented Nezahualcoyotl as a link between Quetzalcoatl and the Virgin of Guadalupe. The Creoles in the seventeenth and eighteenth centuries who followed the Franciscan, apostolic, or the Virgin of Guadalupe tradition often drew from whichever tradition most adequately served their ideological needs.

In the second half of the seventeenth century, don Carlos de Sigüenza y Góngora is probably the most important Creole who exhibited an interest in the indigenous past, and he based his work on that of Alva Ixtlilxochitl. Up to this point, the Quetzalcoatl–Saint Thomas myth had been an abstract hypothesis based on Judeo-Christian history, but Sigüenza y Góngora attempted to verify it through archaeological research, indigenous pictorial texts, and oral traditions (Lafaye 1976:64). In this formulation of the Quetzalcoatl–Saint Thomas myth, the strong influence of Alva Ixtlilxochitl's descriptions of Nezahualcoyotl is evident. In Sigüenza y Góngora's Quetzalcoatl–Saint Thomas myth, Nezahualcoyotl appeared as a follower of Quetzalcoatl–Saint Thomas and expressed his dedication to the omnipotent god through his songs. In his major work, *Paraíso occidental* (1995:52–53), Sigüenza y Góngora included an oration dedicated to Nezahualcoyotl's unknown god. An Italian scholar, Lorenzo Boturini Benaducci (1990:23–24, 228), who was able to access Alva Ixtlilxochitl's manuscript, which Sigüenza y Góngora had preserved, described Nezahualcoyotl as an expert in astrology, a prophet who anticipated the conquest, and a legislator who fairly administered the law. Creole historian Mariano Fernández de Echeverría y Veytia (1944:212), who closely followed Alva Ixtlilxochitl's history of pre-Hispanic Mexico, fully accepted the Quetzalcoatl–Saint Thomas myth and presented Nezahualcoyotl as the disciple of Quetzalcoatl. Mexican Creoles in the eighteenth century, however, faced a more sophisticated challenge from the European Enlightenment.

Famous English and French enlightened philosophers such as George-Louis Leclerc Comte de Buffon, Corneille de Pauw, William Robertson, and

Guillaume-Thomas Raynal "proclaimed a peculiar degeneration of American nature, discovered a natural inferiority in native American creation of works of culture, and attacked the religious fanaticism of the Spaniards" (Florescano 1994:190).[14] This criticism of the American and indigenous people also came from Spanish enlightened philosophers and politicians of the Bourbon dynasty in Spain. They described both the Aztecs and Incas as barbarians whose political tyranny, sanguinary religion, and primitive and crude artistic works demonstrated their own exceptional inferiority. To counter imperial prejudice and enlightened philosophers, Mexican Creoles actively defended their native land and history. One of the most important Creole projects in the eighteenth century was to save the indigenous past from European calumnies. They reevaluated the indigenous past, emphasizing the excellence of indigenous ruling, legal, cultural, and artistic systems and presented them as counterexamples against European denunciation. The most popular method the Creoles used to prove the high level of indigenous society was to compare it to European equivalents. Among many pre-Hispanic heroes and kings, Nezahualcoyotl was the ideal and stood out the most. Numerous Creole historians such as Friars Juan José de Eguiara y Eguren (1944:87–88), Joseph Joaquín Granados y Gálvez (1987:42–49, 90–94), and Francisco Javier Clavijero (1991:113–16) emphasized Nezahualcoyotl's advanced and efficient government institutions, religious ideas, and artistic activities, which demonstrated the American native's high level of intellect and thus contradicted the climatic determinism and American exceptionality propagated by European Enlightenment philosophers. By doing so, the Creoles, as natives of America and descendants of the glorious past, could then argue that they had a political, intellectual, religious, and literary past as advanced as the Europeans.[15] Later, when these Mexican Creoles converted their patriotism for their homeland into a nationalist ideology, Nezahualcoyotl continued to be one of the most popular and significant pre-Hispanic figures, but now representing a glorious and memorable national past in newly independent Mexico.

Mexican Creoles played a decisive role in the independence movements at the end of the eighteenth and the beginning of the nineteenth centuries. They formed the prominent social group with military power and intellectual inclination to build a nation. Many Creoles belonged either to the liberal party, which supported a democratic republic based on eighteenth-century Enlightenment politics, or to the conservative party, which supported a traditional monarchy like that of Spain.[16] Both groups were very different in terms of their ideal political system, but they both despised indigenous people and their past as barbarous and savage. Against these major groups, there existed some Creole patriots such as Fray Servando Teresa de Mier and Carlos María de Bustamante who promoted pre-Hispanic heritage as a valuable national tradition, arguing that the independent nation should be based on the indigenous tradition (Brading 1985:48–50, 1991:601–2).

In order to promote Mexican independence, the Mexican Creole patriots such as Mier developed the tradition of the Virgin of Guadalupe. Mier (1946:47–54) argued that the cape on which her image was painted did not originally belong to Juan Diego but rather to Quetzalcoatl–Saint Thomas, who left it in Tepeyac after preaching the Gospel to the New World. According to this theory, the Creoles, natives of the land in which Saint Thomas had preached before the arrival of the Spaniards, have more of a right to rule their own land than the Spaniards.[17] In this Creole patriot's nationalist discourse, Nezahualcoyotl appears as the heir of Quetzalcoatl's legacy, because this indigenous king's peaceful religious practices and his prohibition of human sacrifice are presented as clear examples of the kinds of teachings that Quetzalcoatl–Saint Thomas had introduced to the New World before the conquest (Mier 1990:587, 591–92, 669). On the other hand, other Creole patriots such as Carlos María de Bustamante (1970:introduction) promoted the pre-Hispanic indigenous political system as the model for independent Mexico. In his writing, Nezahualcoyotl appears as the most righteous and ideal governor and thus as a role model for Mexican political leaders.

After independence in 1821, Mexico suffered a series of civil wars between liberals and conservatives. In the first half of the nineteenth century, the North American historian William H. Prescott published his famous book, *History of the Conquest of Mexico*.[18] This book was translated into Spanish and published in Mexico City in the middle of the nineteenth century, and it motivated many Mexican scholars to take an interest in Aztec and colonial history. In his book, Prescott (n.d.:99–116) extols the conquest as the victory of Christianity over paganism and of the civilized Europeans over the barbaric Indians. However, he presents Nezahualcoyotl as one of the true great men in human history who maintained the most civilized political, legal, religious, and cultural systems despite the domination of the barbarous and sanguinary Mexica.

In the second half of the nineteenth century, Nezahualcoyotl continued to appear as a pre-Hispanic sage and the city of Texcoco as a center of pre-Hispanic indigenous civilization. Manuel Orozco y Berra (1960, 1:121, 299–300) repeated the account of Nezahualcoyotl's highly advanced governing system and thus presented his city, Texcoco, in opposition to the capital of the warlike Mexica, Tenochtitlan. At the same time, Nezahualcoyotl began to appear as a Mexican hero and as the most representative Nahua poet in pre-Hispanic times. José Joaquín Pesado makes a first attempt to incorporate pre-Hispanic literature into Mexican national literature by publishing pre-Hispanic poems translated into Spanish (Campos 1998:xii). In his book, *Las Aztecas* (1998:39–62), Pesado paid special attention to Nezahualcoyotl by collecting several of his poems in a separate chapter. José María Vigil (1957) studied Nezahualcoyotl and published a biography that included songs attributed to him. He described this indigenous king as one of the most illuminated figures in Mexican national history. During this period, Nezahualcoyotl, as a national hero, began to gain international fame as a poet. Uruguayan scholar Pedro Mascaró y Sousa (1972) compared Nezahualcoyotl's poetry to European poetry and argued that Nezahualcoyotl was a universal elegiac poet. A North American anthropologist and linguist, Daniel G. Brinton, translated the *Cantares mexicanos* and published them in *Ancient Nahuatl Poetry* (1887), which presents Nezahualcoyotl as the most distinguished Nahua poet and includes several poems that have traditionally been attributed to him and that repeatedly appear in historical texts.

Current Nahua Studies and Nezahualcoyotl

Nahua scholars in the twentieth century significantly improved our understanding of indigenous history, culture, religion, philosophy, and literature before the European invasion. They recognized the importance of original indigenous sources such as pre-Hispanic monuments, pictorial scripts, and Nahuatl alphabetic texts. They extensively studied, translated, and used these sources and thus were able to provide a more accurate interpretation of pre-Hispanic indigenous society. Even in this new era of Nahua studies, however, there still exist significant misinterpretations or misrepresentations of Aztec culture and history because many scholars rely primarily on the chronicles of the Spanish friars, mestizos, and Creoles, whose writings adopt Judeo-Christian historical perspectives and/or certain indigenous groups' regionalism. I argue that current Nahua studies related to Nezahualcoyotl, on such subjects as Nahua history, poetry, and religion, contain some highly conspicuous misrepresentations and are in urgent need of revision.[19]

The study of Nezahualcoyotl from the twentieth century to the present has flourished more than in any previous period. Innumerable biographies of this king have been published, and many historians, anthropologists, literary critics, and creative writers have studied his traditionally recognized achievements in pre-Hispanic politics, law, religion, philosophy, and the arts. Most of them used firsthand sources such as pictorials and Nahua song texts, but they continue to rely on Alva Ixtlilxochitl, Torquemada, or Creole historians' texts and research to interpret those original sources. Thus, they merely repeat and reinforce the depictions of Nezahualcoyotl that were based on a Judeo-Christian perception of history and Texcoca regionalism after the conquest.

In Mexico, the Mexican Revolution (1910–1920) sparked a national interest in the indigenous past. The Mexican government supported the study of indigenous history, leading to significant developments in Mexican archaeology and anthropology. Many leading anthropologists and historians of pre-Hispanic civilizations, such as Manuel Gamio, Alfonso Caso, Wigberto Jiménez Moreno, Rubén Campos, and Angel María Garibay K., emerged in this context.[20] Among them, Campos and Garibay significantly developed the study of Aztec literary production. They paid special attention to the original Nahuatl texts and translated them into Spanish. Campos (1936), who lamented the inequality and the miserable situation of indigenous people, even after the Mexican Revolution, presented Aztec literary texts as a clear example of the advanced level of pre-Hispanic civilization. In the poetry section, he collected all the poems that were traditionally attributed to Nezahualcoyotl and also translated into Spanish about thirty Nahua songs from the *Cantares mexicanos*. Of these songs, Campos attributed two to Nezahualcoyotl. Campos's study appeared to replicate what Brinton had done about thirty years earlier, but it made a further contribution to the study of Nahua poetry in that it was the first direct translation from Nahuatl that identified Nezahualcoyotl as the author of some of the poems. Garibay (1992, 1993), however, made the most influential contribution to the study of Nezahualcoyotl and more generally to the study of Nahua poetry and literature. Before him, the historians and chroniclers who dealt with Nezahualcoyotl or included his poems in historical texts did not present any evidence to show that this king was actually a poet. They included at most one or two fragmented poems attributed to Nezahualcoyotl, which were supposedly translated from Nahuatl into Spanish. By translating the existing Nahua song texts, the *Cantares mexicanos* and the *Romances de los señores de la Nueva España*, into Spanish in the early 1940s, Garibay was able to formulate arguments identifying many pre-Hispanic poets, among whom he presented Nezahualcoyotl as the most prolific and representative. His work, however, is not always reliable because he interprets and translates Nahua texts based on colonial chronicles and thus inadvertently perpetuates the European perspective that informs those texts. Garibay's study of Nahua literature and poetry and of Nezahualcoyotl influenced later literary critics such as José Alcina Franch (1957, 1968) and Miguel León-Portilla, whose works will be examined in detail later.

While twentieth-century Mexican scholars focused on the role of Nezahualcoyotl as a poet, German and American historians and anthropologists stressed Nezahualcoyotl's nonliterary activities described in the colonial chronicles. The American anthropologist George C. Vaillant summarizes the general role of Nezahualcoyotl as typically described during the colonial period:

> In 1472, early in the reign of Axayacatl, the life of a great figure in American Indian history, Nezahualcoyotl, came to an end. This Texcoca chief had begun his manhood in political exile fleeing from Tepanec vengeance, but had fought and intrigued his way back into power. He even restored the fortunes of his people who, in the previous century, had rivaled the Culhuacanos in the formative years of Aztec civilization. Nezahualcoyotl had a broad judicial sense which enabled him successfully to elaborate the administrative structure of a far-flung realm. Since the Texcoca, before the Tepanec domination in 1419–28, already had a chain of tribute-paying vassals, this resumption

of control in after years was not so much a conquest as the forceful exercise of due right.

He took a lively interest in the construction of temples and public buildings so that, for all its tattered decay today, Texcoco was one of the most imposing cities on the central Plateau. His palace near by and his bath, hewn from the solid rock of Texcotcingo, are visible proof of the rich luxury of his life.

Nezahualcoyotl took a profound interest in religion and arts. He transformed theological speculation into a philosophy of religion and worshipped a single god, the force through which nature manifests itself and from which the lesser gods derived their power and being. He encouraged the arts and in his own right attained great renown as a poet and orator. The lore of the stars fascinated him, and he had a deep knowledge of the astrological astronomy of his day and age. In contrast to the bleakly austere records of the Tenochca overlords, his career was a model of wise administration. Not the least of Nezahualcoyotl's achievements was his keeping the peace with his arrogant island ally, Tenochtitlan, which was ever ready by intrigue, murder or open warfare to add to its wealth and power. (Vaillant 1953:101–2)

Vaillant reproduces the same colonial descriptions of Nezahualcoyotl that first appeared four centuries earlier in the sixteenth century. The German historian Walter Krickerberg (1995:105, 107–8) studied Nezahualcoyotl's advanced legal system, architectural achievements such as dikes and the temple in Tetzcotzinco, and the religious practice of the unknown god. Krickerberg also traced Texcoca genealogy based on Texcoca pictorial codices in his narration of Chichimec history. Nezahualcoyotl, the inheritor of Xolotl, the great lawmaker, and the religious reformer, continued to be the focus of leading scholars in the second half of the twentieth century. Burr Cartwright Brundage (1972:13–18, 62–65) recorded Texcoca supremacy over central Mexico before and during Nezahualcoyotl's reign, and he also emphasized Nezahualcoyotl's unknown god as a religious system unique to Texcoco (Brundage 1979:67–68). Jerome A. Offner (1983) examined Texcoca law and politics and presented Nezahualcoyotl as the legislator and governor who maintained the most advanced system, quite different from that of Tenochtitlan, in pre-Hispanic Mexico. Offner's work had a significant impact on studies of the Aztec legal system, such as that of Richard F. Townsend (1992:80–81, 84–85).

The most important scholar to study Nezahualcoyotl in the twentieth century is the Mexican anthropologist, historian, and literary critic Miguel León-Portilla. As a disciple of Garibay, he continued the line of research initiated by his mentor. León-Portilla identified more poets and began to reinterpret pre-Hispanic culture and history starting in the 1960s. León-Portilla argued that poems in Nahuatl (*in xochitl in cuicatl*) in the *Cantares mexicanos* and the

Romances should be understood as symbolic representations of a peaceful indigenous ideology inherited from Quetzalcoatl before the conquest and thus as a clear contrast to the sanguinary and militaristic ideology of the Mexica and their god Huitzilopochtli. León-Portilla presented the composers of the poems as *tlamatinime* (wise men) who opposed human sacrifice and military dominance in Aztec society. At the center of this interpretation, he presented Nezahualcoyotl as the most civilized and peaceful sage-poet based on an interpretation of his poetry as an articulation of an ideology of nonviolence. In León-Portilla's works, all the positive images of Nezahualcoyotl formed from the conquest to the present were compiled, systematically reorganized, and verified. His works were, however, unfortunately based on the chronicles of Alva Ixtlilxochitl and Spanish friars such as Motolinia and Torquemada. Nevertheless, León-Portilla's translations and studies have decisively contributed to making Nezahualcoyotl one of the most popular pre-Hispanic, as well as Mexican national, figures in present times.

León-Portilla's major works, such as *Los antiguos mexicanos a través de sus crónicas y cantares* (1996), *La filosofía nahuatl estudiada en sus fuentes* (1966), *Trece poetas del mundo azteca* (1967b), and *Quince poetas del mundo nahuatl* (1994), were published and translated into various foreign languages, and innumerable Nahua scholars, literary critics, and creative writers have relied on León-Portilla's study and translation of Nahua poetry. Most of these studies include Netzahualcoyotl's songs and present them as poignant examples of Nahua philosophy, which was dedicated chiefly to the beauty and ephemerality of earthly life and thus contrasted starkly with Mexica practices such as human sacrifice and military expeditions. In the Spanish-speaking world, many literary critics such as José Luis Martínez (1996) and creative writers such as José Emilio Pacheco (1973) and Ernesto Cardenal (1992) were inspired by León-Portilla's study and translation of Nahua poetry. The immediate translation of León-Portilla's works on Nezahualcoyotl and Nahua poetry into other languages also captured the attention of numerous leading historians, anthropologists, and literary critics. Georges Baudot (1979:53–56) and Le Clezio (1993:111–15) in the French-speaking world and Francis F. Berdan (2005:162–65), Michael D. Coe and Rex Koontz (2002:222–24), Michael E. Smith (2003:262–65), Davíd Carrasco (1998:164–66, 2003:136–37), Hugh Thomas (1993:13–14), and Benjamin Keen (1971:25–26, 38–48) in the English-speaking world recycled selected or entire descriptions of Nezahualcoyotl as the representative poet and *tlamatini* that León-Portilla had proposed.

Rethinking Nezahualcoyotl and Pre-Hispanic History, Poetics, and Religion

Only a few scholars have challenged the colonial depictions of Nezahualcoyotl that originated in the Judeo-Christian interpretation and the perspective of

Texcoca regionalism. Alfredo Chavero (1958:xlvii–xlviii) simply mentioned that Alva Ixtlilxochitl had invented a history for his own hometown and that the two poems that Alva Ixtlilxochitl attributed to Nezahualcoyotl were fake, but he did not provide any supporting evidence. He also suggested that Nezahualcoyotl's reign should be understood as part of Texcoca regional history, not as the most "civilized" representation of pre-Hispanic Mexico (1958:666–73). In the twentieth century, Gordon Brotherston (1972) and John Bierhorst (1985) challenged the description of Nezahualcoyotl as a poet by arguing the impossibility of detecting individual poets in the composing process and performance of Nahua songs. Nigel Davies (1980:42–71, 1987:42–47), on the other hand, challenged the version of pre-Hispanic history based on the Texcoca dynasty from Xolotl to Nezahualcoyotl by arguing that Texcoca pictorial sources and chroniclers invented a genealogical connection between the Chichimec hero, Xolotl, and their Texcoca ancestors. Thus, Davies even doubted the existence of the Texcoca empire described in Texcoca sources and widely accepted by later historians, even to the present. These studies, however, only partially challenged the canonical descriptions of Nezahualcoyotl and in many cases are in need of revision themselves. By reviewing the history of and research about Nezahualcoyotl from the colonial period to the present, I identify eight elements that need reconsideration. Each chapter of this book focuses on one of these eight elements, which are organized into four sections: (1) sources, (2) pre-Hispanic history, (3) Nahua poetry, and (4) Nahua religion.

The first section reexamines the sources of the main chronicles about Nezahualcoyotl and demonstrates that the canonical descriptions of Nezahualcoyotl were derived mainly from Texcoca sources, influenced by the political and religious interests of the chroniclers. The second section consists of three chapters and deals with pre-Hispanic history. I challenge the notion that the two foundational figures of the Texcoca dynasty were Quetzalcoatl and Xolotl. Both were symbolic cultural and political figures of the ethnic groups or city-states in pre-Hispanic central Mexico, but I argue that Texcoca scribes appropriated them from other regional groups by making them the exclusive founders of their own dynasty. This argument naturally leads to a reexamination of Texcoca culture and politics before and during Nezahualcoyotl's reign. I argue that before Nezahualcoyotl, Texcoco did not have much military or cultural supremacy over its neighboring cities. In addition, I argue that the Texcoco of Nezahualcoyotl's time participated in the same cultural and political institutions that characterized the Mexica. By demonstrating that there were many similarities rather than differences between Texcoco and Tenochtitlan in terms of political and cultural traditions, and that Nezahualcoyotl himself actively introduced the Mexica system to his city, I seriously challenge the idea that Nezahualcoyotl's Texcoco maintained a ruling system very different from that of the Mexica in Tenochtitlan.

The third section revises the current study of Nahua poetry. I argue that the method of seeking individual authorship of Nahua songs was based on the European perception of poetry composition and was motivated by Alva Ixtlilxochitl's attempt to make Nezahualcoyotl into an analogue of the biblical King David, the well-known composer of psalms. Moreover, I demonstrate that León-Portilla's canonical interpretation of Nahua poetry as a peaceful act, in contrast to Mexica religious and military practices, is impossible, because Nahua poetry itself was created and performed from the perspective of Nahua cosmology, and thus promoted battles and human sacrifice regardless of its regional origin. The fourth section reexamines Nezahualcoyotl's religious practices and his unknown god. I present many examples that contradict earlier descriptions of Nezahualcoyotl's unknown god and his rejection of human sacrifice. I demonstrate that both colonial and modern arguments or explications that present Nahua songs as evidence of a belief in a single, "unknown" god and an articulation of a peaceful ideology are misinterpretations. In addition, there is no historical evidence to confirm the construction of the famous temple dedicated to an unknown god. Along with the four main sections of this study, I include an epilogue in which I examine the poetry of the Nicaraguan poet Ernesto Cardenal as the most representative example of the ideological use of colonial descriptions and current Nahua scholarship on Nezahualcoyotl. As a liberation theologian, Cardenal introduces Nezahualcoyotl as a universal symbol of peace that contrasts with any kind of viciousness in human history such as Aztec human sacrifice, North American capitalism, or Latin American dictatorships.

Owing to the images that colonial chroniclers invented, Nezahualcoyotl has now become one of the most well-known pre-Hispanic indigenous figures in Mexico as well as in the world. In Mexico, there is a *colonia* named after Nezahualcoyotl, and indigenous poets celebrate an annual poetry contest in his honor. In addition, Nezahualcoyotl is the only pre-Hispanic historical figure to appear on Mexican currency: he appears on the one-hundred-peso bill along with a fragment of his poem. Nezahualcoyotl undoubtedly gained his position as a national hero as a part of everyday life in Mexico. Outside of Mexico, in the United States and Europe, Nezahualcoyotl is widely considered the symbolic figure of pre-Hispanic indigenous civilization. From history to literature courses about pre-Hispanic Mexico, scholars and students study Nezahualcoyotl as the most representative ruler, poet, and philosopher. The current images of Nezahualcoyotl, however, stem from colonial manipulation, and thus I would argue that the more Nezahualcoyotl's images gain validity, the more urgently scholars and students need to pay attention to their colonial origins.

part one

The Sources

THE SCHOLARS WHO STUDY NEZAHUALCOYOTL AND HIS CITY, TEXCOCO, draw their information mainly from the chronicles of Spanish friars such as Toribio de Benavente (Motolinia), Andrés de Olmos, and Juan de Torquemada and some of the Texcoca chroniclers such as Juan Bautista Pomar and don Fernando de Alva Ixtlilxochitl. Most scholars, however, ignore the colonial context in which these chronicles were written and in which their primary indigenous sources were reproduced. By reviewing the possible sources and informants for the main chronicles about Nezahualcoyotl, chapter 1 demonstrates how the major chroniclers of Nezahualcoyotl selected and manipulated their sources according to European historical criteria and Texcoca regionalism in the context of colonial society.

CHAPTER ONE

The Sources, Colonial Ideology, and Texcoca Regionalism

Long before the European invasion, the natives of central Mexico, like other peoples of Mesoamerica, were already recording their history using pictorial script. The painter-scribes, tlacuiloque, painted or wrote the indigenous pictorial texts, *tlacuilolli*, either on native paper or on animal skin.[1] In addition, they preserved their history by memory, which could be either parallel or complementary to pictorial histories or independent accounts. After the conquest, this indigenous historical tradition survived and a large number of pictorial codices were produced following the pre-Hispanic historiographical tradition. In addition to producing pictorial codices and continuing their oral traditions, the indigenous people quickly adapted European alphabets to transcribe these texts. Moreover, there emerged a new hybrid textual tradition that combined native pictorial and European alphabetical modes, such as that exhibited in the *Códice Aubin* (1963).[2]

On the other hand, indigenous history written in Spanish from within the European historiographical tradition began with the conquest. In their letters and chronicles, the conquistadores included comments on native politics, religion, customs, and geography of the New World. As explained briefly in the introduction, this European historiography began more systematically with the arrival of Spanish friars who had been trained in sixteenth-century humanism. In the 1530s and 1540s, with the help of indigenous informants, these Spanish friars, such as Toribio de Benavente (Motolinia) and Andrés de Olmos, started writing indigenous histories based on pictorial codices and oral accounts.[3] They also began to teach the European alphabet to the sons of the ruling class as part of their efforts to convert them. Under Spanish rule, then, alphabetic literacy spread to many indigenous people. As a result, by the end of the sixteenth century historical books solely in alphabetic script began to replace native pictorial codices. By the early seventeenth century, when major indigenous and Spanish chroniclers such as don Fernando de Alva Ixtlilxochitl, don Fernando Alvarado Tezozomoc, don Domingo de San Antón Muñón Chimalpahin, and Fray Juan de Torquemada produced their alphabetic texts, the pictographic mode had virtually disappeared (Glass 1975:4).[4]

The available sources used by the chroniclers to write pre-Hispanic indigenous history vary depending on the time period when they were writing. For instance, indigenous pictorial texts and oral traditions were the primary sources for Motolinia and Olmos in the 1530s and 1540s, while at the end of the sixteenth century and the beginning of the seventeenth century, Alva Ixtlilxochitl, Torquemada, Alvarado Tezozomoc, and Chimalpahin drew from alphabetic texts in Nahuatl, as well as in Spanish, that European and Europeanized chroniclers had written, in addition to the surviving indigenous oral traditions and pictorial texts. As many scholars demonstrate (Adorno 1986, 1989a, 1989b; Florescano 1994:100–83; Klor de Alva 1989; Mignolo 1989a, 1989b, 1993a, 1993b), however, all the sources employed by the chroniclers were collected, painted, written, interpreted, and even transformed during the colonial period, and thus in one way or another they should be understood in that context. Only certain oral traditions and some pictorial texts survived and were reproduced after the conquest, while others were prohibited, and those who violated the prohibition were severely punished. At the same time, the primary indigenous historiographical traditions of pictography and oral performance lost their unique role and meaning. The form, historical values, and topics of indigenous historiography were evaluated according to the criteria of European historiography. This colonization of indigenous historiography is manifested especially in the indigenous history of Spanish friars because (1) they initiated the transpositioning of pictorial scripts and oral traditions into alphabetic texts; (2) they introduced a European methodology of collecting information exclusively based on European historiography; and (3) they established criteria to judge and record indigenous history and thus provided later chroniclers with a ideological framework for understanding indigenous history. The Spanish friars Olmos and Motolinia, who were the first chroniclers of indigenous history in alphabetic texts, described Nezahualcoyotl as a lawmaker and a religious skeptic, and they served as a model for later historians.

Motolinia and Olmos collected their data from the native informants who could read pictorial scripts or recite indigenous history by memory. As Louise Burkhart explains, the Spanish friars controlled all the processes of collecting the data by deciding what would be investigated and recorded:

> In discussing their culture, the colonial Nahuas did not speak freely, for Europeans created the context within which information was set down. They sought answers to particular questions, determining not only what matters would be recorded but the form the records would take. Investigators, especially those who were priests, tended to

respond to what they learned about indigenous religion with shock or zeal, depending on their own values. (Burkhart 1989:6–7)

The questions that the Spaniards asked constrained the responses by the indigenous informants, thus limiting the information collected to certain aspects of the past that happened to conform with European expectations. Burkhart (1989:7) also suggests that the indigenous informants intentionally modified the information that was explicitly solicited by the Spaniards: "Even if the Indians were encouraged to be honest, they soon understood what their interlocutors thought about some of their most cherished traditions." Burkhart focuses on the context of the conversation between the colonizers and the colonized in which the latter could preserve their "cherished traditions" by disguising them as analogous or even equivalent to those of the colonizers. In addition to the asymmetrical power relationship between the Indians and the Spaniards, regional antagonisms between colonized indigenous groups themselves who were competing for political advantage within the colonial system also influenced the specifics of indigenous histories produced by the informants from different areas. Each indigenous group surely promoted its traditions as the best or the most representative of pre-Hispanic Mexico.

This indigenous history, doubly manipulated by the Spanish interlocutors and the indigenous informants, is frequently misleading. I present the representations of Nezahualcoyotl in the colonial chronicles as the most poignant example of this doubly manipulated indigenous history. Given what is known of the pre-Hispanic period and the religious and political context of the colonial period, the image of Nezahualcoyotl as a lawgiver, fair legal practitioner, and religious skeptic first formulated by the Spanish friars and further developed by later Texcoca chroniclers is speciously convenient and should raise serious questions about the sources of this image.

Motolinia (Toribio de Benavente), Andrés de Olmos, and Their Sources

As the first chroniclers of indigenous history, Motolinia and Olmos state that their accounts were based on indigenous oral traditions and/or pictorial codices. In the preface of his book, *Memoriales*, dedicated to the Count of Benavente, don Antonio Pimentel, Motolinia writes that the natives had their own way of recording their history:

> Había entre estos naturales cinco libros, como dije de figuras y caracteres: el primero hablaba de los años y tiempos: el segundo de los días y fiestas que tenían en todo el año: el tercero que hablaba de los sueños y de los agüeros, embaimientos y vanidades en que creían: el cuarto era del bautismo y nombres que daban a los niños: el quinto es de los

ritos, ceremonias y agüeros que tenían en los matrimonios. Los cuatro de estos libros no los ha de creer vuestra ilustrísima señoría como los Evangelios, porque ni los escribieron Juanes, ni Lucas, ni Marcos, ni Mateos, mas fueron inventados por los demonios. El uno, que es de los años y tiempos, de éste se puede tomar crédito, que es el primero, porque en la verdad aunque bárbaros y sin escrituras de letras, mucha orden y manera tenían de contar los mesmos tiempos y años, fiestas y días, como algo de esto parece en la primera parte del tratado y sexto [sic] capítulo. Asimismo escribían y figuraban las hazañas e historias de guerra [y también] del subceso de los principales señores, de los temporales y pestilencias, y en qué tiempo y de qué señor acontecían, y todos los que subjetaron principalmente esta tierra e se enseñorearon hasta que los españoles entraron. Todo esto tienen escrito por caracteres e figuras. (Benavente 1971:5)

There were among these natives five types of books, as I said, of figures and characters: the first book spoke of the years and times; the second, of the days and feasts that the natives had during the entire year; the third spoke of the dreams and the omens, trickery, and vanities in which they believed; the fourth book was of the baptism and names that they gave to the children; the fifth is of the rites, ceremonies, and omens that they had in their marriages. Your Illustrious Lordship must not believe that four of these books are like Gospels, because they were written neither by Johns, nor Luke, nor Mark, nor Mathew, but were invented by the demons. The first one, which is of the years and times, can be given credit because, although the natives were barbarian and without alphabetic writings, truly they had much order and a way to tell the same times and years, feasts and days, as something similar to this appears in the first part of the treaty and sixth [sic] chapter. They themselves also wrote and drew the exploits and histories of war [and also] of the events of the main lords, of the weather and pestilences, and in what time and under which ruler they occurred, and all those who principally subjected this land and took possession until the Spaniards entered. The natives have all this written by characters and figures. (author's translation)

Motolinia was fully aware that the indigenous people had five different types of pictorial books, each of which was dedicated to a specific topic such as religion or history. Among the five types, the one that describes the achievements of the rulers may have been a source for the discussion of Nezahualcoyotl's legal practice in Motolinia's book. Along with the pictorial books, Motolinia was also aware that there existed certain indigenous people who could recite their history from memory without pictorial scripts. For his book, therefore, Motolinia needed indigenous informants who could either recite their history by memory or read pictorial scripts for him:

> Estos indios; demás de poner por memorial las cosas ya dichas en especial el suceso y generación de los señores y linajes principales, y cosas notables que en sus tiempos acontecían, por figuras, que era su modo de escribir, había también entre ellos personas de buena memoria que retenían y sabían aun sin libro, contar y relatar como buenos biblistas o coronistas el suceso de los triunfos e linaje de los señores, y de éstos topé con uno a mi ver bien, hábil y de buena memoria, el cual sin contradicción de lo dicho, con brevedad me dio noticia y relación del principio y origen des estos naturales, según su opinión y libros. (Benavente 1971:9)

> These Indians; in addition to recording the already mentioned things by figures, which was their way of writing, especially, the event and generation of the lords and principal lineages, and remarkable things that occurred in their times, there were also among them people of good memory who retained and knew, even without books, how to tell and to relate like good Bible readers or chroniclers the event of the victories and lineage of the lords. Among these people, I ran into one, in my opinion, capable and of good memory, who, without contradiction and with brevity, gave me information and an account of the beginning and origin of these natives, according to his opinion and books. (author's translation)

Motolinia clearly states that these indigenous pictorial scripts and indigenous informants were the primary sources for his history. In the process of using these sources for his book, Motolinia seems to have functioned as a compiler and editor who formulated questions and organized information about indigenous history. The real author of most of Motolinia's text then would have been the indigenous informants who recounted the history by memory or read the pictorial scripts for the Spanish priest. The reliability of this information, however, depended heavily on the regional origin or political interest of the informants or the painters of the pictorial scripts, because each of the major pre-Hispanic city-states had its own historical tradition. And, in fact, Motolinia seems to have distinguished the information from the informants or the pictorial scripts according to their regional origin. For instance, when he discusses the indigenous religious ceremonies, he divides them into several chapters, each of which is titled relative to the ceremonies of either Mexica or Tlaxcala or Cholula. However, whether Motolinia checked the reliability of the information that his informants provided or had sufficient knowledge to understand pictorial scripts is doubtful, nor did he have any intention of verifying the information as long as he found it useful for the purpose of his writing. Motolinia, a follower of Franciscan millennialism, collected and reorganized indigenous histories in order to demonstrate that the intellectual capacity of the natives was such that they were perfectly suited to the establishment of a Christian kingdom in the New World. As is evident in Motolinia's description of Nezahualcoyotl, this process of collecting data on indigenous history reveals the regional political interests of the indigenous informants.

Motolinia (Benavente 1971:321–22, 352–59) describes Nezahualcoyotl as a fair legal practitioner during the pre-Hispanic period. According to Motolinia, Nezahualcoyotl introduced many just laws and administered them strictly but fairly. For instance, he executed his four sons who had sexual relationships with his concubines, and Motolinia makes an implicit comparison to King David who sentenced his own son to death due to the same type of misconduct. Motolinia must have acquired this information from Texcoca native informants and pictorial texts. I argue that these informants must have been Texcoca royal families, because after the conquest they would have been the only social group able to access pictorial texts about the history of their ancestral kings. According to Baudot (1995:284), the postconquest Texcoca rulers, such as don Hernando and don Antonio Pimentel Ixtlilxochitl, maintained a close personal relationship with Motolinia and furnished him with necessary codices and oral traditions. The Spanish friar himself actually reveals his relationship with the Texcoca nobles in his book. Motolinia (Benavente 1971:146–47) records that he attended don Hernando Pimentel Ixtlilxochitl's Christian wedding in 1526 in Texcoco and enjoyed the *netotoztli* (dance) at the banquet after the wedding. In addition, the Spanish family name, Pimentel, that the Texcoca nobles adopted also demonstrates the close relationship between Motolinia and the Texcoca rulers. The family name actually came from Motolinia's benefactor, the Count de Benavente Pimentel, to whom he dedicated his book. In addition, when Motolinia (Benavente 1971:322) describes Nezahualcoyotl's legal system and practice, he introduces the Texcoca king as the grandfather of the Texcoca ruler Antonio Pimentel Ixtlilxochitl. Motolinia presents Nezahualcoyotl as a legislator solely based on Texcoca regional sources that the Texcoca noble class provided and interpreted for him.

The other Franciscan, Andrés de Olmos, whose works served as a basis for several other chroniclers in the sixteenth century began to present Nezahualcoyotl and his son, Nezahualpilli, as skeptics of indigenous religion. Olmos's original description of Nezahualcoyotl, which is now missing, was collected in the later chronicles of Gerónimo de Mendieta, Juan de Torquemada, and Alonso de Zorita (Baudot 1995:75–81).[5] These chroniclers clearly acknowledged Olmos's text as their main source. I examine here Mendieta's chronicle because it provides the most detailed version of Olmos's original description of Nezahualcoyotl. According to Mendieta, Olmos employed the same methodology as Motolinia in writing his history:

Pues es de saber, que en el año de mil y quinientos y treinta y tres, siendo presidente de la Real Audiencia de México D. Sebastián Ramírez de Fuenreal (obispo que á la sazon era de la isla de Española), y siendo custodio de la órden de nuestro Padre S. Francisco en esta Nueva España el santo varon Fr. Martín de Valencia, por ambos á dos fue encargado el padre Fr. Andrés de Olmos de la dicha órden (por ser la mejor lengua mexicana que entonces habia en esta tierra, y hombre docto y discreto), que sacase en un libro las antigüedades de estos naturales indios, en especial de México, y Tezcuco, y Tlaxcala, para que de ello hubiese alguna memoria, y lo malo y fuera de tino se pudiese mejor refutar, y si algo bueno se hallase, se pudiese notar, como se notan y tienen en memoria muchas cosas de otros gentiles. Y el dicho padre lo hizo así, que habiendo visto todas las pinturas que los caciques y principales de estas provincias tenian de sus antiguallas, y habiéndosele dado los mas ancianos respuesta á todo lo que les quiso preguntar, hizo de todo ello un libro muy copioso. (Mendieta 1971:75)

Then one should know that in 1533, both D. Sebastián Ramirez de Fuenreal (bishop who was of the island of Española at that time), who was the president of the Real Audiencia of Mexico, and the saintly man, Martin of Valencia who was the custodian of the order of our Father S. Francis in this New Spain, ordered the Father Fr. Andrés de Olmos of the mentioned order (for being the best interpreter of the Mexican language who was in this land at that time and an erudite and discreet man), that he record in a book the antiquities of these native Indians, especially, of Mexico-Tenochtitlan, Texcoco, and Tlaxcala, so that there might be some memory and that any bad and irrational thing might be better refuted, and if anything good were found, it could be noted, as many things of other gentile ones were noted and preserved in memory. And the above mentioned father did it as follows: having seen all the paintings, which the caciques and nobles of these provinces had as their old account, and also having been given by the oldest men an answer to everything he wanted to ask to them, from all this he wrote a very copious book. (author's translation)

Just like Motolinia, Olmos used indigenous pictorial texts and oral traditions as his main sources, and most of these sources probably originated from Tenochtitlan, Texcoco, and Tlaxcala. Olmos's description of Nezahualcoyotl as a religious skeptic appears to be based mainly on Texcoca sources.

Mendieta (1971:83) explains that there were pre-Hispanic Indians such as Nezahualcoyotl and his son Nezahualpilli who doubted the ability of their indigenous gods because the gods never granted their requests. In chapter 6 of his book, Mendieta includes this information but does not show its source. In chapter 4, entitled "De la creación de las criaturas, especialmente del hombre, segun los de Tezcuco" (About the Creation of Creatures, Especially of Man, According to Those of Texcoco), however, he provides a clue when he states that the Texcoca protested against the version of the human creation story that Olmos had previously collected:

> Los de Tezcuco dieron después por pintura otra manera de la creación del primer hombre, muy á la contra de lo que antes por palabra habian dicho á un discípulo del padre Fr. Andrés de Olmos, llamado D. Lorenzo, refiriendo que sus pasados habian venido de aquella tierra donde cayeron los dioses (según arriba se dijo) y de aquella cueva de Chicomoztoc. Y lo que después en pintura mostraron y declararon al sobredicho Fr. Andrés de Olmos, fue que el primer hombre de quien ellos prodcedian habia nacido en tierra de Aculma, que está en término de Tezcuco dos leguas, y de México cinco, poco mas, en esta manera. (Mendieta 1971:81)

> Those of Texcoco later gave in painting another version of the creation of the first man, which is very contrary to what they had verbally said before, to a disciple of the Father Fr. Andrés de Olmos, called D. Lorenzo, mentioning that their ancestors had come from the place where the gods (as mentioned above) fell and from the cave of Chicomoztoc. And what they later showed in painting and declared in this way to the above-mentioned Fr. Andrés de Olmos was that the first man from whom they originated had been born in the land of Acolman, which is in relation to Texcoco two leagues and a little more than five leagues from Mexico-Tenochtitlan. (author's translation)

The Texcoca who provided this alternate version of the human creation story in chapter 4 also appear to be the main source for the description of Nezahualcoyotl as a religious skeptic in chapter 6. At the conclusion of the description of Nezahualcoyotl in chapter 6, Mendieta (1971:83) suggests that he presents Nezahualcoyotl's skepticism as one of the diverse, unexpected attitudes of the natives toward their gods: "De manera que acerca de sus dioses y de la creación del hombre diversos desatinos decian y tenian" (Of the way they said and believed various types of nonsense about their gods and the creation of the man). This suggestion shows that Mendieta still deals in chapter 6 with the same topic, "about the indigenous gods and the creations of human beings," as chapter 4, in which the Texcoca provide an alternative version of the creation of humans in pre-Hispanic Mexico (Mendieta 1971:83). One might logically believe that the Texcoca, who dared to correct the Spanish friar Olmos regarding the origin of human beings in pre-Hispanic Mexico, provided the information about Nezahualcoyotl as a religious skeptic. By presenting their ancestor

Nezahualcoyotl as a religious skeptic, the Texcoca would make their city the center of anti-indigenous religion and thus make it the most appealing place for the Spanish friar among the cities in New Spain.

The first texts that present Nezahualcoyotl as a legislator, a fair legal practitioner, and a religious skeptic originated from a mutual interest between the Franciscan friars and Texcoca informants. As shown in the case of Motolinia and Olmos, the Franciscans studied indigenous traditions in order to decide which beliefs and practices were acceptable and which should be extirpated in order to facilitate their religious goal of issuing in the millennium (Baudot 1995:185). They denounced indigenous religion but commended other traditions such as the efficient system of government and the strict legal administration. The Spanish friars naturally, then, attempted to eradicate indigenous religion while preserving the other good indigenous traditions that would expedite the establishment of the Christian kingdom on earth. The representation of Nezahualcoyotl as a religious skeptic, a fair practitioner of laws, and a legislator must have appeared in this preestablished Franciscan framework of indigenous history. For Motolinia and Olmos, the fair legal system that Nezahualcoyotl practiced and the skeptical attitude of this king toward the indigenous gods are certainly worth being remembered in indigenous history and would have been a valuable tool in the evangelization of the king's vassals.

On the other hand, Texcoca informants seem to have been aware of what the Spanish friars wanted to know about their past, and they tailored their accounts accordingly. By presenting their ancestral king, Nezahualcoyotl, as a good legal practitioner as well as a religious skeptic, Texcoca informants could claim that their city-state was the most civilized and the most pious place in pre-Hispanic Mexico according to European criteria. Several decades later, toward the end of the sixteenth century, their descendants such as Pomar and Alva Ixtlilxochitl made every effort to prove that Texcoco maintained the most civilized political and legal system and practiced peaceful religious rites without conducting human sacrifice. According to them, Nezahualcoyotl was responsible for this civilized and peaceful Texcoco.

Juan Bautista Pomar, don Fernando de Alva Ixtlilxochitl, and Their Sources

The sources available to the Texcoca chroniclers such as Juan Bautista Pomar and don Fernando de Alva Ixtlilxochitl include indigenous oral traditions, pictorial scripts, and alphabetic texts in Nahuatl as well as in Spanish. Both of them claimed to be mestizo descendants of the Texcoca royal family and Spanish conquistadores.[6] In 1582, Pomar (1993:152) finished his *Relación geográfica de Texcoco*, which included in its appendix *Romances de los señores de la Nueva España*, native songs in Nahuatl. This is one of the most typical works made by request of the Spanish authorities. King Philip II, who wanted to know more about his

American colonies, prepared a series of questions and ordered that each city send him its answers.[7] Pomar was assigned by Spanish officials to answer the questionnaire. In some of his answers to the questions about pre-Hispanic Texcoco, he describes Nezahualcoyotl as a pious man with a skeptical attitude toward indigenous gods that required human sacrifice. Pomar also describes Nezahualcoyotl as a philosopher-poet who left his peaceful religious ideas in his songs, as a legislator and wise practitioner of law, and as a good governor who maintained a well-organized government system. This Texcoca chronicler combines the representations of Nezahualcoyotl that Olmos and Motolinia had set forth previously and adds three more dimensions to this pre-Hispanic figure: poet-philosopher, anti-Mexica sage, and good governor.

Pomar claims that his *Relación* was based primarily on indigenous oral traditions:

> La cual se hizo con la verdad posible y habiendo primero hecho muchas diligencias para ello; buscando indios viejos y antiguos, inteligentes de lo que en dicha institución se contiene; buscando cantares antiquísimos, de donde coligió y tomó lo más que se ha hecho y escrito. (Pomar 1993:152)

> He [Pomar] wrote the relación with as much truth as possible having first made many efforts to do so: seeking old, elderly, and intelligent Indians whom the said institution contains; seeking very ancient songs, from which he deduced and took most of what has been made and written. (author's translation)

He states that he could not obtain more information on pre-Hispanic religious ceremonies and practices because the indigenous priests had already died and Hernán Cortés and his soldiers had burned the pictorial scripts in the palace of Nezahualpilli during the conquest (1993:153). And later some Texcoca nobles burned the surviving scripts out of fear of the first archbishop, Juan de Zumárraga, who executed the Texcoca noble don Carlos Ometochtzin for the practice of idolatry. However, Pomar was still able to consult some surviving pictorial codices, and he included some illustrations in his original work.[8] In addition to these sources, Pomar must have used the chronicles of Olmos and Motolinia or the same Texcoca sources upon which these Spanish chroniclers had relied. In sum, here again, all the sources that Pomar used to record pre-Hispanic indigenous history originated exclusively from Texcoco.[9]

Don Fernando de Alva Ixtlilxochitl's writings record the most comprehensive history of Texcoco from its origin to the Spanish conquest. In this history, the chronicler pays special attention to the reign of Nezahualcoyotl and describes it as a golden age. Alva Ixtlilxochitl wrote five works that have been collected in his *Obras completas*: *Sumaria relación de las cosas de la Nueva*

España, Relación sucinta en forma de memorial, Compendio histórico del reino de Texcoco, Sumaria relación de la historia de esta Nueva España, and *Historia de la nación chichimeca.* The editor of Alva Ixtlilxochitl's works, Edmundo O'Gorman (1997:229–33), establishes a hypothetical chronology of these works. He argues that the first four texts were written between 1600 and 1625, but he is unable to determine the date of the last work. Throughout the five works, Alva Ixtlilxochitl thoroughly describes the entire life of Nezahualcoyotl from birth to death and presents him as a religious skeptic, legislator, builder of a large empire, poet, and prophet. Alva Ixtlilxochitl portrays Nezahualcoyotl's government as a highly advanced political system in which science, law, religion, education, and art flourished. According to Alva Ixtlilxochitl, Nezahualcoyotl's Texcoco was a cultural and political center superior to Tenochtitlan. Nezahualcoyotl appears as the most powerful ruler in the Basin of Mexico whose laws and councils even the Mexica imitate. Moreover, developing the peaceful, thus anti-Mexica, image of Nezahualcoyotl proposed by previous chroniclers, Alva Ixtlilxochitl argues that Nezahualcoyotl not only rejected human sacrifice but also anticipated the destruction of the bloody Aztec empire. Alva Ixtlilxochitl's works contain the most important and detailed information on Nezahualcoyotl of any other colonial chronicles.

Alva Ixtlilxochitl frequently asserts in his works that his indigenous history is true because it is based on reliable indigenous pictorial and oral traditions. The following statement is one of many such assertions:

> Por cuya causa he conseguido mi deseo con mucho trabajo, peregrinación y suma diligencia en juntar las pinturas de las historias y anales, y los cantos con que las observaban; y sobre todo para poderlas entender, juntando y convocando a muchos principales de esta Nueva España, los que tenían fama de conocer y saber las historias referidas; y de todos ellos [en] solos dos hallé entera relación y conocimiento de las pinturas y caracteres y que daban verdadero sentido a los cantos, que por ir compuestos con sentido alegórico y adornados de metáforas y similitudes, son dificilísimos de entender. (Alva Ixtlilxochitl 1997, 1:526)

> For that reason I have obtained my desire with much work, pilgrimage, and great diligence to bring together the paintings of the histories and annals, and the songs with which the nobles maintained them; and above all to be able to understand them, I met with and called many nobles of this New Spain, those who were famous for knowing and understanding the mentioned histories; and among all of them I found only two who had a complete account and knowledge of the paintings and figures and who gave true meaning to the songs, which are extremely difficult to understand being composed with allegoric meaning and adorned with metaphors and analogies. (author's translation)

Just like the Franciscan friars and Pomar, Alva Ixtlilxochitl states that he used indigenous sources such as pictorial scripts and songs, and he sought out nobles who could interpret these sources for him. Thus, his version of Nezahualcoyotl's story resulted from the typical way of collecting information on pre-Hispanic indigenous history. Unlike the previous chroniclers of Nezahualcoyotl, however, Alva Ixtlilxochitl seems to have included more diverse sources by drawing from works produced by non-Texcoca chroniclers: meeting with and calling "many nobles of this New Spain, those who were famous for knowing and understanding the mentioned histories." Alva Ixtlilxochitl offers detailed information on his sources about Nezahualcoyotl.[10] When he deals with the death of Nezahualcoyotl in the *Historia de la nación chichimeca*, he explicitly identifies his source of information:

> Autores son de todo lo referido y de lo demás de su [Nezahualcoyotl] vida y hechos los infantes de México, Itzcoatzin y Xiuhcozcatzin, y otros poetas e históricos en los anales de las tres cabezas de esta Nueva España, y en particular en los anales que hizo el infante Quauhtlatzacuilotzin primer señor del pueblo de Chiauhtla, que comienzan desde el año de su nacimiento hasta el tiempo del gobierno del rey Nezahualpiltzintli, y asimismo se halla en las relaciones que escribieron los infantes de la ciudad de Tetzcuco don Pablo, don Toribio, don Hernando Pimentel y Juan de Pomar, hijos y nietos del rey Nezahualpiltzintli de Tetzcuco, y asimismo el infante don Alonso Axayacatzin señor de Iztapalapan hijo del rey Cuitlahuac y sobrino del rey Motecuhzomatzin; y últimamente, en nuestros tiempos, lo tiene escrito en su historia y Monarquía indiana el diligentísimo y primer descubridor de la declaración de las pinturas y cantos, el reverendo padre fray Juan de Torquemada padre del santo evangelio de esta provincia. (Alva Ixtlilxochitl 1997, 2:137)

> The authors of all the above-mentioned things and others of his [Nezahualcoyotl's] life and achievements are the princes of Mexico-Tenochtitlan, Itzcoatl and Xiuhcozcatzin, and other poets and historians of the annals of the three heads of this New Spain, especially the annals made by the prince Quauhtlatzacuilotzin, first lord of the town of Chiauhtla, the annals which begin from the year of his birth and go to the time of the government of the king Nezahualpilli, and he himself is found in the *relaciones* that the princes of the city of Texcoco don Pablo, don Toribio, don Hernando Pimentel, and Juan de Pomar, children and grandchildren of the king Nezahualpilli of Texcoco wrote, and likewise the prince don Alonso Axayacatzin, ruler of Iztapalapa and son of the king Cuitlahuac and nephew of the king Moctezuma; and finally, in our times, the reverend Father Fray Juan

de Torquemada, first discoverer of the declaration of the paintings and songs and father of the holy gospel of this province, has written Nezahualcoyotl's life and achievements in the book *Monarquía indiana*. (author's translation)

The previously mentioned sources employed by Alva Ixtlilxochitl in narrating Nezahualcoyotl's life can be divided into three groups according to their geographical origin: the Texcoco, the Spanish, and the Mexica. As Alva Ixtlilxochitl demonstrates, most of the sources originated from Texcoco. Among them, the *relaciones* of don Hernando Pimentel and Pomar are particularly important because the former provided Motolinia with the information about Nezahualcoyotl as a legislator and fair legal practitioner while the latter actually furnished the schematic descriptions of Nezahualcoyotl that Alva Ixtlilxochitl developed more extensively in his texts. The other relaciones seem to have provided information not much different from that of Hernando Pimentel and Pomar, because all of them belonged to the Texcoca royal family, who could claim to be descendants of Nezahualcoyotl. The annals of Chiauhtla, which originated from Chiauhtla near Texcoco, also seem to record history from a Texcoca perspective. According to Alva Ixtlilxochitl's description, these annals must have been the original copy of the currently surviving pictorial source, the *Codex en Cruz* (1981). Both the annals and the *Codex en Cruz* originated from Chiauhtla and depicted major Texcoca historical events year by year from the birth of Nezahualcoyotl. The only difference between the two sources is that the annals of Chiauhtla ended with Nezahualpilli's reign while the codex continues until several decades after the conquest. Taking into account the similarities between these two sources, the annals of Chiauhtla that Alva Ixtlilxochitl consulted also expressed a Texcoca perspective.

The only Spanish source mentioned in Alva Ixtlilxochitl's list of sources is the *Monarquía indiana*, written by his contemporary friar, Juan de Torquemada. Torquemada presents Nezahualcoyotl as a religious skeptic, legislator, poet, and great empire builder. Torquemada's description of Nezahualcoyotl is very similar to that of Alva Ixtlilxochitl. A close comparison between Alva Ixtlilxochitl's and Torquemada's works reveals that they used many of the same sources, such as the *Codex Xolotl* and the *Mapa Quinatzin*, and their interpretations of these pictorial sources vary only slightly. In addition, Torquemada's book *Monarquía indiana*, which compiled the works of major Franciscan chroniclers, included the two initial descriptions of Nezahualcoyotl as a religious skeptic and legislator that Olmos and Motolinia first formulated and that later their Franciscan successors such as Mendieta reproduced.[11] Thus, in Torquemada's book, Alva Ixtlilxochitl could have found more evidence to support the descriptions of Nezahualcoyotl that he wanted to promote in his own writings.

The Mexica sources that Alva Ixtlilxochitl used to reconstruct Nezahualcoyotl's life in his chronicles are songs, annals, and relaciones. Fortunately, many of these kinds of Mexica sources survive abundantly. The surviving Mexica sources, which will be examined later in this chapter, do not, however, support the images of Nezahualcoyotl that Alva Ixtlilxochitl describes in his chronicles. Rather, they portray Nezahualcoyotl as the closest ally of the Mexica who administered a very similar political, artistic, and religious system. Thus, Nezahualcoyotl and the Mexica cannot be distinguished from each other in the way Alva Ixtlilxochitl proposes in his chronicles. I argue that Alva Ixtlilxochitl was selective in his use of information and thus misinterpreted the Mexica sources. Alva Ixtlilxochitl himself wrote that

> con cuya [los principales] ayuda pude después con facilidad conocer todas las pinturas e historias y traducir los cantos en su verdadero sentido, con que ha satisfecho mi deseo, siguiendo siempre la verdad; por cuya causa no me he querido aprovechar de las historias que tratan de esta materia, por la diversidad y confusión que tienen entre sí los autores que tratan de ellas, por las falsas relaciones y contrarias interpretaciones que se les dieron. (Alva Ixtlilxochitl 1997, 1:526)

> with their [the nobles'] help, later I was able to easily recognize all the paintings and histories, and to translate the songs in their true meaning, which has satisfied my desire, always pursuing the truth; For this reason, I have not wanted to use the histories that deal with this matter because of the variety and confusion that exists even among the authors and because of the false accounts and contrary interpretations that they gave. (author's translation)

Alva Ixtlilxochitl states that the indigenous sources he consulted could have a different or even contrary interpretation. However, he did not include any alternative interpretations in his writings because according to his criteria, they were not true. Alva Ixtlilxochitl adopted the same perspectives and the same tactic of selective reading as the previous chroniclers upon whom he relied. He takes a biblical perspective, like Spanish friars such as Torquemada, and a Texcoca regional perspective, like Texcoca sources such as the texts produced by Hernando Pimentel and Juan Bautista Pomar. Moreover, Alva Ixtlilxochitl merely excluded or modified information from sources that contradicted the images of Nezahualcoyotl that he wished to promote. Just like the first Franciscan chroniclers, Motolinia and Olmos, who described Nezahualcoyotl as a religious skeptic and lawmaker for their own ideological needs, Alva Ixtlilxochitl significantly reinforced and developed the biblical and civilized images of Nezahualcoyotl for his own political need.

Alva Ixtlilxochitl (1997, 1:526) argues that the reason he decided to write Texcoca history from its origin to the conquest was simply to learn about the past of his ancestor and namesake that had been forgotten with time. But his writing was a highly political act whose main objective was to document the contribution of his ancestors, especially don Fernando Cortés Ixtlilxochitl, to the Spanish conquest and thus to demonstrate that he and his fellow nobles, as descendants of Cortés Ixtlilxochitl, were deserving of merit and recompense. Alva Ixtlilxochitl's history claims that Nezahualcoyotl instructed his grandson, Cortés Ixtlilxochitl, in his Christian-like religious, political, and cultural practices. Throughout all of his works, these Christian-like beliefs serve as a prelude to the arrival of the Spaniards and led the Texcoca to welcome Cortés and help him destroy Tenochtitlan. During the conquest of Tenochtitlan, Cortés Ixtlilxochitl appears as a reincarnation of Nezahualcoyotl, who had detested the bloodthirsty indigenous gods and rejected human sacrifice. Alva Ixtlilxochitl records, for example, that Cortés Ixtlilxochitl destroyed the temple of Huitzilopochtli with Cortés:

> Y subieron a la torre y derribaron muchas ídolos, especialmente en la capilla mayor donde estaba Huitzilopoxtli, que llegaron Cortés y Ixtlilxúchitl a un tiempo y ambos envistieron con el ídolo, Cortés cogió la máscara de oro que tenía puesta este ídolo con ciertas piedras preciosas que estaban engastadas en ella. Ixtlilxúchitl le costó la cabeza al que pocos años antes adoraba por su dios. (Alva Ixtlilxochitl 1997, 1:466)

> And they went up in the tower and they knocked down many idols, especially in the main chapel dedicated to Huitzilopochtli, at which Cortés and Hernando de Cortés Ixtlilxochitl arrived at the same time and both attacked the idol, Cortés took the mask of gold set with certain precious stones that had been put on this idol. Ixtlilxochitl took the head of the idol that not many years ago he worshipped as his god. (author's translation)

Then, as the well-instructed descendant of Nezahualcoyotl, Cortés Ixtlilxochitl dedicated his life and exhausted his fortune in order to destroy the evil world of Huitzilopochtli that Nezahualcoyotl had rejected and whose destruction he had already anticipated:

> Otras muchas entradas hicieron los nuestros fuera de las referidas que por no haber habido en ellas cosas señaladas no se ponen aquí, y por evitar prolijidad, ayudando Ixtlilxúchitl, sus hermanos, deudos y vasallos en todas ellas, en donde le costó hartos trabajos y grandísimos gastos en sustentar y pagar a los españoles, que se puede decir esto con mucha verdad, pues es notorio que demás de que ayudó con su persona y vasallos a los cristianos en servicio de Dios y del emperador nuestro señor, los sustentó y dio a todos ellos cuantos oro y plata y joyas había en los palacios de su padre y abuelo. (Alva Ixtlilxochitl 1997, 1:491)

Our people [the Texcoca] conducted many other conquests beyond the ones mentioned—which are not dealt with here because they did not involve significant events and in order to avoid prolixity—in all of which Ixtlilxochitl, his brothers, relatives and vassals participated, where he exerted much effort and spent tremendous expense in supporting and paying the Spaniards, which can be told with a great deal of truth, because it is well known that in addition to helping the Christians in the service of God and of the emperor our lord personally and with his vassals, he supported them and gave to all of them as much gold and silver and jewels as there were in the palaces of his father and grandfather. (author's translation)

According to Alva Ixtlilxochitl, don Cortés Ixtlilxochitl's military and financial contributions to the conquest and the king, which were inspired by Nezahualcoyotl's instructions, were crucial in the establishment of New Spain. However, despite such decisive contributions by the Texcoca to the conquest, their descendants did not receive due consideration from the Crown. When Alva Ixtlilxochitl was writing his chronicles in the beginning of the seventeenth century, the Texcoca nobles no longer enjoyed a lifestyle appropriate to their status.

Alva Ixtlilxochitl records how the Texcoca royal descendants suffered poverty even though they were loyalist vassals of the Spanish king:

De manera que desde los españoles llegaron a esta Nueva España, siempre y continuamente les obedecieron [Los Texcoca], y siempre fueron y han sido leales vasallos de su majestad, porque nunca dimos guerra a los españoles, sino que siempre los hemos obedecido, y desde el primer día que oímos nombrar el emperador nuestro señor, siempre lo hemos tenido por nuestro rey y señor, y siempre hemos obedecido a sus reales mandatos, y los gobernadores que en su real nombre han venido a esta Nueva España siempre hemos obedecido y tenido por señores, y habemos hecho y obedecido sus mandamientos.

Y siendo como somos señores y naturales, y primero que México, y haber tenido y poseído mucha cantidad de tierras y pueblos, poblándolos por nuestra autoridad, y otras habiéndolas ganado como hombres de Guerra, y teniéndolas debajo de nuestra jurisdicción y mando, y siendo los mejores indios de la Nueva España, y los que con mejor título éramos señores de lo que teníamos, después de haber venido españoles en esta Nueva España, y habiéndonos tornado cristianos de nuestra propia voluntad, porque tenemos conocido el error en que primero estábamos, y hallándonos el capitán don Hernando Cortés señoreando, mandando y reinando en los pueblos y provincias de sus declaradas, y teniendo en ellos nuestras casas y heredadas, tributándonos como nos tributaban como a señores que éramos suyos, después de haber puesto debajo del dominio de su majestad y ser como somos cristianos y leales vasallos de su majestad se nos han quitado todos los pueblos y tierras y mando que teníamos y nos han dejado solamente con la cabecera de Tezcuco con otros cuatro o cinco sujetos, y aun los cuales, viendo el poco favor que se nos da y en cuán poco somos tenidos, se nos quieren alzar y poner por sí, y se nos han quitado los pueblos de nuestra haciendas y heredades, en los propios pueblos que nosotros de nuestras propias gentes hicimos y poblamos, de lo cual habemos recibido y recibimos notorio agravio, y vivimos muy pobres y necesitados sin ninguna renta, y vemos que los pueblos que eran nuestros y nuestras propias tierras, la gente que en ellos estaba era nuestros renteros y tributarios, y los calpixques que nosotros teníamos puestos, vemos que ahora son señores de dones, siendo como eran mazehuales, y tienen renta de los dichos pueblos, y nosotros, siendo señores, nos vemos pobres sin tener qué comer. (Alva Ixtlilxochitl 1997, 1:392–93)

So since the Spaniards arrived at this New Spain, the Texcoca always and constantly obeyed them, and they always were and have been loyal vassals of your majesty, because we never fought against the Spaniards, but we have always obeyed them, and since the first day that we heard our lord named emperor, we have always considered him our king and lord, and we have always obeyed his royal orders and we have always obeyed and considered as lords the governors who in your royal name have come to this New Spain, and we have fulfilled and obeyed their commands.

And being as we are rulers and natives, we had owned and possessed more than Mexico-Tenochtitlan, a lot of land and towns, populating them with our authority and having earned others as fighting men, and having them under our jurisdiction and command, and we are the best Indians of New Spain, as the lords with the best title of what we had. After the Spaniards having come to this New Spain, we have become Christians willingly, because we have recognized the error in which we were. And the captain don Hernando Cortés found and ruled us, dominating and reigning the towns and provinces of his declaration in which we had our houses and inheritance and having them pay us tribute as their rulers, as we were, as they used to do. After having been placed under the control of your majesty and being Christians and loyal vassals of your majesty, we have had taken away from us all the towns, lands, and command that we had, and they have left us only with the *cabecera* of Texcoco with other four or five subject towns. And even these towns, seeing the little favor given to us and how little we owned, want to rebel against us and to be independent, and they have taken our haciendas and estates in the very towns that we ourselves built and populated. Since we have received and receive evident insult from them, we live very poor and needy without any income. And we see the towns that were ours and our own lands, the people in them were our tenants and tributaries, and the tax collectors [*calpixques*] whom we had placed. We see that these calpixque now are nobles, being as they were commoners [*mazehuales*] and they have income of the said towns, while we, being nobles, find ourselves poor without food. (author's translation)

Alva Ixtlilxochitl complains that the king did not recognize the constant obedience and service of the Texcoca rulers:

Lo cual pensamos que su majestad, sabiendo quién nosotros somos, y servicios que le habemos hecho, nos hubiera hecho mercedes, y nos hubiera dado más de lo que teníamos; y vemos que antes nos han desposeído de lo nuestro y desheredado, y héchonos tributarios donde no lo éramos, y que para pagar los tributos donde no lo éramos. (Alva Ixtlilxochitl 1997, 1:393)

We think that your majesty, knowing who we are and the services that we have done for you, would have shown us mercy and would have given more than what we had; and we consider that they have taken before what was ours and our inheritance, and they made us tributaries where we were not before. (author's translation)[12]

For this reason Alva Ixtlilxochitl decided to write the history of his hometown, Texcoco, just like the chroniclers of other regions such as Alvarado Tezozomoc of Tenochtitlan and Chimalpahin of Chalco; as Susan Schroeder explains,

For Nahua intellectuals in the capital at the turn of the century there was surely a keen sense of urgency to keep to tradition while securing vestigial positions of high status within the colonial system. Writing local histories seemed to furnish at least temporary solutions for both concerns. Typically, each author focused on his home region in order to champion his particular royal lineage and the unique qualities of his own *altepetl* (kingdom, ethnic state). (Schroeder 1997:6)

The sources for the major chronicles related to Nezahualcoyotl originated mostly from Texcoco and were selected and interpreted by the authors of these chronicles according to their religious and political perspectives. The Franciscan friars such as Motolinia and Olmos began to represent Nezahualcoyotl as a religious skeptic, a legislator, and a fair legal practitioner, and later friars such as Las Casas, Mendieta, and Torquemada recycled Motolinia's and Olmos's descriptions of Nezahualcoyotl, sometimes without changing a single word. With this representation of Nezahualcoyotl, the Franciscans tried to prove that the natives were capable of building a Christian kingdom in the New World, and the Dominican Las Casas presented it as clear evidence of rationality. The Texcoca chroniclers such as Alva Ixtlilxochitl, on the other hand, built on the Franciscan image of Nezahualcoyotl, adding a Christian dimension to their ancestors' achievements in order to obtain favor from the king. The regional perspectives inflected with a Christian ideology that inform the work of Motolinia, Olmos, Pomar, and Alva Ixtlilxochitl make it necessary to (1) review the surviving sources that these chroniclers used or might have used, and (2) cross-check the Texcoca history of these chroniclers with that of the native chroniclers of other regions as well as Spanish chroniclers. A comprehensive review of the surviving Texcoca sources and a comparison between Texcoca sources and those of other regions support neither the initial nor the expanded representation of Nezahualcoyotl.

Texcoca Pictorial Scripts: The *Códice Xolotl, Mapa Quinatzin,* and *Mapa Tlotzin*

The three main chroniclers of Nezahualcoyotl, Juan Bautista Pomar, don Fernando de Alva Ixtlilxochitl, and Fray Juan de Torquemada, and even earlier chroniclers, such as Andrés de Olmos and Toribio de Benavente (Motolinia), frequently claimed pictorial scripts as the most authentic indigenous sources, and they insisted that their works were reliable by virtue of this fact. The currently available pictorial scripts from Texcoco and its dominated areas that the chroniclers might have used include the following: from Texcoco, the *Códice Xolotl* (1996), *Mapa Quinatzin* (Aubin 1886a), *Mapa Tlotzin* (Aubin 1886b), *Boban Calendar Wheel* (Dibble 1990), and *Códice Ixtlilxochitl* (1996); from Texcoca-dominated cities, the *Codex en Cruz* (1981) from Chiauhtla, *Tira de Tepechpan* (1978) from Tepechpan, *Códice de Tepetlaoztoc* (1992) or *Codex Kingsborough* from Tepetlaoztoc, and *Códice de Xicotepec* (1995) from Xicotepec. The geographical diversity of these sources represents almost all of the Texcoca territory and the relationship between Texcoco and its subject cities. Among these scripts, the *Códice Xolotl*, *Mapa Quinatzin*, and *Mapa Tlotzin* are particularly important because (1) they were painted no later than 1546, which suggests that the Franciscan chroniclers might have relied upon them for their Texcoca histories; (2) they provide the most important and detailed information on Texcoco and Nezahualcoyotl of all the surviving pictorial sources; and (3) Alva Ixtlilxochitl and Torquemada clearly demonstrate that certain parts of their works were direct alphabetic transcriptions of such texts.[13] However, the determination of the importance and reliability of these pictographic texts requires careful consideration of the fact that all three sources were postconquest products, and thus their information on the pre-Hispanic period could have been affected by the colonial context.

Before the conquest, the peoples of Mesoamerica produced several different types of pictorial texts: screenfold, strip, and *lienzo*. The screenfold books are classified generically either as annals, *xiuhtlapohualli*, or as ritual books, *teoamoxtli* (Brotherston 1992:51).[14] The annals document certain historical events, moving forward year by year through the indigenous calendar, that is, the combination of thirteen numbers and twenty day signs. The ritual books, on the other hand, are closely associated with religious philosophy as well as with human life and labor. According to Brotherston (1995:16), they supply "a cosmogonical base for the economics of day-to-day life, both the labour tribute regulated by the *tonalamatl*, and the commodity tribute or offerings made over the cycle of annual feasts." The lienzo type of native text, which generally represents maps, records the locations of subject cities and other independent neighboring nations. These books were important for military expeditions as well as for tribute and tax assessment by the native government. After the conquest, most native books were destroyed by the Europeans. Spanish friars fanatically burned the religious books, sometimes along with their owners.[15] The other types of pre-Hispanic texts such as annals and maps, however, continued to be produced by the natives for their own use and for that of the Spaniards until the end of the sixteenth century.

Most of the texts used by the main chroniclers of Nezahualcoyotl were annals or maps that generally narrated regional genealogical and cultural histories. They typically depict a genealogy of local rulers and their political and cultural achievements. These regional annals and maps, however, frequently construct their past so as to establish an uninterrupted genealogical succession up to the generation of the patrons for whom they were painted in order to justify their right to rule, even after the conquest. The regional histories also exaggerate local achievements, treating them as if they referred to the whole of pre-Hispanic Mexico in order to enhance the profile of their particular ethnic group in pre-Hispanic times. With their regional pictorial annals and maps, which Spanish colonial authorities accepted as legal documents, indigenous nobles attempted to defend their own political status as governors and to expand their own or their cities' privileges. The painters and the patrons of the annals and maps were targeting both indigenous and Spanish readers.[16] The major Texcoca pictorial sources, such as the *Códice Xolotl* (1996), the *Mapa Quinatzin* (Aubin 1886a), and the *Mapa Tlotzin* (Aubin 1886b), fall into this category, narrating the pre-Hispanic history of central Mexico exclusively from a Texcoca perspective.[17] And Alva Ixtlilxochitl and Torquemada use these three Texcoca texts as their main sources when they deal with Nezahualcoyotl and his city of Texcoco.

After the conquest, the Spaniards did not impose their own governing system, but rather took advantage of existing indigenous sociopolitical organizations (Lockhart 1992:14–58). The first Hispanic governing unit, the *cabecera-sujeto* system, is based on the indigenous *altepetl* organization. In this system, the cabecera can be identified with the leading city in which the pre-Hispanic ruler, *tlatoani*, resided, and the sujeto with the basic ethnic or kinship community, *calpulli*, or with the subject cities (Gibson 1964:34). After the conquest, the tlatoani, who was usually a descendant of pre-Hispanic nobility, ruled over his subject cities, sujetos. As in pre-Hispanic times, the tlatoani was able to collect tribute from his subject cities and to demand their labor and service. This cabecera-sujeto system, however, had a significant impact on the political status of the capital city of the Aztec empire, Tenochtitlan, and its main allies, Texcoco and Tlacopan, because the Spanish system was not based on the pre-Hispanic Aztec imperial hierarchy. The rulers of Tenochtitlan, Texcoco, and Tlacopan were *hueitlatoque* (great rulers), which meant that they controlled most lower-level *tlatoque* (plural of tlatoani) before the conquest. In the colonial system, however, these rulers were demoted to the status of a regular tlatoani under the cabecera-sujeto system (Gibson 1964:34, 50). In the colonial context, Texcoca rulers argued that their city had dominated the eastern Basin of Mexico but that it lost its control after the conquest of Coatlichan, Huexotla, Chiauhtla, and Tezoyucan, each of which had its own tlatoani under the cabecera-sujeto system. From the early 1550s on, Texcoco and its royal descendants launched a legal campaign arguing that these Acolhuacan cities had been subject to Texcoco before the conquest. Texcoco won its first legal suit against Huexotla and was able to convert this city into its sujeto. Later, however, Huexotla was able to regain its independent status. Texcoco lost its legal battles with other cities in most cases (Gibson 1964:51–52).

As Susan Spitler (1998) and Eduardo de Douglas (2003) demonstrate, the three Texcoca pictorial texts, the *Códice Xolotl* (1996), the *Mapa Quinatzin* (Aubin 1886a), and the *Mapa Tlotzin* (Aubin 1886b), focus on pre-Hispanic history but actually also address postcolonial issues such as the Texcoca royal family's political status, land, tribute, and genealogy. The painters of the Texcoca pictorial texts or their patrons were royal descendants, and they created these texts around 1546 (Robertson 1994:138–39). When these texts were being painted, they had already lost, or at least been challenged on, their alleged dominant position as *hueitlatoani* (great ruler) in the Acolhuacan region. All three maps attempt to document the allegedly original dominance of the Texcoca royal family by depicting Texcoca supremacy over other cities in the pre-Hispanic period. For this pre-Hispanic history, each text focuses on the Texcoca rulers and their highly significant role in Texcoca history. And all three texts pay particular attention to Nezahualcoyotl, describing in detail his life, his conquests, and his system of government. In these three texts, then, Nezahualcoyotl appears as the historical protagonist who built a great empire, collecting tribute from Acolhuacan as well as many other regions.

The *Mapa Quinatzin* (Aubin 1886a) depicts most explicitly this Texcoca supremacy over neighboring cities. In leaf 2 of the map, the painter-scribe depicts the court of Nezahualcoyotl and Nezahualpilli and their tributaries.

The two kings are depicted on the authority mat inside their palace while the rulers of Huexotla, Coatlichan, Chiauhtla, Acolman, Tezoyucan, and many others are sitting in the Texcoca kings' courtyard as their tributaries without the authority mat. The *Mapa Tlotzin* (Aubin 1886b) also describes the rulers of Texcoco as the only tlatoque in the Acolhuacan region by depicting them on the authority mat, *icpalli*, but not the rulers of other major cities such as Huexotla and Coatlichan (Spitler 1998:76). The text pays special attention to Nezahualcoyotl by depicting him as the first tlatoani. Most of the major cities on this map in the eastern Basin of Mexico such as Huexotla, Coatlichan, Chiauhtla, and Tezoyucan are cities that Texcoco tried to convert into its sujeto cities through legal suits in the 1550s. However, as many colonial sources, such as the *Relaciones geográficas* (1982–1988), and secondary sources, such as Gibson (1964:52), argue, these cities had their own independent governments and thus their own tlatoani before the conquest. The painter-scribe of the two maps manipulated pre-Hispanic history in order to assert Texcoca supremacy over neighboring cities after the conquest.

The *Códice Xolotl* (1996) presents the Texcoca supremacy more ambitiously by extending its territorial domain from Acolhuacan in the eastern Basin of Mexico to the entire basin and even beyond. This text presents the legendary Chichimec leader Xolotl, who conquered the entire Basin of Mexico in the twelfth century and founded the Texcoca dynasty. In this codex, Texcoca rulers inherited their legitimacy from Xolotl and controlled vast areas of the Basin of Mexico, including major cities such as Tenayuca, Azcapotzalco, Coatlichan, Huexotla, and Coatepec. In this scheme, the Texcoca painter argues that the original Texcoca territory was not limited to the Acolhuacan area, the east side of the basin on which the *Mapa Quinatzin* and the *Mapa Tlotzin* focus, but that it actually covered the entire Basin of Mexico.

This ambitious claim, however, appears to be a postconquest invention. As the *Códice Xolotl* (1996) itself and the texts of other regions show, the city-state of Texcoco was founded at the end of the thirteenth century, far later than other Chichimec cities in the Basin of Mexico such as Tenayuca, Azcapotzalco, Coatepec, Coatlichan, Huexotla, and many others that Xolotl founded much earlier. In fact, as a relatively late settlement, Texcoco originally fell under the influence of neighboring cities such as Coatlichan and Huexotla, but in the first half of the fifteenth century the inhabitants of Texcoco were able to reverse their political fortune. In the 1420s and 1430s, Nezahualcoyotl allied with Tenochtitlan to make a series of conquests in the Basin of Mexico. Thus, as Spitler (2000:622–30) explains, the Texcoca scribe of the *Códice Xolotl* attempted to legitimate Nezahualcoyotl's conquests of the fifteenth century in the basin by suddenly transforming the political status of the Texcoca rulers and thereby expanding the territory to which they could legitimately lay claim.

The Texcoca royal descendants who were conducting a legal campaign to gain control of the Acolhuacan area in the 1540s painted or commissioned the trilogy of the *Códice Xolotl*, the *Mapa Quinatzin*, and the *Mapa Tlotzin* (Douglas 2003:286; Robertson 1994:139, 143). They tried to demonstrate that the Texcoca rulers, from Xolotl through the Spanish conquest, exhibited the same political superiority and that, therefore, their city should play a role as cabecera over Coatlichan, Huexotla, and other Acolhuacan cities. In this way, the Texcoca royal descendants attempted to convince the Spanish colonial authorities that Texcoco should be privileged over other competing indigenous groups in the colonial system of government. Alva Ixtlilxochitl and Torquemada faithfully transcribe this Texcoca version of the pre-Hispanic history of central Mexico into their alphabetic texts. Alva Ixtlilxochitl, in particular, in some cases further embellishes his home city's past by misinterpreting his pictorial sources.

Nezahualcoyotl in Other Sources

From the 1530s and 1540s, when Motolinia and Olmos produced their histories, to the beginning of the seventeenth century, when Alva Ixtlilxochitl and Torquemada were writing, there appeared many other texts that dealt with Nezahualcoyotl. These sources, however, do not corroborate the peaceful and civilized image of Nezahualcoyotl that characterizes the accounts set down by the Franciscans, Alva Ixtlilxochitl, and Torquemada. Mexica chroniclers and other Franciscans, such as Fray Bernardino de Sahagún, either present Nezahualcoyotl in a much different light or exclude him altogether from the history of the Basin of Mexico.

In the 1540s, Fray Bernardino de Sahagún, who came to New Spain in 1529, five years later than Motolinia and Olmos, began to prepare the *Florentine Codex*, the most extensive and encyclopedic of all colonial sources. He used both information from indigenous sources that he collected himself and the chronicles of his Franciscan fellows, Motolinia and Olmos. The *Florentine Codex* consists of twelve volumes. Each volume has its own title that reflects its contents. Although Sahagún compiled the work just as his Franciscan fellows did previously, he employed indigenous informants in collecting data and writing the text in Nahuatl. The data of the codex are collected from three major places, Tepepulco of Texcoco, Tlatelolco, and Tenochtitlan, where Sahagún lived. The codex is able to cover other regions, however, because many of the indigenous informants were from other areas, including Chalco, Azcapotzalco, and Cuauhtitlan.[18] The indigenous scribes recorded the information they collected in their own language, Nahuatl. The codex describes almost every aspect of indigenous society, including religion, politics, history, geography, astrology, commerce, and medicine. Book Eight (*Florentine Codex* 1950–1982, 8:1–14) deals with the indigenous rulers of Tenochtitlan, Tlatelolco, Texcoco, and Huexotla from pre- to post-Hispanic times. The Mexica rulers and their conquests are recorded beginning with the first ruler, Acamapichtli, through the sixteenth, don Cristóbal Cecepatic. The history of the Texcoca rulers begins with Tlatecatzin, who probably represents Quinatzin Tlaltecatzin, and ends with the thirteenth ruler, don Hernando Pimentel, who was a close friend of Motolinia. Among these rulers, Nezahualcoyotl appears as a progressive leader of Texcoco who conquers many other indigenous nations in cooperation with the Mexica ruler Itzcoatl.

This detailed indigenous history collected in the *Florentine Codex*, however, does not record the religious skepticism nor the fair legal system that Sahagún's contemporary Franciscans attributed to Nezahualcoyotl. In the first three volumes, Sahagún deals with indigenous gods and religious ceremonies just like Motolinia and Olmos did in their books, but Nezahualcoyotl's skepticism appears nowhere. Sahagún (*Florentine Codex* 1950–1982, 8:41–42) describes the court of justice that the rulers supervised, but he does not present Nezahualcoyotl as a fair legal practitioner or legislator. Rather, Sahagún presents Moctezuma Xocoyotzin as an exemplary ruler who punished corrupt judges. Sahagún's silence about Nezahualcoyotl's religious and legal practices calls into question the initial representation of Nezahualcoyotl as a religious skeptic and fair legal practitioner. Sahagún spent a few years in Tepepulco, which is located in the Texcoca region, and he worked in the same areas from which his Franciscan predecessors had collected their sources. Sahagún surely would have been familiar with Motolinia's and Olmos's versions of indigenous history in which Nezahualcoyotl figured so prominently, but evidently his own research did not confirm the previous accounts.

Excluding the Texcoca sources, the most abundant data about Nezahualcoyotl come from Mexica sources. These Mexica sources, both pictorial and alphabetic, generally focus on the historical events that concern their own ethnic group. Thus, they do not record the activities of Nezahualcoyotl in as much detail as do the Texcoca sources, but they provide some fragmented information on Nezahualcoyotl regarding his political and cultural relationship with the Mexica. Surviving Mexica pictorial scripts include the *Tira de peregrinación* (1964) or the *Codex Boturini*, the *Códice Aubin* (1963), the *Codex Mendoza* (1992), the *Codex Mexicanus* (Menguin 1952), the *Codex Azcatitlan* (1995), and the *Codex Telleriano-Remensis* (1995). The first three codices—the *Tira de peregrinación*, *Códice Aubin*, and *Codex Mendoza*—contain no description of Nezahualcoyotl, but they describe the Mexica cultural, religious, and political system, which provides useful information for reconstructing that of Texcoco during Nezahualcoyotl's reign. For instance, the elements of Mexica life depicted in the *Codex Mendoza*, such as education, employment, and crimes and punishments, are almost identical with the Texcoca practices described in the Texcoca pictorial map, *Mapa Quinatzin*, and the chronicles of Pomar and Alva Ixtlilxochitl. The other three Mexica codices—the *Codex Azcatitlan*, *Codex Mexicanus*, and *Codex Telleriano-Remensis*—depict certain historical events related to Nezahualcoyotl such as his birth and death, his military activities with the Mexica rulers Itzcoatl, Moctezuma Ilhuicamina, and Axayacatl, and his construction work undertaken for the Mexica, including the aqueduct of Chapultepec. These historical events depicted in the Mexica sources are fragmented and limited, but they clearly demonstrate Nezahualcoyotl's close relationship with the Mexica. The Mexica tlacuiloque maintain an exclusive focus on the Mexica kings and nobles and their achievements. If they depict non-Mexica rulers, they do so only because these rulers have an important relationship with the Mexica. For instance, the *Codex Azcatitlan* (1995:plate 13) records the Azcapotzalca ruler Tezozomoc who presided over the inauguration of the Mexica rulers Acamapichtli and Cuacuauhpitzahuac, which was an important event in Mexica history. And among all the non-Mexica political figures to appear in Mexica texts, Nezahualcoyotl is the most predominant. The record of Nezahualcoyotl's achievements in Mexica sources suggests that they considered him on a par with other Mexica kings due to the close political relationship that they maintained.

The major Mexica alphabetic texts—such as the *Anales de Tlatelolco* (1948), *Historia de los mexicanos por sus pinturas* (1941), *Legend of the Suns* (1992), *Histoire du Mechique* (1965), and *Crónica mexicana* (Alvarado Tezozomoc 1987)—record briefly or in detail Nezahualcoyotl's political and religious activities. Just like the pictorial scripts, these alphabetic texts focus on Nezahualcoyotl's conquests carried out in alliance with Mexica rulers such as Itzcoatl, Moctezuma Ilhuicamina, and Axayacatl and his participation in religious ceremonies in Tenochtitlan. All these texts confirm that Nezahualcoyotl's political and religious activities were not different from, but rather were quite similar to, those of the Mexica. The *Crónica mexicana* (1987) by Fernando Alvarado Tezozomoc, for example, describes in detail the close religious and political relationship that Nezahualcoyotl had with the Mexica.[19] Alvarado Tezozomoc describes him as the closest political ally who participated in almost every Mexica political activity from conquests to royal ceremonies and also as the most important non-Mexica supporter of the cult of the main Mexica god, Huitzilopochtli. In this chronicle, Nezahualcoyotl appears and acts just like a Mexica ruler.

There are some texts from regions other than Texcoco and Tenochtitlan that record certain historical events related to Nezahualcoyotl. The *Annals of Cuauhtitlan* (1992), which is a part of the *Codex Chimalpopoca*, was written in Nahuatl in 1570 by a native from Cuauhtitlan (Bierhorst 1992:3). The annals record the history of central Mexico and are based on unidentified sources from Texcoco, Cuitlahuac, Colhuacan, and Tenochtitlan. The anonymous author focuses mainly on two groups, the Mexica and the people of Cuauhtitlan, but he also pays much attention to the Texcoca rulers, including Nezahualcoyotl. He describes the assassination of Nezahualcoyotl's father, Huehue Ixtlilxochitl, the persecution of Nezahualcoyotl by the Azcapotzalca king Tezozomoc, and Nezahualcoyotl's role as one of the closest Mexica allies. These annals provide fairly detailed information on Nezahualcoyotl, comparable to the Texcoca chronicles, such as those written by Pomar and Alva Ixtlilxochitl. Chimalpahin, a descendant of a noble family from Chalco-Amecameca, writes several annals in Nahuatl. He focuses on two native groups: the Mexica and the Chalca. Thus, he deals with Mexica history beginning with the peregrination through the end of the sixteenth century, and he represents a variety of ethnic groups, their origins in Chalco, and their relationship to the Mexica. Chimalpahin's *Relaciones originales de Chalco Amaquemecan* (1965) presents Nezahualcoyotl as the closest ally of the Mexica in several military expeditions.

There are some texts, such as the two indigenous songbooks *Romances de los señores de la Nueva España* (1993) and the *Cantares Mexicanos* (1985), that deal with Nezahualcoyotl and are not tied to a specific geographic region. The songs recorded in these texts are drawn from various areas. The songs of the *Romances* were collected by Pomar and are attached to his chronicle as an appendix. He collected the songs from several different regions of central Mexico, but the majority of them come from Texcoco and its allied cities, Tenochtitlan and Tlacopan. According to Garibay (1993, 1:xii–xvii), among the thirty-eight Texcoca songs, Nezahualcoyotl may have composed twenty-eight. These twenty-eight poems constitute the majority of the extant songs attributed to Nezahualcoyotl. The *Cantares Mexicanos* is a more extensive collection than the *Romances* and is collected from the three city-states Tenochtitlan, Texcoco, and Tlacopan and their neighboring regions, Chalco, Huexotzinco, and Tlaxcala. The songs from subject cities such as Chalco and Huexotzinco were gathered as tribute. According to Bierhorst (1985:112–18), the *Cantares Mexicanos* served as historical sources for many chroniclers such as Torquemada and Alva Ixtlilxochitl. The book contains some songs contributed or written by Nezahualcoyotl, which are similar to those of the *Romances*. These songs from *Cantares* and *Romances* indicate the close relationship between Nezahualcoyotl and the Mexica because they were performed at court to celebrate the comradeship between the Mexica and Texcoca rulers. Nezahualcoyotl appears in the songs as a muse who offers artistic inspiration to the Mexica as well as the Texcoca poets.

The representations of Nezahualcoyotl as a religious skeptic, lawmaker, peaceful poet, anti-Mexica sage, and prophet of the destruction of the Aztecs, which many scholars currently accept as valid, have their origin mainly in Texcoca sources produced in the colonial context. The Franciscans who initiated these images and Pomar, Alva Ixtlilxochitl, and Torquemada, who expanded them, all base their description about Nezahualcoyotl exclusively on Texcoca oral, pictorial, and alphabetic sources. In addition, these chroniclers of Nezahualcoyotl interpreted the Texcoca sources from their own ideological perspectives. Moreover, some of their sources such as the *Códice Xolotl*, *Mapa Quinatzin*, and *Mapa Tlotzin*, upon which Alva Ixtlilxochitl and Torquemada relied, already contained a Texcoca regional bias. The texts from other regions, however, do not support these representations of Nezahualcoyotl, and in some cases they explicitly contradict them. The pictorial as well as alphabetic sources from Mexica Tenochtitlan are particularly clear about how Nezahualcoyotl was a faithful follower of indigenous religion and thus could not be distinguished from his contemporary Mexica rulers on the basis of political or religious practices. And texts from Cuauhtitlan and Chalco corroborate the Mexica version. In addition, some of the major Franciscan chroniclers such as Sahagún, who was very familiar with Texcoco and its history, completely silenced the achievements of Nezahualcoyotl. By reviewing and comparing the colonial chronicles and their sources on Nezahualcoyotl, the next chapters present a revision of the history, poetry, and religion of Nezahualcoyotl that has been widely accepted by scholars and students of Aztec studies.

part two

Revising Pre-Hispanic History

From the colonial period to the present, many Nahua scholars have described Texcoco as one of the most politically powerful and culturally advanced city-states of pre-Hispanic Mexico. In this pre-Hispanic history, they present the Chichimec emperor Xolotl as the founder of the Texcoca political dynasty and the Toltec god and ruler Topiltzin Quetzalcoatl as the impetus behind Texcoca cultural advancement. In their works, as the inheritor of these two traditions, Nezahualcoyotl's Texcoco in the fifteenth century appears as a political and cultural center with highly advanced legal, government, religious, and artistic systems. On the other hand, these texts denigrate the Mexica rulers as representative of indigenous military barbarism. However, I demonstrate in the next three chapters that this version of Texcoca history was invented during the colonial period by European and Europeanized Texcoca chroniclers such as Juan Bautista Pomar and Fernando de Alva Ixtlilxochitl. The political and cultural system that Nezahualcoyotl instituted in his city actually originated in the Mexica city of Tenochtitlan.

CHAPTER TWO

Founding the Texcoca Dynasty
Chichimec Xolotl and Toltec Topiltzin Quetzalcoatl

From the fall of the Toltec empire in the 1170s to the establishment of the Aztec empire in the 1430s, central Mexico became an arena of struggle in which multiple immigrant groups, such as the Chichimecs, and the native residents, such as the Toltecs, competed for land and political power. They frequently conducted wars against each other and sometimes peacefully assimilated with each other through intermarriage. The Toltecs, who migrated from Tula, the capital of the Toltec empire, and established themselves in central Mexico earlier than the Chichimecs, maintained a politically and culturally advanced lifestyle. Numerous pictorial codices depict the use of cotton cloth and the cultivation of corn as identifying symbols of Toltec culture. The Chichimecs, who migrated from the north later than the Toltecs, were hunter-gatherers rather than cultivators. Their identifying features in the pictographic medium were arrows, bows, and animal skin clothing. In most cases, the Chichimecs abandoned their original lifestyle and adopted the advanced Toltec political, religious, and cultural systems (Kirchhoff 1948; León-Portilla 1967a). The Chichimecs even gave up their mother tongue for Nahuatl, the language of the Toltecs. Due to this Toltecization, Colhuacan, the capital city of the Toltecs in the basin, was venerated as the place of ancestors. When the Mexica founded Tenochtitlan in 1325, most Chichimec groups in central Mexico had already settled down, assimilated to Toltec culture, and in many cases established ethnically diverse city-states. Despite their political independence, these city-states claimed both the Toltecs and the Chichimecs as their foundational ancestors. Some of them, such as Texcoco and Tenayuca (*Códice Xolotl* 1996), Tepetlaoztoc (*Códice de Tepetlaoztoc* 1992), and Chalco (Chimalpahin 1998), begin their foundational history with the immigration of their Chichimec ancestors. On the other hand, other city-states, such as Cuauhtitlan (*Annals* of *Cuauhtitlan* 1992), Cholula (*Historia Tolteca-Chichimeca* 1989), and Tlaxcala (Muñoz Camargo 1986), begin their regional histories with the Toltecs. Both versions, however, demonstrate that sooner or later the Chichimecs adopted the Toltec lifestyle, and the Toltecs accepted the Chichimecs as immigrants or were forced to accept them as neighbors in their territory. In some cases, these sources call their ancestors the Toltec-Chichimecs.

In their pictorial and alphabetic texts, the Texcoca demonstrate their Chichimec and Toltec origin more than any other regional group in the Basin of Mexico. They present one of the most powerful Chichimec rulers, Xolotl, as the founder of the Texcoca dynasty. Along with Xolotl, they also present Topiltzin Quetzalcoatl, the symbolic figure of the Toltec civilization, as another founder of their dynasty. In this way, the Texcoca argue that their city, Texcoco, inherited not only the vast Chichimec land, Chichimecatlalli, from the great Chichimec emperor Xolotl, but also the advanced political and religious systems from the last Toltec ruler, Topiltzin Quetzalcoatl. Don Fernando de Alva Ixtlilxochitl, in particular, repeatedly attests that the Texcoca dynasty is the legitimate heir of both Chichimec and Toltec traditions. This claim, however, was motivated by the desire to embellish Texcoco's regional history by exaggerating and in many cases even inventing the political and cultural achievements of Texcoca rulers. In addition, Alva Ixtlilxochitl's making Topiltzin Quetzalcoatl a founder of the Texcoca dynasty was a postconquest invention motivated by a Christian perception of history: this Texcoca Topiltzin Quetzalcoatl was not a pre-Hispanic Toltec ruler but rather the postconquest figure Quetzalcoatl–Saint Thomas, whom Spanish friars introduced in their evangelization efforts.

Making Xolotl the Founder of the Texcoca Dynasty

Most Nahua scholars from the colonial period to the present have accepted Xolotl as the founder of the Texcoca dynasty, but this acceptance is based solely on the colonial Texcoca sources that overlook the continuous revision of the foundational history of the Texcoca dynasty. The Texcoca pictorial texts, *Mapa Quinatzin* (Aubin 1886a), *Mapa Tlotzin* (Aubin 1886b), and *Códice Xolotl* (1996), present Quinatzin as the founder of Texcoco, but they differ in regard to the founder of the ruling Texcoca dynasty. The *Mapa Quinatzin* depicts Quinatzin as the founder of both Texcoco and its dynasty: it records no previous rulers or ancestors before Quinatzin, and he appears seated on the authority mat, icpalli (figure 2.1).[1] The *Mapa Tlotzin* clearly establishes that the Texcoca dynasty begins with Tlotzin, who cofounds the city-state of Texcoco along with his son Quinatzin (figure 2.2). The *Códice Xolotl* also depicts Quinatzin as the founder of Texcoco but traces its dynastic genealogy further back to Xolotl of Tenayuca (figure 2.3). Don Fernando de Alva Ixtlilxochitl (1997), Fray Juan de Torquemada (1975), and other colonial chroniclers whose writings are based on these three codices construct a coherent Texcoca genealogical history by making a logical

Tlailotlaca

Quinatzin

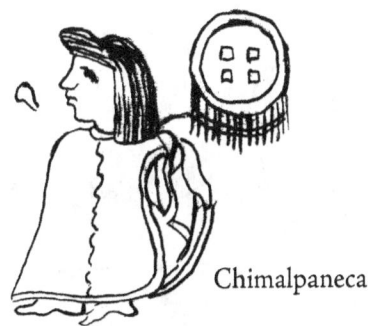

Chimalpaneca

FIG. 2.1

Quinatzin as the first ruler of Texcoco and his reception of the two immigrant groups, Tlailotlaca and Chimalpaneca, from the *Mapa Quinatzin*. Reproduced from M. Aubin (1886a) with permission of the Bibliothèque nationale de France.

Quinatzin is depicted here as a growling deer head. He is the first ruler to sit on an *icpalli* (authority mat). His authority mat appears very small and primitive compared to that of his son Techotlalatzin and his great-great-grandson Nezahualcoyotl in the same text. The rustic nature of his authority mat in contrast to that of later rulers indicates that under Quinatzin's rule Texcoco began as a small city-state. As the first ruler of Texcoco, he receives two immigrant groups, the Tlailotlaca (Returning People) and Chimalpaneca (People of Shield Place). The cultural and ethnic difference between Quinatzin and these immigrants is evident: the former is a Chichimec group wearing animal skin while the latter are either Toltecs or a Tolteczied people wearing cotton clothes.

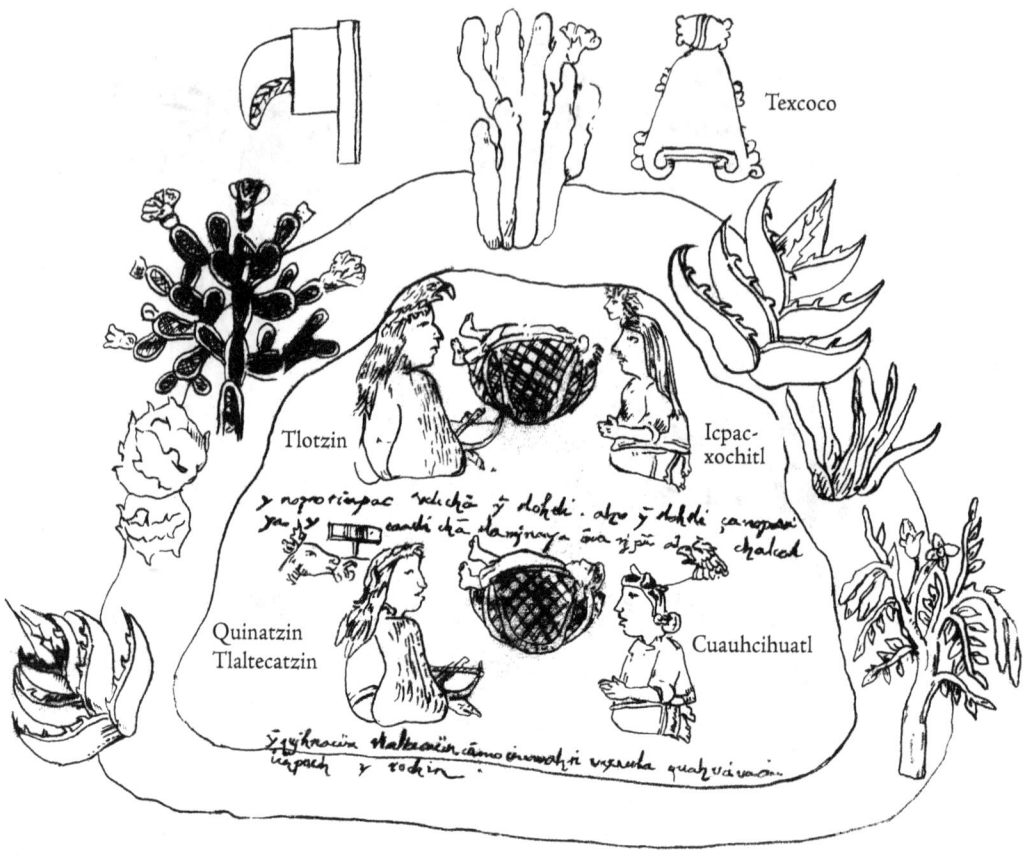

FIG. 2.2

Tlotzin's and Quinatzin's foundation of Texcoco from the *Mapa Tlotzin*. Reproduced from M. Aubin (1886b) with permission of the Bibliothèque nationale de France.

In a cave in the Texcoca region, Tlotzin (Falcon) and his wife Icpacxochitl (Chaplets [Flower on the Head]) are watching over their baby, Quinatzin, who appears between them. Below them, Quinatzin and his wife, Cuauhcihuatl (Eagle Woman), face each other with their own son Techotlalatzin between them. The *tlacuilo* of the map describes the four figures as the founders of Texcoco because they are depicted in a cave separated from their descendant Texcoca rulers who appear outside the cave. For the Chichimecs, a cave generally symbolizes the place of their origin and foundation. The most significant example of the Chichimec cave origin can be found in the departure of all of the Chichimec groups from the famous cave Chicomoztoc (Seven Caves).

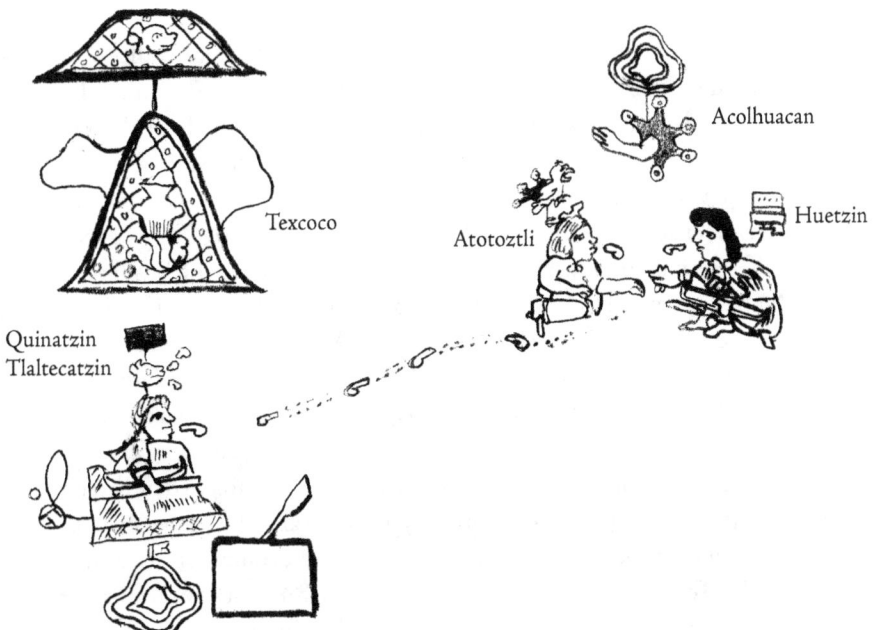

FIG. 2.3

Quinatzin-Tlaltecatzin's founding of Texcoco from the *Códice Xolotl* (1996: map 3). Reproduced with permission of the Bibliothèque nationale de France.

Under Texcoco, Quinatzin (Growling Deer Head)–Tlaltecatzin (Resident on the Earth) founds his city Texcoco in 1 Flint, which is depicted by a square of land with a founding stick. He is talking to Huetzin, ruler of Acolhuacan (Coatlichan). He appears to ask Huetzin permission to found Texcoco. As the codex frequently indicates, the speech glyph of the ruler who has authority always extends toward his subject rulers or those who have lower political status. Huetzin's speech glyph extends toward Quinatzin-Tlaltecatzin, not the other way around. The *Códice Xolotl* is the only pictorial source to depict Quinatzin's genealogical connection with Xolotl of Tenayuca and by reading this codex, Alva Ixtlilxochitl argues that Quinatzin received the land from his great-grandfather Xolotl. This figure seems to demonstrate this relationship. A head of a dog, which depicts Xolotl, inside the small hill connected to Texcoco shows that Texcoco belonged to Xolotl. However, in this figure Quinatzin talks to Huetzin rather than Xolotl about his foundation of Texcoco. This discrepancy seems to be caused by Texcoca historians' modification of history. As Alva Ixtlilxochitl and the *Códice Xolotl* describe, Texcoco might have been a part of Xolotl's territory before the foundation of Texcoco, but two or three generations later, Texcoco had become part of Acolhuacan or Coatlichan, the oldest and most powerful city-state in the eastern Basin of Mexico. Thus, when Quinatzin was founding Texcoco at the end of the thirteenth century, he needed to ask permission from Huetzin, not Xolotl. Nevertheless, the colonial Texcoca Alva Ixtlilxochitl and the *tlacuilo* of the *Códice Xolotl* needed to articulate their historical relationship to Xolotl because they needed a way to historically legitimize their own political dominance over Coatlichan or Acolhuacan during Nezahualcoyotl's reign in the fifteenth century. Such a modification of history is evident several times in the *Códice Xolotl*. This figure is an example. The tlacuilo of the codex describes his ancestor Quinatzin as a ruler by depicting him on the *icpalli* while Huetzin appears without the icpalli, in spite of the fact that Quinatzin is asking him permission to found Texcoco.

FOUNDING THE TEXCOCA DYNASTY

connection between the rulers depicted on the Texcoca codices. They assume that the main figures, such as Nopaltzin, Tlotzin, and Quinatzin, in each of the Texcoca codices refer respectively to the individuals of the same name in the other ones. For them, for instance, the three Quinatzins who appear as the founder of Texcoco in the *Mapa Quinatzin*, the *Mapa Tlotzin*, and the *Códice Xolotl*, respectively, are the same person. In addition, the *Mapa Tlotzin* records a different name, Amacui, for the person who comes to the Basin of Mexico with Nopaltzin and Tlotzin, but the colonial chroniclers identify him with Xolotl. Moreover, they also suppose that Xolotl (Amacui), Nopaltzin, and Tlotzin have a genealogical relationship in which Xolotl appears as the father of Nopaltzin, grandfather of Tlotzin, and great-grandfather of Quinatzin, the founder of Texcoco. According to Alva Ixtlilxochitl's interpretation of the three Texcoca codices, the genealogy of the Texcoca dynasty extends two or three generations further back than that of the *Mapa Quinatzin* and the *Mapa Tlotzin*. This genealogical extension appears to enhance the importance, prestige, and legitimacy of the Texcoca dynasty, but this revised history causes serious chronological problems in Texcoca historiography, which resulted in apparent contradictions in the three codices.

In the *Códice Xolotl* (1996), Quinatzin appears as a contemporary of his great-grandfather, Xolotl, during whose reign Quinatzin participated in several wars. According to the *Mapa Tlotzin* (Aubin 1886b), on the other hand, Quinatzin is not a contemporary of Xolotl or Amacui or even his son, Nopaltzin. In this map, Quinatzin first appears as a baby in a cradle while his supposed great-grandfather, Amacui or Xolotl, already had his son, Nopaltzin, and fully grown grandson, Tlotzin (figure 2.4). Alva Ixtlilxochitl, who consulted these three texts for his chronicles, demonstrates such a chronological confusion. He often describes Quinatzin in a completely different period from that of Xolotl, but he sometimes presents the former as a clear contemporary of the latter.[2] He even records that Quinatzin received land from Xolotl to found Texcoco (Alva Ixtlilxochitl 1997, 1:426). Alva Ixtlilxochitl's own chronology ironically demonstrates the impossibility of the interaction between Xolotl and Quinatzin: Xolotl died in the year 13 Flint (1127) at the latest, while Quinatzin became the ruler of Texcoco in 1 Rabbit (1140) at the earliest (O'Gorman 1997:100–101).[3] This chronological discrepancy between the Texcoca sources with regard to Texcoca genealogy appears to have been created by the Texcoca painter-scribes' attempt to establish a genealogical connection between their founder, Quinatzin, who lived at the end of the thirteenth century, and Xolotl, who was revered as one of the most powerful rulers among the Chichimec groups in the twelfth century.[4] All the existing Texcoca sources record the same rulers, from Quinatzin through Techotlalatzin and Huehue Ixtlilxochitl to Nezahualcoyotl, with no chronological discrepancy. The chronological discrepancy in the Texcoca genealogy among the Texcoca codices only occurs before the reign of Quinatzin, that is, before the foundation of

FIG. 2.4

Three Chichimec leaders of the eastern Basin of Mexico from the *Mapa Tlotzin*. Reproduced from M. Aubin (1886b) with permission of the Bibliothèque nationale de France.

The three leaders, Amacui (Paper Grasper), Nopaltzin (Cactus), and Tlotzin (Falcon), stay in a cave near Cuauhyacac (Peak on a Tree) with their wives, Malinalxochitl (Twisted Flower), Cuauhcihuatl (Eagle Woman), and Icpacxochitl (Chaplets [Flower on the Head]), respectively. Following Alva Ixtlilxochitl, the previous readers of the *Mapa Tlotzin* such as Aubin (1886b) and Ramírez (2001, 2:293–313) identify Amacui as father of Nopaltzin and grandfather of Tlotzin, but this map does not depict such a relationship. However, Amacui is probably the leader of the other two because he is always depicted first in the map as the above figure demonstrates.

the city-state of Texcoco. This implies a certain manipulation of the Texcoca sources in their history before Quinatzin's reign.

The *Mapa Tlotzin* (Aubin 1886b) suggests that the individuals who appear with the same names in the three Texcoca codices might not be identical. This map describes two Chichimec leaders, Amacui and Nopaltzin, who came to the Basin of Mexico with Tlotzin and stayed together in Cuauhyacac for a certain time. However, it does not convey any genealogical relationship between the three figures. Rather, the notes in Nahuatl below the figures suggest that each leader is independent of the others, because each of them simultaneously founded his own city-state:

> Oncan mochtin motlalico in Quauhyacac: oc cencatca. Qui noncan onehuac in Amacui; nehuan icihuauh yaque in Cohuatlichan. Quin no oncan onehuac in Nopal; nehuan icihuauh yaque in Huexotla. Quin no oncan onehuac in Tlotli; nehuan icihuauh yaque in Oztoticpac. (Aubin 1886b:309)

> All came to establish themselves there in Cuauhyacac: All were still there together; later Amacui left there; he and his wife went to Coatlichan. Later Nopal left there; he and his wife went to Huexotla. Later Tlotli left there; he and his wife went to Oztoticpac. (author's translation)

According to the *Mapa Tlotzin*, then, Nopaltzin and Amacui founded Huexotla and Coatlichan, respectively, while Tlotzin established himself in Texcoco. In previous correlations of the information in this map with that which appears in the *Codex Xolotl* (1996), Amacui is generally identified with Xolotl, and Nopaltzin with Nopaltzin. The *Mapa Quinatzin* (Aubin 1886a), however, suggests that the Amacui/Xolotl and the Nopaltzins depicted in the *Mapa Tlotzin* and the *Códice Xolotl* could be different people. The *Códice Xolotl* gives the names of Xolotl's and Nopaltzin's respective wives as Tomiyauh and Azcaxochitzin, but the *Mapa Tlotzin* records different names: Malinalxochitl for Xolotl's wife and Cuauhcihuatl for Nopaltzin's wife. In addition, Azcaxochitzin in the *Códice Xolotl* is a Toltec princess from Colhuacan, while Cuauhcihuatl in the *Mapa Tlotzin* is a Chichimec. Furthermore, the *Códice Xolotl* describes Tlotzin's wife as a Toltec Pachxochitzin, while the *Mapa Tlotzin* describes her as a Chichimec Icpacxochitl. If we consider again the fact that these maps were created in the 1540s by the same Texcoca royal descendants, then this inconsistency among the Texcoca sources, with regard to the history of the Texcoca dynasty before the reign of Quinatzin, raises serious questions about their claims that Xolotl was the founder of the Texcoca dynasty.

According to the *Códice Xolotl* (1996) and the chronicles of Alva Ixtlilxochitl (1997) and Torquemada (1975), which are based on this codex, Xolotl was the first Chichimec ruler to establish an enormous empire extending beyond the

Basin of Mexico. These texts describe Xolotl as a powerful Chichimec leader who arrived at the basin and settled in Tenayuca with six vassals in the year 5 Flint (1172), four years after the destruction of Tula (figure 2.5). He founded his first city, Xoloc, and began to explore the basin and areas beyond. The first map of the *Códice Xolotl* shows Xolotl's ambitious domain, which went far beyond the basin and covered Chiuhnautecatl in the Nevado de Toluca to the southwest, Poyauhtecatl in the state of Veracruz to the southeast, Tenanitec in the state of Puebla to the northeast, and Metztitlan and Atotonilco in the state of Hidalgo to the northwest. The second map of the codex records that Xolotl conquered major cities, such as Colhuacan, which had been constructed by the Toltec descendants of Tula and played a leading role as a political and cultural center in the basin. Following the geopolitical description in the first and second maps of the *Códice Xolotl*, Alva Ixtlilxochitl (1997) and Torquemada (1975) recorded the extensive nature of Xolotl's empire. According to these Texcoco-based sources, the Texcoca rulers were the genealogically legitimate heirs of Xolotl's political power and his Chichimecatlalli (Chichimec land). Xolotl's Chichimecatlalli described in Texcoco-based sources, however, seems to be considerably inflated.

Several scholars suggest that Xolotl was merely one of many Chichimec leaders, not, as the Texcoca sources claim, a dominant emperor who controlled a vast territory. Charles Dibble (1954–1955:286) argues that Xolotl might have been a leader of nomadic Chichimec groups to the east and north of the Texcoca lake, because only Texcoca sources contain details about Xolotl; accounts from other regions, such as the writings of Sahagún from Tepepulco, completely ignore him. Dibble concludes, therefore, that Xolotl could not have controlled such extensive territory nor held such political and military supremacy over the basin as described in the Texcoca sources. Following Dibble, Jiménez Moreno (1954–1955:230) also argues that Xolotl could not have ruled an empire and that, even if he had, it must have been minor and short-lived.[5] Brotherston (1995:62–71) suggests that Xolotl was one among several regional leaders in the Basin of Mexico. By comparing the native texts produced in several regions that claim Chichimec origins, he proposes five principal Chichimec arenas: the Highland Basin, the Cholula Plain, Tlaxcala, Coixtlahuaca, and Cuextlan. Brotherston demonstrates that Xolotl was one of the leaders who came to the Basin of Mexico. At the same time, by examining the *Tlatelolco Map*, the *Códice de Tepetlaoztoc* (1992), and the *Annals of Cuauhtitlan* (1992), Brotherston also demonstrates how neighboring Chichimec leaders challenged Xolotl. The *Tlatelolco Map* indicates the northern boundary of Xolotl's domain by depicting his confrontation with Cuauhtzin (Little Eagle), who was the Chichimec leader of Xoloc near Xaltocan. The *Códice de Tepetlaoztoc* describes the political independence of Tepetlaoztoc until the middle of the fifteenth century, which, according to the *Códice Xolotl* (1996), was supposed to have been taken by Xolotl two centuries earlier. The *Códice de Tepetlaoztoc* even claims that the Chichimec

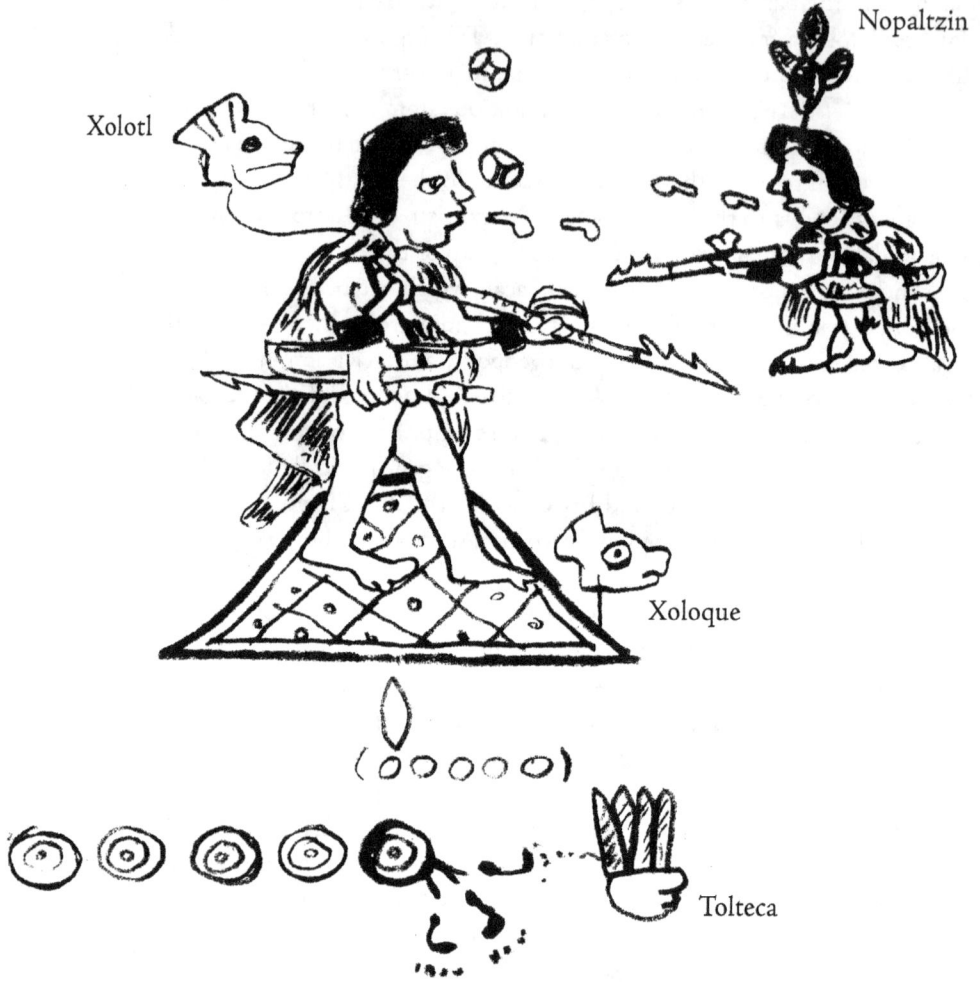

FIG. 2.5
Xolotl's arrival at the Basin of Mexico from the *Códice Xolotl* (1996:map 1). Reproduced with permission of the Bibliothèque nationale de France.

The meaning of the name Xolotl is unknown, but his glyph is the head of a dog. He arrived at the Basin of Mexico in 5 Flint, that is, five years after the fall of the Toltecs (Tolteca: People of Tula). He founded Xoloc or Xoloque (Place of Xolotl) and spoke to Nopaltzin about more conquests in the Basin of Mexico. Many colonial and modern historians identify Nopaltzin as a son of Xolotl because the first reader of the codex, Alva Ixtlilxochitl, suggested this relationship, and Nopaltzin succeeded Xolotl after the latter's death. However, the codex does not depict such a relationship (Dibble 1996:7). As the first Chichimecs in the basin, they carried bows and arrows and wore a cloth of animal skin, but their descendants exchanged them for shields, swords, and cotton clothing as they assimilated to the culture of their Toltec neighbors.

leaders of Tepetlaoztoc, such as Tonatiuh and Ocotochtli, arrived in the basin earlier than Xolotl. Thus, in contrast to the image of Xolotl as an emperor who controlled an enormous area beyond the Basin of Mexico, Brotherston argues that he was a regional leader who competed with many other Chichimec leaders for land and power within the basin.

Xolotl may, however, have been one of the strongest regional Chichimec leaders in the Basin of Mexico. The *Códice Techialoyan García Granados* (1992) from the Azcapotzalca area located in the eastern basin also depicts that Xolotl's power reached various regions beyond the basin, such as Tula in the state of Hidalgo, Zacatlan in the state of Puebla, and Tlaximaloyan in the state of Michoacan. The *Códice Techialoyan* obviously exaggerates Xolotl's territory, as in the *Códice Xolotl* (1996), but its corroboration of the existence of Xolotl and his founding of several city-states in the basin provides significant evidence for determining the role of Xolotl in the Basin of Mexico. The two codices originated from different regions: the *Códice Xolotl* from Texcoco and the *Códice Techialoyan* from Azcapotzalco. This different origin demonstrates that Xolotl maintained considerable territory on both the west and the east sides of the basin and that he exercised power over several major city-states. This information is more reliable when one takes into consideration that Texcoco and Azcapotzalco were major enemies during the Tepanec-Acolhuacan war, but they claim the same person, Xolotl, as their genealogical founder.

If Xolotl founded not only Texcoco but also many other cities in the Basin of Mexico, then these cities could also claim Xolotl as the founder of their dynasty or their city. This claim that the cities were founded by Xolotl is even more convincing when one takes into account that Xolotl either installed his own descendants as, or married his daughters to, the rulers of these cities. The Texcoca historian's claim that the Texcoca dynasty exclusively inherited Xolotl's political legitimacy should be reconsidered in the broader context of pre-Hispanic history, because there were many other city-states that could claim they were also legitimate heirs of Xolotl, and in fact some of them did so. The *Códice Xolotl* (1996) and the *Códice Techialoyan* (1992) show Xolotl as the conqueror of existing cities and at the same time the founder of new cities that would play major political roles in the Basin of Mexico. According to the second map from the *Códice Xolotl*, Xolotl granted the three Chichimec leaders, Aculhua, Chiconcuauh, and Tzontecomatl, the authority to found Azcapotzalco, Coatlichan, and Xaltocan, respectively (figure 2.6).[6] And he married his two daughters to Aculhua and Chiconcuauh. Moreover, Xolotl also distributed land to the six vassals who had accompanied him on his journey to the basin, and they founded important cities as well. One of them, Acatomatl, is worth mentioning. He was awarded Zohuatepec, near Coatepec, which was one of the leading cities in the eastern basin, and in the *Relaciones geográficas* (1982–1988, 6:41), he was recorded as one of the cofounders of Coatepec. The *Códice Techialoyan* cites many cities in the basin that were founded either

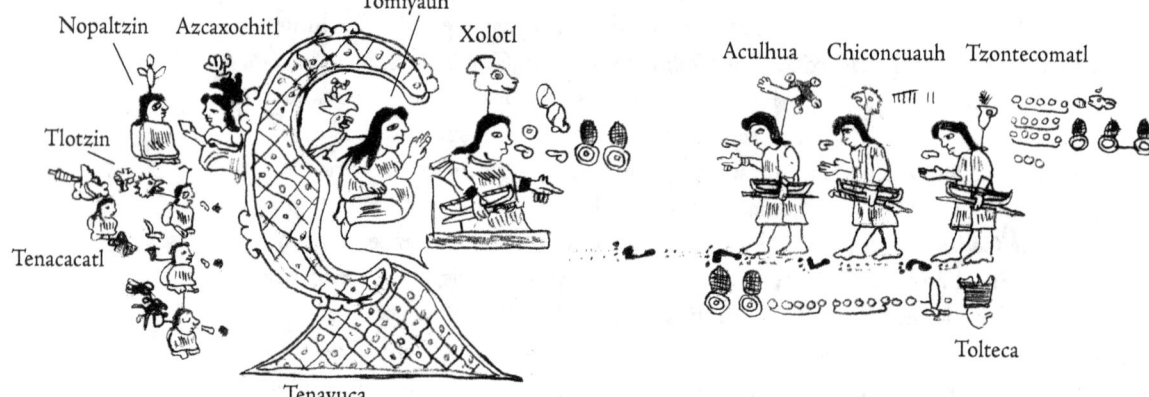

FIG. 2.6
Xolotl's reception of the three Chichimec leaders from the *Códice Xolotl* (1996:map 2). Reproduced with permission of the Bibliothèque nationale de France.

While Xolotl and his wife, Tomiyauh (Our Maize Flower), moved from Xoloque to live in Tenayuca, the three Chichimec leaders, Aculhua (One Who Lives near Bent Water), Chiconcuauh (Seven Eagle), and Tzontecomatl (Head [hair gourd]), came to ask for land from Xolotl. Xolotl gave them Azcapotzalco, Xaltocan, and Coatlichan (also known as Acolhuacan), respectively, and he married his two daughters to Aculhua and Chiconcuauh. The arrival of the three leaders and the distribution of land occurred in 1 Flint, that is, fifty-two years after the destruction of the Toltecs. Behind Tomiyauh, Nopaltzin is sitting with his wife, Azcaxochitl (Ant-Flower), and below them their three children appear. The first one is called Tlotzin Pochotl (Falcon, Silk-Cotton Tree). Behind Tlotzin appears Nopaltzin's other son, Tenacacaltzin (Wall), Tlotzin's half brother. This figure provides a clue for the future political map of the Basin of Mexico after Xolotl's death. Even though Nopaltzin succeeded Xolotl in Tenayuca, the three cities, Azcapotzalco, Xaltocan, and Coatlichan, challenged Tenayuca's dominance and began emerging as political centers in the west, north, and east of the Basin of Mexico. This figure also illustrates the dispersion of Xolotl's descendants. Both Nopaltzin's sons, Tlotzin and Tenacacaltzin, and Aculhua's and Chiconcuauh's children could claim Xolotl's political legacy as his grandchildren. In fact, Tenacacaltzin succeeded Nopaltzin in Tenayuca, and thus the rulers of Tenayuca could have claimed to be the legitimate heirs of Xolotl. In addition, in the beginning of the fifteenth century, Aculhua's son Tezozomoc claimed Xolotl's title, *chichimecatecuhtli* (Chichimec lord). Alva Ixtlilxochitl consistently claimed, and later historians widely accepted, that Tlotzin succeeded Nopaltzin, and thus Tlotzin and his descendant Texcoca rulers were the legitimate heirs of Xolotl. From the beginning of Chichimec history in the Basin of Mexico, however, there were many of Xolotl's descendants who would later lay claim to Xolotl's legacy just like the Texcoca rulers did.

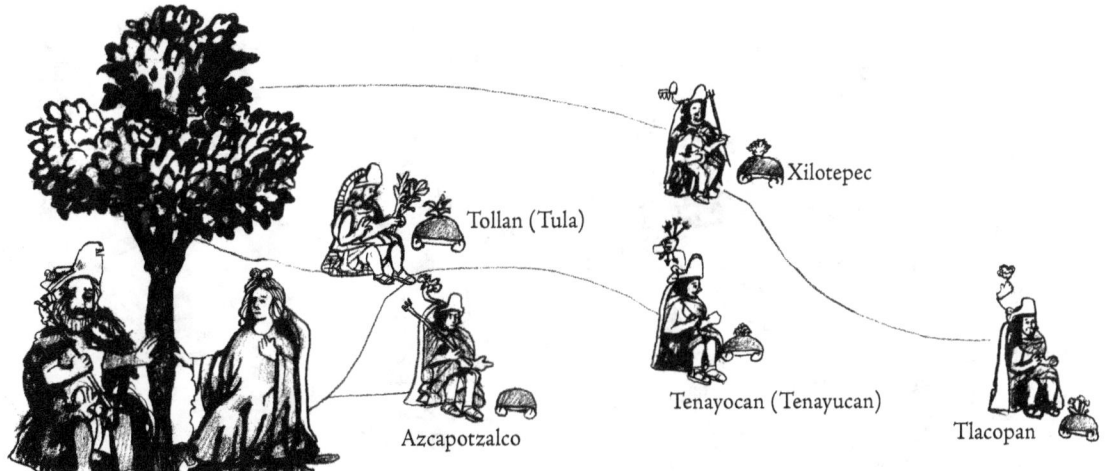

FIG. 2.7
Xolotl's subject city-states from the *Códice Techialoyan García Granados* (1992). Reproduced with permission of El Colegio Mexiquense A.C.

Xolotl and the rulers of the city-states are depicted like European kings, but the codex still maintains essential indigenous concepts of genealogy and foundation. A dynasty born from a tree is a common notion in Mesoamerica (Brotherston 1995:98–117). The *Códice Techialoyan* seems to participate in this tradition by depicting Xolotl under the big tree from which his subject cities are derived. Along with the Texcoca sources from the eastern Basin of Mexico, this codex from the Azcapotzalca area in the western basin is significant in that it verifies the existence of Xolotl and his territorial domain, about which numerous modern historians remain skeptical.

---

by Xolotl himself or under his influence, such as Azcapotzalco, Xilotepec, Tenayuca, Tlacopan, and many others (figure 2.7).

In the founding history of Texcoco described in the *Códice Xolotl* (1996), the *Mapa Quinatzin* (Aubin 1886a), and the *Mapa Tlotzin* (Aubin 1886b), Quinatzin's inauguration as the first ruler of Texcoco appears ambiguous. The *Mapa Tlotzin* depicts Quinatzin as a youth in Tlatzallan-Tlalanoztoc and records him and his father, Tlotzin, as cofounders of Texcoco, but it does not depict when and why he moved to Texcoco from Tlatzallan-Tlalanoztoc, where he was born, or where his father was ruling. Based on the *Códice Xolotl*, however, Alva Ixtlilxochitl insists that Quinatzin went to Tenayuca with his father, Tlotzin, when his grandfather, Nopaltzin, died and returned from Tenayuca as soon as his father died in 1 Rabbit (1298). Alva Ixtlilxochitl (1997, 1:310, 2:28) provides two versions of Quinatzin's departure from Tenayuca where Quinatzin's great-grandfather, Xolotl, governed his empire: (1) Quinatzin left and conceded the throne to his uncle, that is, Tlotzin's half brother, Tenacacaltzin; and (2) Tenacacaltzin forcibly

FOUNDING THE TEXCOCA DYNASTY

FIG. 2.8

Tenacacaltzin's succession to Nopaltzin and his departure from Tenayuca from the *Códice Xolotl* (1996:map 4). Reproduced with permission of the Bibliothèque nationale de France.

Nopaltzin died in Tenayuca after reigning for thirty-two years, and Tenacacaltzin succeeded him. He fought a war against the Mexica in 2 Reed (1351), but he was defeated and fled from Tenayuca with his fellow Chichimec Zayollin (Fly). Tenacacaltzin's succession clearly undermines the Texcoca rulers' claim that they are the legitimate heirs of Xolotl, which Alva Ixtlilxochitl tried to verify throughout his chronicles. Tlotzin (Falcon) seems to have stayed in Tenayuca but without any political authority. He is depicted under Nopaltzin's mummy bundle without an *icpalli*.

---

took the throne from Quinatzin, the legitimate heir of Tlotzin, and exiled him to Texcoco. Alva Ixtlilxochitl's two versions are not supported by the *Códice Xolotl*, which clearly depicts Tenacacaltzin's ascension as heir of Nopaltzin (figure 2.8). Quinatzin's father, Tlotzin, did not succeed Nopaltzin, but rather Tlotzin's half brother, Tenacacaltzin, sits on the authority mat, the icpalli, while Tlotzin is sitting without any authority mat below the mummy bundle of his father's body. Thus, Tlotzin's son, Quinatzin, does not seem to ascend to the throne of the *chichimecatecuhtli* (Chichimec lord) in Tenayuca.[7] Alva Ixtlilxochitl misreads the codex in order to justify the position of Texcoco as a legitimate heir of Xolotl. Tenacacaltzin's succession to the throne describes that Tenayuca, rather, seems to have been Xolotl's legitimate heir.

Because Xolotl founded or assisted with founding many city-states in the Basin of Mexico, they can all claim the Chichimec ruler as their founder as well as the genealogical origin of their ruling dynasty. After the Mexicas' conquest of Tenayuca, the capital of Xolotl's empire, in 2 Reed (1351) under the patronage of the Azcapotzalca ruler, Acolnahuacatzin, several powerful Chichimec rulers might have claimed themselves as Xolotl's heirs. Alva Ixtlilxochitl (1997, 1: 310–12) himself records that Aculhua in Azcapotzalco conquered Tenacacaltzin's Tenayuca and made himself chichimecatecuhtli (Chichimec lord), which was Xolotl's title. This is an important event in Chichimec history in the basin because this conquest of Xolotl's original city-state allows Azcapotzalco to lay claim to Xolotl's legacy. It also explains why in the beginning of fifteenth century Aculhua's son, Tezozomoc, could call himself Xolotl (Alva Ixtlilxochitl 1997, 1:402). The *Annals of Cuauhtitlan* (1992:48–50) also record that Tezozomoc was called Xolotl. When Coyohua, who served as Nezahualcoyotl's tutor and guardian after Huehue Ixtlilxochitl's assassination, went to talk to Tezozomoc, he called this Azcapotzalca ruler "Xolotzin" (the honorific form of Xolotl) several times. By misinterpreting the *Códice Xolotl*, Alva Ixtlilxochitl argues that Tezozomoc took away the Texcoca rulers' legitimate land and title that they inherited from Xolotl. The historical context in which Coyohua identifies Tezozomoc as Xolotl, however, reveals the symbolic role that Xolotl played in the Chichimec tradition. When Coyohua met Tezozomoc at the beginning of the fifteenth century, this Azcapotzalca ruler was the most powerful Chichimec leader in the Basin of Mexico, having conquered almost all the major city-states in the basin, such as Xaltocan, Tenayuca, Tenochtitlan, Coatlichan, Huexotla, Texcoco, and Coatepec, which, according to Texcoca sources, Xolotl had originally controlled in the twelfth century. Thus, after his death, the name "Xolotl" appears to acquire a symbolic significance referring to the position of power occupied by the most dominant leader among the original Chichimec city-states. Following this Chichimec tradition, the Texcoca sources try to position Nezahualcoyotl as the exclusive heir of Xolotl, by which they would have justified his authority over the other Chichimec city-states when this Texcoca ruler dominated the Basin of Mexico in alliance with the Mexica during his reign. If the Texcoca took advantage of the Chichimec Xolotl in order to justify their political dominance, they also linked themselves to the Toltec Topiltzin Quetzalcoatl in order to establish their cultural and religious preeminence.

Topiltzin Quetzalcoatl as Cofounder of the Texcoca Dynasty

Topiltzin Quetzalcoatl played an important political, religious, and cultural role in Mesoamerica during pre-Hispanic times. The existing Aztec pictorial and alphabetic texts show that he was a historical ruler and priest who maintained a close connection with Tula during the postclassical period, but the archaeological record in many previous urban centers such as Chichen Itza, Teotihuacan, and Xochicalco also demonstrates that his symbolic representation as "Feathered Serpent" enjoyed a long and continuous tradition in Mesoamerica (Brundage 1979:102–28; Carrasco 2000; Florescano 1999; López Austin 1973; Nicholson 2001). The role of Topiltzin Quetzalcoatl before the conquest is, however, difficult to determine with any specificity because he appears as the mythical god

Quetzalcoatl, or the historic Toltec ruler-priest Topiltzin, or in many cases as a combination of the two. In addition, Topiltzin Quetzalcoatl also appears with different names such as Ce Acatl (1 Reed) Topiltzin in the Toltec and Aztec traditions; Gucumatz, Kukulcan, or Nacxitl in the Maya tradition; and 9 Wind in the Mixtec tradition. Moreover, Spanish conquistadores, who tried to justify the conquest by taking advantage of the prophecy of Quetzalcoatl's return, and Spanish friars, who tried to make him into the Christian apostle Saint Thomas, made the roles of Topiltzin Quetzalcoatl even more complicated by projecting their own political and religious ideas onto the pre-Hispanic figure. Numerous accounts record that Topiltzin Quetzalcoatl engaged in many civilized practices such as religious penitence, fasting, calendar making, painting (writing), dancing, singing, and so forth (Brotherston 1979:269–74; Florescano 1999:29). At the same time, they also show that he was both a great warrior king who established a formidable empire, conquering vast regions, and a typical indigenous god that required human sacrifice (Florescano 1999:116–93; Nicholson 2001:255–67). As Eloise Quiñones Keber points out (1988:329), however, "it becomes evident from the texts that in the course of the sixteenth century the political and militaristic roles ascribed to Topiltzin Quetzalcoatl in the earliest written sources progressively diminish as his representation as a pacific and penitential figure becomes increasingly Christianized and mythologized in later documents." Texcoca chroniclers such as Alva Ixtlilxochitl claim that Texcoca rulers are the legitimate heirs of Topiltzin Quetzalcoatl, and they reproduce the pacific and "civilized" image that had already been Christianized, thus eliminating the political role of the indigenous Topiltzin Quetzalcoatl.

The role of Quetzalcoatl in Texcoca history seems to be very limited before the publication of Alva Ixtlilxochitl's works (1997) at the beginning of the seventeenth century. The earlier Texcoca pictorial texts such as the *Códice Xolotl* (1996), the *Mapa Quinatzin* (Aubin 1886a), and the *Mapa Tlotzin* (Aubin 1886b) mention neither the god Quetzalcoatl nor the ruler Quetzalcoatl. These texts simply describe the Toltecization of the Texcoca Chichimec ancestors by depicting the change from a nomadic to a sedentary lifestyle and the Texcoca rulers' acceptance of Toltec cultural and religious traditions. Moreover, Pomar (1993:159–67), who wrote his *Relación* in 1582, two decades earlier than Alva Ixtlilxochitl, pays very little attention to Quetzalcoatl. Pomar presents other indigenous gods, such as Tezcatlipoca, Tlaloc, and Huitzilopochtli, as the major gods worshiped in Texcoco. He merely mentions that Quetzalcoatl was the chief priest in the Texcoca temples (1993:173). The existence of the Toltec tradition in Texcoco was evident, but during the first eighty years after the conquest, Texcoca historians did not promote their Toltec heritage nor its symbolic figure, Topiltzin Quetzalcoatl. Rather, they emphasized their Chichimec heritage and widely promoted it.

Alva Ixtlilxochitl was the first to make a close connection between Texcoco and Topiltzin Quetzalcoatl's Toltecs. Alva Ixtlilxochitl makes every effort to present Texcoco as the cultural center of pre-Hispanic Mexico, successor of the Toltec civilization. Alva Ixtlilxochitl's Topiltzin Quetzalcoatl, however, does not follow previous Texcoca sources or any other indigenous image of Topiltzin Quetzalcoatl, but rather the Quetzalcoatl–Saint Thomas myth that the Spanish friars had created several decades earlier. By describing Texcoco as having put into practice the teaching of the Quetzalcoatl–Saint Thomas Christian missionary, Alva Ixtlilxochitl attempts to demonstrate that the Texcoca had already accepted Christian teachings even before the conquest and that therefore they would be the most receptive to the Spanish evangelical project and an important asset to the colonial administration.

When Alva Ixtlilxochitl began to write his chronicles at the end of the sixteenth century, the Quetzalcoatl–Saint Thomas myth was widely accepted. He incorporates this myth in the history of Texcoco in order to Christianize his Texcoco before the conquest. As Henry B. Nicholson points out (2001:113–29), Alva Ixtlilxochitl's history distorts the historical role played by Topiltzin Quetzalcoatl in pre-Hispanic contexts. In his chronicles, Alva Ixtlilxochitl records two different Quetzalcoatl-like figures, Quetzalcoatl and Topiltzin. The chronicler explicitly represents Quetzalcoatl as a white-bearded Christian apostle who introduced Christian doctrine to the people:

> Y estando [los Olmeca-Xicalanca] en el mayor prosperidad llego a esta tierra un hombre a quien llamaron Quetzalcohuatl y por otro nombre, Huemac, virgen, justo y santo, el que vino de la parte del oriente y enseñó a la ley natural y constituyó el ayuno evitando todos los vicios y pecados; el primero que colocó y estableció la cruz a que llamaron dios de las lluvias y de la salud; el cual, viendo el poco fruto que hacia en la enseñanza de estas gentes, se volvió por la aparte de donde vino. (Alva Ixtlilxochitl 1997, 1:529–30)

> When the Olmeca-Xicalanca were in their greatest prosperity, there arrived in this land a man whom they called Quetzalcoatl and who is also known as Huemac, virgin, just and holy, who came from the place of the east, taught the natural law, and introduced fasting, in order to avoid all vices and sins; he was the first person to place and establish the cross, and whom they called the God of the rains and of health; when he noticed what little success he was having in teaching these peoples, he returned to the place from whence he came. (author's translation)

There is no doubt that Alva Ixtlilxochitl follows the Quetzalcoatl–Saint Thomas myth. On the other hand, the Texcoca chronicler also presents another Quetzalcoatl-like figure, Topiltzin, who was a virtuous sage and ruler of the Toltecs (1997, 1:276, 282, 350, 420). In Alva Ixtlilxochitl's chronicles,

Quetzalcoatl and Topiltzin appear as different figures in different chronological periods, but they share many common characteristics that Spanish friars had highlighted in the Quetzalcoatl–Saint Thomas myth: both were described as religious sages and lawmakers, and both left their governing city and told their descendants that they would come back to the land they had once preached in or ruled. Alva Ixtlilxochitl rewrites Toltec history with two Christianized Quetzalcoatls: Quetzalcoatl the missionary and Topiltzin the Toltec ruler.

In his chronicles, Alva Ixtlilxochitl often amends the dates of major pre-Hispanic historical events, so he must have been very careful in how he incorporated the two Quetzalcoatl figures into his history. If Quetzalcoatl was the missionary, then he must have come to and left Tula around the beginning of the Christian era. Many indigenous and Spanish sources prior to Alva Ixtlilxochitl, however, record that Topiltzin Quetzalcoatl was the last ruler of Tula before it fell, which was not a remote historical event for the sixteenth-century indigenous and mestizo chroniclers; for them, the Toltecs were their immediate ancestors. According to Alva Ixtlilxochitl's chronology, however, the fall of Tula happened in the tenth century at the earliest (O'Gorman 1997:96). To resolve this chronological problem, he presented two Quetzalcoatls, Quetzalcoatl the missionary at the beginning of the Christian era and Topiltzin as Quetzalcoatl's disciple at the end of the Toltec empire. Since Alva Ixtlilxochitl needs Quetzalcoatl to be a Christian apostle, he records that Quetzalcoatl the missionary arrived in the New World slightly after Jesus' incarnation, which corresponds to the end of the Olmeca-Xicalanca and the beginning of the Toltec era:

> Y según parece por las historias referidas y por anales, sucedió esto algunos años después de la encarnación de cristo, señor nuestro; y desde este tiempo acá entró la cuarta edad, que dejaron llamarse Tletonatiuh porque se ha de acabar con fuego. En esta cuarta edad llegaron a esta tierra la nación tulteca. (Alva Ixtlilxochitl 1997, 1:530)

> And according to the above-mentioned histories and annals, this [Quetzalcoatl's departure] seems to have happened some years after the incarnation of Christ, our lord; and from this time here began the fourth age (sun), which is called Tletonatiuh because the world of this age will end by fire. In this fourth age, the Toltec nation arrived at this land. (author's translation)

Because the missionary Quetzalcoatl left the Toltecs long before the actual fall of Tula in the twelfth century, Alva Ixtlilxochitl presents another Quetzalcoatl-figure, Topiltzin, as the last ruler of Tula at the end of the twelfth century. Alva Ixtlilxochitl's Toltec chronology, which began with Quetzalcoatl the missionary and ended with the Quetzalcoatl-like Topiltzin, suggests a continuous succession of Christian practice in the Toltec period. The chronicler records that the Toltec kings shared the same ethnic origin with the white missionary Saint Thomas because they "eran altos de cuerpo y blancos, barbados como los españoles" (they were tall and white with beards like the Spaniards) (Alva Ixtlilxochitl 1997, 1:271). Alva Ixtlilxochitl's adaptation and modification of the Quetzalcoatl–Saint Thomas myth was not motivated by a desire to Christianize the entire history of pre-Hispanic Mexico, but rather by an interest in constructing a Texcoca regional history inflected with an apostolic ideology.

After Christianizing the Toltecs, Alva Ixtlilxochitl (1997, 1:301, 2:18) makes a connection between the Texcoca and the Toltec dynasties. According to this chronicler, Topiltzin was forced to flee from Tula with his son Pochotl. After Topiltzin died, his son, Pochotl, married Toxochipantzin, a daughter of the Colhuacan ruler Nauhyotl. This couple had a daughter, Azcaxochitzin, whom they married to Nopaltzin, the son of Xolotl. Nopaltzin's marriage to the granddaughter of Topiltzin in Alva Ixtlilxochitl's history allows him to argue that the Texcoca dynasty is the legitimate heir to Topiltzin's Toltec legacy. The *Códice Xolotl* (1996:map 2), which the chronicler consulted, does record the marriage between Pochotl and Azcaxochitzin, but it does not seem to corroborate that Pochotl was a son of Topiltzin. Alva Ixtlilxochitl (1997, 1:297–98) records that Pochotl lived in Cuauhtitenco, adjacent to Tula, but the footprints depicted in the codex show that he came from the west, not from the north.

In the same way that he made the Texcoca rulers into the legitimate heirs of Xolotl, Alva Ixtlilxochitl also presents them as the legitimate heirs of Topiltzin and his Toltec civilization. But there were many other Chichimec rulers from the Basin of Mexico who married Toltec princesses and hence could also claim to be the legitimate heirs of Topiltzin and his civilization. When the Chichimecs came to the Basin of Mexico, they began assimilating the more advanced Toltec political, religious, and cultural systems. The most common vehicle for this assimilation was the practice of intermarriage between the ruling classes of the two groups (Davies 1980:338–39; Gillespie 1989:20–21).[8] In most cases, the Colhuaque, who were the actual biological heirs of the Toltecs in the Basin of Mexico, provided the Chichimecs with women to generate offspring who could legitimately inherit positions of authority as the descendants of both the Chichimecs and the Toltecs. The *Códice Xolotl* (1996) indicates that most Chichimec leaders in the Basin of Mexico engaged in this practice of intermarriage. Map 2, which describes the marriage between Nopaltzin and the Colhuacan princess, Azcaxochitzin, also depicts various marriages of Chichimec leaders, such as Tzontecomatl in Coatlichan and Acatomatl in Coatepec, to female descendants of the Toltecs, Cihuatetzin and Cohuazanac, respectively. Sometimes, the intense competition among the Chichimec leaders for a Colhuacan princess caused a *chichimecayaoyotl* (Chichimec war) as described in Map 3 of the *Códice Xolotl* (figure 2.9). Huetzin of Coatlichan and Yacanex of Tepetlaoztoc fought for

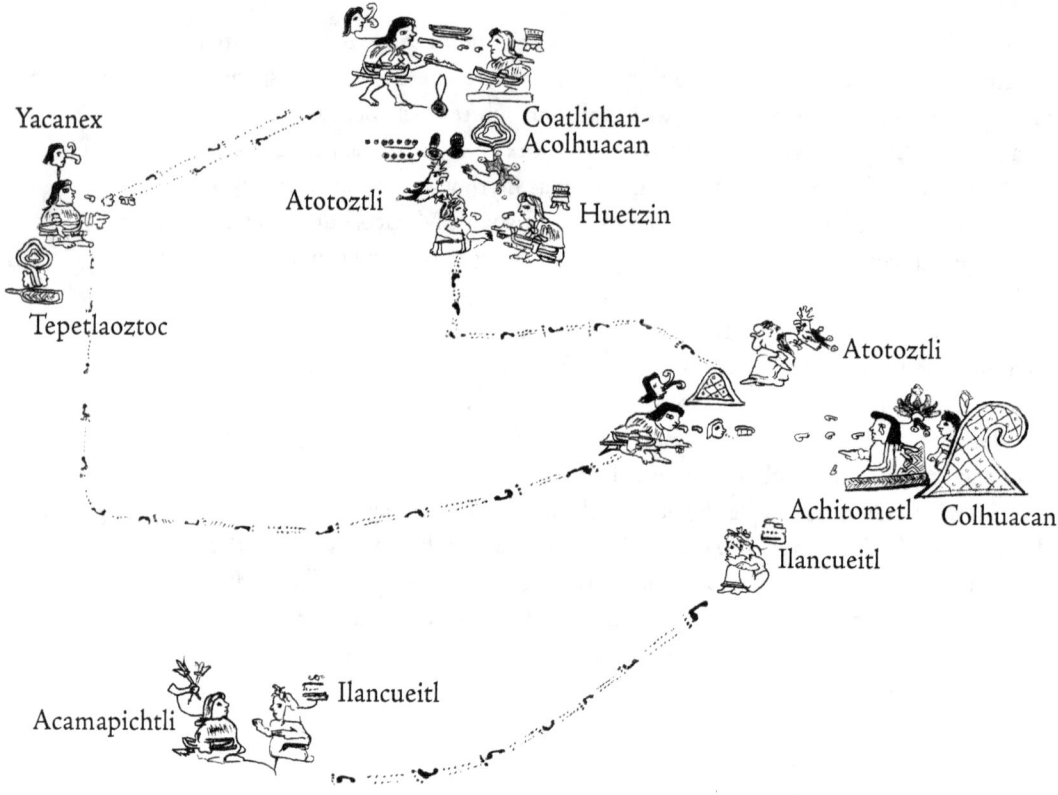

FIG. 2.9

Chichimec leaders searching for the Colhua princess from the *Códice Xolotl* (1996: map 3). Reproduced with permission of the Bibliothèque nationale de France.

The two Chichimec rulers, Yacanex (Ash Nose) from Tepetlaoztoc (Cave of the Stone Mat) and Huetzin (Drum) from Acolhuacan (Place of Those Who Live near Bent Water), competed for Atotoztli (Water-Bird), the daughter of the Colhuacan ruler Achitometl (Water Maguey). In Colhuacan, Yacanex seems to be threatening the Colhuacan ruler Achitometl because the latter is in tears and his daughter, Atotoztli, is crying. But Achitometl married Atotoztli to Huetzin of Acolhuacan. Yacanex got angry and went to Acolhuacan to talk to Huetzin. Between Yacanex and Huetzin a bow and arrow is depicted, which demonstrates that their conversation was not peaceful. This conversation occurred in 1 Flint, and a war broke out between them in the same year. On the other hand, Achitometl's other daughter, Ilancueitl (Old Woman Skirt), marries Acamapichtli (Reed Fist) of Tenochtitlan. These marriages between the Chichimec immigrants and the native Toltec Colhuaque were solicited and sometimes forced by the former groups, who were militarily more powerful. Chimalpahin (1991:39) records that Huetzin conquered Colhuacan, which probably explains why Atotoztli married Huetzin, not Yacanex.

Atotoztli, a daughter of the Colhuacan ruler Achitometl. Finally Huetzin was victorious and was able to marry Atotoztli. The descendants of Chichimec rulers and Colhuacan princesses, such as those of Huetzin of Coatlichan and Nopaltzin of Tenayuca, therefore, can legitimately claim the Toltecs as their ancestors. They can also claim to be legitimate heirs of Topiltzin Quetzalcoatl, because their mothers' home, Colhuacan, was considered as the capital of the Toltec descendants after the destruction of Tula, and its rulers were considered the heirs of Topiltzin Quetzalcoatl. In this context, not only the Texcoca rulers as descendants of Nopaltzin, but also the rulers of other regions, such as those of Coatlichan, could claim themselves as the legitimate heirs of Topiltzin Quetzalcoatl.

Although the Mexica intermarried with the Colhuaque, as did their fellow Chichimec neighbors, they took greater advantage of the resultant genealogical connection to Topiltzin Quetzalcoatl than any other ethnic group in the Basin of Mexico. Several pictorial and alphabetic sources, both from Tenochtitlan as well as from other city-states, indicate a close relationship between the first Mexica ruler, Acamapichtli, and the Colhuacan princess Ilancueitl.[9] The Texcoca sources such as the *Códice Xolotl* (1996) record that the Colhuacan princess, Ilancueitl, a daughter of Achitometl and thus a sister of Atotoztli, wife of the Coatlichan ruler Huetzin, was married to Acamapichtli. Other sources, such as Alvarado Tezozomoc's *Crónica mexicayotl* (1992:83–85) and Chimalpahin's annals (1998, 1:225), record Ilancueitl as wife or mother of Acamapichtli. Since Ilancueitl was a Colhuacan princess, regardless of whether she was the wife or the mother of Acamapichtli, the later Mexica rulers could claim to be legitimate heirs of their ancestor, Topiltzin Quetzalcoatl.

As Quiñones Keber (1988:332–36) shows, the Mexica rulers indeed tried to promote themselves as the legitimate heirs of Topiltzin Quetzalcoatl, honoring him as their immediate ancestor. Quiñones Keber demonstrates that Mexica rulers, such as Moctezuma Ilhuicamina and Itzcoatl, ordered their images carved in stone following the model of the prototypical images of the Toltec ruler, Topiltzin Quetzalcoatl. She also explains that later Mexica rulers, such as Tizoc and Ahuitzotl, also left their images in the pre-Hispanic Dedication Stone of the Templo Mayor. By comparing the style and attire of the surviving pre-Hispanic rock carving of Topiltzin Quetzalcoatl in the Cerro de la Malinche with those created for Aztec rulers, Quiñones Keber (1988:333) argues that "Its similarity [the image of Topiltzin Quetzalcoatl in the Cerro de la Malinche] to Aztec ruler depictions on dynastic monuments suggests that the rock relief itself be regarded as a dynastic image, whose function was to enshrine the Toltec priest-ruler shown on it as an ancestral patron of the Aztec ruling line." Worshiping or imitating Topiltzin Quetzalcoatl as a model ruler does not seem to be a Mexica invention, but rather a long Mesoamerican tradition in which the ruling class of the central city of the empire invoked Quetzalcoatl in order to justify their political power.

Topiltzin Quetzalcoatl played the symbolic role of legitimizing political power, and more specifically imperial power, in all of Mesoamerica. As Davíd Carrasco (2000:104–47) demonstrates, Quetzalcoatl was an emblematic figure who legitimated the political power of the ruling class throughout recorded Mesoamerican history. His symbolic representation, Feathered Serpent, could be found in the center of the main temple or ruler's palace of each urban empire (i.e., Teotihuacan, Tula, Xochicalco, and Chichen Itza). In Teotihuacan, the presence of Quetzalcoatl's temple in the center of the palace indicates the role Quetzalcoatl played in legitimizing the political order of the city and the imperial expansion of the ruling class. In Xochicalco, Cholula, and Chichen Itza, Quetzalcoatl appears as the principal deity or ruler of the city. According to Davíd Carrasco, Quetzalcoatl was the symbol of authority that sanctioned the supreme power and social order in the imperialist centers many centuries before Tenochtitlan emerged. The Mexica of Tenochtitlan, who were able to construct an urban empire similar to those of Tula and Teotihuacan, followed the pattern of their precursors by worshiping Quetzalcoatl as the origin of their power.

The importance of Topiltzin Quetzalcoatl to the Mexica was not limited to politics; it extended to almost every aspect of Mexica society. They constructed a temple dedicated to Quetzalcoatl in the Templo Mayor in Tenochtitlan in front of the two towers dedicated to Huitzilopochtli and Tlaloc, and they named him the patron of the school or *calmecac*. The Mexica respected the people of Topiltzin Quetzalcoatl, the Toltecs, as the masters of science, arts, medicine, and knowledge. For the Mexica, "The Toltecs were wise. Their works were all good, all perfect, all wonderful, all marvelous" (*Florentine Codex* 1950–1982, 10:165–66). As León-Portilla points out (1995:18–19), the word *toltecayotl*, or "Toltec-ness," represents "el ser de pueblos no ya sólo dueños de rica cultura sino también de una civilización" (the essence of the Indians, as owners of rich culture as well as a civilization) (author's translation). The Mexica of Tenochtitlan clearly claimed themselves as the true heirs of the Toltec civilization and its founder and ruler Topiltzin Quetzalcoatl. Different ethnic groups in the Basin of Mexico also acknowledged the Mexica rulers' political, religious, and cultural campaign to be heirs of Topiltzin Quetzalcoatl. Chimalpahin (1965:122) from Chalco records that "Después de la muerte de Totépeuh y Tópil, durante 100 años nadie reinó en Colhuacan. Durante 52 años el Tópil había tenido a su cuidado y encargo el gobierno real, y 700 años más tarde terminó este gobierno real con la muerte del Mocteuhzoma El Menor, Señor de Tenuchtitlan" (After the death of Totépeuh and Tópil, nobody reigned in Colhuacan for 100 years. Tópil had charge over the loyal government for 52 years, and 700 years later this royal government ended with the death of Moctezuma the Younger, Lord of Tenochtitlan) (author's translation).[10] The names of the two rulers, Totepeuh and Topil, refer to Topiltzin Quetzalcoatl. Totepeuh is another name for Topiltzin Quetzalcoatl, and Topil is a nonhonorific form of Topiltzin. According to Chimalpahin, the Mexica rulers inherited Topiltzin Quetzalcoatl's Toltec kingdom and maintained it until the arrival of the Spaniards.

As explained before, Alva Ixtlilxochitl silences the political role of Topiltzin Quetzalcoatl in Tenochtitlan and his close relationship with the Mexica, the residents of this city. Rather, he tries to make the Texcoca out to be the most fervent followers of Topiltzin Quetzalcoatl. However, even Alva Ixtlilxochitl himself verifies the close connection between the Mexica and the Colhuaque, the symbolic descendants of the Toltecs in the Basin of Mexico, by describing the Mexica several times as the primary descendants of the Toltec Colhuaque. When he records the alliance among the three cities, Texcoco, Tenochtitlan, and Tlacopan, after the Mexica-Tepanec war, Alva Ixtlilxochitl states that each city of the alliance represents a major ethnic-political group in the Basin of Mexico, and he identifies the ruler of the Mexica as the ruler of the Toltec Colhuaque in the following way:

> Y habiendo dado, y tomado sobre este caso, hubo de permanecer el voto y los de la parte de Nezahualcoyotzin, fueron jurados todos tres por sucesores al imperio, y cada uno de por sí por rey y cabeza principal de su reino. Al de Tezcuco llamándose Acolhua Tecuhtli, y dándole juntamente el título y dignidad de sus antepasados, que es llamarse Chichimécatl Tecuhtli que era el título y soberano señorío que los emperadores chichimecas tenían. A su tío Itzcoatzin se le dio de Colhua Tecuhtli, por la nación de los culhuas tultecas. A Totoquihuatzin se le dio el título de Tepanecátl Tecuhtli, que es el título que tuvieron los reyes de Azcapotzalco. (Alva Ixtlilxochitl 1997, 2:82–83)

> Having carefully considered this case, Nezahualcoyotl's judgment and opinion was to prevail, and all the Mexica lords and those of Nezahualcoyotl, all three together were sworn in as successors to the empire, and each one himself as a king and as the head of his kingdom. The king of Texcoco was called Acolhua Tecuhtli and was also given the title and dignity of his ancestors, that is to be called Chichimecatl Tecuhtli, which was the title and sovereign lordship that the Chichimec emperors had. His uncle Itzcoatl was given the title of Colhua Tecuhtli for the kingdom of the Collhua-Toltecs. Totoquihuaztli was given the title of Tepanecatl Tecuhtli, which is the title that the kings of Azcapotzalco held. (author's translation)

Alva Ixtlilxochitl explains that the Mexica ruler Itzcoatl inherited the Toltec tradition while the Texcoca ruler Nezahualcoyotl carried on the Chichimec tradition. This ethnic-political division among these three nations continued to be acknowledged even after the conquest. Nezahualcoyotl's grandson, don

Carlos Ometochtzin, who was burned alive in 1539 due to his idolatrous practice, maintained his political title of chichimecatecuhtli.

When Topiltzin Quetzalcoatl was converted into a Christian-like sage or a Christian apostle at the end of sixteenth century, the close relationship between Topiltzin Quetzalcoatl and the Mexica rulers began to disappear from the colonial historiography of Mexico. The Christianized Quetzalcoatl was designed specifically as a contrast to the Mexica rulers who, according to the Spanish friars, were the promoters of human sacrifice and militaristic ideals. On the other hand, the chroniclers of other regions, such as Alva Ixtlilxochitl of Texcoco, actively assimilated the Christianized Quetzalcoatl into their local histories. Before Alva Ixtlilxochitl's chronicles, Texcoca pictorial and alphabetic texts generally identified the Chichimecs as the primary originators of Texcoca ethnic and cultural identity. Alva Ixtlilxochitl, however, adds one more ethnic and cultural dimension by introducing a Christian interpretation of pre-Hispanic Texcoca history: the Quetzalcoatl–Saint Thomas myth.

Like many historians of other city-states in the Basin of Mexico, the Texcoca historians presented the Chichimecs and Toltecs as their founding ancestors, symbolized by Xolotl and by Topiltzin Quetzalcoatl, respectively. They did so, however, by making Xolotl the exclusive founder of the Texcoca dynasty, omitting his role as the founder of their neighboring and competing city-states in the Basin of Mexico, such as Coatlichan, Huexotla, Coatepec, and Azcapotzalco. They also silence the role Topiltzin Quetzalcoatl played in the origin of other dynasties, and they convert him into a Christian missionary. Most notable is Alva Ixtlilxochitl, who enthusiastically promotes this double heritage in the founding history of Texcoco and the Texcoca dynasty. In his chronicles, Texcoco is the most powerful city-state, having inherited its position from the Chichimec emperor Xolotl, and the most advanced cultural and religious center thanks to the Christian missionary Quetzalcoatl and his descendant Topiltzin. As an example of Chichimec political and Toltec cultural traditions in Texcoco, Alva Ixtlilxochitl presents the Texcoca ruler Nezahualcoyotl. In Alva Ixtlilxochitl's chronicles, Nezahualcoyotl, a descendant of Xolotl, rules the most powerful empire before the conquest, even more powerful and extensive than that of the Mexica. And as a descendant of the Christian-like Quetzalcoatl and Topiltzin, Nezahualcoyotl inherited and further developed their civilized traditions, such as an advanced legal system and peaceful religious practices (Alva Ixtlilxochitl 1997, 1:305). In fact, according to Alva Ixtlilxochitl, just like the Christian apostle Quetzalcoatl once did, Nezahualcoyotl tried to preach his peaceful and civilized religious practices and beliefs to the Mexica of Tenochtitlan, where war and human sacrifice were common.

CHAPTER THREE

REVISITING PRE-HISPANIC CENTRAL MEXICO

Texcoca Reality before Nezahualcoyotl

For the period before Tenochtitlan gained political dominance in the 1430s in the Basin of Mexico, historiographers of central Mexico have relied mainly on Texcoca sources such as the *Códice Xolotl* (1996), the *Mapa Quinatzin* (Aubin 1886a), the *Mapa Tlotzin* (Aubin 1886b), and Alva Ixtlilxochitl's works (1997). These sources, particularly the *Códice Xolotl* and its alphabetic counterpart, Alva Ixtlilxochitl's chronicles, record the historical development of both Texcoco and other major city-states in the basin such as Tenayuca, Coatlichan, Huexotla, Azcapotzalco, Tenochtitlan, and many others. Based on these pictorial and alphabetic sources, many historians such as Fray Juan de Torquemada (1975) at the beginning of the seventeenth century; Lorenzo Boturini Benaducci (1990), Mariano Fernández de Echeverría y Veytia (1944), and Father Francisco Javier Clavijero (1991) in the eighteenth century; and Manuel Orozco y Berra (1960:vol. 3) in the nineteenth century all base their pre-Hispanic histories of central Mexico on Texcoca sources. In these texts, Texcoco is the legitimate inheritor of the great Chichimec conqueror Xolotl and the most powerful city-state in central Mexico during the thirteenth century through the reign of Nezahualcoyotl in the fifteenth century. Numerous historians and twentieth-century literary critics such as Burr Cartwright Brundage (1972), Miguel León-Portilla (1967a), and José Luis Martínez (1996) still follow these Texcoco-based sources in their accounts of pre-Hispanic history in the Basin of Mexico.

By reexamining Texcoca pictorial and alphabetic sources and those of other regions, however, some scholars have challenged this version of pre-Hispanic Mexican history. Gibson (1956:2, 1964:17) states that Texcoco began to appear as a leading city on the east side of the Basin of Mexico in the middle of the fourteenth century during the reign of Nezahualcoyotl's great-grandfather, Quinatzin, and grandfather, Techotlalatzin.[1] Offner (1983:29–35) also argues that Quinatzin was able to make Texcoco a leading city in the eastern basin but that Texcoco's prominence began to wane during the reign of his son, Techotlalatzin. Davies (1980:123, 133) insists that Texcoco displaced its neighboring city, Coatlichan, and assumed a leading role on the east side of the Basin of Mexico only after Quinatzin's reign in the middle of the fourteenth century. In the accounts of these scholars, Texcoco began to appear as the leading city in the eastern basin during Quinatzin's and Techotlalatzin's reigns, that is, in the middle of the fourteenth century, and continued to the end of the Tepanec-Acolhuacan war (1415–1418). They all record that during the war the Texcoca ruler, Huehue Ixtlilxochitl, ruled over neighboring city-states such as Coatlichan, Huexotla, and Coatepec. Gibson, Offner, and Davies revise the Texcoco-based pre-Hispanic history in that according to their accounts, Texcoca supremacy in the Basin of Mexico was limited to the fourteenth century rather than the three centuries from the twelfth to the first half of the fifteenth as the Texcoca sources and later historians have insisted. Many current historians and anthropologists follow this revised version of Texcoca history (Brumfiel 1983:266–67; Evans 2001:91; Smith and Berdan 1996). Gibson, Offner, and Davies's argument that Texcoco played a commanding role in the eastern basin from the middle of the fourteenth century through the end of the Tepanec-Mexica war (1427–1428), however, still seems very early, because prior to Nezahualcoyotl's reign, Texcoco was still competing for power with its neighboring city-states, Coatlichan, Huexotla, and Coatepec. In fact, Texcoco may have been a fairly minor player in central Mexican politics at this time.

Davies (1980) and Offner (1979, 1983) base their revised Texcoca history on the Texcoca pictorial sources, the *Códice Xolotl* (1996), the *Mapa Quinatzin* (Aubin 1886a), and the *Mapa Tlotzin* (Aubin 1886b). They argue that these sources exaggerate Texcoca history. I am in complete agreement with this argument, but at the same time I maintain that the pictorial sources sometimes unintentionally reveal Texcoca reality before the conquest. In some cases, the copyists of the sixteenth century, who reconstructed Texcoca regional history, might have been inconsistent or less than thorough in their revisions of the indigenous sources, leaving traces of the original text. I identify these traces through a detailed examination of the various accounts of Texcoca history, in particular, its relationship with neighboring cities such as Coatlichan and Huexotla as well as more remote cities such as Chalco, Xaltocan, Azcapotzalco, and Tenochtitlan. I demonstrate that Texcoco's cultural and political development occurred relatively late compared to other central Mexican city-states. Thus, Texcoco was not prepared to play a leading role in the basin until Nezahualcoyotl came to power in the fifteenth century. The analysis of Texcoca development before the reign of Nezahualcoyotl illuminates how the Texcoca historians modified Texcoca history to justify Nezahualcoyotl's new political power by eliminating the supremacy of neighboring city-states such as Huexotla and Coatlichan.

Leading City-States before the Tepanec-Acolhuacan War: Tenayuca, Colhuacan, Azcapotzalco, and Coatlichan

As Elizabeth Brumfiel (1983:268–70) and Charles Gibson (1964:20–21) demonstrate, in the thirteenth and fourteenth centuries, the Basin of Mexico suffered frequent wars and changes of power among various city-states due to internal and external conflicts. Both the nobles and the commoners of many city-states often rebelled against their rulers. In addition, the city-states often conducted wars against each other, frequently shifting their alliances to secure their safety or to expand their political territory. During this politically volatile period, political power and cultural prestige were distributed among several major city-states such as Tenayuca, Colhuacan, Azcapotzalco, and Coatlichan. By the beginning of the fifteenth century, however, most city-states in the basin had fallen under the control or influence of either Azcapotzalco or Coatlichan.

The *Códice Xolotl* (1996:map 2) depicts Xolotl founding and residing in Tenayuca. During Xolotl's reign, Tenayuca seems to have enjoyed a brief period of political supremacy in the basin. Its dominance, however, began to wane with the death of Xolotl, while the later Chichimec immigrants established themselves through the foundation of major cities like Coatlichan, Azcapotzalco, and Xaltocan. During the reigns of Xolotl's son, Nopaltzin, and his grandson, Tenacacaltzin, Tenayuca steadily declined in importance. Nopaltzin, for example, seems to have had limited power in Tenayuca. The *Códice Xolotl* (1996: map 3) records Nopaltzin's conquest of Colhuacan and other military actions during Xolotl's reign but nothing during his own reign. Alva Ixtlilxochitl (1997, 2:24) simply enumerates the ruler of each of the major cities over whose founding Xolotl presided, and he repeats Nopaltzin's conquest of Colhuacan during Xolotl's regime. Alva Ixtlilxochitl also describes Nopaltzin as a legislator who instituted five specific laws that do not appear in the codex.

Prior to the founding of Tenayuca by the Chichimec leaders Xolotl and Nopaltzin, Colhuacan in the south of the basin served as a political and cultural center. The literal meaning of Colhuacan, "Place of the Grandfathers" or "Place of the Ancestors," already indicates its long tradition. Colhuacan was the most important ally of the Toltec empire in the basin (Davies 1980:23–30), and after the downfall of the capital of the empire, Tula, it received Toltec refugees and briefly served as the capital. Colhuacan's dominance in the basin, however, was very brief due to the invasion of the barbarous, nomadic Chichimecs from the north. As examined in chapter 2, from the beginning of the contact between the two groups, Colhuacan served as a civilized political and cultural center that provided the Chichimecs with an advanced political and cultural system. At the same time, however, Colhuacan was not able to militarily resist the Chichimecs and was finally conquered by Acolhuaque of Coatlichan in 1253 (Davies 1980:30).

Tenayuca's leadership among the Chichimec city-states was quickly replaced by its neighboring Chichimec city, Azcapotzalco, in the fourteenth century.² During the reign of Aculhua (Acolnahuacatzin in Tlatelolca version), Azcapotzalco received the Mexica and the Tlatelolca and allowed them to found Tenochtitlan in 2 House (1325) and Tlatelolco in 2 Rabbit (1338), respectively. It was a significant event in Azcapotzalca history in that Acolnahuacatzin's successor, Tezozomoc, would make a series of conquests in the basin with the help of these new immigrants. According to the *Anales de Tlatelolco* (1948:47–48), Tezozomoc installed one of his sons, Cuacuahpitzahuac, as a ruler of Tlatelolco in 1 Rabbit (1350). The first ruler of Tenochtitlan, Acamapichtli, may also have a Tepanec connection because some sources record him as a direct descendant of the Tepanec-Azcapotzalca royal family (Zantwijk 1985:185). And Acamapichtli's son, Huitzilihuitl, married one of Tezozomoc's daughters. With these recently arrived migrants, Tezozomoc conquered other major city-states and established a large empire in the northern, western, and southern parts of the basin.

Tezozomoc's son, Cuacuahpitzahuac, the ruler of Tlatelolco, conquered Chimalhuacan in 2 Reed (1351) (*Anales de Tlatelolco* 1948:48). The Tepanec-Mexica conquered Tenayuca in 2 Reed (1351) according to the *Códice Xolotl* (1996:map 4) or 13 Reed (1372) according to the Mexica sources such as *Historia de los mexicanos por sus pinturas* (1941:250). According to the *Annals of Cuauhtitlan* (1992:73), in the year 2 Calli (1377), the Tepanec-Mexica conquered the most historically prestigious city of the basin, Colhuacan, which was under the dominance of Coatlichan. Moreover, according to Jiménez Moreno (1954–1955:231–33) and Carrasco (1984), Azcapotzalco established a considerable empire by conquering the following cities before the Tepanec-Acolhuacan war: Mexicaltzinco, Xochimilco, Cuitlahuac, Cuauhnahuac, Cuauhtitlan, and Xaltocan. The *Anales de Tlatelolco* (1948:22–23) records that Tezozomoc ruled his colonies by installing his sons to rule over them: Acolnahuacatzin in Tlacopan, Teyolcohuatzin in Acolman, Maxtla in Coyoacan, Cuacuauhtzin in Tepechpan, and Moquihuixtzin in Cuauhnahuac. Tezozomoc also placed his grandsons, that is, Cuacuahpitzahuac's sons, in subject cities as rulers: Tezozomoc, whose name is the same as his grandfather in Cuauhtitlan, and Yaocuixtli in Mexicaltzinco. As the *Códice Xolotl* (1996) indicates in maps 5 and 6, around the year 8 House (1409) when Huehue Ixtlilxochitl was inaugurated as the third ruler in Texcoco, Azcapotzalco bordered Texcoco to the northeast and Coatepec to the southeast of the basin.

While Azcapotzalco was dominating the western basin in the fourteenth century, Coatlichan became a leading city in the eastern basin with its third ruler, Huetzin, that is, the grandson of Tzontecomatl to whom Xolotl had granted Coatlichan. The *Códice Xolotl* (1996) provides some clues in regard to Coatlichan's political boundaries during Huetzin's reign. Map 1 of the codex depicts that Huetzin receives tribute from Yacanex of Tepetlaoztoc and his vassals, suggesting that Coatlichan controlled the northeastern basin from the beginning of Huetzin's reign (figure 3.1). Yacanex, however, rebelled against Huetzin and invaded the basin twice (figure 3.2).³ In the first invasion, Huetzin

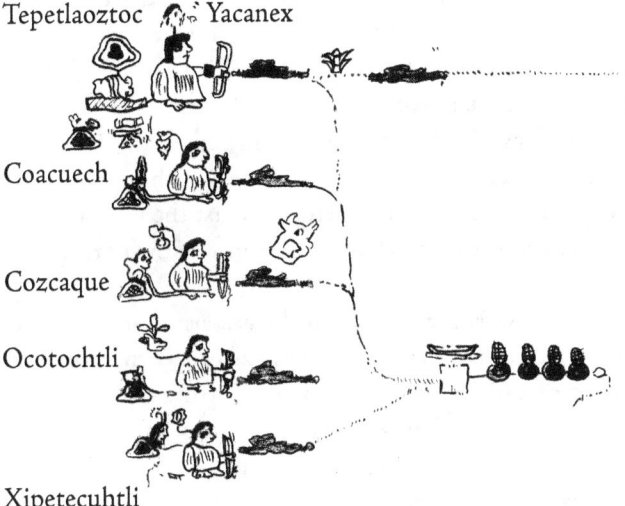

FIG. 3.1
Huetzin receives tribute from Yacanex and his subjects from the *Códice Xolotl* (1996: map 3). Reproduced with permission of the Bibliothèque nationale de France.

Huetzin from Acolhuacan receives rabbits from Yacanex (Ash Nose) of Tepetlaoztoc (Cave of the Stone Mat). Under Yacanex appear his five vassals who are depicted a little smaller than their master, Yacanex: Coacuech (Snake Bell), Cozcaque (One Who Has Necklace), Ocotochtli (Bobcat [Pine Tree Rabbit]), and Xipetecuhtli (Lord of Xipe). Tzontecomatl, to whom Xolotl granted Acolhuacan (Place of Those Who Live near Bent Water), appears in a cave with his wife and the foundation of his city is recorded as occurring in 1 Reed. Yacanex and his vassals began to pay tribute to Huetzin in 1 Reed, that is, eighty-one years after the arrival of the three Chichimec leaders, one of whom is Huetzin's grandfather, Tzontecomatl, the founder of Acolhuacan. The items of tribute were hunted animals that were collectively depicted as rabbits. Two generations after its foundation during Huetzin's reign, Acolhuacan maintained an extensive territory from Tepetlaoztoc in the north to Colhuacan in the south of the eastern Basin of Mexico. This figure demonstrates that Texcoco, which is located between Tepetlaoztoc and Coatlichan, started out as a city-state within Coatlichan's political domain. This explains why the founder of Texcoco, Quinatzin, asks Huetzin permission to found his city as depicted in figure 2.3.

confronted Yacanex in Chiauhtla and defeated him there. Between Yacanex's first and second invasion, Huetzin received a Chichimec leader, Tochintecuhtli, and let him settle down in the neighboring city of Huexotla in the year 13 Reed (1219) according to the *Códice Xolotl* (1996) and 1 Flint (1220) according to the *Memorial breve* (Chimalpahin 1991:37). Tochintecuhtli's arrival in Huexotla was an important event for Coatlichan. Huexotla rapidly developed and became the second most important city in the eastern basin, and Tochintecuhtli helped Huetzin defeat the second invasion of Yacanex, who had allied with neighboring Chichimec groups from Metztitlan, Tototepec, and Tulantzinco.[4] Huetzin's vassal, Tochintecuhtli from Huexotla, defeated Yacanex in Chiconahutla, while Nopal-Cuetlachihui and Huetzin himself defeated the Chichimec invaders from Tototepec and Metztitlan. Huetzin's victory against the Chichimecs from Tepetlaoztoc seemed to secure Coatlichan's dominance in the northeastern basin.

Huetzin built the most powerful city-state in the eastern basin by conquering the Toltec center, Colhuacan, in the southeastern corner of the basin. According to map 2 of the *Códice Xolotl* (1996), Nopaltzin conquered Colhuacan by killing its ruler Nauhyotl in 13 House during Xolotl's reign, and Xolotl placed Achitometl, Nauhyotl's grandson, on the throne. This Texcoca version, however, seems less plausible than that of other regions. According to the *Memorial breve* (Chimalpahin 1991:37), Huetzin conquered Colhuacan with the help of Xolotl and Nopaltzin.[5] The sources of other regions, such as the *Annals of Cuauhtitlan* (1992:44–45), also record Huetzin's control over Colhuacan. The *Crónica mexicayotl* (Alvarado Tezozomoc 1992:49–52, 84) describes in detail how the ruler of Colhuacan maintained a close relationship with Coatlichan even after Huetzin's reign. When the Mexica were defeated in Chapultepec in 1 Rabbit (1298), for example, the Colhuaca ruler was Coxcox, who was a grandson of Huetzin.[6] And one of Coxcox's sons, Acamapichtli, was ruling Coatlichan. Thus, during Huetzin's reign, Coatlichan dominated all the cities from or near Tepetlaoztoc in the north to Colhuacan in the south of the eastern basin.

Coatlichan's supremacy in the east of the basin can be detected in its alternate name, Acolhuacan. In the *Códice Xolotl* (1996), the geographical glyph of Acolhuacan first appears with the arrival of the first ruler of Coatlichan, Tzontecomatl, and shortly thereafter the use of the Acolhuacan glyph indicates Coatlichan's political dominance in the east basin. For instance, Quinatzin of Texcoco, who participated in the war against Yacanex and his allies, was depicted with his own name glyph as well as that of Acolhuacan (figure 3.2).[7] This description indicates Coatlichan's superior political power in the eastern basin not only because the leaders of the major cities participated in the chichimecayaoyotl (Chichimec war) under Coatlichan's leadership, but also because the victory in this war made it possible for Coatlichan to expand and secure its national boundaries to the northeast near Tepetlaoztoc. Coatlichan's

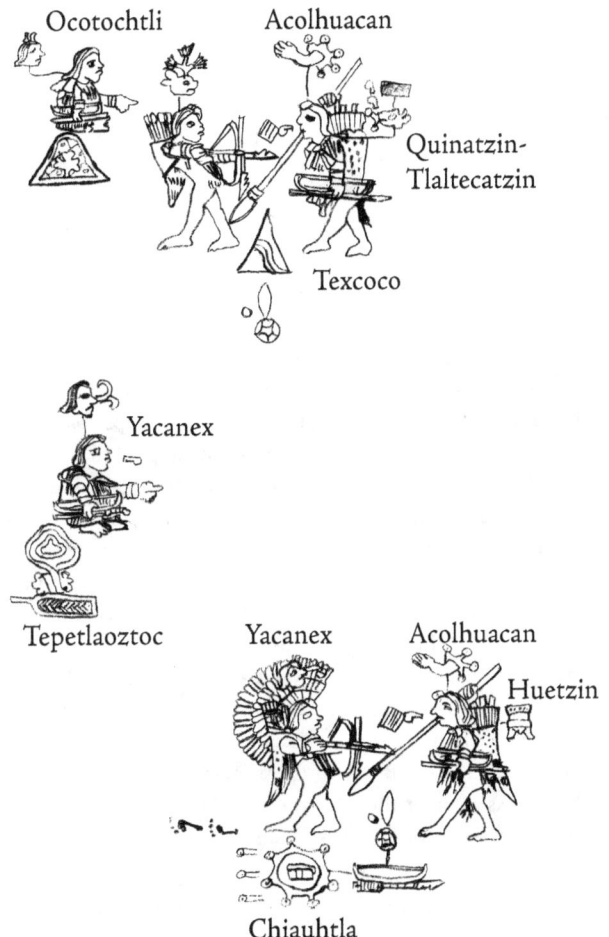

FIG. 3.2
Chichimec war (*chichimecayaoyotl*) between Huetzin and Yacanex from the *Códice Xolotl* (1996:map 3). Reproduced with permission of the Bibliothèque nationale de France.

Yacanex (Ash Nose) and his vassal Ocotochtli (Bobcat [Pine Tree Rabbit]) invaded Acolhuacan in the year 1 Flint. Quinatzin is fighting against Ocotochtli in Texcoco (Craggy Mountain) while Huetzin (Drum) battles against Yacanex in Chiauhtla(n) (Greasy Place). The *tlacuilo* views this war as a rebellion by Yacanex because Huetzin's and Quinatzin's speech glyphs, which represent their status as *tlatoani* (ruler), are being obstructed in some way by Yacanex and Ocotochtli. Both groups are depicted as Chichimecs: they are using the same types of weapons—bows and arrows with quivers on their backs. But the leaders of Acolhuacan, Huetzin and Quinatzin, are now using a long spear like their neighboring Toltecs, which demonstrates that they are in the process of Toltecization. Quinatzin and Huetzin are both depicted under an Acolhuacan glyph, which indicates that Huetzin was in charge of the war as the ruler of Acolhuacan. Here again, Coatlichan appears as the political center in the eastern Basin of Mexico.

FIG. 3.3

Tepanec-Acolhuacan war from the *Códice Xolotl* (1996:map 7). Reproduced with permission of the Bibliothèque nationale de France.

Tezozomoc, the ruler of Azcapotzalco, initiated the Tepanec-Acolhuacan war in 1 Reed (1415). His allied troops, the Tepaneca (People from Tepan [Stone-Flag]), crossed Lake Texcoco by canoelike ships and attacked the allied Acolhuacan troops, the Acolhuaque (Place of Those Who Live near Bent Water). Even though the participating warriors can be divided into two allied groups, each member of each group is still distinguished by their different hairstyles and arms. As a whole, the two groups in the eastern and western basin who had a common Chichimec origin now seem to be fully acculturated in the Toltec lifestyle: both groups abandoned bows and arrows and adopted the *chimalli* (shield), the *maccuahuitl* (obsidian sword), and the *ehuatl* (hanging belt). The result of the war is obvious. The Tepaneca won the war by capturing the Acolhuaque and burning their temples, which occurred in 4 Rabbit (1418). The cities of the primary antagonists in the war are also obvious: each allied troop is depicted with either the Tepaneca or the Acolhuaque, which establishes the cities of the primary antagonists as Azcapotzalco, in the west, and Coatlichan, in the east of the Basin of Mexico.

---

power over the eastern basin, however, seems to gradually wane during the fourteenth century as neighboring cities such as Texcoco and Huexotla extend their territories. Nevertheless, Coatlichan was still the most powerful city in this region until the end of the Tepanec-Acolhuacan war in 4 Rabbit (1418). The allied soldiers who participated in this war are still depicted under the Acolhuacan glyph (figure 3.3). Alva Ixtlilxochitl (1997, 2:53) corroborates that until the end of the Tepanec-Acolhuacan war, Coatlichan maintained control over a large part of the eastern basin, including the provinces of Chalco, Tulantzinco, Otompan, Tepepulco, and Cempoala.

Texcoca Development under Quinatzin and Techotlalatzin in the Fourteenth Century

Before Quinatzin (1298–1357) founded the city of Texcoco, it might have been a small village near a forest where Quinatzin's grandfather, Nopaltzin, had a hunting retreat (Alva Ixtlilxochitl 1997, 2:19). Alva Ixtlilxochitl (1997) boosts the military and political power of Texcoco over the basin during Quinatzin's reign. He focuses on the first Chichimec war, chichimecayaoyotl, which was caused by Yacanex's invasion (see figure 3.2). Alva Ixtlilxochitl argues that Quinatzin commanded the great Chichimec conquerors Huetzin of Coatlichan and Tochintecuhtli of Huexotla in the war and defeated the neighboring Chichimec leaders Yacanex and Ocotochtli of Tepetlaoztoc. However, the *Códice Xolotl* (1996), upon which Alva Ixtlilxochitl based his history, does not corroborate this account. As explained previously (see figure 3.2), Huetzin of Acolhuacan, not Quinatzin of Texcoco, presided over the Chichimec war: according to the *Códice Xolotl*, Quinatzin and Tochintecuhtli battled under the flag of Huetzin's home city-state, Acolhuacan. Huetzin's commanding role in this war even suggests that during the beginning of Quinatzin's reign, Texcoco fell under Coatlichan's jurisdiction. Huetzin extended and secured his territory by defeating Yacanex in Chiauhtla, which was located farther north than Texcoco. After Huetzin's victory in Chiauhtla, then, Quinatzin's Texcoco would have fallen within Huetzin's territory, between Coatlichan and Chiauhtla. Moreover, the defeated Chichimecs of Tepetlaoztoc in the *Códice Xolotl* clearly deny Quinatzin's victory over them in the *Códice de Tepetlaoztoc* (1992:map 3); they insist that they were independent until Nezahualcoyotl conquered them with Moctezuma Ilhuicamina in 4 Reed (1431). Alva Ixtlilxochitl's history tries to give Texcoco a dominant role at the end of thirteenth century, but his account is based on a misinterpretation of his original source, the *Códice Xolotl*.

Alva Ixtlilxochitl intentionally misinterprets the codex in his portrayal of Quinatzin's supremacy. He claims that Tochintecuhtli, the ruler of Huexotla who participated in the Chichimec war with Quinatzin and Huetzin, was Quinatzin's brother (1997, 1:316–19). But as the *Códice Xolotl* (1996:map 3) demonstrates, Tochintecuhtli was sent by Xolotl from Tenayuca to Coatlichan where Huetzin was acting as ruler. Quinatzin had a brother named Tochintecuhtli, but he was a different person.[8] As Dibble (*Códice Xolotl* 1996:36–37) points out, Alva Ixtlilxochitl (1997, 1:424) also insists that Itzmitl, the second ruler of Coatlichan and the father of the great conqueror Huetzin, married Malinalxochitzin, the sister of Quinatzin. But on map 2, the codex shows that Itzmitl married another Malinalxochitzin, the daughter of Cozcacuauh who was one of the six vassals of Xolotl and came with this Chichimec ruler to the Basin of Mexico.

Rather than being a strong ruler, Quinatzin had difficulty in controlling his own family and subjects from the beginning of his establishment in Texcoco. Alva Ixtlilxochitl records a domestic rebellion against Quinatzin:

> Si Tlotzin tuvo muy particular cuidado de que se cultivase la tierra, fue con más ventajas el que tuvo Quinatzin en tiempo de su imperio, compeliendo a los chichimecas no tan solamente a ello, sino a que poblasen y edificasen ciudades y lugares, sacándolos de su rústica y silvestre vivienda, siguiendo el orden y estilo de los tultecas, por cuya

causa muchos de los chichimecas se alteraron, los que hallando de su opinión y parte, de cinco hijos que el rey tenía, los cuatro mayores (cuyos nombre están atrás referidos), y con ellos otros caballeros y gente principal, se levantaron y los primeros que este desacato cometieron, fueron los que estaban poblados en Poyauhtlan, que quemaron muchas labranzas, y luego se confederaron con el tirano Yacánex arriba referido, que había estado recluso con otros bandoleros en las tierras septentrionales; y asimismo hicieron levantar a los de la provincia de Metztitlan, Tototepec y Tepepolco, y otros lugares de menos cuenta. (Alva Ixtlilxochitl 1997, 2:30)

If Tlotzin was particularly careful to cultivate the land, it was Quinatzin who benefited most during his reign of the empire. He compelled the Chichimecs not only to cultivate the land but also to populate and build cities and places, taking them away from their rustic and wild lifestyle in order to follow the order and style of the Toltecs. This demand disturbed many Chichimecs, including the oldest four out of the five sons of the king (whose names are mentioned later), who revolted with other nobles and renowned individuals. And those who first started this contempt were the people who were living in Poyauhtlan. They burned many farms, and then they allied with the above-mentioned tyrant Yacanex, who had been living in reclusion with other bandits in the northern territory; and they also incited the people of the province of Metztitlan, Tototepec and Tepepulco, and other smaller places to rebel. (author's translation)

Quinatzin was not even able to control his own sons, who seriously challenged Quinatzin's political power, thus calling into question the image of Quinatzin as the emperor that Alva Ixtlilxochitl describes in other parts of his text. Moreover, if Huetzin of Coatlichan defeated Yacanex's invasion twice, then this Huetzin would have been a defender of Quinatzin. This again verifies that Texcoco began to develop under Coatlichan's influence from the beginning of its foundation.

The date of the foundation of the city-state of Texcoco by Quinatzin also undermines the theory of Texcoca supremacy in the Basin of Mexico. The diachronic representation of Texcoco in pictographic sources reveals that it was founded much later than other Chichimec cities in the basin. The *Códice Xolotl* (1996) presents Texcoco for the first time on the second map, but it is merely indicated with its glyph with no accompanying rulers. Other cities such as Azcapotzalco and Coatlichan are marked not only with place glyphs but also with glyphs that represent their ruling families. This late foundation of Texcoco has been confirmed by archaeological research. Based on ceramic development in the Basin of Mexico, Jiménez Moreno (1954–1955:219–36) argues that Texcoco began to emerge as a leading city around 1365. Jeffrey Parsons (1970:437–38,

1971:90–91) also demonstrates that the Texcoca area formed a city far later than neighboring cities such as Coatlichan and Huexotla. According to Parsons's research, Texcoco emerged as an urban center capable of competing with other cities in the region, such as Coatlichan and Huexotla, during the late Aztec period (1350–1520). The suggested date for the foundation of Texcoco by archaeological studies corresponds to the beginning of Techotlalatzin's reign, which undermines the political supremacy of Quinatzin.

Techotlalatzin (1357–1409) was Quinatzin's youngest son and successor. As mentioned before, Quinatzin had five sons, but the first four rebelled against their father and joined his enemies. In this critical situation, Quinatzin needed a strong successor. He married his son Techotlalatzin to Tozquentzin, a daughter of the most powerful ruler of Coatlichan in the eastern basin (Alva Ixtlilxochitl 1997, 2:29).[9] Through this marriage, Techotlalatzin appears to have secured his power in Texcoco and expanded his territory. Techotlalatzin participated in the conquest of Xaltocan and its provinces, such as Cuauhtitlan, Tepoztlan, and Xilotepec, with the Azcapotzalca and the Mexica. The *Códice Xolotl* (1996) records this conquest in 5 Flint (1380) while the *Annals of Cuauhtitlan* (1992:75) registers it as occurring in 7 Reed (1395). The *Códice Xolotl* (1996:map 5) depicts that Techotlalatzin attacked Xaltocan from the east (figure 3.4), while Tezozomoc attacked from the west. Tzompantli, the ruler of Xaltocan, fled to the north. According to Alva Ixtlilxochitl (1997, 1:322–23), Techotlalatzin allowed Tzompantli to flee to Metztitlan. This was an important event in Texcoca history because Texcoco appears to free itself from Coatlichan's power by acquiring its own tributary. At the same time, Texcoco began to share a border with Azcapotzalco, ruled by Tezozomoc. Texcoca dominance of Xaltocan, however, seems to have been very brief, because the major cities between Texcoco and Xaltocan, such as Chiconahutla, Tepechpan, and Acolman, were already under Tepaneca control when Huehue Ixtlilxochitl succeeded Techotlalatzin in 8 Calli (1409).

Map 5 of the *Códice Xolotl* (1996) depicts that Techotlalatzin gave eleven villages in the north of Texcoco to the young Huehue Ixtlilxochitl. Based on Alva Ixtlilxochitl's works, Dibble (*Códice Xolotl* 1996:78) identifies them as Cuextecatlichocayan, Tepepulco, Tlalaxapan or Actopan, Tizayocan, Ahuatepec, Axapochco, Cuauhtlatzinco, Teotihuacan, Tezoyucan, Tepechpan, and Chiconauhtla. The *Códice Xolotl* and Alva Ixtlilxochitl's version of this history, however, are not consistent with sources from some of these cities (e.g., Tepepulco, Teotihuacan, Tepechpan, and Chiconauhtla), which claim that they were not part of Texcoco until Nezahualcoyotl conquered them with the Mexica in the fifteenth century. According to the *Relaciones geográficas* (1982–1988, 7:175–76), Tepepulco had been independent until it was conquered first by Tezozomoc of Azcapotzalco and later by Nezahualcoyotl and Moctezuma Ilhuicamina. The same source argues that Teotihuacan had also been independent until the conquest of Nezahualcoyotl and Moctezuma

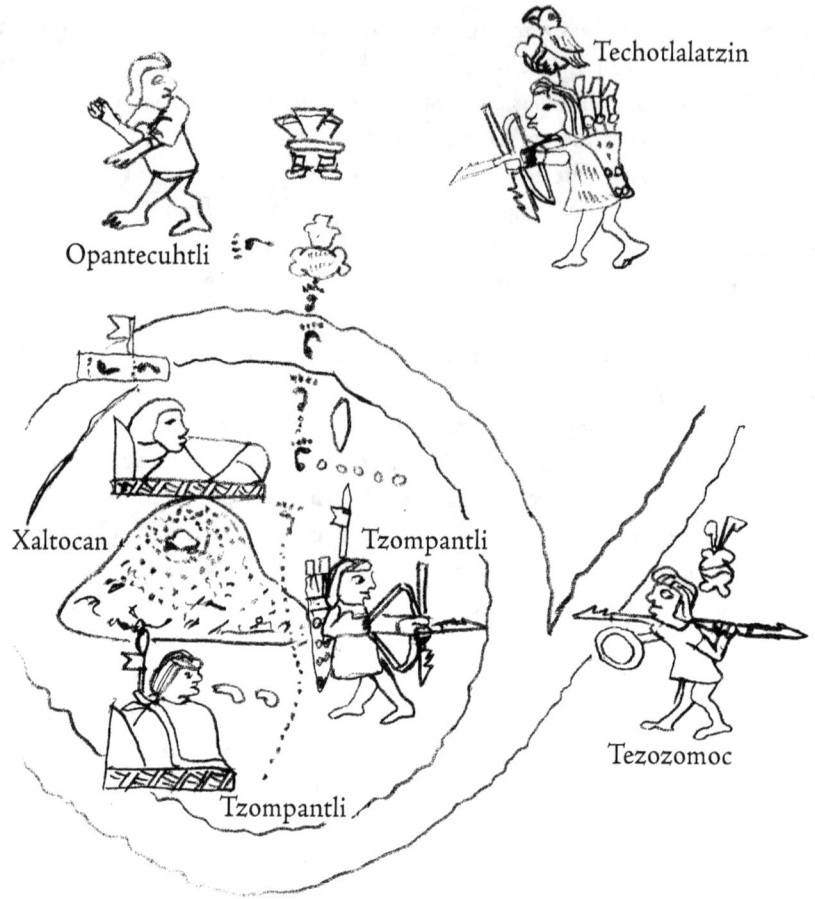

FIG. 3.4

Techotlalatzin's attack on Xaltocan from the *Códice Xolotl* (1996:map 5). Reproduced with permission of the Bibliothèque nationale de France.

On the island Xaltocan (Place of the Sand Spider), its ruler Opantecuhtli (Lord of the Road Flag) dies and his son Tzompantli (Skull Rack) succeeds him. In 5 Flint (1380), he is attacked by Tezozomoc (Angry Stone) from the south and by Techotlalatzin (Stone Dove) from the east. Tzompantli is defeated and flees to the north. The *Códice Xolotl* depicts this event as the first independent military action by the Texcoca ruler since its foundation.

Ilhuicamina (1982–1988, 7:232). The other two cities, Tepechpan and Chiconauhtla, also seem to have been independent for some time until they were conquered by Tezozomoc. As discussed before, Tezozomoc installed his sons as rulers in Acolman and Tepechpan (*Anales de Tlatelolco* 1948:45). This event occurred during Techotlalatzin's reign as the *Códice Xolotl* (1996:map 6) clearly depicts that these two cities were subject to Acolman during Huehue Ixtlilxochitl's reign. In the scene from the *Códice Xolotl* that appears in figure 3.5,

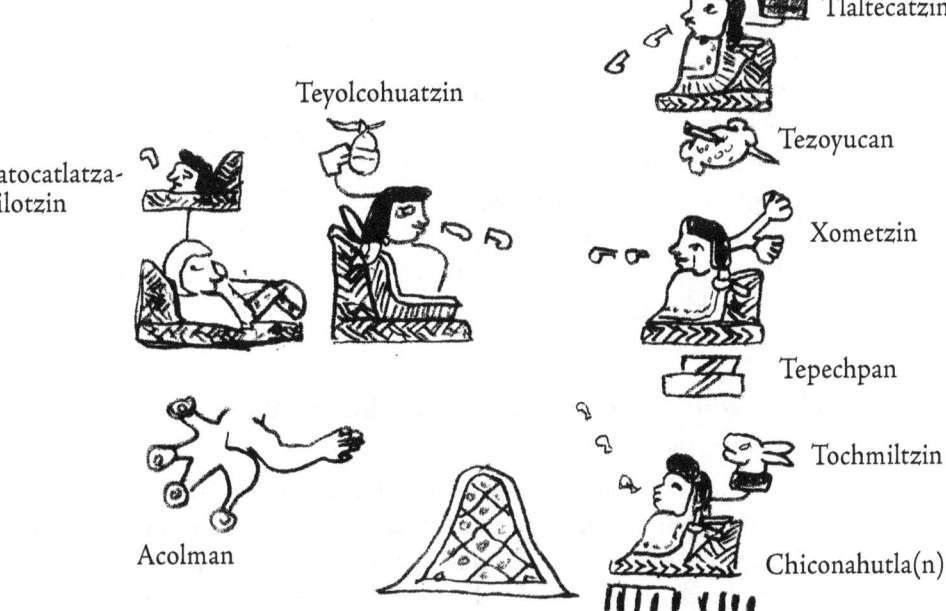

FIG. 3.5

Acolman and its subject cities during Huehue Ixtlilxochitl's and Tezozomoc's reign from the *Códice Xolotl* (1996:map 6). Reproduced with permission of the Bibliothèque nationale de France.

In Acolman (Place of Bent Water), Tlatocatlatzacuilotzin (Kingship) dies and Teyolcohuatzin (Stone Heart) succeeds him. Teyolcohuatzin has three subject cities: Tlaltecatzin's (Resident on the Earth) Tezoyucan (Place of Pierced Stone), Xometzin's (Elder Tree) Tepechpan (Place of Stone Mat), and Tochmiltzin's (Rabbit Field) Chiconauhtla(n) (Place of Seven). Teyolcohuatzin's superior position is evident: his authority mat and speech glyph are depicted as bigger than those of the other three rulers who are facing him. According to the *Anales de Tlatelolco*, Teyolcohuatzin was a son of Tezozomoc of Azcapotzalco and was appointed by his father. With its dominance in Acolman, Azcapotzalco secured a basis upon which to advance into the Acolhuacan area in the northeastern basin while Texcoco had to face the powerful and ambitious ruler Tezozomoc. During the Tepanec-Acolhuacan war, Teyolcohuatzin seemed to make a significant contribution to the Tepanec victory and was appointed after the war as the highest ruler of Acolhuacan along with Tezozomoc's other son Quetzalmaquiztli.

Tezozomoc's son, Teyolcohuatzin of Acolman, was ruling its three neighbor cities, Chiconauhtla, Tepechpan, and Tezoyucan. Thus, the *Códice Xolotl*'s claim that these cities were awarded to the young Huehue Ixtlilxochitl seems to be anachronistic and self-contradictory.

Alva Ixtlilxochitl (1997, 1:325) insists that Texcoco was the most powerful city in the basin, and he records a list of forty-six colonies that Techotlalatzin established. The list, however, appears to be an exaggeration, because it includes many cities, such as Tlacopan, Cuauhnahuac, Xochitepec, Xicotepec, Chiauhtla, Tepetlaoztoc, Tepechpan, and Teotihuacan, that Nezahualcoyotl and his Mexica allies conquered several decades later.[10] Nevertheless, Texcoco was clearly growing more powerful during Techotlalatzin's reign, and it does seem to become one of the leading political and cultural centers in the eastern basin by way of expanding its territory and assimilating more civilized groups. But the city was still competing for power with neighboring cities like Huexotla, Coatlichan, and Coatepec, all of which were independent during Techotlalatzin's reign (Alva Ixtlilxochitl 1997, 1:325).

Huehue Ixtlilxochitl, the Tepanec-Acolhuacan War, and the Tepanec Empire

In 8 Calli (1409), when Huehue Ixtlilxochitl succeeded Techotlalatzin in Texcoco, the city-states in the eastern basin, such as Coatlichan, Huexotla, and Coatepec, witnessed Azcapotzalco's expansion in the western basin. This expansion of Azcapotzalco during Tezozomoc's reign involved a series of wars during the second half of the fourteenth and the beginning of the fifteenth century that resulted in the subjugation of many major city-states in the western, southern, and northern basin. Tezozomoc, who wanted to control the eastern basin, devised an ambitious plan around the same time that Huehue Ixtlilxochitl ascended to the throne. Tezozomoc appears to have tried to subjugate the eastern basin peacefully. As the *Códice Xolotl* (1996:map 7) and Alva Ixtlilxochitl (1997, 1:327–28) show, Tezozomoc sent cotton to the major cities of the eastern basin (Coatlichan, Huexotla, Texcoco, and Coatepec) so that they could make blankets for him. At first these cities accepted Tezozomoc's demand, but they soon rejected his proposal by returning the cotton, and the war began in 1 Reed (1415). According to the *Códice Xolotl* (1996:map 7), the allied cities of the eastern basin were able to successfully defend themselves against Azcapotzalco and its allies, also known as the Tepaneca, and even almost won the war. The codex describes that the allied cities of the eastern basin marched successfully near Azcapotzalco, conquering many villages as they went. Azcapotzalco's attack on Huexotla and Texcoco from Lake Texcoco, however, was the crucial turning point in the war. All the rulers of Acolhuacan's major cities except Huehue Ixtlilxochitl fled to Huexotzinco and Tlaxcala. The Texcoca ruler was captured and slain by the Otompan-Tepaneca and Chalca-Tepaneca.[11]

Alva Ixtlilxochitl (1997, 1:435–36) insists that Texcoco was the leader of the Acolhuacan cities in the Tepanec-Acolhuacan war and that Huehue Ixtlilxochitl played a commanding role in the conflict. His assertion, however, is difficult to accept because there are many recorded events that contradict it. Alva Ixtlilxochitl insists that Huehue Ixtlilxochitl commanded the army of Acolhuacan cities such as Coatlichan, Huexotla, and Coatepec. He argues further that at the beginning of the war, Huehue Ixtlilxochitl was elected as the

Chichimec ruler, chichimecatecuhtli, from among the rulers of the major cities in the eastern basin and that in the year 13 Rabbit (1414) he named his son Nezahualcoyotl the heir to his empire in Huexotla. The scene from the *Códice Xolotl* (1996) "transcribed" by Alva Ixtlilxochitl, however, does not corroborate this chronicler's claim (figure 3.6). The codex does not depict the inauguration of Huehue Ixtlilxochitl as the greatest Chichimec ruler, chichimecatecuhtli, as Alva Ixtlilxochitl claims. Rather, Huehue Ixtlilxochitl seems to declare his son Nezahualcoyotl legitimate heir to Texcoco: the throne is connected to Huehue Ixtlilxochitl's glyph, and he himself is connected to Nezahualcoyotl by a dotted line. But the speech glyphs indicate that he talks to Coatlichan's priest, Tlalnahuacatzin, about this succession. And Huehue Ixtlilxochitl is depicted below Huexotla's ruler, Tlacotzin, and also painted on the same level as two priests, Tlalnahuacatzin of Coatlichan and Tozatzin of Huexotla. The codex does not show Huehue Ixtlilxochitl as having any greater power or authority. Rather, he seems to occupy a lower status than Tlacotzin, the Huexotla ruler, because he is spatially subordinate to Tlacotzin and obligated to pay homage by traveling to Huexotla for the ceremony.[12]

Rather than Texcoco, Coatlichan was the oldest and the most powerful city-state in the eastern basin, and it seems to have played an important role in the Tepanec-Acolhuacan war. Alva Ixtlilxochitl (1997, 1:436) indirectly supports Coatlichan's role by stating that Huehue Ixtlilxochitl named Cihuacnahuacatzin, a son of the Coatlichan ruler Paintzin, as the chief military commander of the Acolhuacan troops. Torquemada (1975, 1:109) also records that this position was occupied by Tochintecuhtli, the son of Coatlichan's ruler. This is significant because command of the military troops in central Mexico was normally assigned to the most powerful ruler's heir. The fact that Cihuacnahuacatzin or Tochintecuhtli of Coatlichan assumed this position indicates the superior position of Coatlichan among the allies in the eastern basin.

After conquering almost the entire Basin of Mexico, Tezozomoc of Azcapotzalco reorganized the Acolhuacan region to facilitate his control. Tezozomoc distributed the newly acquired land to his principal allies, the Mexica and the Tlatelolca. The *Códice Xolotl* (1996) records that Tezozomoc took Coatlichan and gave Texcoco and Huexotla to the Mexica and the Tlatelolca, respectively (figure 3.7). Alva Ixtlilxochitl describes this distribution in detail:

> Acordó el tirano Tezozomoc en esta ocasión de repartir el reino de Tetzcuco en este modo. El pueblo de Coatlichan con todo su llamamiento (que en aquella sazón eran muchos pueblos y lugares que tenían el nombre y apellidos de acolhuas, y corrían desde los términos de la provincia de Chalco hasta los Tolantzinco, en donde entraban las provincias de Otompan, Tepepolco, y Cempoalan), tomó para sí. Huexotla que era la otra cabecera que asimismo contenía muchos pueblos

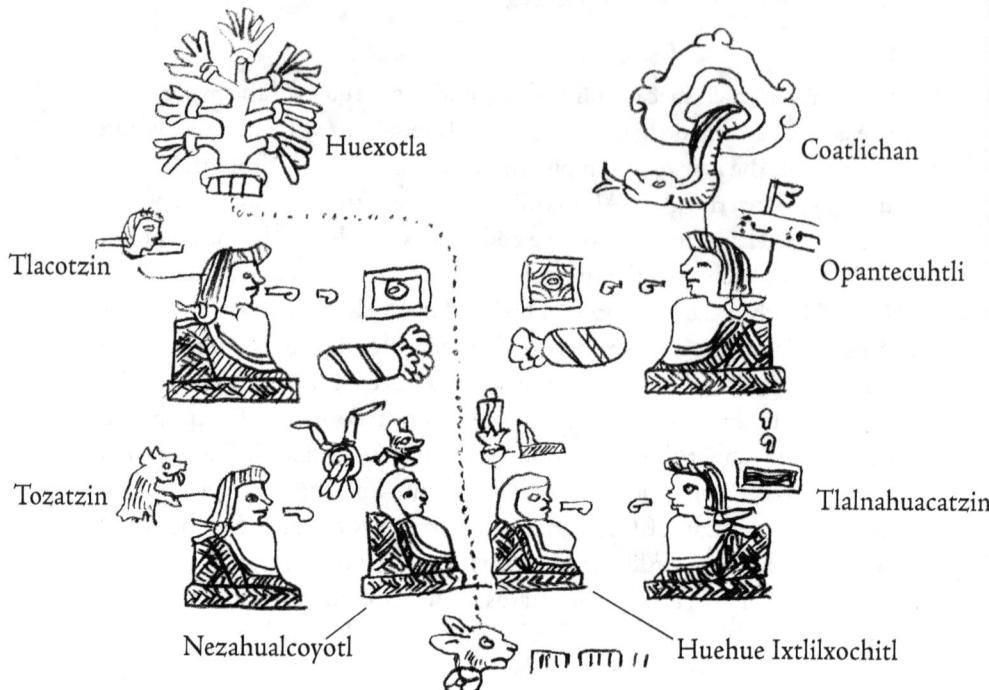

FIG. 3.6

Preparation for the Tepanec-Acolhuacan war and the appointment of Nezahualcoyotl as the legitimate heir of Texcoco from the *Códice Xolotl* (1996:map 7). Reproduced with permission of the Bibliothèque nationale de France.

Before he initiated the Tepanec-Acolhuacan war, Tezozomoc, the ruler of Azcapotzalco, sent war supplies such as cotton to the rulers of the Acolhuacan city-states Coatlichan, Huexotla, Texcoco, and Coatepec, and he asked them to make war supplies for him. The Acolhuacan rulers accepted Tezozomoc's request at first but later reneged on their agreement. The Coatlichan ruler Opantecuhtli (Lord of the Road Flag) and the Huexotla ruler Tlacotzin (Slave) are talking about the materials that Tezozomoc had sent them. Below them, Tozatzin (Gopher), Nezahualcoyotl (Fasted Coyote), Huehue Ixtlilxochitl (Black-Eyes Flower), and Tlalnahuacatzin (Speaking Earth) appear to be talking about a different matter. Alva Ixtlilxochitl and modern readers of the codex interpret this scene as an appointment ceremony in which Huehue Ixtlilxochitl mandates the Tepanec-Acolhuacan war in his role as *chichimecatecuhtli* (Chichimec ruler).

This interpretation, however, is not very convincing because (1) if Huehue Ixtlilxochitl were the most powerful ruler, the rulers and people from other regions such as Coatlichan and Huexotla would have come to Texcoco where the Texcoca ruler resided, but in this scene, Huehue Ixtlilxochitl travels to Huexotla; (2) rather than being depicted in a dominant position, Huehue Ixtlilxochitl appears smaller than, and below, Huexotla and Coatlichan's ruler. His political status is clearly lower than these two rulers and seems to be equal to that of the priests or nobles of Coatlichan and Huexotla, Tozatzin and Tlalnahuacatzin. I would argue that Huehue Ixtlilxochitl went to Huexotla to discuss the appointment of Nezahualcoyotl as the legitimate heir of Texcoco. Huehue Ixtlilxochitl is connected to an *icpalli* (authority mat), and Nezahualcoyotl is now sitting on an authority mat indicating that he is a ruler. The figure does not show any Texcoca supremacy over neighboring cities; rather, it demonstrates that the Texcoca ruler remains dependent upon Coatlichan and Huexotla because he needs their approval in the appointment of his heir.

FIG. 3.7
Tezozomoc's distribution of Acolhuacan cities after the Tepanec-Acolhuacan war from the *Códice Xolotl* (1996:map 8). Reproduced with permission of the Bibliothèque nationale de France.

In the year 6 Flint (1420), after his victory over the Acolhuacan allies, Tezozomoc distributed the major Acolhuacan city-states among his allied city-states. Tezozomoc (Angry Stone) of Azcapotzalco (Place of Ant Mound) claims for himself the most prestigious Acolhuacan city, Coatlichan (Snake Home). He gives Huexotla (Place of Willow) to Tlacateotzin (Human Sun) of Tlatelolco (Place of the Round Earth Mound) and Texcoco (Craggy Mountain) to Chimalpopoca (Smoking Shield) of Tenochtitlan (Place of the Cactus Fruit on the Stone). All three victorious rulers are sitting on the authority mat *icpalli* of a *tlatoani* (ruler) while the defeated appear without the icpalli or any speech glyph of authority. The losers also pay maguey and maize as tribute. The land distribution by Tezozomoc provides some indication concerning the political situation in the 1420s in the Basin of Mexico. The two Mexica cities Tlatelolco and Tenochtitlan, which had been subject cities of Azcapotzalco, now seem to elevate their status to equal partners of the ruling city. This partnership demonstrates that the two Mexica cities developed into major city-states capable of dominating the Basin of Mexico in the 1430s. On the other hand, Texcoco started out as a tributary of Tenochtitlan during the 1420s and from that point on played an important role in Mexica history. In this context, Itzcoatl's appointment of Nezahualcoyotl as the ruler of Texcoco in 4 Reed (1431) would be an act of naming a ruler for one of his many tributaries.

> interpolados con los de la ciudad de Tetzcuco y con los de Coatlichan, le dio a Tlacateotzin, señor de Tlatelolco; y la ciudad de Tetzcuco con los demás pueblos de su llamamiento le dio a Chimalpopoca, rey de México. (Alva Ixtlilxochitl 1997, 2:53)

> The tyrant Tezozomoc agreed on this occasion to distribute the kingdom of Texcoco in the following way. He took for himself Coatlichan with all its subject towns (which at that time were many towns and places that had names and surnames of Acolhuaque and ran from the province of Chalco to the Tulantzinco, which included the provinces of Otompan, Tepepulco, and Cempoala). He gave Tlacateotzin, king of Tlatelolco, Huexotla that was the other capital which itself included many towns interspersed between those of Texcoco and Coatlichan; and he gave Chimalpopoca, king of Mexico-Tenochtitlan, the city of Texcoco with its subject towns. (author's translation)

Tezozomoc took Coatlichan, the capital of the Acolhuacan cities, because Coatlichan controlled the most tributaries from among the Acolhuacan cities. He replaced Coatlichan's ruler with his grandson Quetzalmaquiztli and let him supervise all the tribute collected in the Acolhuacan area. Alva Ixtlilxochitl (1997, 1:344–47) also reports how Tezozomoc tried to consolidate his empire after the conquest of Acolhuacan by reorganizing the political and economic system. He declared himself the monarch of the world and then recognized his longtime subordinates, the Mexica and the Tlatelolca, as his main partners. Tezozomoc elevated two of their cities, Tenochtitlan and Tlatelolco, to the status of cabecera on a par with his own city of Azcapotzalco and declared that the three cities would govern all of the conquered city-states. In addition, he created other cabecera cities such as Acolman, Coatlichan, Chalco, and Otompan. Tezozomoc then divided the land and tribute of the Acolhuacan region into eight parts. He took two of them as the head of the empire and assigned one to each cabecera city. This political and tribute system that Tezozomoc instituted in the 1420s provides an important clue both for understanding the origin of the political and tribute system that the Mexica would employ in their empire and to determine the status of Texcoco in this empire after the 1430s.

Texcoca Politics, Culture, and Religion before Nezahualcoyotl

The Texcoca pictorial sources and alphabetic texts depict Texcoco as a politically and culturally well-stabilized city-state from its beginning, but this city-state actually started its political and cultural development far later than its neighboring city-states such as Coatlichan and Huexotla. Texcoca pictorial sources such as the *Códice Xolotl* (1996), the *Mapa Tlotzin* (Aubin 1886b), and the *Mapa Quinatzin* (Aubin 1886b) indicate that when Quinatzin was founding

Texcoco, his Chichimec group at first continued their hunter lifestyle rather than the agricultural practices of the Toltecs. All of these sources describe the acculturation of the nomadic Texcoca to the more civilized practices of their Toltec neighbors as a gradual process. On map 1, the *Códice Xolotl* divides the entire basin into two areas: the north, occupied by Xolotl's Chichimecs, and the south, occupied by Toltec descendants in Colhuacan, Chapultepec, Tototepec, and Cholula. The Chichimecs wear clothes made of animal skin and carry bows and arrows while the Toltecs wear cotton cloths and live sedentary lives. The Texcoca founder, Quinatzin, first appears on map 2 and is depicted just like his fellow Chichimecs with animal skin clothing and bow and arrows. His son Techotlalatzin on map 4 is depicted in the same way as his father. There is no change in his costume and arms. Huehue Ixtlilxochitl is the one who undergoes a sudden change in his garb on map 6, where he is wearing a cotton cloth just like the Toltecs depicted on map 1. The *Códice Xolotl* demonstrates that the Toltecization of the Texcoca Chichimecs was complete with Huehue Ixtlilxochitl. The *Mapa Quinatzin* and the *Mapa Tlotzin* also depict the Toltecization of the Texcoca Chichimecs. Both maps represent Quinatzin's Chichimec group with clothing made of animal skin rather than cloth. The *Mapa Tlotzin* shows Tlotzin's Toltecization by symbolically depicting him learning how to barbecue hunted animals and how to cultivate crops from his Chalca neighbors (figure 3.8).[13]

As a city-state founded far later than its neighboring cities, Texcoco seems to have needed to establish a general structure of political, cultural, and religious institutions within a short period of time. In this context, the Texcoca rulers were eager to accept more civilized immigrants to their city. Quinatzin welcomed the Toltecized tribes—Tlailotlaca in 4 Reed (1327) according to the *Códice Xolotl* (1996) (figure 3.9), and the Tlailotlaca and the Chimalpaneca according to the *Mapa Quinatzin* (Aubin 1886a) (see figure 2.1). Both sources depict that these recent immigrants were Toltec descendants by distinguishing them from Quinatzin's Chichimecs in terms of their dress. Quinatzin's efforts to Toltecize the nomadic Chichimecs of Texcoco continued during his son Techotlalatzin's reign. Techotlalatzin may have been the first Texcoca ruler who was able to speak Nahuatl, the language of the Toltecs (Alva Ixtlilxochitl 1997, 2:34). Like his father, he welcomed four Toltecized tribes in 4 House (1405) according to map 5 of the *Códice Xolotl* (figure 3.10) and the *Mapa Quinatzin*: the Mexica, the Colhuaque, the Huitznahuaque, and the Tepaneca.[14] Both the *Códice Xolotl* and the *Mapa Quinatzin* indicate that they came from Colhuacan. These four tribes with two, the Tlailotlaca and the Chimalpaneca, who had already come under Quinatzin's reign constituted six principal barrios of Texcoco.

These immigrants seem to have played a decisive role in Texcoca cultural, religious, and political systems. The first immigrants, the Tlailotlaca, were experts of paint writing. In figure 3.9, the Tlailotlaca individual is depicted in

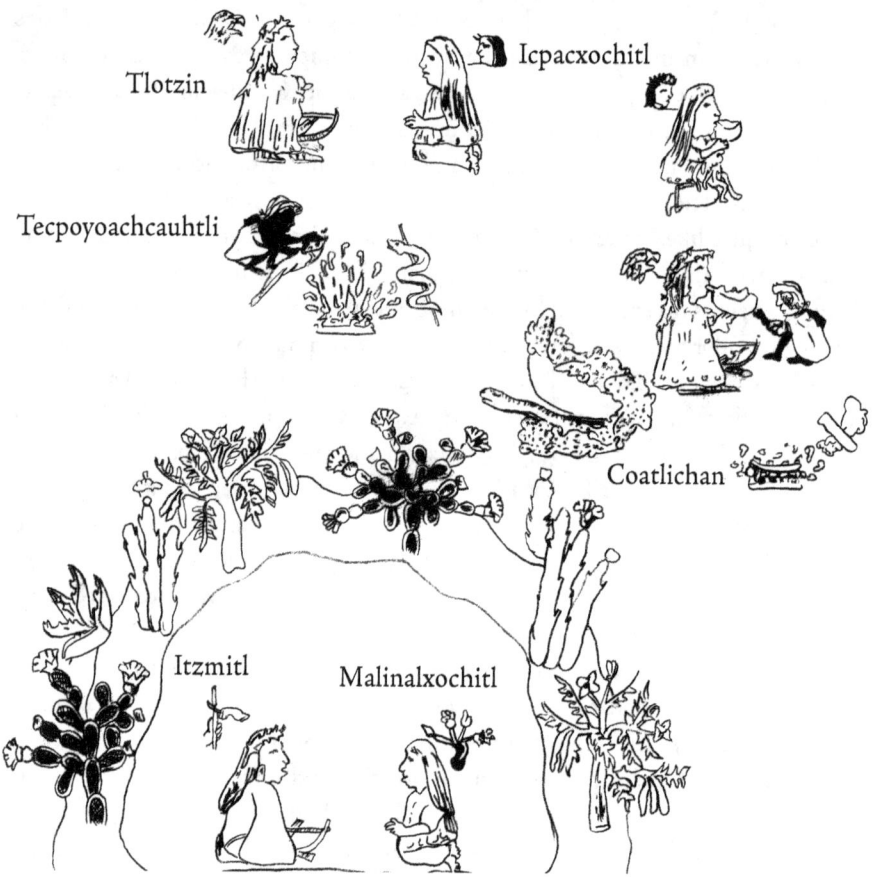

FIG. 3.8

Tlotzin's Toltecization near Coatlichan from the *Mapa Tlotzin*. Reproduced from M. Aubin (1886b) with permission of the Bibliothèque nationale de France.

According to the Nahuatl notes on the map, the Chalca Tecpoyoachcauhtli teach Tlotzin and his wife, Icpacxochitl, two activities associated with Toltec culture: cooking animals such as rabbit and snake and drinking *pulque*. The two Chichimec figures begin to learn the sedentary Toltec lifestyle. This happens near Coatlichan (Snake Home) where Itzmitl (Obsidian Arrow) and his wife, Malinalxochitl (Twisted Flower), are living. These two residents of Coatlichan had already begun the process of Toltecization as indicated by their dress. Itzmitl carries a bow and arrows, but both he and his wife wear cotton cloths while Tlotzin and his wife Icpacxochitl continue to wear animal skins. This difference between the Coatlichan and Texcoca rulers indicates that Coatlichan started the process of Toltecization much earlier than Texcoco.

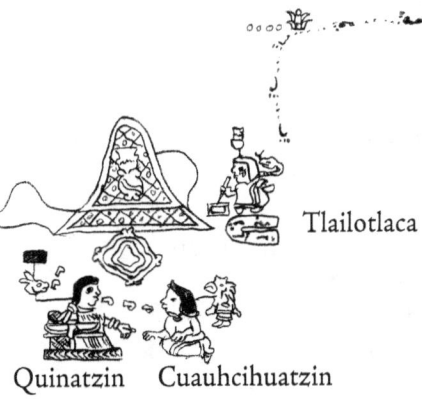 

FIG. 3.9

Quinatzin's reception of the Tlailotlaca from the *Códice Xolotl* (1996:map 4). Reproduced with permission of the Bibliothèque nationale de France.

Tlailotlaca (Returning People) travels from Chalco (Place of Precious Stone) to Texcoco during Quinatzin's reign in 4 Reed (1327). Their Chalca origin is also indicated by a glyph above their heads, and the name of their leader seems to be Coatl (Snake). The Tlailotlaca must have been *tlacuilos* (painter-scribes) as they are depicted with pen and paper. With their arrival, Texcoco probably began to record regional history with pictorial glyphs just like its Toltec or Toltecized neighboring cities did.

---

the act of painting something, which represents the group's specialized skill as tlacuiloque, "painter-scribes." Alva Ixtlilxochitl (1997, 2:32) also confirms their specialty: "Los tlailotlaques por su caudillo a Aztatlitexcan, o según la historia general Coatlitepan, los cuales eran consumados en el arte de pintar y hacer historia, mas que en las demás artes" (The Tlailotlaque, whose leader was Aztatlitexcan, or according to the general history Coatlitepan, were those who were experts in the art of painting [writing] and at recording history, more than in any other arts). According to the *Mapa Quinatzin* (Aubin 1886a), one of the later immigrant groups brought corn to the basin and presumably taught others how to grow it. These immigrants also brought their gods with them to Texcoco. The Tlailotlaca brought their god Tezcatlipoca and the Mexica brought their god Huitzilopochtli. Alva Ixtlilxochitl (1997, 2:32–33) regretfully records that these groups seem to have influenced the Texcoca religious system in a major way by introducing their religious ceremonies that included human sacrifice.

The immigrant groups obviously contributed significantly to Texcoca cultural and religious development, but at the same time they eroded Texcoca

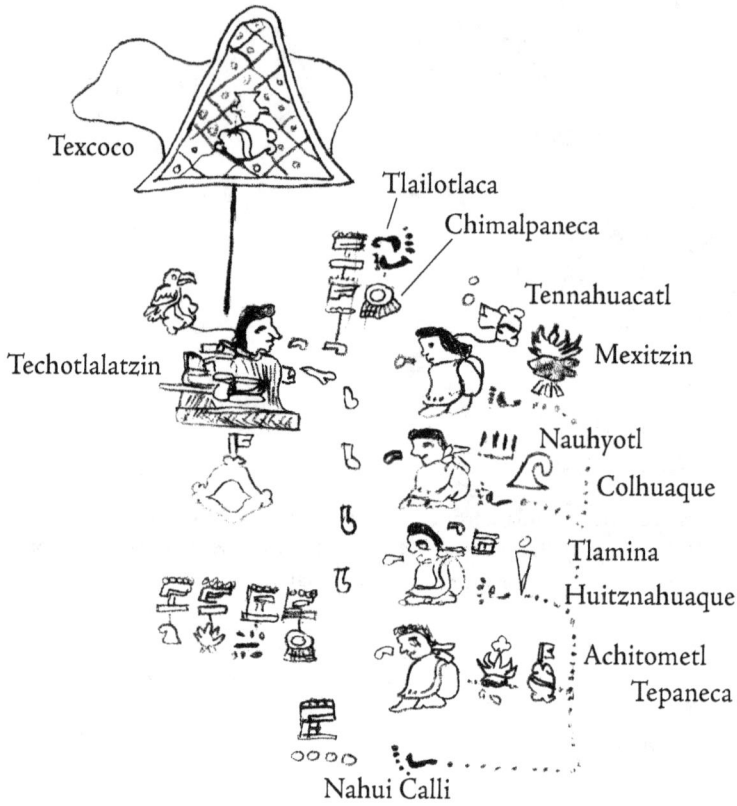

FIG. 3.10

Techotlalatzin's reception of the four immigrant groups from the *Códice Xolotl* (1996: map 5). Reproduced with permission of the Bibliothèque nationale de France.

Techotlalatzin (Stone Dove) is addressing the leaders of the four recently arrived immigrant groups from Chalco: Tennahuacatl (Someone from Tennahuac [Speaking Stone Lip]) of the Mexitzin (People of Maguey), Nauhyotl (Essence of Four) of the Colhuaque (People of Colhuacan), Tlamina (Shooter) of the Huitznahuaque (People of the Place near Thorns), and Achitometl (Water Maguey) of the Tepaneca (People of Tepan [Stone-Flag]). These four ethnic groups with two others, the Tlailotlaca and the Chimalpaneca, who had arrived previously during Quinatzin's reign, formed the six major *calpulli* in Texcoco. These six groups, all of whom were Toltecized or Toltec descendants, induced significant political and cultural transformations in Texcoco. They greatly contributed to Toltecizing Texcoco by introducing maize cultivation, the Toltec language, Nahuatl, and Toltec religious practices. However, some of these immigrant groups also appear to have caused political instability in Texcoco, because they helped the Tepanec invaders conquer their newly adopted city during the Tepanec-Acolhuacan war.

political stability. Because they were newcomers, they did not have much loyalty to Texcoca rulers. According to Alva Ixtlilxochitl (1997, 2:44), when the Tepanec-Acolhuacan war broke out in 1 Reed (1415), the Chimalpaneca, one of the immigrant groups, rebelled against Huehue Ixtlilxochitl and allied with Tezozomoc. They killed Huehue Ixtlilxochitl's subjects and pillaged his palace. Alva Ixtlilxochitl does not record more about the reaction of the immigrant groups to the war, but there were the Mexica who had immigrated to Texcoco and who might have aided the Mexica of Tenochtitlan in their conquest of Texcoco. In addition, Alva Ixtlilxochitl (1997, 1:342–43) records a rebellious group of Huehue Ixtlilxochitl's subjects. They were close allies of Tezozomoc and did not want to help Nezahualcoyotl recuperate his city. These rebellions demonstrate that during Huehue Ixtlilxochitl's reign, Texcoco was not able to completely control its own subjects; it was still in the process of becoming a politically stable city-state.

Texcoco was founded by Quinatzin in the basin of central Mexico at the end of the thirteenth century. The efforts made by the Texcoca rulers such as Quinatzin and Techotlalatzin to develop their city-state politically and culturally made possible Texcoco's rise to power in the short space of one century. Its chance for further growth, however, was eliminated by the assassination of its third ruler, Huehue Ixtlilxochitl, by the Azcapotzalca. Texcoco, however, was able to gain higher political status in the Basin of Mexico by allying with the Mexica during the reign of Nezahualcoyotl in the 1430s. With the Mexica, Nezahualcoyotl conquered many city-states, such as Azcapotzalco, Coatlichan, and Huexotla, which had been more dominant than Texcoco. Contrary to the assertions of Texcoca sources that describe the political supremacy of Texcoco in the Basin of Mexico during the thirteenth and fourteenth centuries, Texcoco was originally a small city that was only able to replace Coatlichan as the capital of Acolhuacan under Nezahualcoyotl's leadership in the fifteenth century.

CHAPTER FOUR

Reexamining Nezahualcoyotl's Texcoco

Politics, Government, and Legal System

Colonial chroniclers of pre-Hispanic Mexico paid special attention to Nezahualcoyotl and praised him as a prudent and sage king who established one of the most elaborate, civilized, and efficient political and legal systems in pre-Hispanic times. As explained in chapter 1, the Franciscan scholar Fray Toribio de Benavente (Motolinia) was the first to describe Nezahualcoyotl as a fair legal practitioner and legislator, which provided the basis for further embellishments. The Texcoca chronicler don Fernando de Alva Ixtlilxochitl (1997) played a decisive role in creating the modern image of Nezahualcoyotl by documenting his councils, his tribute collection system, and his efficient and egalitarian legal system. Alva Ixtlilxochitl also insisted that Nezahualcoyotl established the most powerful empire before the arrival of the Spaniards and that his city-state Texcoco served not only as a model city-state in the basin, but also as a clear contrast to Tenochtitlan, which according to him was only interested in conquering neighboring nations and practicing barbarous human sacrifice.

Following Motolinia and Alva Ixtlilxochitl's perspective, later chroniclers and historians also focused on Nezahualcoyotl and his city-state of Texcoco. The sixteenth-century Spanish chronicler Fray Juan de Torquemada records,

> A estos dos reyes [Nezahualcoyotl y Nezahualpilli], mas que a los otros sus antepasados, estimaron, y tuvieron, en mucho, los de México, por su mucha prudencia, y buen gobierno, y por la mucha antigüedad de su señorío, y los tenían como por padres. (Torquemada 1975:354)

> These two kings [Nezahualcoyotl and Nezahualpilli], more than any other ancestors, those of Mexico-Tenochtitlan esteemed them and held them in high regard for their great prudence, good government,

and for the great antiquity of their kingdom, and they considered the kings parents. (author's translation)

In the eighteenth century, Father Francisco Javier Clavijero (1991:115) describes Texcoco as the Athens of pre-Hispanic Mexico, because he believed that under Nezahualcoyotl and his successor, Nezahualpilli, Texcoco exhibited a more advanced politics and culture than any other city-state in the basin. In the nineteenth century, William H. Prescott (n.d.:93–117) compares Nezahualcoyotl with Solomon and David because, according to this historian, Nezahualcoyotl developed a highly advanced culture and politics in the barbarous and sanguinary environment in which the Mexica dominated and propagated a militaristic ideology.

These images have appeared repeatedly in histories produced throughout the twentieth century. Modern scholars who have studied Nezahualcoyotl, such as Francis Gillmor (1983), José María Vigil (1957), Miguel León-Portilla (1972, 1992a), Jerome A. Offner (1983), and many others, bring into relief the prudent and civilized image of Nezahualcoyotl as well as his anti-Mexica ideology. All of these images, however, are based on the prefabricated contrast between the prudent and civilized Nezahualcoyotl of Texcoco and the more powerful but barbarous Mexica of Tenochtitlan. Comparing Nezahualcoyotl to Solomon or David, the paragons of wisdom in the Bible, automatically places him in a position superior to the Mexica rulers. Moreover, the association between Texcoco and Athens suggests that Tenochtitlan corresponds to Rome, thereby reinforcing Texcoco's cultural superiority. In this way, Nezahualcoyotl and Texcoco have consistently been represented in terms of their differences from, and their cultural and intellectual superiority over, the more barbarous Mexica kings of Tenochtitlan.

That this contrast between Texcoco and Tenochtitlan originated in the work of colonial indigenous chroniclers from Texcoco may come as no surprise. Texcoca chroniclers insisted that their accounts were based on previous pictorial and alphabetic texts. If we examine these original texts in detail, however, we find that they do not support the arguments made by the later Texcoca sources. Rather, these texts demonstrate not only Nezahualcoyotl's close relationship to, and his many conquests with, the Mexica kings, but also similarities between the political, artistic, and legal institutions of Texcoco and Tenochtitlan.

Establishment of Nezahualcoyotl as Ruler of Texcoco

Nezahualcoyotl was born in 1 Rabbit (1402) as Nezahualcoyotl Acolmiztli (Fasted Coyote, Arm of a Lion) (figure 4.1). In 4 Rabbit (1418), when he was only fifteen years old, his father, Huehue Ixtlilxochitl, was assassinated by the Tepaneca. After the assassination of his father, the Tepanec king Tezozomoc

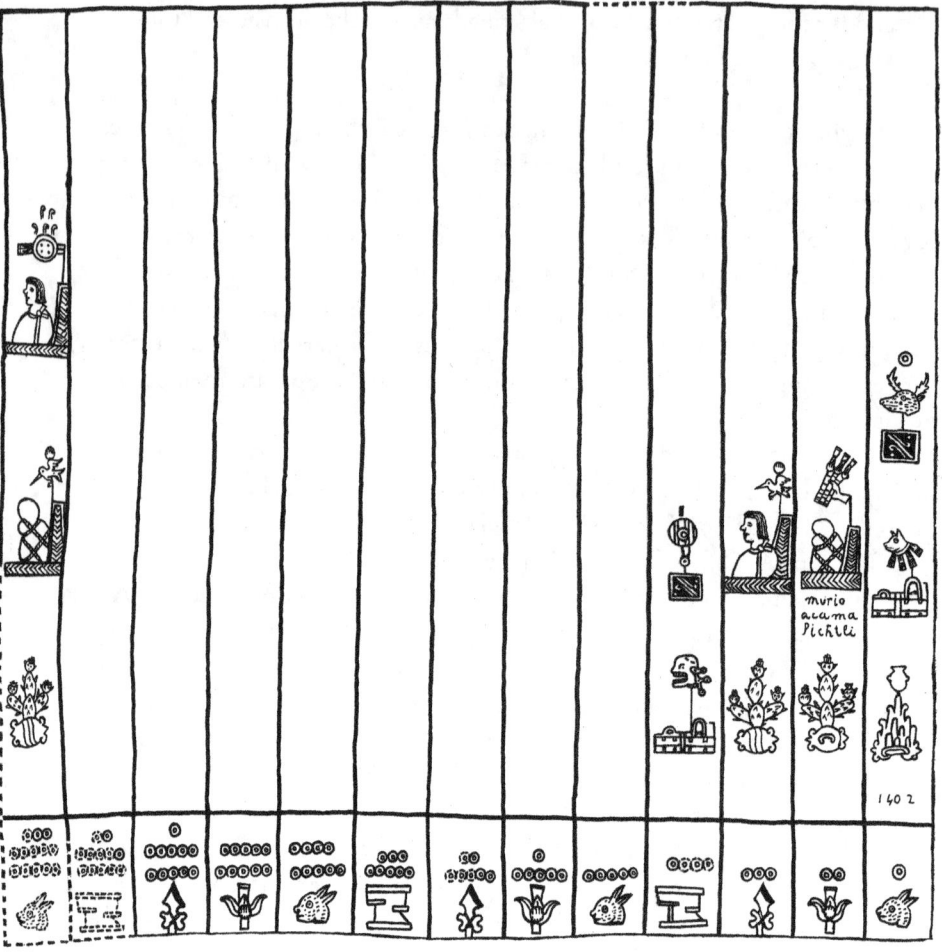

FIG. 4.1

Nezahualcoyotl's birth in 1 Rabbit (1402) from the *Codex en Cruz* (1981). Reproduced with permission of the University of Utah Press.

The *Codex en Cruz* is a clear example of indigenous historical annals, *xihutlapohualli* or *cexiuhtlacuilolli*, which record major historical events year by year. It starts with 1 Tochtli (1 Rabbit, 1402) and reads from right to left. The first column records the birth of Nezahualcoyotl, the most significant event in Texcoco (Craggy Mountain). Above Texcoco appears a cradle connected with Nezahualcoyotl's name glyph, a coyote with a collar (Fasted Coyote), which depicts the birth of Nezahualcoyotl. Above the name glyph is a diagonal that indicates the day, 1 Mazatl (1 Deer). The whole column, then, records that Nezahualcoyotl was born in Texcoco on the day 1 Deer of the year 1 Rabbit. The codex offers the most detailed chronology of events in Texcoco during Nezahualcoyotl's lifetime.

and his successor Maxtla pursued Nezahualcoyotl because, according to the *Códice Xolotl* (1996) and Alva Ixtlilxochitl's works (1997), he was the legitimate heir of Texcoco.[1] His legendary tale, which includes frequent escapes from his enemies and repeated attempts to regain his lost city, appears in the *Códice Xolotl* and alphabetic texts such as the *Annals of Cuauhtitlan* (1992) and the works of Alva Ixtlilxochitl.[2] The latter chronicler records in detail Nezahualcoyotl's life under the Tepanec kings' persecution. Nezahualcoyotl fled to Tlaxcala and spent a couple of years there. Then he went to live in Tenochtitlan, thanks to his Mexica aunts who bribed the Tepanec king, Tezozomoc. Nezahualcoyotl's residence in Tenochtitlan is an important stage in his life because it suggests that he was partially raised and educated as a Mexica. He arrived in the Mexica city when he was seventeen years old, and he stayed in Tenochtitlan for more than ten years, from 6 Flint (1420) until he reconquered Texcoco in 4 Reed (1431). Nezahualcoyotl was clearly at the age when Mexica youth began to study at school, the calmecac. According to the *Codex Mendoza* (1992), the Mexica father took his son to the calmecac when he was fifteen years old (figure 4.2). During the years of his residence in Tenochtitlan, Nezahualcoyotl was exposed to the Mexica educational system, and he would have been thoroughly familiar with Mexica politics and culture. As many scholars demonstrate, the calmecac was the most important Mexica ideological institution, charged with training warriors and priests for Aztec society.[3] Nezahualcoyotl's experiences in Tenochtitlan would later inform the way he governed Texcoco.

After the Tepanec emperor Tezozomoc died in 13 Reed (1427), his son Tayatzin succeeded him, but another son, Maxtla, killed this successor and proclaimed himself the ruler of the Tepanec empire. The Mexica kings, Chimalpopoca of Tenochtitlan and Tlacateotzin of Tlatelolco, sided with Tayatzin. This prompted Maxtla to kill Chimalpopoca and Tlacateotzin and to attempt to take over their cities, thus dissolving the Tepanec alliance with the Mexica in the year 12 Rabbit (1426) (Alva Ixtlilxochitl 1997, 2:56). The desperate Mexica king Itzcoatl who succeeded Chimalpopoca was about to surrender to the Tepaneca when the famous general Tlacaelel rallied the Mexica to defeat the Tepaneca in 1 Flint (1428). Mexica-based sources such as Fray Diego Durán's *The History of the Indies of New Spain* (1994:75–81) and don Fernando Alvarado Tezozomoc's *Crónica mexicana* (1987:46–52, 267–68) record that the Mexica fought the war alone and achieved victory without any allies. Sources from Cuauhtitlan, such as the *Annals of Cuauhtitlan* (1992:95–97), and from Texcoco, such as the chronicles of Alva Ixtlilxochitl (1997, 1:364–71, 2:79–81), however, claim that Nezahualcoyotl contributed greatly to the Mexica victory over the Tepaneca. They report that Nezahualcoyotl played an important diplomatic role in persuading his relatives from Huexotzinco and Tlaxcala to fight against the Tepaneca. This Texcoca version, however, does not seem plausible. Davies (1987:35–34) argues that if Huexotzinco had helped the Mexica conquer Azcapotzalco, they would have claimed prisoners for sacrifice and acquired

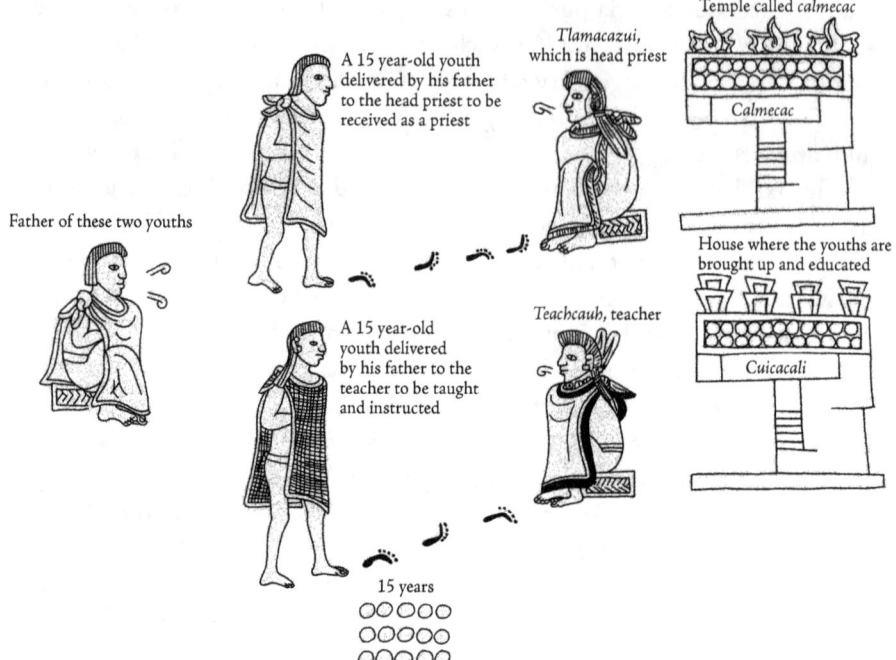

FIG. 4.2

A fifteen-year-old Mexica youth goes to the *calmecac* and *cuicacalli* from the *Codex Mendoza* (1992:f. 61r). Reproduced with permission of the University of California Press.

The father takes one of his sons to the calmecac (House of Cord) and the other to the cuicacalli (Song House) in accordance with the boys' individual inclinations. Based on the clothing worn by the boys and their teachers, the one who attends the calmecac probably wishes to be a priest, while the other who goes to the cuicacalli will be a warrior.

---

political control over part of the conquered region, but there is no indication of any such thing in the extant sources. I would argue that if Nezahualcoyotl had brought military force from Huexotzinco and Tlaxcala, the majority of this force would have been made up of the refugees from Acolhuacan city-states such as Coatlichan, Huexotla, Texcoco, and Coatepec who had fled to Huexotzinco and Tlaxcala after the Tepanec-Acolhuacan war (1415–1418).[4] Alva Ixtlilxochitl records that Nezahualcoyotl met the refugees several times to persuade them to return to their home. Rather than seeking outside help, the Mexica took advantage of the Tepanec civil war. They diplomatically approached city-states such as Tlacopan, which disapproved of Maxtla's usurpation of power, to ensure that they should not support Maxtla. At the same time, the Mexica attacked Azcapotzalco, whose ruler Tayatzin was slain by Maxtla, rather than Coyoacan, where Maxtla had resided before the Tepanec civil war and where he had the most support. Alva Ixtlilxochitl (1997, 2:79–81) insists that Nezahualcoyotl played a pivotal role in destroying Azcapotzalco not only through his diplomatic efforts but also with his own troops in battle. For Alva Ixtlilxochitl, then, Nezahualcoyotl saved the Mexica from Azcapotzalca tyranny. This Texcoca chronicler's claim, however, is not consistent with the historical context. Nezahualcoyotl probably could not have led a large force of his own in the conquest of Azcapotzalco because, as Davies (1987:35) points out, at that time the young Nezahualcoyotl was a refugee in Tenochtitlan and would not have had his own troops. In addition, the ruler and the nobles of his own hometown, Texcoco (i.e., his half sister Tozquentzin and his half brothers Yancuiltzin and Tochpilli), did not support him. In fact, they tried to kill him by allying with Maxtla during the Tepanec-Mexica war (Alva Ixtlilxochitl 1997, 2:76).[5]

Even after the Tepanec-Mexica war, Nezahualcoyotl had to stay in Tenochtitlan because the nobles in Texcoco, such as his brother-in-law Nonohualcatl and Toxihui and the other pro-Tepanec rulers of Coatlichan, Huexotla, and Coatepec, refused to recognize him as the legitimate ruler of Texcoco (Alva Ixtlilxochitl 1997, 1:376–77). As a result of this situation, Nezahualcoyotl was crowned by the Mexica rulers, Itzcoatl and Cuacuauhtlatohuatzin, in Tenochtitlan in 4 Reed (1431) and stayed in Tenochtitlan trying to regain control of Texcoco. Another

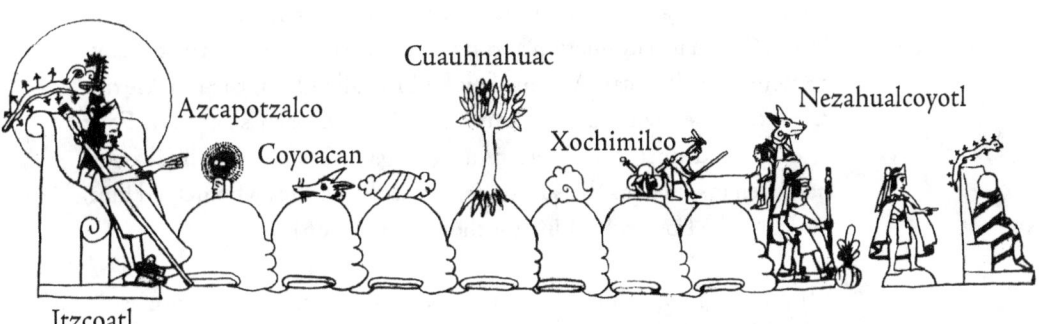

FIG. 4.3

Itzcoatl's appointment of Nezahualcoyotl as the ruler of Texcoco from the *Codex Azcatitlan* (1995:plate 17). Reproduced with permission of the Bibliothèque nationale de France.

This Mexica codex records significant events such as conquests and the construction of temples during the reign of each ruler. This plate depicts these events during Itzcoatl's (Obsidian Snake) reign. He conquered Azcapotzalco (Place of Ant Mound), Coyoacan (Place of One Who Has Coyotes), Cuauhnahuac (Place near Trees), and Xochimilco (Flower Field). In addition to these conquests, the Mexica *tlacuilo* records Nezahualcoyotl's (Fasted Coyote) inauguration as ruler of Texcoco. He is sitting on the chair carrying a long stick of authority just like Itzcoatl does. The codex demonstrates that Itzcoatl appointed Nezahualcoyotl as the ruler of Texcoco, and this appointment is depicted as one of his important achievements.

Mexica source, the *Codex Azcatitlan* (1995), also records Itzcoatl's installation of Nezahualcoyotl as the ruler of Texcoco (figure 4.3). By the time Nezahualcoyotl was finally able to regain control of Texcoco, it had been almost completely destroyed as a result of frequent wars and the exodus of many leaders: "Todo se había trocado, y aún decaecido, mucha parte, las buenas costumbres, y leyes sanas, con que vivían" (Everything had been changed, and many of the good customs and healthy laws with which they lived even declined) (Torquemada 1975, 1:146). According to the *Anales de Tlatelolco*, the Mexica were the ones who helped Nezahualcoyotl in his time of need:

> En el año 4 Acatl Nezahualcoyotzin se sentó como soberano, entonces comenzó y fundó el gobierno, el reinado en Acolhuacan. Fueron Quaquahtlatouatzin e Itzcouatzin quienes lo instalaron como soberano en Acolhuacan. Cuando ellos lo hubieron instalado, vinieron los viejos mexica reuniendo a los acolhuaque que se habían dispersado. Pasaron 4 años hasta que estuvieron reunidos nuevamente. Cuando Nezahualcoyotzin hubo sido instalado como soberano, fueron los mexica quienes le ayudaron erigiéndole las casas. (*Anales de Tlatelolco* 1948:55)

> In the year 4 Acatl, Nezahualcoyotl was established as the sovereign, then he began and founded the government, the reign in Acolhuacan. It was Cuacuahtlatohuatzin and Itzcoatl who installed him as the sovereign of Acolhuacan. When they had installed him, the old Mexica came together with the Acolhuaque who had been scattered. Four years passed until they were reunited again. When Nezahualcoyotl had been installed as the sovereign, it was the Mexica who helped him, building the houses for him. (author's translation)

Thus, when Nezahualcoyotl moved to Texcoco from Tenochtitlan in 6 House (1433), he asked the Mexica to send him government officials and priests:

> Nezahualcoyotzin mandó a ciertos mensajeros que fuesen a México, que trujesen algunos oficiales de todos los oficios para Tezcuco, los cuales, sabiendo la voluntad de Nezahualcoyotzin, fueron muchos, y les dieron tierras en que viviesen, y luego mandó que se hiciese una casa grande para sus ídolos y hicieron, lo cual luego se puso por obra, y se hizo un cu y una casa mayor que ninguna de cuantas hasta entonces se habían hecho. (Alva Ixtlilxochitl 1997, 1:379)

> Nezahualcoyotl sent some messengers to Mexico-Tenochtitlan so that they would bring some officers of all types to Texcoco. Knowing

Nezahualcoyotl's desire, many of them came and he gave them lands to live on and then he ordered that they build a large house for their idols and they did. They started the work and built a temple and a house larger of those any of those that had been constructed until then. (author's translation)

The Mexica and Texcoca source, *Anales de Tlatelolco*, and Alva Ixtlilxochitl's chronicles both record that Nezahualcoyotl reestablished Texcoco's political and religious systems with the help of the Mexica. In addition to government officials and priests, Alva Ixtlilxochitl states that Nezahualcoyotl requested artisans from Tenochtitlan and brought others from other subjected cities:

Y asimismo, para ilustrar más a la ciudad de Tetzcuco, pidió a su tío [Itzcoatl] le diese cantidad de oficiales de todas las artes mecánicas, que trajo a la ciudad de Tetzcuco con otros que sacó de la ciudad y reino de Azcapotzalco, y la de Xochimilco y otras partes. (Alva Ixtlilxochitl 1997, 2:84)

And likewise, to better instruct the city of Texcoco, he asked his uncle [Itzcoatl] to give him many officials of all the mechanical arts, and he brought them to the city of Texcoco with others whom he took from the city and kingdom of Azcapotzalco, Xochimilco, and other places. (author's translation)

These efforts by Nezahualcoyotl to reestablish religious, political, and artistic systems in Texcoco are also shown in the *Mapa Quinatzin* (Aubin 1886a). The note below the artisans reads, "Auh yehuatl in nezahualcoyotzin quincennechico diablo, quincalti in nahutlamantin, ihuan quinnechico in izquitlamantin tlachichiuhque in tolteca" (And Nezahualcoyotl gathered the idols together, gave shelter to the four groups, and gathered all kinds of Toltec artisans) (Aubin 1886a:314; author's translation) (figure 4.4). This means that the reconstitution of Nezahualcoyotl's Texcoco was modeled after the politics, religion, and art of Tenochtitlan. Nezahualcoyotl himself voluntarily introduced Mexica traditions to his city. At the same time, he required further Mexica military support in order to defend his position from other Texcoca nobles and to avoid conflicts with the leaders of neighboring city-states who were reluctant to accept Nezahualcoyotl due to his close ties to the Mexica, with whom they were still hostile (Alva Ixtlilxochitl 1997, 2:85; Barlow 1949a:149–50).

I would argue that the Mexicas' appointment of Nezahualcoyotl as the ruler of Texcoco and their strong support for him was a well-planned Mexica strategy designed to avoid losing control of the Acolhuacan area that they had recently conquered. As explained in chapter 3, Tezozomoc reorganized his empire after his conquest of the eastern basin. In the Acolhuacan area, he

Nezahualcoyotl

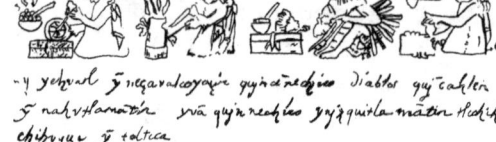

FIG. 4.4

Nezahualcoyotl's reception of the craftsmen from the *Mapa Tlotzin*. Reproduced from M. Aubin (1886b) with permission of the Bibliothèque nationale de France.

Nezahualcoyotl (Fasted Coyote) receives seven master craftsmen, each of whose skills are depicted in front of them. They seem to be gold workers, lapidaries, and feather workers.

Some of the illustrations in Book Nine of the *Florentine Codex* (1950–1982) provide similar pictorial descriptions of these craftsmen. Nezahualcoyotl probably witnessed the work of these artisans in Tenochtitlan or other city-states during his exile, and he enlisted them to help revitalize Texcoco after it had been destroyed by years of war.

established two cabeceras, Coatlichan and Acolman, and appointed his two grandsons, Quetzalmaquiztli and Teyolcohuatzin, as the tlatoani in each city. Tezozomoc ordered all other rulers in Acolhuacan to obey Quetzalmaquiztli and Teyolcohuatzin as their superiors, and he established regional courts in Coatlichan and Acolman where all legal suits had to be adjudicated. Thus, Coatlichan and Acolman maintained a higher status than other Acolhuacan cities such as Texcoco, Huexotla, and Coatepec. After their victory over Azcapotzalco, the Mexica reorganized the Acolhuacan area by replacing the Tepanec institutions with Mexica ones. The Mexica appointed Nezahualcoyotl as the ruler of Texcoco because Nezahualcoyotl was the only candidate who had inherited Mexica blood from his mother, Matlalcihuatzin, daughter of the Mexica king Huitzilihuitl.[6] In addition, the Mexica saw other candidates, such as Nezahualcoyotl's half brothers, Yancuiltzin and Tochpilli, and his half sister's husband, Nonohualcatl, as potentially rebellious because they had served, and received benefits from, Maxtla, and they maintained a close relationship with Azcapotzalco (Alva Ixtlilxochitl 1997, 1:371, 2:76, 85). The Mexicas' appointment of Nezahualcoyotl as the ruler of Texcoco dramatically changed the distribution of power among the Acolhuacan cities. The two leading cities in the eastern Basin of Mexico under the Tepanec empire, Coatlichan and Acolman, lost their dominant position to Texcoco. Throughout the entire fifteenth century, Nezahualcoyotl and his son Nezahualpilli were the Mexicas' most reliable allies, securing the Acolhuacan area and allowing them to focus their attention on extending their empire far beyond the Basin of Mexico.[7]

Nezahualcoyotl, the Triple Alliance, and the Conquests

Texcoca sources such as Pomar (1993:198–99) and Alva Ixtlilxochitl (1997, 2:82–83) record that shortly after Nezahualcoyotl was inaugurated as the ruler of Texcoco in the early 1430s, he formed the Triple Alliance along with Itzcoatl from Tenochtitlan and Totoquihuaztli from Tlacopan. Alva Ixtlilxochitl (1997, 2:86–88) argues that Nezahualcoyotl actually conquered Tenochtitlan, and then proposed the alliance. He also provides a Nahua song as evidence of Nezahualcoyotl's leadership in this endeavor:

> Y para mayor claridad de esta verdad (demás de ser público y notorio), se echa de ver en un canto antiguo que llaman Xopancuicatl, que casi en todos los demás de los pueblos de esta Nueva España en donde se usa hablar la lengua mexicana, lo cantan los naturales en sus fiestas y convites, ser las tres cabezas de la Nueva España los reyes de México, Tetzcoco y Tlacopan que dice así: "canconicuilonican que on intlactícpac conmahuicotitihuya a Tliantépetl Mexico nican Acolihuacan Nezahualcoyotzin Motecuhzomatzin, Tlacopan on in Totoquihuatzin Yeneli ai con-piaco inipetlícpal intéotl a Ipalnemoani, etcétera" que significa conforme a su verdadero sentido: "Dejaron memoria en el universo los que ilustraron el imperio de Mexico y aquí en Acolihuacan, los reyes Nezahualcoyotzin, Moteucuhzomatzin, y en Tlacopan Totoquihuatzin: de verdad que será impresa, eternizada vuestra memoria (por lo bien que juzgasteis y registeis) en el trono y tribunal de dios criador de todas las cosas etcétera." (Alva Ixtlilxochitl 1997, 2:83)

> And for greater evidence of this truth (despite it being public and well known), it is easy to see the kings of Mexico-Tenochtitlan, Texcoco, and Tlacopan as the three heads of New Spain in an old song that the natives call Xopancuicatl and that they sing at their festivals and feasts in almost all the other towns of this New Spain where the Mexica language is spoken. The song says the following: "Canconicuilonican que on intlactícpac conmahuicotitihuya a Tliantépetl Mexico nican Acolihuacan Nezahualcoyotzin Motecuhzomatzin, Tlacopan on in Totoquihuaztli Yeneli ai con-piaco inipetlícpal intéotl to Ipalnemoani, etc," which means, according to its true sense: "Those who enlightened the empire of Mexico, the kings, Nezahualcoyotl and Moctezuma Ilhuicamina here in Acolhuacan, and Totoquihuaztli in Tlacopan, left a monument in the universe: truly, your memory (of how well you judged and governed) will be printed and eternalized in the throne and court of God, creator of everything etc." (author's translation)

This song suggests Texcoca leadership in the Triple Alliance because the three rulers gathered in Acolhuacan, that is to say, Texcoco.[8] Bierhorst, however, reconstructs the original Nahuatl phrase and argues that Alva Ixtlilxochitl deliberately modified his translation to support his claim:

> Zan conicuilotehuaque on in tlalticpac. Conmahuizzotitihui-a atl-o yan tepetl Mexico nican Acolihuacan Nezahualcoyotzin, Moteuczomatzin, Tlacopan on in Totoquihuatzin. Ye nelli a in ipetl in teotl-a Ipalnemohuani, etc.
>
> They went away having painted oh! This earth. They went away having glorified this city of Mexico, they, Acolhuacan's Nezahualcoyotl, Montezuma, and Totoquihuaztli of oh! Tlacopan. Truly they came to guard the mat and throne of the spirit Life Giver, etc. (Bierhorst 1985:116)

According to Bierhorst, Alva Ixtlilxochitl mistranslates the phrase "atl tepetl Mexico nican" (here in Mexico) as "aquí en Acolhuacan" (here in Acolhuacan) in order to place the head of the Triple Alliance in Texcoco rather than in Mexico-Tenochtitlan. In contrast to Alva Ixtlilxochitl, many chroniclers such as Fray Diego Durán (1994:121) record that this alliance was led by the Mexica king Itzcoatl. Durán's claim is more probable than that of Alva Ixtlilxochitl because as a newly inaugurated ruler, Nezahualcoyotl would not have had enough military power to conquer Tenochtitlan; moreover, the Mexica were the ones who established him as a ruler. Records suggest that there was a military conflict between Nezahualcoyotl and Moctezuma, but this was merely a mock war, for Nezahualcoyotl himself burned the temple with the consent of Moctezuma Ilhuicamina (Alvarado Tezozomoc 1987:283–84; Durán 1994:127–29; Chimalpahin 1998:249).

In general, the existence of the Triple Alliance between Tenochtitlan, Texcoco, and Tlacopan has been accepted by modern scholars, but there is some disagreement about the details. Most scholars (Davies 1987:42–46; Carrasco 1999:29–30) argue that the Mexica of Tenochtitlan led the alliance from the beginning, while others (Gibson 1971:383–89; Offner 1983:88–94; Hodge 1996:20–21) insist that the Mexica and the Texcoca shared the leadership role with Tlacopan as a junior member. Susan Gillespie (1998) has argued recently, however, that the Triple Alliance was a post- rather than preconquest tradition. She acknowledges that early colonial documents frequently group the three city-states, Tenochtitlan, Texcoco, and Tlacopan, but she argues that specific references to the Triple Alliance began to appear only at the end of sixteenth century, particularly in the sources from Texcoco and Tlacopan. According to her, under the Spanish cabecera-sujeto system, Texcoco and Tlacopan tried to better their political position by recording that there were only three cabeceras that shared tribute among themselves before the conquest (Gillespie 1998:248–54). I agree with Gillespie that Nezahualcoyotl's Texcoco was actually built by the Mexica and that Texcoco itself was already a Mexica tributary as suggested by the fact that Tezozomoc granted it to the Mexica king Chimalpopoca after the Tepanec-Acolhuacan war. I would argue further that the frequent association of the three cities, Tenochtitlan, Texcoco, and Tlacopan, derives from the Mexica administrative reorganization of the Basin of Mexico after the Tepanec-Mexica war. The Mexica wanted to replace the two Tepanec regional centers, Coatlichan in the eastern basin and Azcapotzalco in the western basin, with the pro-Mexica city-states Texcoco and Tlacopan. In this process, the Mexica took away some privileges from Coatlichan and Azcapotzalco, such as having regional courts, and awarded them to Texcoco and Tlacopan. For instance, Motolinia (Benavente 1971:352) records that only three cities, Tenochtitlan, Texcoco, and Tlacopan, had distinguished legal systems, "porque en cada cibdad de éstas había jueces, a manera de audiencia" (because in each of these cities there were judges, in the way of courts) (author's translation).

In addition to serving as the legal center in the Aztec empire, Texcoco and Tlacopan seem to have also served as centers of tribute collection and war preparation. According to the "Memorial de los pueblos" (*Epistolario de Nueva España* 1940, 14:118–22), which focuses on the Tlacopaneca tributaries, several major cities in the west of and beyond the Basin of Mexico such as Azcapotzalco, Coyoacan, Cuauhtitlan, Tzompanco, Citlaltepec, Tula, Atotonilco, and many others brought tribute to and gathered in preparation for war at Tlacopan. The same was true of Texcoco in the eastern basin. The Mexica must have moved the administrative and political center in the eastern basin from Coatlichan to Texcoco when they reorganized the eastern Basin of Mexico after the Tepanec-Mexica war. Thus, the Triple Alliance described by the Texcoca and Tlacopaneca sources after the conquest was actually based on an administrative division instituted by the Mexica in order to more effectively govern their empire. It was not the division of imperial power that the Texcoca and Tlacopaneca postconquest sources describe. In this Aztec imperial system, Nezahualcoyotl and the city of Texcoco played a more significant role than any other city-state allied to the Mexica. Nezahualcoyotl, for example, provided the Mexica with the most military forces. Nezahualcoyotl's administrative and military contributions made Texcoco the second most powerful city in the Aztec empire.

As an important ally of Tenochtitlan, Texcoco conducted many conquests with the Mexica. During his reign, Nezahualcoyotl participated in military expeditions with the Mexica kings Itzcoatl, Moctezuma Ilhuicamina, and Axayacatl and the Tlacopaneca king Totoquihuaztli. Nezahualcoyotl helped these kings conquer many major cities such as Coatlichan, Huexotla, Coatepec, Xochimilco, Chalco, Cuauhtitlan, and Cuitlahuac in the basin, as well as Cuauhnahuac, Xilotepec, Tula, Tlachco, Coixtlahuacan, and Tochpan outside of the basin. The chroniclers of the *Relaciones geográficas* (1982–1988) confirm that Nezahualcoyotl conquered Coatepec, Acolman, Teotihuacan, and Cempoala with the Mexica ruler Moctezuma Ilhuicamina, and he collected tribute from these areas as an ally of the Aztec empire. Some pictorial sources also record Nezahualcoyotl's conquests with the Mexica kings. The *Codex en Cruz* (1981) from Chiauhtla depicts Nezahualcoyotl's conquest of Cuauhtitlan with the Mexica king Moctezuma Ilhuicamina in 7 Rabbit (1434) (figure 4.5). In addition, the Mexica text, the *Codex Azcatitlan* (1995:plate 18), also depicts Nezahualcoyotl's conquest of Tulantzinco during the reign of Moctezuma Ilhuicamina (figure 4.6). This pictorial description of Nezahualcoyotl's conquest conveys more importance because in indigenous pictorial historiography, the *tlacuilo* (painter-scribe) normally focuses on the history of his own city or altepetl, minimizing the history of other cities. In this plate, the tlacuilo of the Mexica codex, the *Codex Azcatitlan* (1995), places particular emphasis on Nezahualcoyotl, clearly indicating that the Mexica tlacuilo considers Nezahualcoyotl's conquest as a part of Mexica history. Some pictorial sources from other regions also record Nezahualcoyotl's conquests of neighboring cities and other more remote regions. The *Codex en Cruz* (1981, 1:12–13) from Chiauhtla depicts Nezahualcoyotl's subjugation of Tepetlaoztoc (see figure 4.5).[9] The *Códice de Xicotepec* (1995) also depicts Nezahualcoyotl's and his son Cipactli's participation in the conquest of Xicotepec (figures 4.7 and 4.8). All of these conquests that Nezahualcoyotl carried out both with and without the Mexica demonstrate that he was no less a warrior than the Mexica kings and that he made a significant contribution to the Aztec empire.

From the beginning to the end of his reign, Nezahualcoyotl participated in many conquests with his Mexica uncles, and he received many benefits from these conquests. The Mexica chronicler Alvarado Tezozomoc (1987) states that Nezahualcoyotl was the Mexica kings' favorite among the kings of the neighboring cities. Every time the Mexica planned a military expedition, royal funeral, or inauguration, Nezahualcoyotl was notified first, and he gladly participated in these events. Durán also records that

> Three years before his [Acamapichtli's] death, in 1402 [sic], the great lord Nezahualcoyotzin had been born, who later became king of Tezcoco. Besides being a close relative of the rulers of Mexico, Nezahualcoyotl was sympathetic to the Aztec [Mexica] nation and a great friend of its people. Very few other, or none, equaled this relationship. In the following chapters will be told the manner and way in which he perpetuated the confederation and friendship of the Aztecs and how he achieved this without letting the other nations know his intentions. (Durán 1994:57)

Nezahualcoyotl was a great warrior king who was able to expand the old Texcoca geographical frontier from the central basin to the gulf coast. Almost all of his conquests and political triumphs, however, were made possible through his close kinship and political alliance with the Mexica. The peaceful image of

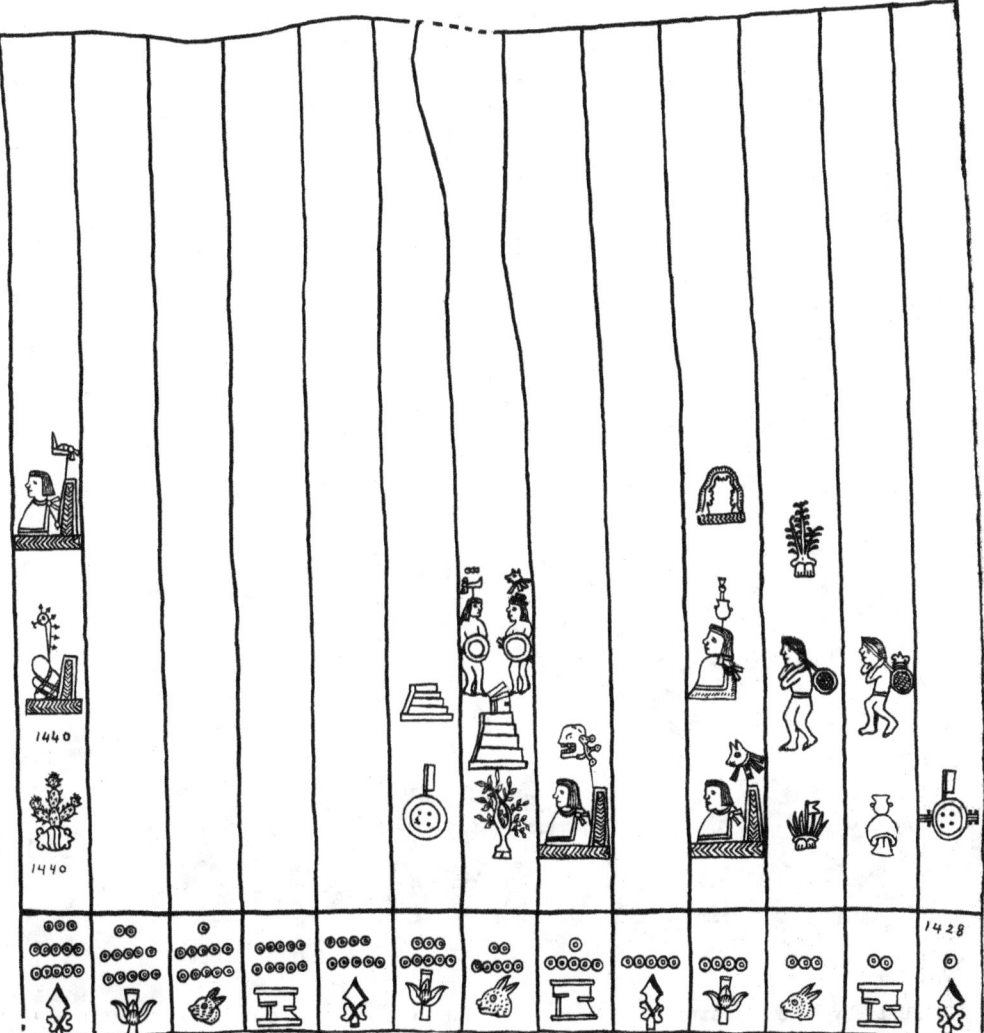

FIG. 4.5
Nezahualcoyotl's conquest of Cuauhtitlan with Moctezuma Ilhuicamina and his appointment of Cocopin as the ruler of Tepetlaoztoc from the *Codex en Cruz* (1981). Reproduced with permission of the University of Utah Press.

In the year 7 Rabbit (1534) the first glyph refers to Cuauhtitlan (Place near Trees). Above Cuauhtitlan is a temple in a state of partial collapse, an image that indicates a conquest. Two warriors, each with an obsidian sword and a shield, stand above. The one to the right is Nezahualcoyotl (Fasted Coyote), and the other is Moctezuma Ilhuicamina (Angry Lord, Sky Shooter). This column demonstrates that Nezahualcoyotl and Moctezuma Ilhuicamina conquered Cuauhtitlan during the year 7 Rabbit (1434).

In the column dedicated to the year 4 Reed (1431), Nezahualcoyotl is seated on the authority mat and above him appears a person named Cocopin (Removing Pot). Above him is Tepetlaoztoc (Cave of the Stone Mat). This column records that Nezahualcoyotl appointed Cocopin as a ruler of Tepetlaoztoc in 5 Reed (1431).

REEXAMINING NEZAHUALCOYOTL'S TEXCOCO 109

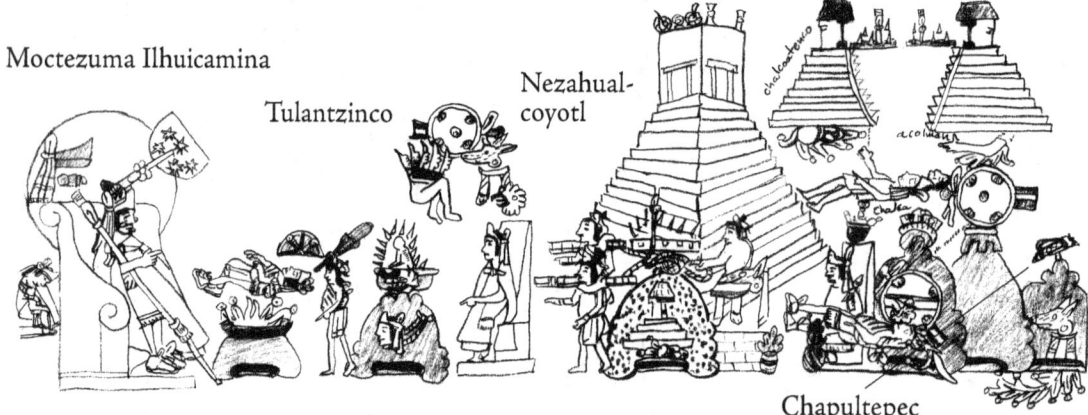

FIG. 4.6

Nezahualcoyotl's conquest of Tulantzinco during the reign of Moctezuma Ilhuicamina from the *Codex Azcatitlan* (1995:plate 18). Reproduced with permission of the Bibliothèque nationale de France.

In the middle of the plate, there appear three distinct glyphs that correspond to Nezahualcoyotl, Tulantzinco (Place of Little Reed), and *chimalli* (shield). According to the image, Nezahualcoyotl conquered Tulantzinco. In the right bottom corner of the plate, another Nezahualcoyotl glyph appears in Chapultepec (Grasshopper Hill) with a long water glyph, which depicts Nezahualcoyotl's construction of the aqueduct in Chapultepec. These events occurred during the reign of the Mexica king Moctezuma Ilhuicamina (Sky Shooter). In this plate, the Mexica *tlacuilo* places particular emphasis on Nezahualcoyotl, clearly indicating that he considers Nezahualcoyotl's achievements as a part of Mexica history.

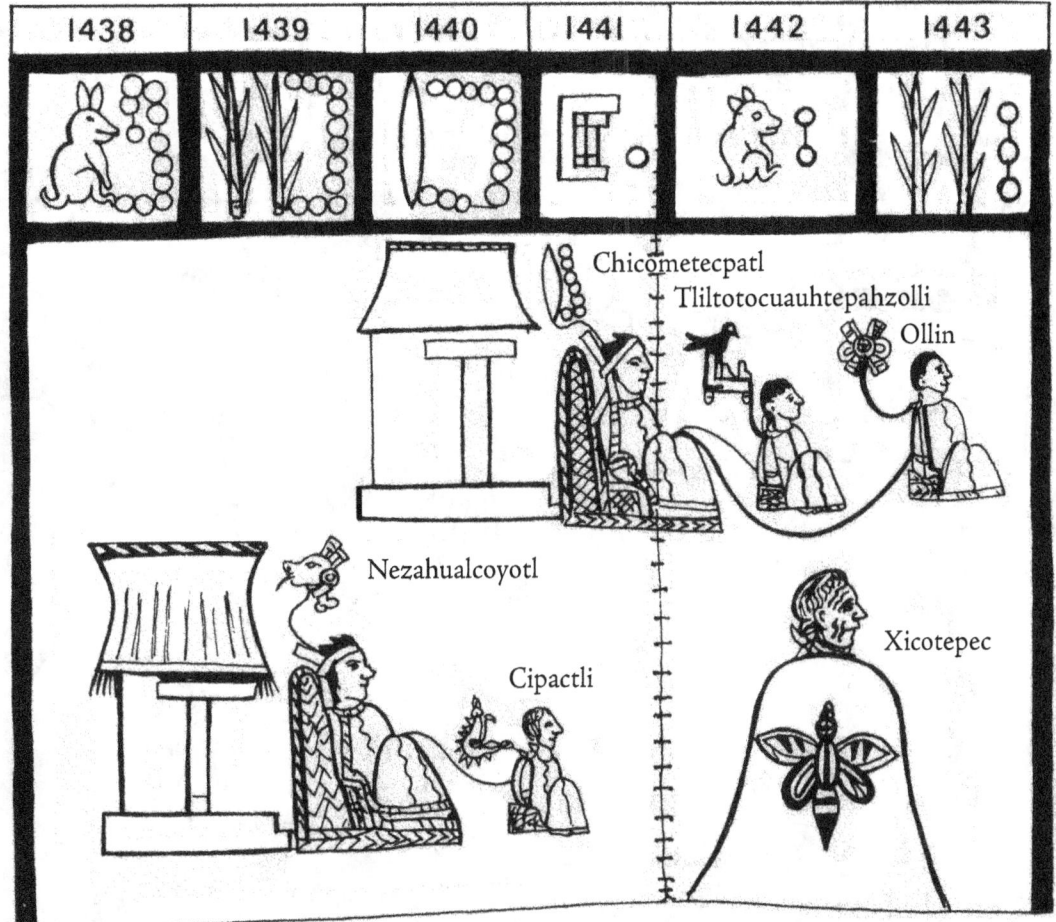

FIG. 4.7
Nezahualcoyotl's arrival at Xicotepec from the *Códice de Xicotepec* (1995:84). Reproduced with permission of the Fondo de Cultura Económica.

Between 11 Rabbit (1438) and 12 Reed (1439), Nezahualcoyotl and his son Cipactli (Crocodile) arrive at Xicotepec (Bumblebee Hill). A couple of years later, probably in the year 13 Flint (1440), Chicometecpatl (Seven Flint) also comes to Xicotepec with his two sons, Tliltotocuauhtepahzolli (Black Bird on a Wood Nest) and Ollin (Movement). Nezahualcoyotl and Chicometecpatl are allies and seem to have equal political status because their costumes are almost identical and the size of the authority mat (*icpalli*) is almost the same.

FIG. 4.8

Nezahualcoyotl's conquest of Xicotepec in the *Códice Xicotepec* (1995:88). Reproduced with permission of the Fondo de Cultura Económica.

In 4 Flint (1441), the five allies, Nezahualcoyotl and his son, Cipactli, and Chicometecpatl and his two sons, Tliltotocuauhtepahzolli and Ollin, attack the local residents, the Huaxteca, who were well known for the perforation of their noses. The allies use the same arms such as *chimalli* (shield) and *maccuahuitl* (hand stick), and they also employ a type of armor to protect the lower body. Chicometecpatl and his two sons seem to make the most decisive contribution to this conquest by capturing the leader of the Huaxteca. Texcoca sources such as the *Mapa Quinatzin* and Alva Ixtlilxochitl's chronicles repeatedly claim Xicotepec as the exclusive tributary of Texcoco, but the local *tlacuilo* of Xicotepec suggests that Chicometecpatl was more instrumental than Nezahualcoyotl in the conquest. In later sections, he describes Nezahualcoyotl's son, Cipactli, as one of several corulers of Xicotepec.

Nezahualcoyotl in contrast to the Mexica warrior kings was invented by Texcoca chroniclers. In fact, in addition to the Mexica and other non-Texcoca sources, there are several Texcoca texts that confirm Nezahualcoyotl's close relationship to, and his collaboration with, the Mexica kings in many military campaigns.

Nezahualcoyotl's Government: Tribute System and Councils

While Texcoco was getting larger and larger by expanding its territories through conquest, Nezahualcoyotl was trying to reform the existing governing systems, including the councils and legal procedures. Alva Ixtlilxochitl (1997, 2:92) insists that Nezahualcoyotl's ruling system was the best that the New World had ever had:

> Esta división y repartición de tierra de los pueblos y lugares del reino del Tetzcuco se hizo también en el de México y Tlacopan, porque los otros reyes y cabezas del imperio fueron siempre admitiendo sus [Nezahualcoyotl] leyes y modo de gobierno, por parecerles ser el mejor que hasta entonces se había tenido; y así, lo que se trata y describe del reino de Tetzcuco, se entiende ser lo mismo el de México y Tlacopan, pues las pinturas, historias y cantos que sigo siempre comienzan por lo de Tetzcuco, y lo mismo hace la pintura de los padrones y tributos reales que hubo en esta Nueva España en tiempo de su infidelidad. (Alva Ixtlilxochitl 1997, 2:92)

> This division and distribution of the land of the towns and places of the Texcoca kingdom was also practiced in Mexico-Tenochtitlan and Tlacopan, because the other kings and heads of the empire were always implementing his [Nezahualcoyotl's] laws and form of government, which to them seemed the best that had existed until then; and thus, what is dealt with and described about the kingdom of Texcoco is understood to apply to Mexico-Tenochtitlan and Tlacopan as well, for the paintings [pictorial books], histories, and songs that I follow always begin with the things of Texcoco and the paintings of the royal census and tributes that existed in this New Spain during the time of its infidelity do the same thing. (author's translation)

This is a rather dubious claim, not only because Texcoco had no experience in governing colonies before Nezahualcoyotl's reign, but also because Texcoco's political and cultural revival relied heavily on the Mexica. Moreover, Nezahualcoyotl's Texcoco controlled considerably fewer colonies than did the Mexica. Thus, the ruling system introduced by Nezahualcoyotl in Texcoco seems to have come from Tenochtitlan, which the Mexica had originally inherited from the Toltec and Azcapotzalca empires.

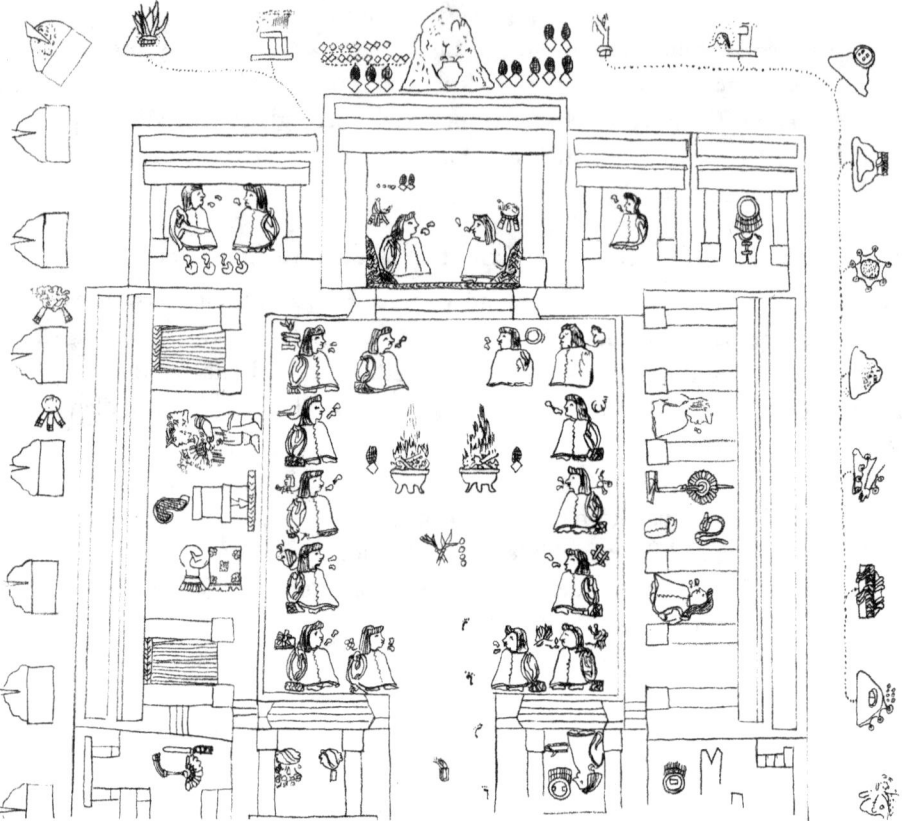

FIG. 4.9
Nezahualcoyotl's and Nezahualpilli's court and their tributaries from the *Mapa Quinatzin*. Reproduced from M. Aubin (1886a) with permission of the Bibliothèque nationale de France.

In the top center of the court, Nezahualcoyotl and his son, Nezahualpilli, face each other sitting on the authority mat. In the courtyard, their fourteen main tributaries appear without authority mats. This court is surrounded by less important tributaries. Alva Ixtlilxochitl (1997, 2:92–97) identifies the role of each room by reading this figure glyph by glyph. He finds rooms for judges, warfare, tribute, science and music, and the Mexica and Tlacopaneca rulers. Following Alva Ixtlilxochitl, later historians interpret the map without taking into consideration the colonial influence that informed it. The fact that the Texcoca royal family originally created this map to demonstrate their political supremacy over their neighboring cities after the conquest suggests that it contains a Texcoca regional bias. Thus, before reading the map, one must first identify this Texcoca regional perspective by comparing the map with other regional histories. Alva Ixtlilxochitl propagates the difference between Texcoco and Tenochtitlan in terms of government system and legal practice. However, the *Codex Mendoza* (1992:f. 69r) indicates that the court structure of Nezahualcoyotl's and Nezahualpilli's palace is very similar to that of the Mexica rulers. Both palaces have a big courtyard and rooms for war councils, judges, and allied rulers. The two pictorial texts clearly manifest the similarity of the governments of the two city-states rather than the difference upon which Alva Ixtlilxochitl insists in his alphabetic chronicles. This is a good example of how pictorial texts are often more reliable than alphabetic texts.

Alva Ixtlilxochitl (1997, 2:108) records the way tribute collected from subjugated cities was distributed among the three kings. According to him, there were cities that belonged exclusively to each of the kings as well as those that they shared. Nezahualcoyotl, who conquered many city-states with the Mexica, possessed very few colonies exclusively. According to the *Mapa Quinatzin* (Aubin 1886a:321–68), there are fourteen cities assigned to maintain the Texcoca court, which suggests that they were under the control of Nezahualcoyotl. Below Nezahualcoyotl and Nezahualpilli, inside their palace on leaf 2, appear the rulers of fourteen cities that Nezahualcoyotl established (figure 4.9). These cities include Otompan, Huexotla, Coatlichan, Chimalhuacan, Tepetlaoztoc, Chiauhtla, Tezoyucan, Teotihuacan, Acolman, Tepechpan, Chiconauhtla, Tulantzinco, Cuauhchinanco, and Xicotepec.[10] Based on his reading of leaf 2 of the *Mapa Quinatzin*, Alva Ixtlilxochitl (1997, 2:89–97) insists that Nezahualcoyotl appointed the ruler of these cities after the Tepanec-Mexica war and that they were the major tributaries of Texcoco. But if we compare this list with the record of the Mexica conquests and tribute in the *Codex Mendoza* (1992), most of these cities were conquered by the Mexica kings or paid tribute to them. According to the *Codex Mendoza*, Huitzilihuitl (1397–1417) conquered Acolman, Otompan, and Tulantzinco. Even though the codex depicts the king's conquests as his own, Huitzilihuitl obviously did not conquer these places by himself, but rather with other Tepanec allies under Tezozomoc. The chroniclers of Acolman and Chiconauhtla in the *Relaciones geográficas* (1982–1988, 6:226, 235) also record that Acolman was conquered again by Moctezuma Ilhuicamina and Nezahualcoyotl and that Chiconauhtla was subdued by Moctezuma Ilhuicamina. The *Codex Mendoza* (1992:f. 69r), however, does not record Chiconauhtla as a Mexica tributary, but rather as a closely allied city. Moctezuma Xocoyotzin reserved a room for the ruler of Chiconauhtla just like he did for the ruler of his closest allied cities such as Texcoco, Tlacopan, and Colhuacan. On the other hand, the *Codex Mendoza* (1992:ff. 21r–22r) records that Acolman and its subject cities, such as Tepechpan, Tepetlaoztoc, and Tezoyucan, paid tribute to Tenochtitlan.[11] Tulantzinco (*Codex Mendoza* 1992:ff. 29v–30r) and Teotihuacan (Hodge 1984:129–30) also paid tribute to Tenochtitlan. In addition, Cuauhchinanco and its neighboring city Xicotepec probably paid tribute to Tenochtitlan. When Ahuitzotl went to conquer the Huaxteca area, the ruler of Cuauhchinanco welcomed the Mexica king and provided him with soldiers and materials, and he himself participated in the conquest (Durán 1994:324–25). Rather than the Mexica sources, however, Alva Ixtlilxochitl (1997, 1:377–80) himself provides the most important evidence for determining the relationship between Texcoco and the fourteen cities. He records that Nezahualcoyotl conquered most of the Acolhuacan cities with his uncle Itzcoatl and his nephew Moctezuma Ilhuicamina, such as Huexotla, Coatlichan, Chimalhuacan, Tepetlaoztoc, Acolman,

Tepechpan, Chiconauhtla, Tezoyucan, Otompan, and Teotihuacan. Thus, all fourteen cities that the *Mapa Quinatzin* reports as the exclusive domain of Nezahualcoyotl were also within Tenochtitlan's political jurisdiction. I would argue that although Texcoco collected tribute from all fourteen of these cities, it did so in its function as the center of tribute collection in the eastern basin for the Aztec empire. In the 1540s, the tlacuilo of the *Mapa Quinatzin* depicted Texcoco as the most powerful city in the eastern Basin of Mexico by converting it from the administrative to the political center of the Aztec empire.

There is no doubt that Texcoco received tribute from the fourteen cities recorded in the *Mapa Quinatzin*. Texcoco, however, did not function independently, and its portion of the total tribute that the fourteen cities paid to the Aztec empire must have been determined by its political status within the empire. Alva Ixtlilxochitl (1997, 1:407), who claims that there was an equitable partnership between Texcoco and Tenochtitlan, reports that the tribute collected for the Aztec empire was distributed among the three cities, Tenochtitlan, Texcoco, and Tlacopan, in a 2:2:1 ratio and that Nezahualcoyotl established this system. On the other hand, Torquemada (1975, 1:146) records the ratio as 8:5:2 and adds that these terms were dictated by Itzcoatl. Both ratios, however, appear to be rather inflated.[12] Alva Ixtlilxochitl records what Nezahualcoyotl did with the tribute he collected as a member of the Triple Alliance:

> Esta provincia y las demás, en donde puso [Nezahualcoyotl] sus mayordomos y cobradores, fueron las que se adjudicaron al reino de Tetzcuco, sin entrar en partición los otros dos reyes; y las en que no puso sus mayordomos fueron las que se repartían sus rentas entre las tres cabezas de esta Nueva España por la orden referida, las cuales rentas se llevaban a la ciudad de México todas juntas, y allí se hacía la repartición y división, en donde los mayordomos y agentes de los tres reyes, cada uno recibía lo que le pertenecía a su señor; y las rentas que eran de la parte del rey Nezahualcoyotl se guardaban en la ciudad de México en sus palacios antiguos, con las que premiaba a todos los señores de su señorío, sus hijos, deudos y otras personas beneméritas *por mano de los señores mexicanos*, para que justificadamente a cada uno se le diese lo que por sus virtudes merecía: éste fue el principal intento de que sus rentas (las que tenía de la partición con los otros dos reyes) se guardasen en la ciudad de México. (Alva Ixtlilxochitl 1972, 2:108, emphasis added)

> This province and the others, where he [Nezahualcoyotl] put his tax collectors and treasurers, were the ones that the kingdom of Texcoco declared its exclusive possessions without sharing them with the other two kings; and the incomes from the provinces in which he did not put his tax collectors were distributed among the three heads of this

New Spain by the above-mentioned order. All the incomes from these provinces were carried to the city of Mexico-Tenochtitlan together where the distribution and division were made and where the tax collectors and agents of the three kings received what each of their lords deserved; and the incomes that belonged to the king Nezahualcoyotl were kept in his old palaces in the city of Mexico-Tenochtitlan. With these incomes, he rewarded all the lords under his dominion such as his sons, relatives, and other deserving people *by the hands of the Mexica lords* so that each one was fairly given what he deserved by his merits. This was the main reason that his income (the one that he shared with the other two kings) was kept in Mexico-Tenochtitlan. (author's translation)

Alva Ixtlilxochitl provides this information in order to present Nezahualcoyotl as the most powerful ruler of the three states and the one who controlled and distributed the entire tribute of the Aztec empire. At the same time, however, the Texcoca chronicler contradicts himself by stating that the entire tribute, not only Nezahualcoyotl's portion but also that of the other two kings, was taken to Tenochtitlan and distributed by the Mexica lords. Alva Ixtlilxochitl seems to insist that Nezahualcoyotl had many exclusive tributaries and thus that he managed many of his own tribute collectors, but as shown, he had very few cities within his exclusive domain. Contrary to his original intention, Alva Ixtlilxochitl demonstrates Nezahualcoyotl's lower political status inside the Aztec empire. Nezahualcoyotl left his portion of the tribute in Tenochtitlan, rather than bringing it to his city of Texcoco. Moreover, he was not in a position to control even his portion of tribute because it was distributed "by the hands of the Mexica lords."

However, Alva Ixtlilxochitl provides important information about the collection and distribution of tribute in the Aztec empire. The tribute was deposited in Tenochtitlan, and the Mexica lords distributed it among the deserving people according to their merit. The Mexica lords who distributed the tribute would have belonged to the highest Mexica social class. Durán (1994:97–98) records that when Itzcoatl overthrew the Tepanec empire, he acknowledged the noble status of twenty of his relatives and granted them land newly acquired from Azcapotzalco. Among them, his nephews Tlacaelel and Moctezuma Ilhuicamina were most prominent. Alvarado Tezozomoc (1987:268–69) provides a list of the same names but with more detailed information about their places in the political hierarchy. He presents the first four names on Durán's list, Tlacaelel, Moctezuma Ilhuicamina, Tlacahuepan, and Cuatlecoatl, as the four principal lords (señores) and the other seventeen as brave warrior captains. Alvarado Tezozomoc (1987:268) records that the four principal lords "fueron como caciques principales y señores de título y nombradía en el señorío y mando y gobierno mexicano" (were like main lords and nobles of title and appointment in the Mexica dominion, command, and government). Durán and Alvarado Tezozomoc record that the Mexica had already followed certain rules governing the distribution of their tribute from the beginning of their political dominance. I would argue that the four principal lords Alvarado Tezozomoc presents were the "señores mexicanos" (Mexica lords) by whose hand the tribute was distributed as recorded in Alva Ixtlilxochitl's chronicle. In this Mexica system of nobility, Nezahualcoyotl was probably treated like one of the four principal lords because, as Durán and Alvarado Tezozomoc record, he was invited as the Mexicas' main guest for important political and religious ceremonies such as royal successions, and he was one of a few non-Mexica rulers who could speak directly with the Mexica kings about the political and religious matters of the Aztec empire. Taking into account the political status of Nezahualcoyotl within Mexica nobility, Alva Ixtlilxochitl's claim that Nezahualcoyotl's Texcoco received two-fifths of the tribute of the Aztec empire seems still to be greatly exaggerated. Furthermore, taking into consideration the rulers of the other allied cities, such as Xochimilco, Tlacopan, and Colhuacan, the portion of the tribute Nezahualcoyotl received must have been much lower than the two-fifths of the total tribute of the Aztec empire.

Pomar (1993:182–87) and Alva Ixtlilxochitl (1997, 1:406–7) record that there were several councils in Texcoco. Pomar describes two: the councils of justice and war. The council of justice was in charge of administering laws, and the council of war, *tecuihuacalli*, dealt with issues related to war. Alva Ixtlilxochitl describes four councils that Nezahualcoyotl established in Texcoco: the councils of government, music, war, and hacienda. The council of government dealt with government officials, the nobles, and the commoners. The council of music was in charge of poets and astrologers, and the third council dealt with war. The last council, the council of hacienda, took care of the tribute that came to Texcoco from the subjugated cities. It controlled the *mayordomos* (tribute collectors) and the merchants in Texcoco. The descriptions of social and political administration in these two chroniclers coincide in two cases: Pomar's councils of war and justice seem to coincide with Alva Ixtlilxochitl's council of government, and they both include a council of war, although the terms for its leader differ—*tlacochcalcatl* in Pomar and *hueitlacochcatl* in Alva Ixtlilxochitl. Both chroniclers confirm, however, that the chiefs of each of these four councils had a close genealogical relationship to the king, usually either his brothers or sons.

This system seems to have existed also in Tenochtitlan, though earlier than in Texcoco. According to Durán (1994:102–3) and Alvarado Tezozomoc (1987:267–71), the Mexica rulers Itzcoatl and Tlacaelel reformed the Mexica government by assigning official titles and distributing the cities to their brothers and generals according to their contribution after the Tepanec war. Itzcoatl established four new titles: tlacochcalcatl, *tlacatecatl, ezhuahuacatl,* and *tlillancalqui*. Durán provides only the names of the titles, but they appear very similar to the system in Texcoco in that the official title immediately subordinate to the king is tlacochcalcatl, and the person who assumes the title is in charge of the council of war just as in Texcoco. Moreover, Durán (1994:103) reports that the Mexica already had a sophisticated social and political system in which existed "Count, Duke, Marquis, court magistrate, *corregidor*, or district manager, mayor, councilman, consul, bailiff, officials of the palace, and ambassadors." This was an important reform in Mexica history in that the Mexica began to prepare their political and social systems to accommodate larger territories, that is, a new empire.

This ruling system, however, actually originated with the Mexicas' former master, the Tepanec empire.[13] After the victory against the Acolhuacan cities, the Tepanec ruler Tezozomoc introduced this system by distributing the administrative responsibilities for the conquered cities to his sons and grandsons. He developed the system to facilitate tribute collection and to distribute it among the eight cabeceras that he designated as the regional centers as explained in chapter 3. Pomar records that it was Tezozomoc who established the first empire in central Mexico and imposed order:

> Las demás guerras y conquistas que tenían, antes de que los españoles viniesen, eran pocas, porque como se ha dicho, tenían toda la tierra casi sujeta, salvo a Michoacán.... Pero todo el resto de esta Nueva España, hasta cerca de Guatemala, tenían llano y sujeto. La orden que tuvieron para ello, en que se fundó su señorío, fue que Tezozomoctli, señor de Azcapotzalco, con mucho poder que tuvo y el largo tiempo que vivió, y la suerte que le favoreció, se enseñoreó antiguamente de casi toda la tierra. (Pomar 1993:198)

> The other wars and conquests that they had, before the Spaniards came, were few because, as mentioned before, they had dominated almost all the land except Michoacán.... But they had pacified and conquered all the rest of this New Spain up to near Guatemala. The order that they had for their conquered land began with Tezozomoc, king of Azcapotzalco, who founded his kingdom with a lot of power and with the long life he lived, and with the luck that favored him, anciently he lorded over almost all the land. (author's translation)

The Mexica who experienced and administered the imperial system of the Tepanec empire under Tezozomoc adopted it for their own empire. As a political partner of Tenochtitlan, Nezahualcoyotl requested from his uncle, Itzcoatl, the aid of Mexica governmental officials in reestablishing order in Texcoco. Thus, the Texcoca chroniclers' claim that their system of government was the best in New Spain and was imitated by the Mexica stems from the desire to represent their city as more civilized and therefore different from the barbarous Mexica of Tenochtitlan.

Nezahualcoyotl's Legal System: Laws and Punishments

The most impressive achievements of Nezahualcoyotl presented by the Texcoca chroniclers Pomar and Alva Ixtlilxochitl, as well as Spanish chroniclers, were legislative in nature.[14] In the following passage, Pomar does not mention Nezahualcoyotl specifically, but the reader can easily infer that *"reyes"* refers to Nezahualcoyotl and his son Nezahualpilli:

> Las leyes y ordenanzas y buenas costumbres y modo de vivir que generalmente se guardaban en toda la tierra procedían de esta ciudad. Porque los reyes de ella procuraban siempre que fuesen tales cuales se ha dicho y por ellas se gobernaban las demás tierras y provincias sujetas a México y Tacuba. Y comúnmente se decía que en esta ciudad tenían el archivo de sus Consejos, leyes y ordenanzas y que en ellas les eran enseñados para vivir honesta y políticamente y no como bestias. (Pomar 1993:94)

> The laws, regulations, good customs, and way of living that were generally kept in all the land came from this city. Because the kings of the city always tried to maintain them, it has been said that by them the other lands and provinces subject to Mexico and Tacuba were governed. And it was commonly said that in this city they had the archive of their Councils, laws, and ordinances, and that they were taught how to live honestly and politically, not as beasts. (author's translation)

Alva Ixtlilxochitl, who always claims that the Texcoca legal system was the most advanced and efficient, insists that the other two kings of Tenochtitlan and Tlacopan adopted Nezahualcoyotl's laws and governmental system. He records that Nezahualcoyotl enacted eighty laws and that he was strict in enforcing them (1997, 1:385, 405–6, 2:101–2). Among these laws, the chronicler deals with major crimes and their punishments such as treason against the king, adultery, robbery, superstition, misuse of inherited properties, homicide, homosexuality, alcohol abuse, and military misconduct. In addition, his alphabetic texts are supported by a pictorial source, leaf 3 of the *Mapa Quinatzin*.[15] The majority of the crimes and punishments that appear in Alva Ixtlilxochitl's texts are clearly depicted in this leaf (Barlow 1994:261–76). A comparison between the description of the crimes and punishments and the third part of the map reveals that the alphabetic texts are exact transcriptions/translations of the map. Regarding adultery, the *Mapa Quinatzin* (Barlow 1994) describes three types and their respective punishments depending on the context of the adultery or the status of the adulterers (figure 4.10). According to Alva Ixtlilxochitl's interpretation, adulterers were flattened by a large and heavy stone (figure 4.10a) or were stoned in the *tianquiztli* (market) (figure 4.10c); or if the adulterers had killed their spouses, then the male was burned to death and the female was hanged (figure 4.10b).

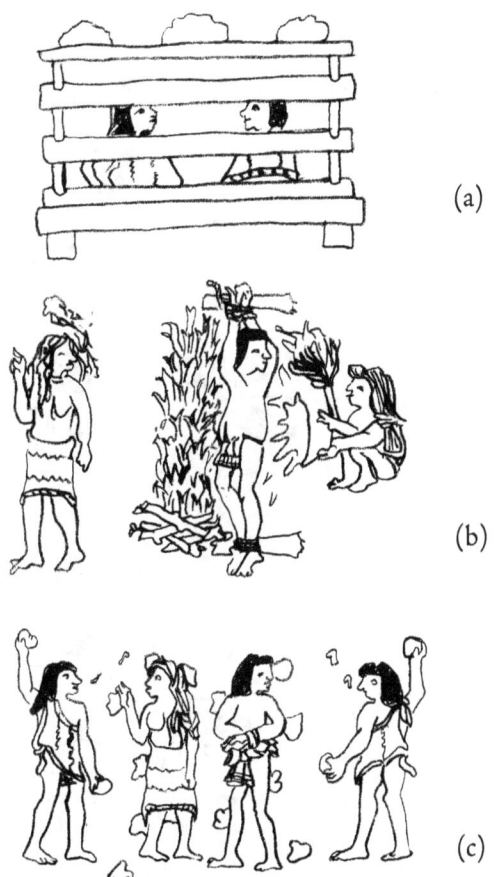

FIG. 4.10
Three types of adultery and punishments from the *Mapa Quinatzin*. Reproduced from Barlow (1994:leaf 3) with permission of the Bibliothèque nationale de France.

The *Mapa Quinatzin* (Barlow 1994) depicts three types of robbery: if a man stole a package from a woman in the marketplace (figure 4.11c) or he stole from a *petlacalli* (woven box) (figure 4.11b) or he broke into a house at night and stole (figure 4.11a), then he would be hanged (figure 4.11). According to Alva Ixtlilxochitl (1997), the thief was hanged because of his misconduct. The *Mapa Quinatzin* (Barlow 1994) provides information about a noble son's misconduct: the good son takes care of things, while the bad son is lazy, adulterous, and thieving (figure 4.12). Alva Ixtlilxochitl briefly records that if a noble son misused the wealth or property of his parents, he was sentenced to death by hanging. Based on his reading of the *Mapa Quinatzin*, therefore, Alva Ixtlilxochitl sees Nezahualcoyotl as the greatest lawmaker in all of pre-Hispanic Mexico.

This claim, however, is rooted in a misinterpretation of Texcoca sources motivated by a desire to portray the city in a more "civilized" way. The first

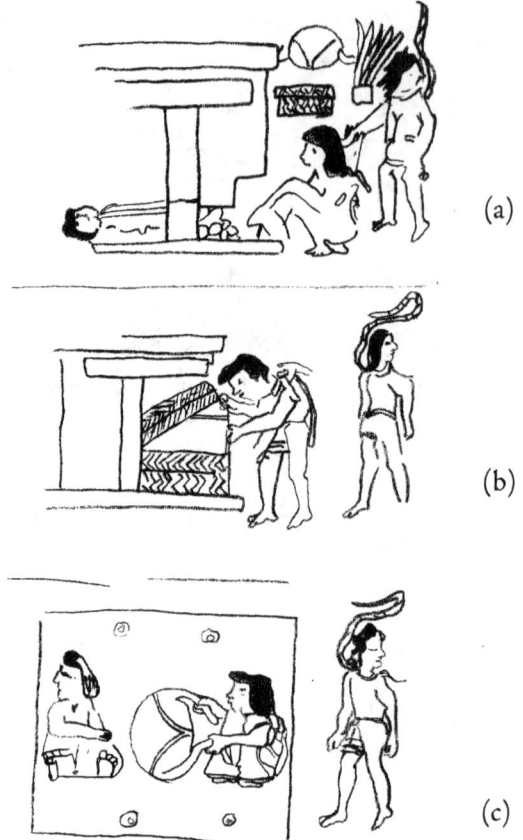

FIG. 4.11

Three types of robbery and punishments from the *Mapa Quinatzin*. Reproduced from Barlow (1994:leaf 3) with permission of the Bibliothèque nationale de France.

chronicler to provide a detailed description of the indigenous legal system is Motolinia (Benavente 1971:353), who presents Nezahualcoyotl as a legislator and fair legal practitioner. This chronicler deals with almost the same crimes and punishments that Alva Ixtlilxochitl examines in his texts and seems to support Alva Ixtlilxochitl's argument. Motolinia (Benavente 1971:352), however, clearly states that the Texcoca legal system was not different from but rather similar to that of two other cities, Tenochtitlan and Tlacopan: "Poca diferencia tenían en las leyes y modo de juzgar, y diciendo la orden que en una parte se guardaba quedar entendido de todas" (There was little variation in the laws and ways to judge, and given the order that in one part was kept, one can easily understand all of them). One of the reasons that Motolinia (Benavente 1971:352–53) focuses only on the Texcoca area is simply because he lived there and because, according to him, information about indigenous society was much

FIG. 4.12
Nobleman's misconduct and punishment from the *Mapa Quinatzin*. Reproduced from Barlow (1994:leaf 3) with permission of the Bibliothèque nationale de France.

more abundant in Texcoco. Another Spanish chronicler, Torquemada (1975, 2:377–85), presents a synthesis of all the offenses and the punishments mentioned by the previous chroniclers. Torquemada provides the extensive information on indigenous legal practices. He deals with basically the same crimes and punishments, though in more detail than Alva Ixtlilxochitl and Motolinia, but nowhere does he mention that the legal practice in pre-Hispanic Mexico originated from Texcoco or that Nezahualcoyotl was a legislator. Rather, Torquemada states that these laws and punishments were widely practiced before the conquest in New Spain.[16]

In the Mexica tradition, the *Crónica mexicana* (Alvarado Tezozomoc, 1987:102–3) records ten commandments of Huitzilopochtli that include two crimes and their punishments similar to those of Texcoco: (1) adultery was prohibited, and the adulterers were hanged, stoned, or beaten to death; and (2) thieves were hanged or enslaved depending on the type of robbery. Another Mexica source, *Historia de los mexicanos por sus pinturas* (1941:73–76), records in extensive detail the legal practices of Tenochtitlan. They are divided into two parts: *leyes en la guerra* (laws of war) and *leyes en sus tianguis o mercados* (laws of their markets). The first part deals with laws similar to those that Alva Ixtlilxochitl included in Nezahualcoyotl's military code: disobedient soldiers and those who stole captives were killed in the Mexica tradition and were either hanged or beheaded in the Texcoca tradition. Many offenses and punishments in the second part reflect those mentioned in Alva Ixtlilxochitl's works: (1) if a noble son sold the property of his father, he was killed secretly by suffocation; (2) those who stole in the tianquiztli were killed with rocks or hanged; (3) adulterers were stoned to death; (4) drunkards were hanged; (5) incest was prohibited and the incestuous were hanged; (6) homosexuals were hanged. The crimes and punishments that Ixtlilxochitl deals with are almost identical to those in this Mexica source, that is, adultery, robbery, incest, and military misconduct.

The particular parallel between the behavior chapter of the *Codex Mendoza* (1992) and the third part of the *Mapa Quinatzin* (Barlow 1994) also helps us to see the similarities in dealing with crimes and punishments between Texcoco and Tenochtitlan (Barlow 1994:263; Mohar B. 2000:227–42). The codex describes how to instruct youth: the majordomo teaches them not to be idle because idleness leads them to be vagabonds, ballplayers, thieves, and gamblers (figure 4.13). This is a similar description to the one of the bad son and the good son that appears in the *Mapa Quinatzin* (Barlow 1994). The codex (f. 71r) also depicts the punishments for some acts of misconduct according to the laws and customs in Tenochtitlan. If a young man or woman is drunk with pulque, he or she should die, according to the laws (figure 4.14a). Thieves and adulterers were killed by stoning (figure 4.14 b and c).

All of the offenses and punishments mentioned in both the Texcoca and Mexica sources demonstrate the many similarities between these two cities. Although some chroniclers, including Alva Ixtlilxochitl and Pomar, insist that Tenochtitlan imitated the Texcoca legal system, these similarities should be understood within the continuity of the larger Mesoamerican tradition rather than in the tradition of a particular city-state such as Tenochtitlan or Texcoco. According to Brotherston (1995:140–42), the good or bad qualities of many human activities had already been established, were inculcated in Mesoamerican culture, and were depicted in various religious texts. Based on the *Codex Borgia* from Cholula or Tlaxcala and the *Codex Fejérváry-Mayer*

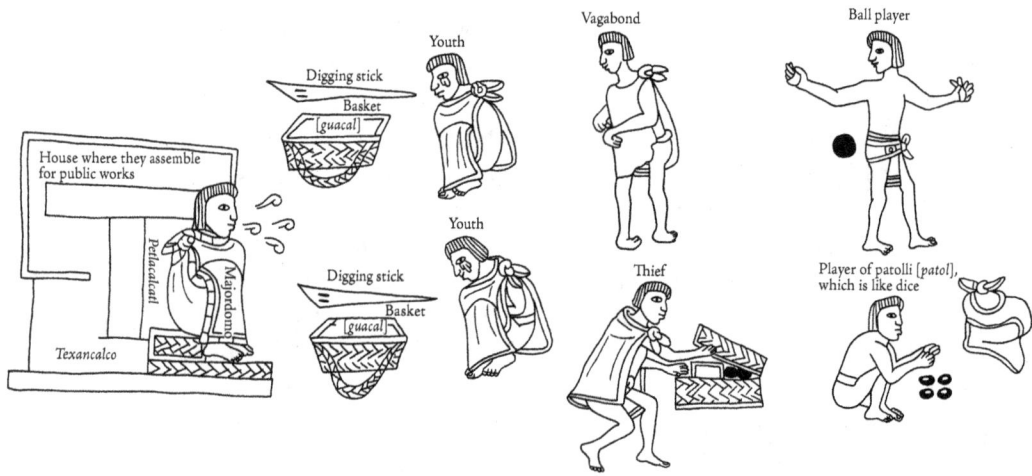

FIG. 4.13

Mexica examples of misconduct from the *Codex Mendoza* (1992:f. 71r). Reproduced with permission of the University of California Press.

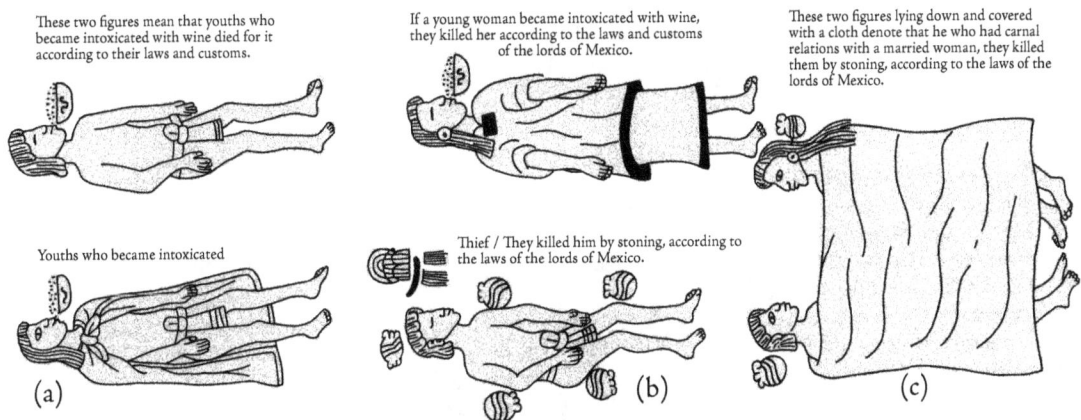

FIG. 4.14
Mexica punishments for drinking, robbery, and adultery from the *Codex Mendoza* (1992:f. 61r). Reproduced with permission of the University of California Press.

from the Mixtec area, Brotherston shows that drinking pulque, stealing, and adultery were clearly described as bad behaviors, as opposed to good behaviors such as producing maize. These codices do not describe the punishments for the offenses, but as the scribes distinguished the bad from the good behaviors, there must have been punishments appropriate to each.

There is another good reason to challenge the image of Nezahualcoyotl as a lawmaker. The pictorial source that Alva Ixtlilxochitl used for his chronicles, leaf 3 of the *Mapa Quinatzin* (Barlow 1994), shows no indication of Nezahualcoyotl as a lawmaker. Alva Ixtlilxochitl based his arguments solely on the top right of the first column of the leaf, where the glyphs of Nezahualcoyotl and his son Nezahualpilli were depicted above the house where a judge is sitting. Other than these glyphs, there is no other appearance of Nezahualcoyotl on the leaf, and the appearance of the glyphs of Nezahualcoyotl and Nezahualpilli do not guarantee their authorship of the laws. It only suggests that all the depicted crimes and punishments were conducted during the reigns of these kings. For instance, the map depicts how the three nations of the Triple Alliance began the war against a rebellious ruler (figure 4.15). According to Offner (1983:71–75), first the Mexica ambassadors from Tenochtitlan on the top left (a) were sent to the ruler in the center of the figure (f).[17] The Mexica did not talk to the ruler, but rather to the elders—Huehuetzin (d) and Ilamatzin (e)—of the city and tried to subjugate them peacefully. If they did not agree, then the Texcoca ambassadors (b) were sent with war equipment to intimidate the ruler. If the ruler still did not surrender to the Triple Alliance, then finally the Tlacopaneca ambassadors (c) were sent to talk to the eagle soldiers (g) and the jaguar soldiers

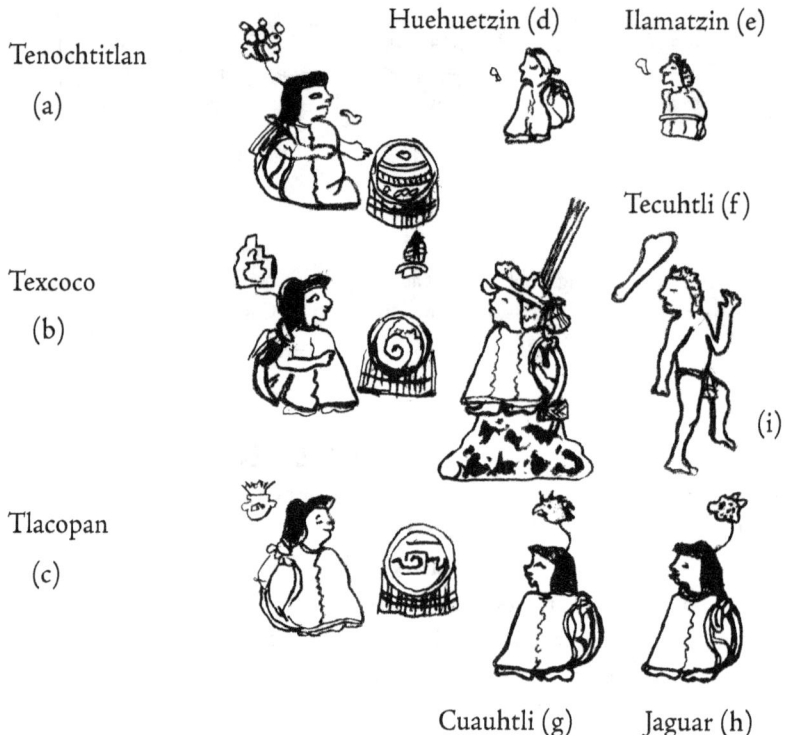

FIG. 4.15
Mexica allies and the way they begin warfare in the *Mapa Quinatzin*. Reproduced from Barlow (1994:leaf 3) with permission of the Bibliothèque nationale de France.

The Mexica ambassadors from Tenochtitlan (Place of the Cactus Fruit on the Stone) first spoke with Huehuetzin (Old Man) and Ilamatzin (Old Woman). The *chimalli* (shield) between them indicates that they talked about the war. The Texcoca (Craggy Mountain) ambassadors came to talk to the ruler of the region about the war again. Finally, the ambassadors of Tlacopan (Place of Sticks) discussed the coming war with *cuauhtli* (eagle warriors) and *jaguar* (jaguar warriors). If the ruler still does not submit to the allied troops, then the war begins. The participation in the war of the three city-states, each of which had regional supreme courts, seems to legally justify the Aztec invasion of other regions.

(h) of the ruler. If all these efforts failed, then the ruler was captured and killed (i). Alva Ixtlilxochitl (1997, 2:101–5) included this Triple Alliance war procedure as one of the "ochenta leyes que estableció Nezahualcoyotzin" (eighty laws that Nezahualcoyotzin enacted). But this is an unsupported claim. As shown before, the Mexica normally planned a war and then notified their allies, the Texcoca and the Tlacopaneca. This means that the Mexica took the initiative in conducting wars, and they established this practice among the nations of the Triple Alliance. At the end of the seventeenth century, Fray Agustín de Vetancurt (1971:57–58) includes this Triple Alliance practice of waging war in his description of Mexica traditions. Again, the laws described in the *Mapa Quinatzin* (Barlow 1994) were not made by Nezahualcoyotl but were applied in his city as well as in neighboring cities.

The claim that Nezahualcoyotl enacted many laws is inconsistent with most other sources; rather, the king seems to have reestablished the laws that Texcoco had lost as a result of the interruption of the Tepanec invasion. Nezahualcoyotl adopted the Mexica legal system and its laws as part of the reconstruction of his city. Thus, as Motolinia records (Benavente 1971:352–53), he may have been an important legislator in Texcoca history, but not in all of pre-Hispanic Mexico. The use of Nezahualcoyotl as a symbol of Aztec law is the result of the misinterpretation of indigenous pictorial sources.

Nezahualcoyotl was a great ruler in Texcoca history because he not only restored his lost city, but also expanded Texcoca territory far beyond the area his ancestors had ruled. Through an alliance with the Mexica, Nezahualcoyotl was quickly able to make his city second only to Tenochtitlan. As a rebuilder of the city-state, his efforts were key to restoring and maintaining Texcoca social, political, and religious order. Texcoca chroniclers in the colonial period record Nezahualcoyotl's achievements in detail. But they also exaggerate his local accomplishments in Texcoco by representing him as an influential figure in the history of the entire Basin of pre-Hispanic Mexico. Furthermore, influenced by European friars, colonial Texcoca chroniclers attempted to suppress Nezahualcoyotl's close relationships to the Mexica and transform their regional hero into a peaceful, wise king quite different from his Mexica allies. The chroniclers learned this perspective from the European colonizers, who always used the barbarous pagan religious practices of the Mexica to justify the conquest. The colonizers supplied the colonized with a mentality such that the latter now saw their culture from the perspective of the former. Some Spanish chroniclers welcomed and even reinforced the Europeanized image of Nezahualcoyotl, and later historians accepted their accounts without challenging the perspective that derived from this colonial situation.

part three

Revising the Study of Nahua Poetics

IN THE STUDY OF NAHUA POETRY, NEZAHUALCOYOTL ALWAYS APPEARS AS the most important representative poet whose main concerns are peace and metaphysical issues such as the ephemerality of earthly life. Most Nahua scholars from the colonial period to the present view Nezahualcoyotl's poetry as a clear contrast to the dominant political and cultural practices such as ritual war and human sacrifice associated with the Mexica. In the next three chapters, however, I argue that Texcoca chroniclers such as Juan Bautista Pomar and don Fernando de Alva Ixtlilxochitl invented this image of Nezahualcoyotl in order to make their pre-Hispanic regional history similar to that of the European colonizers. I demonstrate that individual authors of Nahua poetry are impossible to identify, because this notion is irrelevant to the context of production and performance in which such songs emerged. I also argue that the alleged poets, who belonged to the highest noble class, actually promoted dominant political and religious practices such as war and sacrifice. The poems attributed to Nezahualcoyotl thus are no different from those attributed to the Mexica. In fact, they reveal that as the ruler of Texcoco, Nezahualcoyotl was a close political ally of the Mexica and that he actively participated in the same sociocultural and political activities.

In addition to exploring these issues in the study of Nahua poetry, I need to review the translations of Nahua poems currently available in both English and Spanish. Several scholars have translated songs from the two collections *Cantares Mexicanos* and *Romances de los señores de la Nueva España*, and among them the translations of Angel María Garibay K., Miguel León-Portilla, and John Bierhorst are most used by scholars as well as students. Garibay and León-Portilla translated into Spanish only a selection of Nahua poems extracted from the two collections. In some cases, the translated excerpts are not even complete poems. In addition, because they saw little European influence in the Nahua poems, they downplayed or sometimes deleted Christian elements in their translations. Thus, the translations must necessarily be checked against the original Nahuatl manuscript or a modern transcription. Bierhorst translated into English for the first time the entire collection of the *Cantares* and included a meticulous transcription, but his rather narrow perspective, which views Nahua poetry as a part of indigenous revitalizing movements during the colonial period, leads him to disregard the pre-Hispanic influence on the songs and thus mistranslate some Nahuatl terms in order to make them fit his interpretation of these texts (Dakin 1986; Lockhart 1991). In this book, I use mostly the translations of Garibay, León-Portilla, and Bierhorst as they were published, but I have tried to minimize their limitations by consulting the original Nahuatl collections or transcriptions for my analysis, and I have included original Nahuatl words where necessary.

CHAPTER FIVE

NEZAHUALCOYOTL AND THE NOTION OF INDIVIDUAL AUTHORSHIP IN NAHUA POETRY

In colonial Mexico during the transition from the Aztec pictorial and oral tradition to the European alphabetic writing system, many indigenous artistic representations lost their unique form and content. They were often distorted by European or Europeanized chroniclers who interpreted the indigenous cultural tradition from the colonizer's perspective. The notion of individual authorship in Nahua song-poetry, known as "in xochitl in cuicatl" (flower and song), constitutes a clear example of this phenomenon.[1] By reexamining the poems attributed to Nezahualcoyotl, this chapter demonstrates that individual authorship was an invention of Europeanized colonial chroniclers and modern scholars who relied on uncritical readings of these colonial sources.

The representation of Nezahualcoyotl as a poet began with the Texcoca chroniclers Juan Bautista Pomar (1993) and don Fernando de Alva Ixtlilxochitl (1997) and the Spanish chronicler Fray Juan de Torquemada (1975). Pomar (1993:174–75) records that "algunos principales y señores" (some nobles and kings) were skeptical about the indigenous gods, even though they offered human sacrifices to them. According to Pomar, among these skeptics, Nezahualcoyotl, the most skeptical of all, conveyed his incredulity about the bloody indigenous gods in his songs. In his chronicle, Pomar revives the image of Nezahualcoyotl as a religious skeptic, an image that first appears in the writings of the Franciscan Andrés de Olmos in the 1530s. But Pomar also provides Nahua songs as evidence of Nezahualcoyotl's skepticism about the indigenous gods in an appendix to his chronicle titled *Romances de los señores de la Nueva España* (1993).

Alva Ixtlilxochitl further develops this idea.[2] He insists that Nezahualcoyotl was one of the principal philosophers or sages in pre-Hispanic times and that he was not only a skeptic but also an open antagonist of the indigenous religion and the sacrificial practices of the Mexica (1997, 1:447). In addition, Alva Ixtlilxochitl records that Nezahualcoyotl frequently warned his descendants of the ephemerality of human life by lamenting the transitory nature of the Aztec empire and the Azcapotzalca king Tezozomoc. The chronicler insists that Nezahualcoyotl expressed his religious and philosophical ideas in songs, and, like Pomar, he includes some fragments of Nezahualcoyotl's songs in his chronicles. According to Alva Ixtlilxochitl (1997, 2:125), Nezahualcoyotl left a record of his religious ideas and his anticipation of the conquest in "sesenta y tantos cantos" (sixty some odd songs). Torquemada (1975, 1:156) records a poem by Nezahualcoyotl in a similar context. After constructing a new palace in Texcoco, Nezahualcoyotl invited many kings and captains from all over pre-Hispanic Mexico for an inaugural banquet. There, he asked singers to sing a song that he himself had composed. The song, which beautifully described the transitory nature of earthly life and thus implicitly anticipated the future destruction of the Aztec world, moved all the guests so deeply that they had to leave the table.

These three chroniclers provided the primary basis for later studies of the Nahua song tradition. First, they initiated the idea that there were some indigenous poets or song composers and identified Nezahualcoyotl as a poet. Second, Pomar and Alva Ixtlilxochitl presented these poets as philosophers and sages who rejected, or were skeptical about, human sacrifice and the Mexica who symbolized this practice. These sages and philosophers allegedly dedicated themselves to the composition of poems that focus on beauty and peace. Third, they also established the notion of ephemerality as one of the most distinctive themes in their poems, rather than war and sacrifice. Alva Ixtlilxochitl, in particular, presents Nezahualcoyotl as the most representative of the peaceful, nonviolent sages. The main concern of this chapter is the first issue, the notion of individual authorship.

Making Nezahualcoyotl a Poet: A Brief Review

Since Alva Ixtlilxochitl and Torquemada identified Nezahualcoyotl as a poet in the seventeenth century, a few songs that have been translated into Spanish and were supposedly composed by him have been published.[3] After the discovery of the *Cantares Mexicanos* at the end of the nineteenth century, scholars such as Brinton (1887) and Vigil (1957) tried to translate some of the Nahua songs attributed to Nezahualcoyotl, but their versions were unreliable because of the faulty original they used. Martínez (1996:151) points out that Brinton used for his English translation an imaginative Spanish version translated from Nahuatl, and Vigil translated Brinton's English version into Spanish.[4] Garibay (1993) and his disciple León-Portilla were the ones who reinforced and confirmed the idea of Nezahualcoyotl as a poet in the 1960s, when they translated selections of Nahua songs from *Romances de los señores de la Nueva España* and

Cantares Mexicanos into Spanish, and they identified several individual poets or song composers.

To identify individual poets from the pre-Hispanic period, Garibay and León-Portilla began with the premise that most of the songs in the *Cantares Mexicanos* and the *Romances de los señores de la Nueva España* were preconquest products. They insist that the existing songs were composed in pre-Hispanic times, conserved orally, and recorded after the conquest. In *Historia de la literatura nahuatl* (1992:21), Garibay classifies most of the songs from *Cantares Mexicanos* (1985) and *Romances* (1993) as pre-Hispanic, dating from between 1430 and 1521, the times "en que la lengua y la literatura náhuatl se desenvuelven sin intromisión extraña, o al menos no europea" (in which Nahuatl language and literature developed without foreign or at least European, interference). Garibay insists that the songs are truly indigenous because their literary style is totally different from the Spanish in terms of worldview, religious ideas, social reflection, images, metaphors, and so forth. Following Garibay's arguments regarding the origin of the Nahua songs, León-Portilla (1992b:31) states, "It is important to note that no compositions of a clear Euro-Christian inspiration are detectable in the manuscript [*Romances*], with perhaps the exception of a few glosses or obvious interpolations of single words such as the recurrent dios (god) in Spanish."

Garibay and León-Portilla exclude the possibility of colonial influence on the existing songs, and they identify authorship by applying the same methodology used in the seventeenth century by Alva Ixtlilxochitl to identify Nezahualcoyotl as a poet. In his chronicles, for example, Alva Ixtlilxochitl (1997, 2:132) cites the following song fragments as evidence of Nezahualcoyotl's authorship: "Tlacxoconcaquican hani Nezahualcoyotzin, etcétera que traducidas a nuestro vulgar castellano, conforme al propio y verdadero sentido, quieren decir: oid lo que dice el rey Nezahualcoyotzin" (Tlacxoconcaquican hani Nezahualcoyotzin, etc that, translated into our vernacular Spanish according to their own and true sense, mean: listen to what the king Nezahualcoyotzin says). The invitation in this stanza is very typical in its message and lexicon and can be found easily in the songs of the *Romances* and the *Cantares*. The phrase "ni Nezahualcoyotl" is very common in the songs attributed to Nezahualcoyotl. Even though Alva Ixtlilxochitl translates the phrase as "the king Nezahualcoyotl," it literally means "I, Nezahualcoyotl." Thus, the whole Nahuatl verse reads in Spanish: "oíd lo que digo yo Nezahualcoyotl" (listen to what I, Nezahualcoyotl, say). Here, the self-identification of the poet seems to be the basis upon which Alva Ixtlilxochitl attributes authorship to Nezahualcoyotl. Just like Alva Ixtlilxochitl, Garibay identifies Nezahualcoyotl as the poet based simply on the argument that

> cuando leemos: *Yo soy* Tecayehuatzin, no tenemos motivo para negarlo. Y tampoco, acaso menos, cuando leemos: *Yo soy Nezahualcoyotl, soy el poeta de gran cabeza de loro* (5,1). (Garibay 1993:xxxix)

when we read "I am Tecayehuatzin," we do not have reason to deny it. And neither, perhaps less, when we read "I am Nezahualcoyotl; I am the poet of great head parrot" (5,1). (author's translation)

In this way, he was able to identify many other poets before the conquest such as Nezahualpilli, Tecayehuatzin, Cuacuauhtzin, and Xicotencatl.[5]

Following Garibay's lead (1993), León-Portilla confirms the individual authorship using three criteria:

A triple procedure will be followed to discern the reliability of the attributions made in the glosses and other referential statements. The first has to do with the person to whom the song is attributed. One has to find in other independent testimonies reliable information about his or her existence. Related to this is the possibility of adducing testimonies asserting the fame of the same individual as a composer of songs. The third procedure is a search for eventual independent renditions of one or more of the songs attributed to the same person. (León-Portilla 1992b:42)

Based on this methodology, León-Portilla (1967b) published *Trece poetas del mundo nahuatl*, an edition of Nahua poems with a brief study of Nahua poetry, and later an expanded version, *Quince poetas del mundo nahuatl* (1994). Among these identifiable poets, León-Portilla paid particular attention to Nezahualcoyotl because of his achievements as a ruler and the special religious vision that León-Portilla regards as being quite different from his contemporaries. Garibay and León-Portilla seem to be successful in establishing the authorship of these Nahua poems, but they do so by basing their arguments on the chronicles of Pomar (1993) and Alva Ixtlilxochitl (1997), by faithfully following the glossator's notes within the song texts, and by studying the lives of the poets. Following the work of Garibay and León-Portilla, many scholars have studied individual Nahua poets, and among them, Nezahualcoyotl has been the most popular.[6]

Bierhorst (1985:60–64), however, has seriously challenged the attribution of individual authorship of Nahua poetry, focusing on its origin, its unique structure, and the unreliability of the glossator's notes. Bierhorst insists that most of the songs in the *Cantares* appeared as the result of an indigenous revitalization movement in response to the plagues and devastation of Aztec culture and society after the conquest in the middle of the sixteenth century. The songs are only passively subversive because the poets were forced to adopt a syncretic form comparable to the Christian tradition so that the colonial authorities would not perceive the songs' cultural and political significance. Considering these postconquest circumstances, Bierhorst argues that the majority of the songs are postconquest products and that the historical events or figures represented are fictions that resonate with the sixteenth-century colonial context. In this argument about the origin of the songs, the phrase "ni Nezahualcoyotl" (I Nezahualcoyotl) should be understood figuratively.

Bierhorst (1985:97–105) also argues that the performance structure of Nahua poetry challenges the notion of individual authorship. He explains that the songs were typically performed by multiple singers, not by a single singer. Thus, if the singer says, "I am Nezahualcoyotl," he speaks with the voice of Nezahualcoyotl, either recognizing Nezahualcoyotl's spirit as his muse or merely filling in a needed portion of the dramatic monologue.[7] Therefore, according to Bierhorst (1985:101), identifying the performer/singer with the role he played is one of the "most destructive misconceptions about Aztec poetry." Bierhorst blames Alva Ixtlilxochitl and his readers such as Torquemada for representing Nezahualcoyotl as a poet-king. Bierhorst also demonstrates that many songs of the *Cantares* were reproduced in whole or in part in the other songs of the same collection or in the *Romances*. This phenomenon of borrowing undermines the claim of individual authorship by demonstrating that the songs were passed on orally and were frequently remade. In addition, Bierhorst indicates that the glossator's notes and descriptive titles of the songs do not confirm individual authorship, but rather provide information about the content of the song. According to Bierhorst (1985:98), those who wrote the notes and the titles had "a European preoccupation with authorship."

Both of these arguments about authorship put forth by Garibay and León-Portilla on the one hand and Bierhorst on the other help illuminate in one way or another the nature of the songs collected in the *Cantares* and the *Romances*. I would argue, however, that neither is completely satisfactory. By dating most of the songs to pre-Hispanic times, Garibay and León-Portilla do not take into account the colonial situation under which most of the existing songs were collected and modified. On the other hand, by viewing the songs as purely colonial products, Bierhorst does not consider the long and rich indigenous song tradition nor the indigenous cultural values in which the song composers participated. Rather than designating the majority of the songs as pre- or postconquest products, I would suggest that all the songs be viewed as transcultural texts caught up in the dynamics of cultural contact, which means that we need to take into account both pre- and postconquest traditions in order to analyze them.

Bierhorst is absolutely correct in his assertion that searching for and identifying individual authorship in Nahua poetry is a European preoccupation. Nahua song-poems are quite different from the European poetic tradition in terms of structure and performance: European poems were individually authored and read, while Nahua poems were created anonymously and oriented toward collectivity and performance. I apply this general conception of Nahua poetry to the poems attributed to the allegedly most prolific Nahua poet, Nezahualcoyotl. I focus on the importance of the singer, rather than the composer, in the process of producing and performing songs. By doing so, I demonstrate that the notion of individual authorship that informs the analysis of modern scholars such as Garibay (1993) and León-Portilla (1967b, 1992b) is inconsistent with the principles of Nahua poetics. In addition, I reexamine the glossator's notes that seem to verify the authorship of Nezahualcoyotl in several songs, and I offer an alternative interpretation.

Revising the Interpretation of Nezahualcoyotl as a Poet

Nahua songs were performed collectively as part of religious or secular fiestas and were always accompanied by dance and music. The Nahua song, *cuicatl*, was composed and sung by *cuicani* or *cuicapicqui* (singer-composer). According to Pomar (1993:190), both the nobles and the commoners could be song composers. As a noble, Nezahualcoyotl might have composed songs, but rulers typically had their own personal composers. Fray Diego Durán explains that

> It was common to dance in the temples, but on solemn occasions it was more common in the royal or lordly dwelling places. All these had their own singers who composed chants about their own glorious deeds and those of their ancestors, and especially of Moctecuzoma, the lord about whom we know most, and Nezahualpiltzintli of Tetzcoco. In their kingdoms songs had been composed describing their feats, victories, conquests, genealogies, and their extraordinary wealth. (Durán 1971:299)

Rather than being song composers, the rulers let the composers and singers sing their own heroic accomplishments or those of their ancestors, and they served as poetic inspiration for others who would sing their heroic achievements and those of their ancestors.

The singer was probably distinguished from the composer, but a singer–oral performer was considered a much more important factor in the song production process than a composer-author. Regarding cuicani, the informants of the *Florentine Codex* (1950–1982, 10:28–29) focus much more on the quality of his voice and the overall oral performance than on his ability to compose. There are no existing pictorial song texts, but the word *cuicatlan* (song place) is represented pictographically in some texts. Brotherston (1992:21) identifies four cuicatlan glyphs from pictorial codices (*Codex Mendoza*, the *Tepexic Annals*, and the *Codex Nuttal*) and an inscription at Monte Alban (figure 5.1). All four of these glyphs include a speech scroll, which demonstrates the importance of orality in cuicatl. The importance of the singer is also indicated in the performance of the songs. According to Fray Bernardino Sahagún's *Primeros memoriales* (1997b:89), the religious authorities controlled the singer; the priest *epcoacuacuilli tepictoton* was responsible for supervising and evaluating song composition and performance: "The Epcoacuacuilli Tepictoton saw to the songs.

FIG. 5.1
Pictorial representation of Cuicatlan (Song Place) (after Brotherston 1992:21):
(a) *Codex Mendoza*; (b) *Tepexic Annals*; (c) *Codex Nuttal*; (d) inscriptions at Monte Alban. Reproduced with permission of Cambridge University Press.

When anyone was to fashion a figure [of a mountain] he told [the priest] so that he could assign, he could order the singers. When they were going to sing at the home of someone who was to make a figure, it was he who passed judgement [on the song]." Fray Toribio de Benavente (Motolinia) (1971:382–85) and Fray Diego Durán (1971:295) record that songs were performed with dances and were accompanied by many musical instruments such as the *huehuetl* (an upright skin drum) and the *teponaztli* (the horizontal long drum).[8] The importance of the singer and the involvement of musical instruments in Nahua song are clearly reflected in the songs of *Romances* (1993) and *Cantares* (1985), which contain some drum notations such as *ti, to, co,* and *qui*.[9]

Richard Haly (1986) also demonstrates the importance of the singer rather than the composer by identifying certain formulas among the songs of the *Cantares* and the *Romances*. According to his research, Nahua poetry is closely connected to a musical rhythm that equates "linguistic stress with drumbeat" (1986:125). By carefully examining the rhythm of three variations of the same song, "Xopancuicatl" (*Cantares* 1985, [song] 69, [stanzas] 9–16), "War Song" (*Cantares* 1985, 63), and "Number 6, second part" (*Romances* 1993, 37),[10] Haly insists that

> Throughout the songs there is a tendency toward variation at the points of the lyric which try to be most specific, for example, where an action is associated with a proper name, or a particular flower or bird is described. From this evidence and from the fact that the substitutions are, for the most part, metrically equivalent, it may be assumed

that the metrical requirements at these points in the lyric have been filled formulaically. (Haly 1986:106)

The flower and the bird mentioned by Haly are metaphors for a sacrificed warrior. Haly (1986:106) argues that the singer could substitute this kind of specific word within a certain formula, depending on "the demands of the occasion and audience." For instance, the main thematic figure in the "Easter Song for Huehuetl" (*Cantares* 1985, 14), Jesucristo, is a substitution of an indigenous god or hero. Such revisions made by the singer were actually understood as "composing" or "originating" in Nahua poetics, which suggests that songs were not considered songs until the singer "gave them form" (*Florentine Codex* 1950–1982, 10:29). In such an oral tradition, the notion of authorship is largely irrelevant. Our modern notions of composition and performance converge in the traditional oral singer.

Nahua poetic performances that involved various singers in a single song make the verse or the role of each singer independent, as if each were a poem itself. The following song from *Cantares* demonstrates this special feature:

> Here begin the so-called plain songs that used to be performed in the palaces of Mexico, Acolhuacan, and the Dry Lands in order to entertain the rulers.
> 1. Strike it up in pleasure, singer! Sing in pleasure. May you all be pleasured. Life Giver is entertained.
> 2. Be pleasured. Life Giver adorns us. All are dancing as flower bracelets.
>   They're Your flowers! They're strewn: our songs are strewn within this house of bracelets, scattered in this house of gold. The flower tree is quaking: it shakes. Let the quetzal inhale. Let troupials, let swans, inhale.
> 3. You've become a flower tree, you scatter, bending down: you've appeared! You dwell before God's face, you, a multitude of flowers!
> 4. Live and blossom here on earth. As you move, shaking, flowers fall. Eternal are the flowers, eternal the songs that I, the singer, lift. Parceled out, dispersing, they turn to gold: the troupial enters this house.
> 5. Let there be flowers, raven flowers. You're scattering them, you're shaking them down in this house of flowers.
> 6. Alas, I am rich, I, Prince Nezahualcoyotl: I've assembled jewels, broad plumes, and I recognize their faces: these are jades, these are princes.
> 7. I gaze at the faces of all these eagles, these jaguars, and I recognize their faces: these are jades, these are bracelets.

8. These jades, these bracelets beads are shimmering-these, your hearts, your words, O prince, O Nezahualcoyotl, O Montezuma. You're to leave your vassals grieving.
9. For a moment be rich, near and in the presence of God Life Giver. Not twice does one become a lord on earth. You're to leave your vassals grieving.
10. For a moment be rich, be adorned, O prince, O Nezahualcoyotl. Borrow the flowers of Ipaltinemi. He'll be growing tired and weary here in time: He'll conceal His fame, His glory. The borrowing is brief, O princes.
11. For a moment be rich, be adorned, O prince, O Nezahualcoyotl. Borrow the flowers of Ipaltinemi. He'll be growing tired and weary here in time: He'll conceal His fame, His glory. The blooming is brief, O princes.
    Compose them, O Nezahualcoyotl! It would seem that God Life Giver takes this mat and seat to his home and goes on ruling earth and sky. And he shall be content, spreading out his riches there beyond.
12. We're to pass away. I say, "Be pleasures!"—I that am Nezahualcoyotl. Ah, do we truly live on earth?
13. Not forever on earth, but briefly here. Even jades are shattered. Gold, broken. Ah! Plumes, splintered. Not forever on earth, but briefly here. (*Cantares*, 20, 1–13)

In stanza 1, a leading person calls a singer to sing, which is a conventional beginning for Nahua songs. A singer appears to sing from stanzas 2 through 5. Then, another singer identified as Nezahualcoyotl suddenly appears and sings stanzas 6 and 7. Again another—possibly the first—singer performs stanzas 8, 9, 10, and 11, and then again Nezahualcoyotl appears in stanzas 12 and 13. We do not know exactly how many singers might be involved in the performance of this song but there should be at least two: one to fill the role of Nezahualcoyotl and another for the other parts. Motolinia (Benavente 1971:382–85) explains that normally these songs were performed by various singers, one in the role of leader and the others as his followers; he also notices variations of pitch and tempo. He focuses on the performance of the ritual songs, but we can be sure that the nonritual songs like the song examined here were performed in the same way, because the structure of the two forms is very similar, and both types were performed by various singers and with the same musical instruments. The following ritual song, the "Song of Huitzilopochtli," exhibits the same characteristics as the song cited previously:

1. Huitzilopochtli, wayfaring warrior.
2. None is equal.

3. Not for nothing did I take the yellow parrot feather garb.
4. Because of me the sun has shone...
5. He is terror!
6. Now the Mextec, the Pichahuaztec have one foot.
7. There he's gone! (Sahagún 1997b:130–31)

Like the secular song, a leading singer introduces the god Huitzilopochtli in lines 1 and 2, and then a second singer identified as the god takes his turn and sings lines 3 and 4. Another singer appears to sing lines 5, 6, and 7. The song continues to be sung in this way until the end. To the uninitiated modern reader, the appearance of various unidentified singers in a song causes ambiguity and confusion, but indigenous audiences in the sixteenth century and before would have been familiar with this kind of structure. According to Sahagún (1997b:84), even commoners were trained by a priest, barrio by barrio: "The Custodian, Tlapixcatzin, was in charge of the songs of the devils—all the sacred songs. He took great care to see that no one made a mistake when he taught the sacred songs. He summoned the commoners together so that they would know the songs well." Motolinia also records collective performance in Nahua songs:

> Proveían los cantores, algunos días antes de la fiesta, lo que habían de cantar. En los grandes pueblos eran muchos los cantores, y si había cantos o danzas nuevas, ayuntábanse otros con ellos, porque no oviese defecto el día de fiesta. (Benavente 1971:382–83)

> The singers provided, some days before the feast, what they would sing. In the large towns there were many singers, and if there were new songs or dances, other singers joined with them, so that there would be no mistakes on the day of the feast. (author's translation)

Garibay (1993, 2:1), León-Portilla (1972:67, 1992b:96), and their followers identify two poems by Nezahualcoyotl in the thirteen-stanza song reproduced above. First, they separate stanzas 6 and 7 from the song and entitle them "I Am Wealthy" by translating the first Nahuatl word of verse 6, *nonocuiltonohua*. Second, they separate stanzas 12 and 13 and entitle them "I Ask It" by translating the fourth word of verse 12, *niquittoa*.[11] This extraction, however, presents obstacles to the understanding of Nahua poetry. First, this song does not provide any convincing evidence that Nezahualcoyotl composed only those four stanzas (6, 7, 12, and 13) and not the rest. Second, if we accept the authorship of Nezahualcoyotl for those stanzas, then we also have to accept that many sacred songs, like the "Song of Huitzilopochtli," were composed by the gods. Third, separating a few stanzas from a song removes these stanzas from the original poetic context. This separation destroys the most distinctive feature in Nahua poetry, that is, the intercommunication among the singers involved in the song.

The structure that Garibay and León-Portilla present is no longer for public performance but rather for solitary individual reading. As Frances Karttunen and James Lockhart argue, only the whole song, not an individual stanza separated from a song, can constitute a complete poem:

> La independencia e integridad de la entidad del verso son tan fuertes que éste se podrá considerar un poema en sí. Su carácter parece implicar cuando menos una etapa del desarrollo histórico en que un solo verso era un tipo de canto o poema muy difundido; unos ejemplos de este fenómeno se ve en la *Historia Tolteca-Chichimeca*. Pero en el repertorio de los *Cantares* y los *Romances*, los poemas son agrupaciones de versos. Esto se ve en el hecho de que las variantes o duplicados generalmente contienen todos los mismos versos, o la mayor parte de ellos, lo que establece definitivamente su unidad. Además, la inspección directa demuestra una congruencia temática entre los versos de un solo poema, y lo que resulta aun más conclusivo, muestra que los conjuntos de versos como se presentan en las colecciones tienen una organización numérica muy fuerte. Ciertas agrupaciones numéricas, repetidas a cada paso, vienen a construir formas poéticas o tipos estructurales que definen la entidad más grande, o poema. (Karttunen and Lockhart 1980:17–18)

> The independence and integrity of the verse itself are so strong that this can be considered a poem in itself. Its nature seems to at least imply a stage of the historic development in which a single verse was a type of well-diffused song or poem; some examples of this phenomenon can be seen in the *Historia Tolteca-Chichimeca*. But in the collection of the *Cantares* and the *Romances*, the poems are groups of verses. This can be explained by the fact that the variants or duplicates generally contain all the same verses or most of them, which definitively establishes their unity. Besides, a close inspection demonstrates a thematic coherence among the verses of a single poem, and even more conclusive is that it shows that the verse groupings as presented in the collections have a very strong numerical organization. Certain numerical groupings, repeated at each step, come together to build poetic forms or structural types that define the larger entity, that is, the poem. (author's translation)

Along with the structural impossibility of extracting certain stanzas from a song, the content of the song itself suggests that Nezahualcoyotl was not the poet. In most of the poems attributed to this king, he is already dead and is remembered. In the song quoted above, the singer recalls his flowers, which symbolize his dead ancestors. They are descending from the sky where they "dwell before God's face" (stanza 4), which means that they were already dead and went to the sky in order to live near god. Nezahualcoyotl is recalled as one of these flowers, or dead ancestors. The following stanza shows more clearly from where Nezahualcoyotl comes: "See me! I've arrived, I, a white-flower chachalaca. This is my plume fan. I'm Nezahualcoyotl. The flowers are scattering down. I've come from Tamoanchan" (*Cantares* 1985, 72, 1). Nezahualcoyotl comes from Tamoanchan, the Land of the Dead, where god lives.[12]

The "ni Nezahualcoyotl" (I, Nezahualcoyotl) formula in which this king is spiritually incarnated also supports the idea that the rulers in pre-Hispanic times served as inspirational sources, not as authors of songs or specific stanzas. The people who appear in the formula are almost always dead rulers or high-ranked captains: "I grieve, I, Moctezuma" (*Cantares* 1985, 28, 2); "I say that I pleasure you, I, Totoquihuaztli!" (*Cantares* 1985, 36, 7); "I blow my conch for turquoise swans, I Cuacuauhtzin" (*Cantares* 1985, 62, 17); "I, Lord Xicotencatl, am the one who's saying" (*Cantares* 1985, 68, 49). The people recalled in these examples were powerful rulers in pre-Hispanic times. With these heroes, the Nahua singers preserved and maintained their collective memory:

> The unnamed singer is clearly differentiated from the protagonist in a large number of songs, and even when he is not, the whole point of view of this main core of the corpus concerning famous men of the altepetl is retrospective, the notion being to perpetuate their memory and bewail their passing, thereby honoring both them and the group to which they belonged. (Lockhart 1992:397)

Authorship and the Glossator's Notes

In addition to the fact that the notion of individual authorship is inconsistent with Nahua poetics, the marginal glosses and the titles of some songs that seem to confirm authorship in Nahua song-poetry, and upon which many colonial chroniclers and modern literary critics based their arguments, are not reliable in many cases. As stated before, the existing song collections, *Romances* and *Cantares*, contain some marginal glosses. I would like to make this point clearer by examining two songs that have been consistently attributed to Nezahualcoyotl. First, *Romances* presents song 36 on folios 21r–22v with the note, "Of Nezahualcoyotl while fleeing from the lord of Azcapotzalco." León-Portilla (1992b:88–91) identified Nezahualcoyotl as the author and entitled the song "In chololiztli icuic" (Song of the Flight) based on the note. This song, however, does not contain any evidence that Nezahualcoyotl composed it. Except in the notes, Nezahualcoyotl does not make a single appearance in this song.

The descriptive title corresponding to another song attributed to Nezahualcoyotl is also very misleading. Song 79 from *Cantares* (ff. 66v–67r) contains the following gloss: "Ycuic in Acolhuacan, in Nezahualcoyotzin ic quitlapalco in huehue moteuczomatzin, Mexico yquac mococohuaya" (Song of Nezahualcoyotl of Acolhuacan coming to visit the elder Montezuma of Mexico when he was sick). This title seems to identify the author of the poem as Nezahualcoyotl, but as many scholars like Bierhorst (1985:495) and Karttunen and Lockhart (1980:51) point out, the content of the song does not match the information in the note. The title was formulated based on a misreading of the term *mococo-cauh* (your sustenance) that appears in stanzas 5 and 6 as *mococoxcauh* (your sick person). Based on this misleading title, León-Portilla (1972:91–99) and his followers, such as Martínez (1996:219–21), assign the authorship of this song to Nezahualcoyotl.

I would argue that the glossator's notes and the titles of some songs do not indicate authorship, but rather give information on the main themes of the songs. Many songs both in *Cantares* and in *Romances* were accompanied by many kings' names: in *Romances*, "De Cacamatzin último rey de Tezcoco" (About Cacamatzin, the Last King of Texcoco) (8), "Tlacateotzin" (9), "Chalcayotl tlatocacuicatl" (Songs of Chalca Nobles) (11), "Huexotzincayotl tlatocacuicatl" (Songs of Huexotzinca Nobles) (12), and "De Nezahualcoyotzin" (29); in *Cantares*, "Canto de Tetlepanquetzanitzin" (Song of Tetlepanquetanitzin) (6), "Ycuic Axayacatzin Ytzcoatl Mexico tlatohuani" (Song of Axayacatl Itzcoatl, Ruler of Mexico) (47), "Ycuic Tlaltecatzin Quauhchinanco" (Song of Tlaltecatzin of Cuauhchinango) (48), "Ytotocuic Totoquihuatzin Tlacopā tla'toani" (King of Totoquihuaztli of Tlacopan's To-to Song) (49), and so on. If we take these titles literally, then all these songs were composed by these kings. The preposition *de* or "of," however, does not necessarily translate to "authored by" but can be interpreted as "about" or "pertaining to" (Bierhorst 1985:102). The following song in *Romances*, which has the note "De Nezahualcoyotzin," clearly supports this interpretation:

> You paint your songs, your word,
> Prince Nezahualcoyotl.
> Your heart is in the painting,
> With flowers of all colors
> You paint your songs, your word,
> Prince Nezahualcoyotl (*Romances*, ff. 18v–19r, in León-Portilla 1992b:71)

This song does describe Nezahualcoyotl, but nowhere does it identify him as the author. Rather, it describes how Nezahualcoyotl paints or composes songs.

Song 36 from *Romances* has a glossator's note on folios 21r–21v that states, "De Nezahualcoyotl cuando andaba huyendo del rey de Azcapotzalco" (Of Nezahualcoyotl when he was fleeing the king of Azcapotzalco). This note does not indicate the authorship of Nezahualcoyotl, but rather contains a description of this king. This song, a partial reproduction of an *icnocuicatl* (bereavement

FIG. 5.2

Huehue Ixtlilxochitl's death from the *Códice Xolotl* (1996:map 7). Reproduced with permission of the Bibliothèque nationale de France.

Huehue Ixtlilxochitl (Black-Eyes Flower) is killed by the Tepanec (People from Tepan [Stone-Flag])–Chalca (People of Precious Stone) and the Otompan (Place of the Otomíes)–Tepaneca (People from Tepan [Stone-Flag]). Nezahualcoyotl (Fasted Coyote) is witnessing the assassination of his father. Across the stream, a Tlailotlaca (Returning People) named Chichiquil (Guiding Feathers on a Spear) burns Huehue Ixtlilxochitl on the day 11 Ollin (Movement). Nezahualcoyotl was later rescued by his Mexica nephews Itzcoatl and Moctezuma Ilhuicamina.

---

song) presented in *Cantares*, fits the historical context in which Nezahualcoyotl lived. As examined in chapter 3, Nezahualcoyotl was born in 1402 and named as the legitimate heir of the Texcoca king, Huehue Ixtlilxochitl. Nezahualcoyotl's father, however, was captured and murdered during the Tepanec-Acolhuacan war against the Azcapotzalca king Tezozomoc in 1418. According to the *Codex Xolotl* (1996:plate 7), Nezahualcoyotl witnessed the assassination of his father while hiding in a big tree (figure 5.2). He was able to escape from his enemies, but he was pursued by the assassin, Tezozomoc, for a decade. When Nezahualcoyotl was in flight, he was in a desperate and lonely situation. The icnocuicatl or bereavement song, then, would have been an appropriate genre in which to commemorate his experience. As Brotherston (1979:263) argues, "in examples of the orphan mode as it was cultivated at the Aztec court we find the remembrance of dead heroes who have left on the irreversible journey past death and whose characteristic bravery acts as encouragement to those left behind." The poet of the song reflects this type of encouragement by remembering his dead ancestors:

> Solamente busco,
> hago memoria de mis amigos...
> ¿vendrán una vez más?
> ¿Han de volver a vivir?
> ¡Una sola vez desapareceremos:
> una sola vez estamos en esta tierra!
> Que no se aflijan sus corazones
> al lado, y junto a aquel por quien todo vive. (*Romances*, 36, 8)

> I only seek,
> I recall my friends...
> Will they come back one more time?
> Will they return to life?
> We will only disappear once:
> We are only in this land once!
> May your hearts not grieve
> beside, and close to he by whom everything lives. (author's translation)

The poet remembers his dead ancestors and asks if they will come back in the future, but he himself answers his question by describing that "we," including himself and his dead ancestors, live and die only once on earth. Then, separating himself, the poet asks his dead ancestors not to grieve, because they have gone to the sky where god provides them with an eternal life filled with joy and happiness (*Florentine Codex* 1950–1982, 6:13). This asking can also be applied to the poet himself because he will also enjoy eternal life with god after his death, just like his ancestors do. In this context, Nezahualcoyotl, whose father was assassinated, whose land was conquered, who himself was persecuted for several years by the Azcapotzalca, might have been consoled and encouraged by this type of song.

I would also argue that the glossator's notes provide information on the ownership of the songs. Durán (1971:299), who records that the Aztec nobles, especially kings, had their own private song composers, also records that these composers were professionals who received salaries from the rulers. Thus, if one of Nezahualcoyotl's own song composers had created a song, it might have been considered his; that is, the songs that a ruler had his poets compose might be associated with him. Don Domingo de San Antón Muñón Chimalpahin Cuauhtlehuanitzin records that the Chalca had to go to the palace of the

Mexica ruler Axayacatzin in Tenochtitlan in order to entertain him with songs and dances. They sang a war song that was very popular in Chalco. After listening to the song, Axayacatzin loved it and asked the Chalca to give it to him:

> Al tlatohuani Axayacatzin le gustó mucho "el Cantar de las guerras chalcas," gozaba escuchándolo; en repetidas ocasiones mandó pedir y solicitar a los principales chalcas dicho canto, y en especial a los amaquemecas, porque el "Cantar de las guerras chalcas" era propiedad de los de Tlailotlacan. Allá lo había compuesto un principal llamado Quiyauhtzin Cuauhquiyahuacatzintli, gran poeta [y músico]. En el canto se mencionaba el nombre de Huehue Ayocuantzin Chichimecateuctli, tlatohuani de Itztlacozauhcan Totolimpan; pero cuando Axayacatzin lo solicitó, le hicieron cambios al canto, sacando y borrando de él el nombre del tlatohuani Huehue Ayocuantzin e introduciendo [en su lugar] el nombre de Axayacatzin. En este dicho año el tlatohuani Axayacatzin se apropió el canto, y luego lo hacía ejecutar en su tecpan cuando deseaba alegrarse; ... Este canto pasó [después] a ser propiedad de Tezozomoctli Acolnahuácatl, hijo de Axayacatzin, y de su hijo don Diego de Alvarado Huanitzin, nieto de Axayacatzin, que fue [primero] tlatohuani de Ecatépec y después gobernador de México Tenochtitlan. (Chimalpahin 1998, 2:111–13)

> The tlatohuani Axayacatzin liked "The Song of the Chalca Wars" very much and enjoyed listening to it; on repeated occasions he asked for and requested the said song from the Chalca nobles, and especially from the Amaquemeca, because the "Song of the Chalca wars" was property of those of Tlailotlacan. There it was composed by a noble called Quiyauhtzin Cuauhquiyahuacatzintli, a great poet [and musician]. In the song, the name of Huehue Ayocuantzin Chichimecateuctli, tlatohuani of Itztlacozauhcan Totolimpan was mentioned; but when Axayacatzin requested it, they made changes to the song, removing and erasing from it the name of the tlatohuani Huehue Ayocuantzin and introducing [in its place] the name of Axayacatzin. In this said year the tlatohuani Axayacatzin took possession of the song, and then he had it performed in his palace when he wanted to be merry; ... This song [later] became the property of Tezozomoctli Acolnahuacatl, son of Axayacatzin, and of his son don Diego of Alvarado Huanitzin, grandson of Axayacatzin, who was [first] tlatohuani of Ecatepec and later governor of Mexico Tenochtitlan. (author's translation)

This information provides an important clue to the meaning of the glossator's notes in the song collections. Some songs seem to have been associated with individual rulers, even though they were of popular origin like this Chalca war song, which could also be called the song of Axayacatl because he possessed it and left it to his descendants as part of his legacy. This may explain why the majority of the songs were attributed to famous rulers, as in the song of Axayacatl Itzcoatl, ruler of Mexico (*Cantares* 1985, 47) and the song of Moctezuma (*Cantares* 1985, 76) in which the poets remember the ancestors of these kings. As one of the most powerful rulers in central Mexico, then, Nezahualcoyotl might have possessed many songs, and the glossator in the sixteenth century would have identified Nezahualcoyotl as the owner, not the composer, of the songs that had belonged to him. This suggests that the "de" in the glossator's notes could also be interpreted as an indication of possession rather than of authorship. I would argue, therefore, that Alva Ixtlilxochitl's reference (1997, 2:132) to Nezahualcoyotl's "sesenta y tantos cantos" (sixty some odd songs) should be understood as indicating possession rather than authorship.

Authorship and Preconquest and Postconquest Context

There is another good reason to challenge the notion of individual authorship in Nahua poetry from the pre-Hispanic period. The European concept of "individual authorship" did not exist in the process of artistic performance or book production before the conquest. The artistic performances that involved songs, dances, and music were collective, and the state strictly supervised them through the control of the performers. In the process of book production, the closest Nahuatl equivalent to "author" would be "tlacuilo," which literally means "one who paints something." The tlacuilo painted books with precise ideograms, but these books needed a specialist, a tlamatini (sage), who could read and interpret them by memory (León-Portilla 1992a:39–81; Boone 2000:24–27). The authorship in this process is ambiguous because the painted books could not be considered books until the tlamatini interpreted them, just as songs could not function as songs until they were sung. In this pre-Hispanic society, the notion of authorship is meaningless, which explains why most Nahua alphabetic and pictorial texts published in the sixteenth century were anonymous. The pre-Hispanic song tradition was a collective endeavor, and if any song identifies its singer or composer, then the identification must be a postconquest invention.

In *Cantares* (1985), there appear several glossator's notes and titles that provide reliable information on the authorship of some songs. Surprisingly, these notes explicitly identify a composer or singer of the songs, but most of them also record the postconquest date on which they were composed and sung:

> Here begins songs known as plain Huexotzincan pieces, in which the lords of Huexotzinco who were "hands" used to be spoken of as braves. They were divided into three kinds: lord songs or eagle songs, flower songs, and bereavement songs. And the drum is beaten thus: when a

stanza ends and another stanza is to follow, it's three beat. And when it actually begins, it's one-beat. But as it comes back in, then the drum falls beneath it, and the hand just keeps on going. But when it is in the middle, again the voice of the drum emerges. This, however, must be seen from the hand of the singer who knows how it is beaten. And newly, again, this music was in the home of Don Diego de León, gobernador of Azcapotzalco. Don Francisco Plácido beat it out in the year 1551. (*Cantares* 1985:14)

Here begins a jewel song concerning the nativity of our lord Jesucristo. Don Francisco Plácido put it together in the year 1553. (*Cantares* 1985:55)

Female apparition song, in which the holy word is set in order. It was sung at the feast of Espíritu Santo. The singer Cristóbal de Rosario Xiuhtlamin put it together in August of the year 1550. (*Cantares* 1985:56)

Here begins what is called a cradle song, with which in olden times the Tepanecs lauded the Mexican ruler Ahuitzotl. It's a composition of Nonohuiantzin of Nextenco, who was a singer and a lord. (*Cantares* 1985:57)

Here begins a bringing-out song, in which the holy word is translated. Thus was celebrated the feast of San Felipe, when His Majesty's gift arrived from Spain—the coat of arms that he presented to the city of Azcapotzalco Tepanecpan in the year 1564. The one who composed it was Don Francisco Plácido, gobernador of Xoquipilco, and the year in which was sung was 1565. At that time the gobernador of Azcapotzalco was Don Antonio Valeriano. (*Cantares* 1985:58)

Female song, concerning the resurrection of our lord, composed by Don Baltasar Toquezcuauhyo, tlatoani of Culhuacan, who in the year 1536 gave succor to our poor sought one, Don Diego de León, who was tlatoani here in Azcapotzalco Tepanecpan. (*Cantares* 1985:59)

Song of Nezahualpilli when he went to take captives in Huexotzinco. A Huaxtepec piece, composed by the singer Tececepouhqui. (*Cantares* 1985:67)

Bierhorst (1985:97–98) points out that five out of seven notes record the names of singers or composers of the songs but that all of them were composed or sung only after the conquest during the period between 1536 and

1565. The other two notes for songs 57 and 67 do not actually identify the author. Bierhorst explains that the name of the author of song 57, Nonohuiantzin of Nextenco (Mr. Everywhere of Hearthside), does not refer to any concrete person of a specific place but rather to the metaphorical representation of "Mr. Everywhere of Vagina." Bierhorst also argues that the title of song 67 appears to deal with the pre-Hispanic king Nezahualpilli, but its actual content focuses on the colonial period. Thus, according to Bierhorst, all the songs in *Cantares* that appear to indicate an individual author or singer were actually composed after the conquest.

The marginal glosses and song titles are helpful, however, in tracing how the European concept of authorship was introduced into Nahua poetry. Of the six notes that include dates of composition or oral performance, song 59 from 1536 is the earliest. But this date is probably an error introduced by a copyist because it is much earlier than the dates of the other songs (Garibay 1992:156; Bierhorst 1985:107). Leaving aside this anomaly, the songs can be divided into two categories based on the dates indicated: songs of 1550s and those of the 1560s. The notes for the songs 14–19 (1551), 55 (1553), and 56 (1550) of the first group conform to the pre-Hispanic song tradition in their emphasis on the roles of cuicani, singer. The notes provide information about how they were sung rather than how they were composed. The notes for songs 14–19, in particular, focus on the way the singer sings the song. Identifying the singer in these songs is still impossible, however, because they still involve multiple singers rather than one singer, as explained previously. Thus, don Francisco Plácido and Cristóbal de Rosario Xiuhtlamin, who are identified as the singers of the songs, actually represent the individuals who appear to be in charge of the performance. The former beats the drum out in accordance with the type of the song and the latter "puts the song together" for the feast of Espíritu Santo. On the other hand, the notes for the songs 58 (1565) and 59 (1563), of the second group, use the term "composed" and song 58 actually distinguishes the composer don Francisco Plácido from the unknown singer. All five glosses apply the European concept of authorship to the Nahua songs and song performances in the middle of the sixteenth century.

The introduction of this European notion of authorship in the 1550s and 1560s was probably facilitated by the process of evangelization and the formation of Nahua scholars in the sixteenth century. Spanish friars took advantage of indigenous traditions of song and music to educate and preach Christianity to the natives.[13] Immediately after the conquest, they founded monastery schools in which native children learned reading, writing, and Christian doctrine, sometimes through singing, dancing, and music. Among the first Franciscan friars in Mexico, Pedro de Gante first introduced singing and music in the evangelization and education of the Indians (Ricard 1995:193–94; Burkhart 1996:364; Anderson 1993:xv–xix). In this process of education, the students who learned to read and write alphabetic script would have been well aware of the European concept of authorship. In particular, the alumni of the Colegio de Santa Cruz de Tlatelolco, which was founded in 1536, would have been familiar with this concept because, like their European contemporaries, they studied reading, writing, music, Latin, rhetoric, logic, and philosophy (Ricard 1995:336). Alumni who had studied in the Colegio for the first ten years after its founding between 1536 and 1546 became the most important Nahua scholars of the sixteenth century and collaborated in the production of many Nahuatl texts of Christian doctrine with Spanish priests such as Sahagún in 1550s and 1560s.[14] According to Burkhart (1989:195–202), most of the Nahuatl doctrinal books from the colonial period were published in collaboration with Nahua scholars in this period. It may be no coincidence, therefore, that the glosses of the *Cantares* begin applying the concept of individual authorship to Nahua poetry at precisely the same time, that is to say, the 1550s and 1560s.[15] As collaborators with the priests, indigenous intellectuals were not able to claim authorship of the doctrinal texts, but they certainly would have understood the concept of individual authorship in the publication process.[16] In addition, they would have been familiar with the notion of authorship from reading and reciting sacred poems and psalms from the Bible, which are identified as having been written by the kings such as David and Solomon. This Judeo-Christian influence in the application of the notion of individual authorship to Nahua poetry is evident since four out of the seven notes that provide an author's or singer's name actually deal with Christian doctrine, such as the birth and resurrection of Jesus.

The Texcoca chroniclers Pomar (1993) and Alva Ixtlilxochitl (1997), who first promoted the notion of individual authorship in Nahua poetry, were heavily influenced by the European literary and religious tradition. By viewing their indigenous cultural traditions from a European perspective, they had a vested interest in making their ancestor, Nezahualcoyotl, into an Old Testament–type hero as "the Psalm King, the Mexican David . . . with a good singing voice" (Brotherston 1972:406). Later historians and literary critics have relied uncritically on Pomar's and Alva Ixtlilxochitl's writings, thus perpetuating the Europeanized description of indigenous cultural concepts and practices. The notion of individual authorship in Nahua poetry has gained popularity within scholarly as well as popular culture, especially after contemporary scholars such as Garibay (1993) and León-Portilla (1967b, 1992b) claimed to have established the authorship of many poems by providing a historical background consistent with the poets identified. The evidence, however, suggests that the notion of individual authorship in Nahua poetry originated with Europeanized chroniclers, and its perpetuation by modern scholars has severely distorted the collective structure and performance of the Nahua artistic tradition along with many other aspects of indigenous civilization after the conquest.

CHAPTER SIX

A Reinterpretation of Nahua Poetics
Nahua Cosmogony, Nahua Songs, and Nezahualcoyotl

As introduced in chapter 5, the Texcoca chroniclers Juan Bautista Pomar (1993) and don Fernando de Alva Ixtlilxochitl (1997) began to present a group of sages or philosophers as poets who were incredulous about indigenous gods and religious ceremonies such as human sacrifice. According to the chroniclers, these sages left their peaceful ideas in their poems, and their peace-loving philosophy demonstrates a clear contrast to Mexica practices such as war and human sacrifice. Among these sages and philosophers, Pomar and Alva Ixtlilxochitl argue that Nezahualcoyotl was the most distinctive and prolific. I would argue, however, that Nezahualcoyotl and other poet-sages did not dissent from the dominant religious and political system. Rather, as members of the highest social and political class of their city-states, they were committed to maintaining the existing universal order of Nahua cosmogony. Nezahualcoyotl of Texcoco and the poets of other regions in central Mexico shared with the Mexica the same religious and cultural traditions in which war and human sacrifice were institutionalized. In fact, the Nahua poems attributed to Nezahualcoyotl celebrate these religious and political traditions in the same way as poems ostensibly from other regions, including Tenochtitlan.

Nezahualcoyotl, Song Composers, and Nahua Cosmogony

In the 1960s, Angel María Garibay K. and Miguel León-Portilla relied on and further developed Pomar's and Alva Ixtlilxochitl's view that Nezahualcoyotl and other song composers had religious and philosophical perspectives different from the dominant religion and philosophy of the Mexica. To demonstrate the warlike and sanguinary Mexica tradition, Garibay and León-Portilla focused on the rise of imperial Mexico-Tenochtitlan, that is, the Mexica ruler Itzcoatl's reign between 1428 and 1440. Garibay pays particular attention to Itzcoatl's burning of the ancient pictorial texts and his political and cultural reforms:

> Ideas religiosas, normas de régimen, percebimientos de conservación literaria, poemas y relatos, quedan sometidos a la nueva mano que rige. Nada más natural suponer que la nueva documentación datará de esta época y que lo que ha de llegar hasta nosotros proviene de la nueva cultura, si cabe darle este nombre. (Garibay 1992:23)

> Religious ideas, norms of the state, ordering of literary conservation, poems and stories remain subject to the new hand that governs. It is natural to suppose that the new documentation will date from this epoch and that which would arrive to us stems from the new culture, if it can be given this name. (author's translation)[1]

León-Portilla develops this perspective in detail by focusing on the role of Itzcoatl's half brother, Tlacaelel. According to León-Portilla, Tlacaelel was the one who instituted the mystic-militaristic tradition among the Mexica. By convincing the Mexica that they were the chosen people of the sun, Tlacaelel established Huitzilopochtli as their principal deity and enforced human sacrifice dedicated to this god:

> As can be seen, Tlacaelel's reforms relate to three basic areas: political and legal organization, changes in the economic administration, and modifications in the priestly organization and the forms of worship that should be rendered the gods. With respect to this last point, it is worth recalling that human sacrifice was already practiced before Mexica times. However, with regard to the frequency of this rite, as already noted, it seems that it was Tlacaelel who increased its rate, in accordance with the idea of preserving the life of the Sun with the blood of human victims. (León-Portilla 1992a:103–4)

Against Tlacaelel's reforms, León-Portilla presents a group of tlamatinime (wise men) who preserved the ancient religion and cultural practices from before the time of the Mexica, those of the peaceful and artistic Toltec culture and their deity Quetzalcoatl. According to León-Portilla, these wise men left their peace-loving philosophy and aesthetics in "in xochitl in cuicatl":

> In fact, these sages and poets, who also spoke Nahuatl and were participants in the same Toltec heritage, condemned more than once the martial attitude of the Mexica. Steeped in the ancient Toltec heritage, these wise men, rejecting the martial-mystical interpretation of world or cosmic affairs, oriented their thinking along philosophical lines that

yielded a different nature for the divine, with a less conflictive image of
its relationship to humankind, a less aggressive image of human nature,
a more ambivalent purpose for humanity's existence, and some hope
that an escape from the anguish produced by the transitory nature of
all things was possible.... Their meditations and dialogues also led
them to forge a distinct method by which to approach a comprehension of the fundamental enigmas: poetic expression. Thus they came
to use "flowers and songs," poetry, as a means of gaining a view of ultimate reality and as a way of expressing the results of their inspiration.
By doing this they were able to articulate deity, especially its omnipresence, and the knotty beliefs concerning the value of humanity in the
eyes of the divine. (León-Portilla 1992a:163–64)

León-Portilla argues that Nezahualcoyotl is the most representative example of these tlamatinime, and consequently the songs or poems attributed to him show this perspective more than anyone else's.[2]

Viewing Nezahualcoyotl and his fellow poets as a contrast to the dominant religion and politics of pre-Hispanic Mexico has been an influential perspective in the interpretation of the songs that have been attributed to him. Following Garibay and León-Portilla, Martínez (1972:131–32) argues that Nezahualcoyotl composed very few songs about battle or war and avoided metaphors related to war. In addition, by focusing on the song "Canto a Nezahualcoyotl" from *Cantares*, which I will examine in detail in chapter 7, Martínez finds a clear contrast between the artistic practices of Nezahualcoyotl and his fellow poets, on the one hand, and the militaristic practices of the Mexica, on the other:

> Algún tiempo después de la muerte de Nezahualcóyotl, un poeta cuyo nombre ignoramos dedicó a su memoria al "Canto a Nezahualcoyotl" que es uno de los poemas elegiacos más hermosos de la poesía náhuatl. Intervienen en el canto varios poetas y, en ficción, el mismo Nezahualcóyotl. En la primera intervención de uno de los poetas se personifica a Nezahualcoyotl como la Flor del Canto, esto es, la gala de la poesía. Y en la segunda hay una declaración reveladora, y excepcional en la poesía náhuatl: "destruyen nuestros libros los jefes guerreros," que denuncia probablemente cierta oposición entre la casta guerrera, a la manera azteca, y los poetas, historiadores y filósofos que se interrogan por la existencia y buscaban la belleza. (Martínez 1972:134)[3]

> Sometime after the death of Nezahualcoyotl, a poet, whose name we do not know, dedicated to his memory the "Song to Nezahualcoyotl," which is one of the most beautiful elegiac poems of Nahua poetry. Various poets intervene in the song and, in fiction, Nezahualcoyotl himself.

In the first intervention, one of the poets personifies Nezahualcoyotl as the Flower of the Song, this is to say, the most pleasing part of the poetry. And in the second there is a revealing statement uncommon in the Nahua poetry: "The warlike leaders destroy our books," which probably denounces certain opposition between the Aztec-style warrior caste and the poets, historians, and philosophers who contemplated existence and sought beauty. (author's translation)

There are many other scholars who rely upon Garibay and León-Portilla in their interpretations of Nahua poetry, particularly songs attributed to Nezahualcoyotl. Birgitta Leander (1976:6–7) compares Nezahualcoyotl's worldview, characterized by the beauty and goodness of Quetzalcoatl, with Tlacaelel's worldview, characterized by war, sacrifice, and worship of Huitzilopochtli.[4] The famous Nicaraguan poet, Ernesto Cardenal (1972, 1992) also perpetuates the image of Nezahualcoyotl as a peaceful and civilized poet-king opposed to the Mexica, which will be examined in more detail in the epilogue. This contrast between Nezahualcoyotl and the Mexica rulers, however, is misleading because it ignores the political, cultural, and religious background that Nezahualcoyotl and the Mexica rulers shared.

León-Portilla (1992a:164) studies some "anti-Mexica" philosophers and poets such as Nezahualcoyotl and Nezahualpilli of Texcoco, Totoquihuaztli of Tlacopan, Tecayehuatzin of Huexotzinco, Ayocuan of Tecamachalco, and Xicotencatl of Tlaxcala. Historically, however, there was no difference between the Texcoca and Tlacopaneca rulers on the one hand and the Mexica rulers on the other; they participated in the same cultural and religious practices, and they maintained close political ties with the Mexica. As explained in chapter 4, Nezahualcoyotl himself was established as the Texcoca ruler by his uncle, the Mexica leader Itzcoatl, and he adopted the Mexica political and religious system in his newly recovered nation, an event that is confirmed even by Alva Ixtlilxochitl (1997, 1:379). In addition, Texcoco had already been exposed to the Mexica and their main god Huitzilopochtli even before Nezahualcoyotl's recovery of his kingdom. As shown in chapter 3, Nezahualcoyotl's grandfather, Techotlalatzin, received the Tolticized immigrants known as the Mexica, and they became one of the six main ethnic groups in Texcoco.

The allegedly "anti-Mexica" philosophers and poets studied by León-Portilla were rulers whose real purpose was to maintain the existing political, religious, and cultural order. According to the *Florentine Codex* (1950–1982, 8:51–58), the rulers determined and arranged how war would be conducted; they praised and rewarded brave warriors according to their merits; they rehearsed the sacrifice of captives to their gods and consoled the families whose members died in war; they appointed judges and monitored trials; and they ordered dancing and singing. Pomar also records that Texcoca rulers performed almost the same mission:

> Y despedidos [los nobles], con esto de allí adelante mandaba [el nuevo rey] y gobernaba como le parecía que convenía, poniendo todo su cuidado principalmente en tres cosas: la primera, en los negocios de la guerra, lo segundo, en el culto divino, y lo tercero, en los frutos de la tierra, para que siempre hubiese mucha hartura. Oía todos los días de cosas de gobierno, porque las de justicia oían los jueces, de quien ya se ha dicho. Despechaba con pocas palabras y jamás se excedía en lo que mandaba. (Pomar 1993:186)

> And once they [the nobles] were dismissed, he [the new king] began to rule and govern from then on as he saw fit, placing all his attention primarily on three things: first, on the business of war, second, on divine worship, and third, on the products of the land, so that there would always be great abundance. He tended daily to issues of government, because the judges dealt with legal issues. He spoke with few words and never was excessive in his commands. (author's translation)

Pomar does not mention ordering dancing and singing as a part of the ruler's mission, but Alva Ixtlilxochitl (1997, 1:406) records that the Texcoca ruler also regulated these activities through a council of music. In addition, as shown in chapter 5, the rulers controlled singing and dancing through the priest, epcoacuacuilli, who judged recently composed songs and their performances (Sahagún 1997b:89). I would argue that the songs, whose writing and performance were controlled by this ruling class, reflect its worldview and promote the dominant ideology.

As the major enemies of the Mexica in central Mexico, the Huexotzinca and Tlaxcalteca might have maintained different political, social, and religious traditions from those of the Mexica, and they might have been peaceful and nonviolent. León-Portilla (1992a:172–84) presents the famous meeting among Nahua poets in the palace of the Huexotzinca ruler Tecayehuatzin. In this meeting, the poets such as Tecayehuatzin from Huexotzinco, Ayocuan from Tecamachalco, and Aquiauhtzin of Ayapanco consider poetry the only truth in the world, which, according to León-Portilla, expresses a philosophy completely different from that of the Mexica. If this were the case, they might have condemned the Mexica for their human sacrifice just like Nezahualcoyotl supposedly did: "Nezahualcoyotl the lord of Tezcoco, Tecayehuatzin of Huexotzinco, and various other thinkers, who were given to conceiving the mysteries of the World through poetry, were deeply concerned with the supreme enigma of the divine. For them the cult of human sacrifices, imposed by the Mexicas, could hardly be satisfactory" (León-Portilla 1992a:184). This idea seems convincing if we were to consider only the hostile relationship that these nations had with Mexico-Tenochtitlan. This simple conclusion, however, completely ignores the religious background and the worldview that the Huexotzinca and the Tlaxcalteca inherited from their immediate ancestors, the Toltecs of Tula and Teotihuacan, and the broader context of the Mesoamerican tradition.

Most of the city-states in central Mexico, including Tenochtitlan, Texcoco, Tlacopan, and Chalco in the Basin of Mexico, and Huexotzinco, Cholula, and Tlaxcala in the Puebla-Tlaxcala Valley, inherited almost the same cultural and religious tradition. They were formed by immigrant ethnic groups such as the Chichimecs, the Otomíes, and the Mexica from the north, and the Toltec descendants who had been living in the Basin of Mexico and the Puebla-Tlaxcala Valley for some time. These city-states developed a rich cultural and religious blend of various ethnic groups by conquering neighbors or assimilating themselves to neighboring groups or voluntarily accepting immigrants. Thus, as shown in chapter 2, the two major groups, the Chichimecs and the Toltecs, established many ethnically heterogeneous city-states such as Texcoco, Tenayuca, Azcapotzalco, Coatlichan, and Cuauhtitlan in the Basin of Mexico, and Cholula, Huexotzinca, and Tlaxcala in the Puebla-Tlaxcala Valley. The Mexica, who claimed Aztlan as the place of their ethnic origin, were no exception. The acculturation of the Mexica in the Basin of Mexico with other ethnic groups in the Valley of Puebla-Tlaxcala began in the early stage of their immigration, even before their arrival at Tenochtitlan.

According to Mexica sources such as the *Codex Azcatitlan* (1995:plate 3), the *Tira de la peregrinación* (1964), and Alvarado Tezozomoc's *Crónica mexicana* (1987), the Mexica initiated their pilgrimage or immigration to the promised land along with eight other ethnic groups: the Matlatzinca, the Tepaneca, the Tlahuica, the Malinalca, the Colhuaque, the Xochimilca, the Chalca, and the Huexotzinca (figure 6.1). Many of them, such the Tepaneca, the Colhuaque, the Xochimilca, and the Chalca, established their own city-states in the Basin of Mexico, while the Huexotzinca and Matlatzinca settled in the Valley of Puebla-Tlaxcala. According to the *Tira de la peregrinación* (1964), Huitzilopochtli ordered the Mexica to separate themselves from the other groups and journey alone (figure 6.2). The common regional origin of the Mexica and the other groups, especially the Huexotzinca, who became a major enemy of the Mexica, suggests that they must have shared certain religious and cultural traditions even before they arrived in the Basin of Mexico and established their own city-states. Another major Mexica enemy in the Valley of Puebla-Tlaxcala, the Tlaxcalteca, also shared a certain ethnic connection with them. According to Alvarado Tezozomoc (1987:18–21), the Tlaxcalteca were one of the seven groups who originated from the caves in Aztlan and Teocolhuacan. The Tlaxcalteca departed their cave as the sixth group, and the Mexica as the last.

In addition to their common historical roots, the majority of the residents of the basin and the valley, and most importantly the rulers of the city-states, all spoke the same language, Nahuatl, and they shared the same religious calendar. They used the *tonalpohualli* (day count), which consists of thirteen numbers and twenty day signs, to name days and years. They also served the same or

FIG. 6.1

Mexica immigration with eight different ethnic groups from the *Tira de la peregrinación* (1964:plate 2). Reproduced with permission of the Instituto Nacional de Antropología e Historia.

In this image, the Mexica leave Aztlan, their place of origin, and go to Huei Colhuacan. In Huei Colhuacan, the Mexica join with eight different ethnic groups or families as shown above: Matlatzinca (People of Matlatzinco [Place of the Net]), Tepaneca (People of Tepanecpan [Place of the Stone]), Tlahuica (People of the Arch), Malinalca (People of Malinalco [Twisted Place]), Colhuaque (People of Colhuacan [Place of Ancestors]), Xochimilca (People of Xochimilco [Flower Field]), Chalca (People of Chalco [Place of Precious Stone]), and Huexotzinca (People of Huexotzinco [Place of Little Willow]). The Mexica along with these eight groups started their immigration under the guidance of four priests: Tezcacoatl (Mirror Snake), Cuauhcoatl (Eagle Snake), Apanecatl (Someone from River), and Chimalma (Shield-Hand). Tezcacoatl carries the Mexica god Huitzilopochtli (Hummingbird Left) on his back. The *tlacuilo* of this codex focuses on Mexica history by excluding the gods of the other groups. However, the sources of the other groups record that they also continued worshipping their own gods during the immigration. In other sources, for instance, the Huexotzinca carry their god Camaxtli in the same way that the Mexica carried their god Huitzilopochtli.

FIG. 6.2

Separation of the Mexica from the eight ethnic groups from the *Tira de la peregrinación* (1964:plate 3). Reproduced with permission of the Instituto Nacional de Antropología e Historia.

The Mexica and the eight groups or families continued their immigration together, and at one point, they stayed under a big tree for five years. Under this tree, the Mexica built a *teocalli* (sacred house) dedicated to Huitzilopochtli. When they were eating one day, the big tree broke with great noise. Considering this incident as a bad omen, the Mexica priests got together in tears and asked their god Huitzilopochtli what they should do. The god told them that they should separate themselves from the accompanying eight groups and that these groups must go back. One of the Mexica priests, Aacatl (Water Reed), talks to a leader from the other groups about the separation. This leader weeps at the prospect of the separation. According to the footprints depicted in the codex, the eight accompanying groups go back the way they came following Huitzilopochtli's order. From this moment on, the codex focuses on the journey of the Mexica until they reach Colhuacan in the Basin of Mexico. However, other sources indicate that the eight accompanying groups continued their migration and settled down in central Mexico as well. These sources depict the Mexica as the last group to arrive in the basin. The *tlacuilo* of this Mexica codex, however, appears to reverse this order, making the Mexica the first to arrive.

similar gods and performed the same religious ceremonies. The main Mexica god, Huitzilopochtli, has features in common with the principal Huexotzinca god, Mixcoatl, and the Tlaxcalteca god, Camaxtli. Both Huitzilopochtli and Camaxtli had the same calendar name, 1 Flint (*Florentine Codex* 1950–1982, 2:38), and both gods played a militaristic-tutelary role (Nicholson 1971:426). Thus, as Davies (1987:203) points out, "Camaxtli was little more than Huitzilopochtli under another name, and to have forcibly replaced the latter deity by the former would have been an almost meaningless gesture." In addition, the Mexica, the Huexotzinca, and the Tlaxcalteca shared other major gods including Tezcatlipoca, Tlaloc, Quetzalcoatl, Xochipilli, and many others. They also observed religious ceremonies dedicated to these gods as determined by the same calendar cycles, and human sacrifice was the most important part of these ceremonies:

> All the prisoners and captives of war brought from the towns we have mentioned were sacrificed in this manner, until none were left. After they had been slain and cast down, their owners—those who had captured them—retrieve the bodies. They were carried away, distributed, and eaten, in order to celebrate the feast. There were at least forty or fifty captives, depending upon the skill which the men had shown in seizing and capturing men in war. The same sacrifice was practiced by the men of Tlaxcala, Huexotzinco, Calpan, Tepeaca, Tecali, Atotonilco, and Cuauhquecholan with men from the region of Mexico they had captured. The same feast, the same rites, were performed in front of their god, just was done in Mexico. All the provinces of the land practiced the same ceremonies. (Durán 1971:92–93)[5]

Considering that the Mexica and their enemies, the Tlaxcalteca and the Huexotzinca, practiced human sacrifice in the same ceremonies, to find that the most important warrior groups in the ceremonies, jaguar and eagle knights, were institutionalized in both city-states, Tenochtitlan and Tlaxcala, is not at all surprising (Brumfiel 2001:308).

To understand all the religious similarities among the city-states in central Mexico, their commonly held Mesoamerican cosmogony must be examined. According to the Mexica sources *Legend of the Suns* (1992), *Historia de los mexicanos por sus pinturas* (1941), and *Histoire du Mechique* (1965), there existed four suns or ages before the present sun.[6] The first sun was Oceltonatiuh (Jaguar Sun); the people of this sun were eaten by jaguars and the sun was destroyed. The second sun, Ehecatonatiuh (Wind Sun), was destroyed by wind, and the people were turned into monkeys. The third sun, Quiauhtonatiuh (Rain Sun), was destroyed by a fiery rain, and the people were changed into turkeys. The fourth sun, Atonatiuh (Water Sun), terminated in a great deluge, and the people turned into fish. All these suns were presided over by the gods

Tezcatlipoca, Quetzalcoatl, Tlaloc, and Chalchiuhtlicue. After the destruction of the fourth sun, the gods united together and restored human life to the world again. Quetzalcoatl went to the land of the dead and stole male and female bones. He took them to Tamoanchan, the paradise where the gods lived. There, all the gods did penance together to revive human beings. After the re-creation of human beings, Quetzalcoatl turned into an ant to steal a kernel of corn from Food Mountain and took it to Tamoanchan. There again all the gods got together, chewed the corn, and put it on the lips of the people. In this way, the gods created and nourished human beings. The world, however, was not perfect yet. The sun ceased to move, asking the gods for "their blood, their color, their precious substance" (*Legend of the Suns* 1992:148). All the gods got together and they nourished the sun by sacrificing themselves. In this way, the fifth sun, Ollintonatiuh (Movement Sun), which is the present sun, the present era, was born. This self-sacrifice of the gods set an important precedent in pre-Hispanic religion and ceremony because "the death of the gods was not sufficient in itself to satisfy the insatiable craving of the sun and the earth for blood and hearts. Man himself must bear the chief burden here, and to this end, war was instituted for the primary purpose of obtaining victims for sacrifice" (Nicholson 1971:402).[7] The Nahuas perceived these gods' contribution to the creation of the world and of human beings as their divine burden on earth; that is to say, they should maintain the universe by nourishing the sun and the earth with their blood.[8] The conversation between Nahua priests of Tenochtitlan and the twelve Franciscan friars, which presumably occurred in 1524 but was written in the *Coloquios y doctrina cristiana* by Fray Sahagún in 1560, explains in detail the indigenous perception of the world:[9]

> Ellos [nuestros primogenitores] nos enseñaron,
> todas sus formas de culto,
> sus modos de reverenciar [a los dioses].
> Así, ante ellos acercamos tierra a la boca,
> así nos sangramos,
> pagamos nuestras deudas,
> quemamos copal,
> ofrecemos sacrificios.
> Decían [nuestros primogenitores]:
> que ellos, los dioses, son por quien se vive,
> que ellos nos merecieron
> ¿Cómo, dónde? Cuando aún era de noche.
> Y decían [nuestros primogenitores]:
> Que ellos [los dioses] nos dan
> nuestro sustento, nuestro alimento,
> todo cuanto se bebe, se come,
> lo que es nuestra carne, el maíz, el fríjol,

los bledos, la chía.
Ellos son a quienes pedimos
el agua, la lluvia,
por las que se producen las cosas en la tierra. (Sahagún 1986:151)

They [our ancestors] taught us
all their forms of worship,
their modes of honoring [the gods].
Thus, in front of them we bring earth to our mouths
Thus, we bleed ourselves,
we pay our debts,
we burn resin,
we offer sacrifices.
They [our ancestors] said:
that they are the gods, by whom people live,
that they merited us.
How? Where? While it was still night.
And they [our ancestors] said:
that they [the gods] give us
our sustenance, our food,
all that we eat, drink,
that which is our flesh, corn, beans,
amaranth and the *chia*.
They are those to whom we ask for
water, rain
by which the things on earth are produced. (author's translation)

The Nahua priests insist that their offerings, including human sacrifice, are the way to pay their debt to the gods who provide them with nourishment. The priests also insist that the gods' favor to humans began even before the formation of the universe and has continued through the times of their ancestors to the present. The gods have provided the earth with necessary materials so that the earth produces food for the humans. The indigenous priests assert that their survival depends on the faithful execution of their service to their gods. According to the *Florentine Codex* (1950–1982, 6:12), the Mexica nobles knew that they were assigned to nourish the universe from the beginning of their existence on earth: "Be not mistaken about them [the noblemen], for they have been dedicated [on earth], there promised, born at this time, sent to such a place to provide drink, to provide food, to provide offerings for the sun, for the lord of the earth."

The indigenous solar deities in central Mexico, such as Huitzilopochtli, Tezcatlipoca, and Mixcoatl or Camaxtli, required human hearts and blood in order to nourish the universe. In this sense, the Mexica, the Texcoca, and their enemies, the Huexotzinca and Tlaxcalteca, shared the same worldview, and they all practiced human sacrifice in their respective cities. Again, all these ideas and ceremonies were administered by the most important social class, the priests and the rulers, who, according to León-Portilla, were also the poets or song composers of pre-Hispanic times.

In xochitl in cuicatl as Symbolic Representation of Nahua Cosmogony

The rulers and nobles of the Nahua city-states in the Basin of Mexico and the Valley of Puebla-Tlaxcala strictly observed religious ceremonies involving war and human sacrifice dedicated to the gods in order to preserve the universal order. In return for their service, the gods provided food for the men to survive on the earth. As the primary creators and consumers of the songs during the pre-Hispanic period, the Nahua noble class encouraged and promoted this Nahua cosmology. Their song practice itself implies an interrelationship between gods and humans. The first song of *Cantares Mexicanos*, "Cuicapeuhcayotl" (Beginning of the Songs), reveals how closely Nahua poetics reflect indigenous cosmology.

I present this song as an example of the pre-Hispanic tradition: it does not contain any Spanish words or any direct translations of Spanish words, which is quite different from other songs. In addition, the song faithfully reflects indigenous cultural and religious views from pre-Hispanic times, as will be seen later. In the song, the poet (cuicani) wonders where he can find good sweet flowers, which represent poems. He searches for the quetzal hummingbird, the jade hummingbird, and the troupial butterfly to ask where he can find good songs. He travels around seeing and hearing these birds singing: "And there the mockingbird is throbbing with song, reverberating with song. The bellbird echoes these precious ones, these sundry songbirds: they're rattle-shrilling: they're eulogizing world Owner" (*Cantares* 1985, 1, 2). Then, the singer asks these birds where he can find songs, and they respond shrilly: "They're here. Let's go show them to you, singer. Perhaps with these you'll entertain our lordly fellow braves" (*Cantares* 1985, 1, 3). Then, they take the singer to a land of flowers (Xochitlalpan) and tell him: "Cut whatever flowers you want. Entertain yourself, singer! And when you arrive you'll give them to our lordly comrades who'll entertain World Owner" (*Cantares* 1985, 1, 4). The singer replies to the birds: "And when I arrive I'll spread the word among our friends. We'll always come here to cut these sundry sweet and precious flowers, to get these sundry good ones, these songs. With these we'll entertain our friends on earth, the eagle-jaguar princes" (*Cantares* 1985, 1, 5).

The poet in this song travels to the flower land (Xochitlalpan) searching for good flowers, songs. This is not a physical but rather a spiritual journey to the land in the sky where the poet's dead ancestors live with the gods. There, the singer meets all kinds of birds and butterflies that guide him to find various flowers or songs. According to the *Florentine Codex*, these birds and butterflies in the land of flowers are in fact warriors who died in the battlefield or were sacrificed in religious ceremonies:

> The third place to which they went was there to home of the sun, in heaven. Those went there who died in war, who perhaps right there indeed died in battle, in the warring place.... Perchance one was slain in gladiatorial sacrifice, or cast into the fire, or pierced by darts, or offered up on the barrel cactus, or shot by arrows, or encrusted [and burned] with pieces of resinous wood: all went to the home of the sun...
>
> And when they had passed four years there, then they changed into precious birds—hummingbirds, orioles, yellow birds blackened about the eyes, chalky butterflies, feather down butterflies, gourd bowl butterflies; they sucked honey [from flowers] there where they dwelt. (*Florentine Codex* 1950–1982, 3:49)

The sun, which represents the sun god (Huitzilopochtli in Tenochtitlan, Mixcoatl in Huexotzinco, or Camaxtli in Tlaxcala), rises accompanied by all kinds of birds and butterflies who are sacrificed warriors. In their animal forms, these warriors guide the poet to where the flowers/songs are and ask the poet to take these flowers/songs to the earth. Thus, Nahua songs, flowers, have a divine origin; they come from the sky where the gods and dead warriors live. León-Portilla acknowledges the divine origin of Nahua poetry, but he does not relate it to the indigenous tradition. For him, in xochitl in cuicatl is always a peaceful and nonviolent act, and hence he cannot identify the divine with the indigenous sun god. Rather, like Alva Ixtlilxochitl, he divorces Nezahualcoyotl's poetry from its original historical context; he interprets this divinity as something unknown, a different god that does not require human sacrifice, but accepts only a peaceful act of in xochitl in cuicatl.

Although the first song, "Cuicapeuhcayotl," appears to derive from a regional tradition from Tenochtitlan, numerous Nahua songs, regardless of their regional provenance, claim a divine origin like the following songs from Otomi and Chalco:

> There I hear the root song, I, singer. Ah, it's not on earth that these good songs have begun. What the precious bellbird sings, what the spirit swans and the troupial bird sing, sounds forth from heaven, where ah! They eulogize the Ever Present, the Ever Near. (*Cantares* 1985, 2, 2)

> Where do they come from, these intoxicating flowers, these intoxicating songs, these good songs? They come from His home in heaven. All the flowers come from His home (*Cantares* 1985, 52, 24).

The Huexotzinca piece that, according to León-Portilla (1992a:172–73), was sung in the palace of the Huexotzinca ruler Tecayehuatzin also manifests this idea: "From the interior of the heavens come the beautiful flowers, the beautiful songs." Some Nahua poems express more explicitly their divine origin by revealing that the flowers/poems are the words of gods. The following stanzas, which appear in the song entitled "Song of Nezahualcoyotl," convey the divine origin of the poetry: "The flowers, Life Giver's words, are dispersed: they shower down on Anahuac. With these You cause the city to endure. The world is in Your hands. It is really you who utter them, O Life Giver" (*Cantares* 1985, 46, 29–30). The poet insists that his poems are the gods' creation and thus that he merely plays the role of the gods' messenger, which reveals the close relationship between the poet and indigenous religion. Many poets, in fact, were the priests who taught the poems to the indigenous noble youth at the school known as calmecac in Tenochtitlan. Here the young Mexica learned and memorized songs through continuous repetition (León-Portilla 1992a:70–71; Leander 1976:27).

If the flowers/songs were actually created by the sun god, then what was the purpose of this creation? As the poet witnesses in "Cuicapeuhcayotl" (Beginning of the Songs), many birds and butterflies, that is to say dead warriors, drink from flowers in the sky. The god generates the flowers in his heaven as an eternal food for these dead warriors. In compensation for the sacrificed warriors, the god creates a paradise, Xochitlalpan, filled with the flowers of joy and happiness:

> And there, always, forever, perpetually, time without end, they rejoice, they live in abundance, where they suck the different flowers, the fragrant, the savory. In this wise the valiant warriors live in joy, in happiness. It is as if they live drunk [with joy and happiness], not knowing, no longer remembering the affairs of the day, the affairs of the night, and no longer giving heed to one year, to two years. Eternal is their abundance, their joy. The different flowers they suck, the choice ones, the flowers of joy, the flowers of happiness: to this end the noblemen go to death—go longing for, go desiring [death]. (*Florentine Codex* 1950–1982, 6:13)

In the gods' heaven where the sacrificed warriors are transformed into all kinds of birds and butterflies and where the Nahua poet searches for the flower-songs, these flowers are created by the gods as everlasting nourishment for the dead warriors. However, the flower-songs serve not only for the sacrificed warriors in the sky but also as spiritual nourishment for the live warriors on earth who will be sacrificed in the future. Again, according to "Beginning of the Songs" ("Cuicapeuhcayotl"), the birds and butterflies, the dead warriors, tell the poet to take back to earth the songs to amuse their lordly comrades, "the eagle-jaguar princes." The songs have a special mission on earth: to entertain these Nahua rulers, captains, and priests, who eventually will serve the gods as future sacrificial warriors. In numerous songs collected both in *Romances de los señores de la Nueva España* (1993) and in *Cantares Mexicanos: Songs of the Aztecs* (1985), the Nahua nobles often met and enjoyed composing or listening to the songs. These nobles frequently mourn the loss of their ancestors and lament the transitory nature of life on earth.

One Nahua song mode in particular, the icnocuicatl (orphan song or bereavement song), reveals this function of Nahua poetry. In typical icnocuicatl songs, the poet laments the death of his lordly friends, primarily rulers or important historical figures who died on the battlefield.[10] A song from Huexotzinco, number 18 in *Cantares* (1985, 18, 1), titled "Icnocuicatl," begins with the sadness of the poet due to the loss of his lordly friends: "I say and think that nothing can compare to this bereavement. How can my heart be eased? How can I, a Huexotzincan, put aside this sadness? Do I have a father? Do I have a mother? Is he waiting for me? Will he ease my heart? And can't I put an end to this bereavement?" The pain and sorrow that the Nahua nobles feel about the death of their ancestors seem contradictory to the eulogy of that death, but the feelings are quite understandable in Nahua cosmology when we consider that the distress felt by the nobles comes from a perceived danger of the demise of the social and religious system. For instance, the Mexica believed that the departure of the ancestors, who served as rulers, priests, judges, and as father and mother of the commoners, might cause the total destruction of their city (*Florentine Codex* 1950–1982, 6:21–24).[11] At the same time, the Mexica nobles recognized the burden and hard duties that their dead ancestors had borne: "They departed leaving the large bundle, the large carrying frame, the great burden, the subject—heavy, frightful, insupportable, intolerable. They departed placing it upon their shoulders, upon their backs; they departed leaving it to their offspring, to him who for yet a little while came to raise up their heads, who came glorifying them" (*Florentine Codex* 1950–1982, 6:22). Thus, this bundle that the ancestors left was a mission for the Mexica to maintain the existing world-sun.

In this harsh human life, Nahua poetry has the special role of entertaining the Nahua nobles on earth. It promotes a brotherhood (*icniuhyotl*) among the nobles: "Aren't we happy on earth? It seems we're each other's friends. So there is happiness on earth. It seems to be that way with all of us who are poor. It seems to be that way with every sufferer here in this company" (*Cantares* 1985, 18, 22). The Nahua nobles find joy and happiness through the company of their friends who share the same philosophical perspective on earthly life. Many poems attributed to Nezahualcoyotl by Garibay and León-Portilla promote this brotherhood in the harshness of earthly life:

No hago más que buscar,
no hago más que recordar a nuestros amigos.

¿Vendrán otra vez aquí?,
¿han de volver a vivir?
¡Una sola vez nos perdemos,
una sola vez estamos en la tierra!
No por eso se entristezca el corazón de alguno:
al lado del que está dando la vida.
Pero yo con esto lloro,
me pongo triste; he quedado huérfano en la tierra.
¿Qué dispone tu corazón, Autor de la Vida?
¡Que se vaya la amargura de tu pecho,
que se vaya el hastío del desamparo!
¡Que se puede alcanzar gloria a tu lado,
oh dios... pero tu quieres darme muerte!
Puede ser que no vivamos alegres en la tierra,
pero tus amigos con eso tenemos gozo en la tierra,
Y todos de igual modo padecemos
y todos andamos con angustia unidos aquí. (*Cantares*, ff. 13r–13v, in
    Garibay 1993, 2:127)

I do nothing but seek,
I do nothing but remember our friends.
Will they come here again?
Will they live again?
We only lose ourselves once,
We are only on earth once!
Because of it, no one's heart should be sad:
Beside the one who gives life.
But with this I cry,
I become sad; I have remained an orphan on earth.
What does your heart command, Author of Life?
Let the anguish of your chest go away,
Let the loathing of the abandonment go away!
Let glory reach your side,
oh God... But you want to give me death!
It is possible that we do not live happily on earth,
but your friends, with that we have joy on earth,
And in the same way we all suffer
and we all live united in anguish here. (author's translation)

The poet laments that he will not be able to see his ancestors on earth anymore. He feels he is left like an orphan. He even expresses a grievance against the god who took his ancestors, but the poet finds consolation in the company of his friends who share the same destiny on earth.

Nahua poetry exalts a brotherhood among the nobles, but this brotherhood is possible only with the flowers/songs that the gods have created for their warrior ancestors in the sky. With these flowers/songs, the poet from Chalco consoles those who suffer human life on earth:

Be pleasured for a moment with our songs, O friends. You sing adeptly, scattering, dispersing from plumes, and the flowers are golden.

The songs we lift here on earth are fresh. The flowers are fresh. Let them come and lie in our hands. Let there be pleasure with these, O friends. Let our pain and sadness be destroyed with these. (*Cantares* 1985, 51, 1–2)

As one of the most inspirational sources for the Nahua poet, the poetic voice of Nezahualcoyotl often expresses the divine origin of the poems and promotes brotherhood among the warrior rulers and nobles. Among such instances, the following is the most conspicuous:

Deleitaos
    con las embriagadoras flores
    que están en nuestras manos.
                  ¡vengan a ponerse en los cuellos
                    collares de flores:
    nuestras flores de tiempo de lluvia:
    estén frescas, abran sus capullos!
    Allí anda el ave: parlotea, trina:
    viene a conocer la casa del dios.

Sólo con nuestras flores démonos placer;
    sólo con nuestros cantos vaya desapareciendo
    Nuestra tristeza, príncipes:
    con ellas huya vuestro hastío.

Las crea el que hace vivir todo,
    las hace nacer el Arbitro Supremo:
    flores placenteras:
    con ellas huya vuestro hastío. (*Romances* 1993, 1, 30)

Enjoy yourselves,
with the intoxicating flowers
that are in our hands.
come to put the necklaces of flowers on your necks:
our flowers from the rainy season:

> Be fresh, open your buds!
> There the bird goes: chatters, sings:
> It comes to know the house of the god.
>
> Only with our flowers we enjoy ourselves;
> only with our songs our sadness starts to disappear, princes,
> with them your loathing goes away.
>
> He who makes all things live creates them,
> the Supreme Arbitrator causes them to be born:
> Pleasant flowers:
> With them your loathing flees. (author's translation)

In the first stanza, the poet describes the fresh flowers that just bloomed and invites his fellow nobles to enjoy them like the bird, the incarnation of a dead warrior, enjoys the flowers in the house of god. In this way, the live nobles are able to familiarize themselves with the world of god. The second stanza shows that the flowers are actually songs and asserts that only these flowery songs give the nobles pleasure, easing pain and grief. The last stanza confirms that these flowers/songs are created by god ("the Supreme Arbitrator causes them to be born") and with them the nobles become pleased and free of boredom.

Even though the songs entertain the nobles on earth, the ultimate role of the songs is to promote the world of the god in the sky. In the last two stanzas of "Cuicapeuhcayotl," the poet reveals that he can enjoy true happiness and joy only in Xochitlalpan (the flower land) that the god creates in the sky:

> I, the singer, went to get all of them, and I flower-crowned the princes, adorned them, filled their hands. And then I lift these good songs in praise of all the princes before the Ever Present, the Ever Near. But where would he whose worth is nothing get delicious flowers? Where would he find them? Could he whose worth is nothing, who is wretched and who sins on earth, accompany me to flower land, the land of plenty? It's the Ever Present, the Ever Near, who causes people to deserve them here on earth. And so my heart is weeping. I, the singer, recall how I went to look around in flower land:
>
> And I say, "Ah, this is not a good place. Ah, it's elsewhere that one goes, where there's happiness. What good is earth? Ah, the place of life where all are shorn is elsewhere. Let me go there. Let me go make music with the sundry precious birds. Let me enjoy the good flowers, the sweet flowers, the heart pleasers, that intoxicate with joy and sweetness, intoxicate with sweet joy. (*Cantares* 1985, 1, 6–7)

FIG. 6.3

Huehuetl and its carved images. Reproduced from Saville (1925:77) with permission of the Museum of the American Indian Heye Foundation.

In the first stanza, the poet states that he brought the flowers, songs, to the nobles from the sky and dips them in the flowers in various ways. However, he wonders if the people or the princes on earth ("he whose worth is nothing") might be able to go to the flower land in the sky with him. In the second stanza, the poet compares two worlds, the earth where the princes and the poet himself live and Xochitlalpan where the god dwells. He shuns the first world where everything is temporary and shorn, while he extols the second world with its everlasting flowers of joy and happiness. With the exaltation of Xochitlalpan in the sky, the poet encourages the warriors to go to Xochitlalpan. That is, he inspires them to die in war or the human sacrifice of religious ceremonies so that they feed the sun with their blood and in return receive eternal life filled with joy and happiness.

This artistic representation of Nahua cosmogony can also be found in one of the main musical instruments, huehuetl (upright drum), which was always used for song performance. The images carved on a huehuetl from Malinalco illustrate how the Nahua songs stimulate the warriors to preserve the present sun, Nahui Ollin (4 Movement) (figure 6.3).[12] The images are grouped into three sections, a row of figures at the top of the drum, a narrow band at the bottom of the drum, and three figures that decorate the legs of the drum extending down from the middle band. The top represents the sky or the sun's heaven where the gods live and the bottom represents the earth. The top and the bottom are divided by the middle that represents war or a battlefield with *chimalli* (shield) combined with *mitl* (arrow) and *maccuahuitl* (club). All three of these elements are intertwined by the sacred war symbol, *atlachinolli* (water fire), and by the sacrificial rope. The three spaces on the legs of the drum figuratively represent the earth and contain the figures of two jaguars and one eagle. These animals, which clearly represent the eagle and jaguar knights, carry sacrificial flags and sing and dance with a war song that is depicted by a speech flower glyph and sacred war symbol, atlachinolli, connected to their mouths and feet. At the top in the sky, one jaguar soldier and one eagle soldier are holding the Nahui Ollin with their hands and feet, facing each other. Behind the jaguar soldier appears a figure with a human face and the body of a bird. This figure holds a flower in his right hand and a feather fan in his left, which represents the Aztec god of music, song, and games, Xochipilli (Nicholson and Quiñones Keber 1983:146). According to Xochipilli's song, this god sings a song for the warriors who will go to Tlalocan (which is a place like Xochitlalpan) where the gods live:

> Now do our friends sing.
> Now through the night the *quetzalcoxcoxtli* sings out
> He's the red Centeotl.
> This means, the sun has shone, the day has dawned. Now there is singing; now Centeotl, the quetzalcoxcoxtli, sings
> Just the lord of the bells with the thigh-skin face paint will yet hear my song
> Cipactonal will yet hear my song.
> This means, let our song be heard here, let the people who are here hear it.
> I bid my farewell to Tlalocan's providers.
>
> This means, I take my leave of the *tlaloque tlamacazque*. Now I go to my home.
> I bid my farewell to Tlalocan's providers. (Sahagún 1997b:139–40)[13]

Xochipilli here appears as Centeotl, god of maize, and his *nahualli*, an eagle-like *quetzalcoxcoxtli*. Just like the singer of Nahua poetry travels from the sky to bring down the songs, Xochipilli comes to the earth from Tlalocan to sing in order to help the sun rise through the night. After the sunrise, he still sings to the people on the earth who provide for the sky, that is to say, the warriors who feed the sun with their blood. Then, Xochipilli goes back to his home. Xochipilli's song helps illuminate the roles of the god as depicted on the huehuetl. He appears in the guise of quetzalcoxcoxtli and sings for the jaguar and eagle soldiers who were guarding or helping the present sun, Nahui Ollin. All the images of the huehuetl, then, could be read as follows: the jaguar and eagle warriors on earth who were sacrificed in the war go up to the sky and guard the present world-sun, Nahui Ollin, and the god of songs and music, Xochipilli, sings to encourage the warriors to accomplish their mission.

The gods created the world and nourished the humans. The humans feed the sun and earth with their blood and bodies. Nahua songs are an artistic representation of this interdependent relationship between gods and humans. The gods nourish the dead warriors with the flowers of joy and happiness while the living warriors nourish the gods by becoming the flowers through death by war or sacrifice. The following stanzas beautifully describe this Nahua cosmology through the image of the flower:

> Allí están echando brotes
> las flores del cacao,
> las flores de maíz tostado:
> en México van medrando,
> están abriendo corola.
>
> Es allí y sólo allí
> el sitio de la realeza:
> los águilas y los tigres
> están medrando,
> están abriendo corola. (*Romances* 1993, 10, 3–4)

There they are putting forth bud
the cocoa flowers,
the flowers of sunburned corn:
In Mexico they are growing,
they are opening their petals.

There and only there is
the place of the royalty:
The eagles and the tigers
are growing,
they are opening their petals. (author's translation)

In the first stanza, the poet describes the work that the gods do for the humans. They grow the cacao and maize flowers, which are the most important staples in indigenous society, to nourish the humans. In the second stanza, just as these flowers bloom on earth and provide food for humans, the warriors grow and open their hearts for the gods as nourishment. These two stanzas demonstrate how Nahua poetics clearly reflect a Nahua cosmological view in which the gods nourish the humans as much as the humans nourish the gods.

Nahua song-poetry is closely related to the indigenous cosmological perception of the universe. The gods created the flowers in the sky as compensation for the nourishment provided through death by war or sacrifice, and the poet on earth travels there and brings back the flowers, which then turn into songs on earth. With these songs, the poet soothes the sadness and pain of the Nahua nobles whose fellows have died. Thus, Nahua songs serve the living nobles, who are future sacrificial warriors, as spiritual nourishment. Nahua song practice is, then, to some extent an act to temporarily create a flower land (Xochitlalpan) on earth for the nobles who will soon make the same sacrifice as their fellow warriors. Regardless of their regional origin, Nahua songs corroborate this mutual relationship between gods and humans. The songs attributed to Nezahualcoyotl are no exception to this phenomenon. Like the other songs, these songs claim that they come from the house of the sun god in the sky and have the purpose of consoling the nobles so that they may better serve their god. In this sense, Nezahualcoyotl's poems can hardly be separated from the others, or vice versa.

CHAPTER SEVEN

A Reinterpretation of Nahua Poetic Themes

Ephemerality, War and Sacrifice, and Nezahualcoyotl

From the colonial period to the present, the lamentation of the transitory nature of earthly life has been considered one of the primary topics of Nahua poetry. Two colonial chroniclers, don Fernando de Alva Ixtlilxochitl and Fray Juan de Torquemada, initiated this interpretive tradition in their discussion of several song fragments that they attributed to Nezahualcoyotl in their chronicles. In these poems, Nezahualcoyotl compares the brevity of earthly life, especially the shortness of the Aztec empire, with the temporal existence of flowers. Indeed, just like these songs allegedly by Nezahualcoyotl, many songs in *Cantares Mexicanos* (1985) and *Romances de los señores de la Nueva España* (1993) compare the brevity of the lives of the rulers and their reigns with that of flowers. Thus, ephemerality clearly constitutes one of the most conspicuous themes in Nahua poetry. Alva Ixtlilxochitl and Torquemada, however, seriously misinterpreted the Nahua concept of ephemerality by separating the songs from the original historical context in which they were composed and performed. According to these chroniclers, Nezahualcoyotl lamented the ephemerality of earthly life, which withers like the flower, and with this insight he anticipated the inevitable destruction of his kingdom that would result from the Spanish conquest. Modern scholars of Nahua poetry such as Miguel León-Portilla continue to subscribe to Alva Ixtlilxochitl's and Torquemada's interpretation of ephemerality in Nahua poetry. These scholars present ephemerality as clear evidence of the song composers' (tlamatinime) worldview: they saw the Aztec world as deeply flawed, and they expressed their disdain for the Mexica practices of war and sacrifice through peaceful songs that bemoan the ephemerality of earthly life. In this chapter, however, I argue that the notion of ephemerality did not serve as a prophecy, nor was it understood as a peaceful concept in opposition to the war-mongering Mexica. Rather, the Nahuas, regardless of their regional and political affiliation, understood the notion of ephemerality as a universal principle consonant with the repeated cycle of creation and destruction of the world in Mesoamerican origin myths and with the cosmological significance of ritual wars and human sacrifice. In fact, I would argue that the practices of ritual war and human sacrifice are the more important themes of Nahua poetry.

Ephemerality, Nezahualcoyotl, and Nahua Poetics

Alva Ixtlilxochitl reproduces a song fragment that expresses the ephemerality of earthly life under the chapter title: "Que trata de algunos profecías y dichos que dijo el rey Nezahualcoyotl" (That Deals with Some Prophecies and Maxims That the King Nezahualcoyotl Said). With this song, the Texcoca chronicler tries to show how Nezahualcoyotl anticipated the conquest:

> Entre los cantos que compuso el rey Nezahualcoyotzin, donde más a la clara dijo algunas sentencias, como a modo de profecías, que muy a la clara en nuestros tiempos se han cumplido y visto, fueron los que se intitulan Xompancuícatl que significa canto de la primavera, las cuales se cantaron en la fiesta y convites del estreno de sus grandes palacios, que empieza el uno así: Tlacxoconcaquican hani Nezahualcoyotzin etcetera, que traducidas a nuestro vulgar castellano, conforme al propio y verdadero sentido, quieren decir: "Oíd lo que dice el rey Nezahualcoyotzin en sus lamentaciones sobre las calamidades y persecuciones que han de padecer sus reinos y señoríos." Ido que seas de esta presente vida a la otra, oh rey Yoyontzin, vendrá tiempo que serán deshechos y destrozados tus vasallos, quedando todas tus cosas en las tinieblas del olvido: entonces de verdad, no estará en tu mano el señorío y mando sino en la de Dios. Y entró [sic, por "en otro"] dijo "entonces serán las aflicciones, las miserias y persecuciones que padecerán tus hijos y nietos; y llorosos se acordarán de ti, viendo que los dejaste huérfanos en servicio de otros estraños en su misma patria Acolihuacan; porque en esto vienen a parar los mandos, imperios y señoríos, que duran poco y son de poca estabilidad. Lo de esta vida es prestado, que un instante lo hemos de dejar como otros lo han dejado; pues los señores Zihuapantzin, Acolnahuacatzin y Quauhtzontezoma, que siempre te acompañaban, ya no los ves en estos breves gustos." (Alva Ixtlilxochitl 1997, 2:132–33)

> In the songs that the king Nezahualcoyotl composed, he clearly said some sentences, in the way of prophecies, which have been fulfilled and seen in our times. These songs are entitled Xompancuícatl, which means "song of spring," and they were sung at the feasts and banquets

of the premiere of their large palaces. One song begins like this: Tlacxoconcaquican hani Nezahualcoyotzin, etc., which, translated to our vernacular Spanish according to their own and true sense, means: "listen to what the king Nezahualcoyotzin says in his lamentations on the calamities and persecutions that his kingdoms and territories will suffer." Although you may leave this life for the other, oh king Yoyontzin, a time will come when your vassals will be undone and destroyed, leaving all your things in the darkness of oblivion: then truly, your kingdom and command will not be in your hand but in that of God. And in another song he said "then there will be afflictions, miseries and persecutions that your sons and grandsons will suffer; and they will sorrowfully remember you, seeing that you left them orphans in the service of other strangers in their own native land Acolhuacan; because in this comes to an end the power, empires, and dominions that last a short while and have little stability. The things of this present life are borrowed and in an instant we will have to leave them as others have left them; thus the nobles Zihuapantzin, Acolnahuacatzin and Quauhtzontezoma, who always accompanied you, you no longer see them in these brief pleasures." (author's translation)

The mode of this song is very similar to that of the orphan or bereavement song that I examined in chapter 6. According to Alva Ixtlilxochitl, this song was sung in Nezahualcoyotl's palace, and Nezahualcoyotl himself is the poet who laments the fleeting nature of life, the demise of kingdoms, and the loss of political dominion. Torquemada presents another song fragment attributed to Nezahualcoyotl that also shows the same mode of Nahua song:

> Después de haber comido, mandó [Nezahualcoyotl] a sus cantores, que viniesen a regocijar los estrenos, y finales de la fiesta; y como era hombre de grande entendimiento, y mucha, y profunda consideración, viendo tanto rey, y señores, y capitanes valerosos juntos, y que las cosas de esta vida se acaban, quiso dárselo a entender a todos, para que movidos de esta consideración, usasen de ellas, como de censo, que es al quitar, y mandó a sus cantores, que cantasen un cantar, que el mismo había compuesto, que comenzaba así: *Xochitl mamani in huehuetitlan*, etc. que quiere decir: entre las coposas, y sabinas, hay frescas y olorosas flores, y prosiguiendo adelante, dice: que aunque por algún tiempo están frescas y vistosas, llegan a sazón, que se marchitan, y secan. Iba prosiguiendo en decir, que todos los presentes, habían de acabar, y no habían de tornar a reinar; y que todas sus grandezas, habían de tener fin, y que sus tesoros, habían de ser poseídos de otros; y que no habían de volver a gozar de esto, que una vez dejasen, y los que habían comenzado a comer con gusto, fenecieron la fiesta con

lágrimas, oyendo las palabras del cantar, y viendo ser así verdad, lo que decía. (Torquemada 1975, 1:156)

After having eaten, he [Nezahualcoyotl] ordered his singers to come to celebrate the beginning and ending of the feast; and, as he was a man of good prudence and much and deep consideration and seeing so many kings, nobles, and valiant captains together, he wanted all the attendees to understand that the things of this life end and to be moved by this consideration so that they would use them like the census. And he ordered his singers to sing a song that he himself had composed and began like this: Xochitl mamani in huehuetitlan, etc., which means: "among the trees and junipers, there are fresh and fragrant flowers," and continuing ahead, it says that although for some time they are fresh and bright, they become ripe, they wither, and dry up. He went on to say that all the attendees would die and would not reign again; and that all their grandeur would have an end, and that their treasures would be possessed by others; and that they would not enjoy this again after leaving it. And those who had begun to eat with pleasure finished the feast with tears, hearing the words of the song and seeing that what he said was true. (author's translation)

According to the historical context of this song fragment reproduced by Torquemada, it was composed by Nezahualcoyotl after he finished constructing his palace in Texcoco. He invited many kings and captains from all over pre-Hispanic Mexico for an opening banquet and asked singers to sing his song. Like the song attributed to Nezahualcoyotl by Alva Ixtlilxochitl, this song in Torquemada's chronicle also concerns the transitory duration of the empire that he just established and of his reign over it. However, a comparison between the two songs and one from *Cantares*, upon which they may be based, requires a very different interpretation of ephemerality in Nahua songs. I present the following song for comparison with songs attributed to Nezahualcoyotl by Alva Ixtlilxochitl and Torquemada because it is entitled "Icuic Nezahualcoyotzin" (Song of Nezahualcoyotl), and its mode and content are almost the same as those of the two songs presented by the chroniclers:

1. I come to set up our drum, prompting eagle jaguars to dance. Now that you've departed, song flowers arise. I am seeking songs to adorn us.
2. O prince, O Nezahualcoyotl, you've departed for the Dead Land, the Place Unknown, beyond.
3. "I, Nezahualcoyotl, weep. Alas, how is it that I go to my destruction in the Dead Land? O spirit that I leave behind me, O Life Giver, by your command I go to my destruction.

4. "How will it endure, this land of Acolhuacan? Will you in time disperse your vassals, O Spirit that I leave behind me?
5. Songs alone are our adornment, and He destroys them, our paintings, the princes. Oh, let there be pleasure! Earth is no one's home. We must leave these delicious flowers."
6. No one when he's gone can enjoy your riches, O Life Giver. Is my heart unaware that you came to borrow them just briefly, O Nezahualcoyotl? Here there is no second time. And if on earth there is no second time, earth is no longer His home. I'm a singer, and I weep, recalling Nezahualcoyotl.
7. Flowers have arrived. He's here: it's God Life Giver. Ah, I weep, recalling Nezahualcoyotl. (*Cantares* 1985, 46, 1–7)

Alva Ixtlilxochitl and Torquemada seem to select the third, fourth, and fifth stanzas and to attribute them to Nezahualcoyotl, thinking that only those stanzas were composed by this Texcoca king. Just like in the songs attributed to him in the chronicles of Alva Ixtlilxochitl and Torquemada, in this song from *Cantares*, Nezahualcoyotl narrates his own demise, the demise of his fellow rulers, and the destruction of his kingdom, Acolhuacan, that is to say, Texcoco. This song from *Cantares*, however, conveys a very different notion of ephemerality from that of the two previous songs from the chronicles. First of all, Nezahualcoyotl as narrator of the three stanzas does not predict any sort of future destruction, but rather recounts it as a fact and a universal rule. He is perfectly aware that it is the god who destroys the rulers and their precious belongings, such as paintings, songs, and even their kingdoms. Thus, he clearly asserts that "Earth is no one's home. We must leave these delicious flowers." However, the poetically created Nezahualcoyotl in these stanzas does not consider this destruction a lament, but a pleasure ("Oh, let there be pleasure!") because he has fulfilled the mission assigned to him by god and thus can go to the god's house where everything is everlasting. The poet of the song in the last two stanzas (6–7) recalls Nezahualcoyotl as a model ancestor who teaches him a good lesson in this transitory, earthly life. The poet learns from Nezahualcoyotl's destruction that he can possesses his riches only briefly while on earth, as Nezahualcoyotl did: as this king cannot reclaim his riches twice on earth ("Here there is no second time"), neither can the poet. From this lesson, the poet finds out that earth is not the god's home ("earth is no longer His home"), because there is no second time on earth; that is, there is no eternal life on earth. The poet weeps to recall the dead Nezahualcoyotl, and through his exemplary life the poet can understand god's will. Here the poet's act of weeping does not necessarily refer to a real but rather a spiritual action that accesses the world of the dead. Alva Ixtlilxochitl and Torquemada appropriated the Nahua notion of ephemerality from the original context of native poetry and converted it into a lamentation, and eventually into an anticipation of the conquest. The original song of *Cantares*, however, says nothing about Nezahualcoyotl's kingdom and his vassals falling under the power of strangers. Nor does it say that his riches and treasures would be owned by others. On the contrary, in the poem from *Cantares*, Nezahualcoyotl clearly states that he, his fellows, and his descendants as well as those who would inherit their riches, treasures, and kingdoms would be destroyed just like themselves. Many other songs from both *Cantares* and *Romances* corroborate this universal Mesoamerican message.[1]

As the comparison between forged songs and original songs in Nahuatl demonstrates, Alva Ixtlilxochitl, Torquemada, and later historians and literary critics transformed Nezahualcoyotl's notion of ephemerality into a prophecy of the conquest. There is also other evidence that the anticipation of the conquest was a colonial invention. Don Carlos Ometochtzin Chichimecatecuhtli, the son of Nezahualpilli, grandson of Nezahualcoyotl, and ruler of Texcoco, clearly rejected his grandfather's alleged anticipation of the conquest. According to the testimonies of the witnesses who accused Ometochtzin of idolatry in 1539, Ometochtzin asserted that his father, Nezahualpilli, and his grandfather, Nezahualcoyotl, never anticipated the conquest nor the arrival of Christianity:

> Mirá, oye, que mi agüelo Nezahualcoyotl y mi padre Nezahualpilli ninguna cosa nos dixieron cuando murieron ni nombraron á ningunos ni quienes habían de venir; entiende hermano que mi agüelo y mi padre miraban á todas partes, atrás y delante—como si dixiese, sabían lo pasado é por venir y sabían lo que se había de hacer en largos tiempos y lo que se hizo, como dicen los padres é nombraron los profetas—que de verdad te digo que profetas fueron mi agüelo y mi padre que sabían lo que se había de hacer y lo que estaba hecho; por tanto hermano, entiéndeme, y ninguno ponga su corazón en esta ley de Dios é Divinidad. (*Proceso inquisitorial del cacique de Tetzcoco* 1980:40)

> Look, listen, my grandfather Nezahualcoyotl and my father Nezahualpilli said nothing when they died, nor did they name anybody nor those who would come; understand, brother, that my grandfather and my father observed everywhere, back and forward—as if it were to say, they knew the past and the future and they knew what should be done during long periods of time and what was done, like the priests say and they mentioned the prophets—for truly I tell you that my grandfather and my father were prophets who knew what should be done and what was done; therefore, brother, understand me, and let no one set his heart on this law of God and Divinity. (author's translation)

This testimony of Ometochtzin clearly contradicts the image of Nezahualcoyotl as a prophet that Alva Ixtlilxochitl and Torquemada promoted. Rather, the image of Nezahualcoyotl described here seems to be very similar to that conveyed in the song "Icuic Nezahualcoyotl" (Song of Nezahualcoyotl) because Nezahualcoyotl serves to encourage his descendant, Ometochtzin, to follow the native tradition just as he does the poet of the song.

Ephemerality Reexamined: Nezahualcoyotl, Tlamatinime, and León-Portilla

Many of the poems attributed to Nezahualcoyotl and published by Garibay and León-Portilla treat the theme of ephemerality. Some of them have been repeatedly quoted as among the most poignant examples of an indigenous core philosophy:

> I, Nezahualcoyotl, ask this:
> Is it true one really lives on the Herat?
> Not forever on earth,
> Only a little while here.
> Though it be jade it falls apart,
> Though it be gold it wears away,
> Though it be quetzal plumage it is torn asunder.
> Not forever on earth,
> Only a little while here. (*Cantares* 1985:f. 17r, in León-Portilla 1992b:80)

Here, the poet first discerns the ephemerality of human life, and then he expresses his insight through beautiful images and metaphors. Just as the most precious and durable things such as jade and gold are worn out, everything on earth including the poet himself is fleeting and transitory. The next poem also expresses the ephemerality of earthly life:

> Like a painting
> We will be erased.
> Like a flower,
> We will dry up
> Here on earth.
> Like plumed vestments of the precious bird,
> That precious bird with the agile neck,
> We will come to an end...
>
> Think on this, O lords,
> Eagles and tigers,
> Though you be of jade,
> Though you be of gold,
> You also will go there,

> To the place of the fleshless.
> We will have to disappear,
> No one can remain. (*Romances* 1993:ff. 35r–36r, in León-Portilla
>   1992b:80–81)

This poem uses more indigenous similes, such as comparisons with a tlacuilolli (painting or pictorial book) and *quetzalli* (quetzal feather), to express the ephemerality of life. In addition, it conveys a more generalized notion of ephemerality in that the insight of the poet is not that of an individual "I," but rather a collective "we," who know that they will go to the house of the gods after this ephemeral life.

As a literary critic, León-Portilla appears very perceptive, and his interpretations of ephemerality in Nahua poems seem persuasive. He considers ephemerality to be the most important concept in understanding Nahua poetics (1996:120–25). Even though the Nahua poets perceive ephemerality in everything on earth, they consider their poems, in xochitl in cuicatl, the only true or everlasting things: "Live and blossom here on earth. As you move, shaking, flowers fall. Eternal are flowers, eternal the songs that I, the singer, lift" (*Cantares* 1985, 20, 4). According to León-Portilla (1963:79), for the Nahua poets, in xochitl in cuicatl is eternal because it originates from the divine and "thus poetry as a vehicle of metaphysical expression relying on metaphors, is an attempt to vitiate the transitoriness of earthly things, the dream of tlaltícpac." At first glance, this appears to be a compelling interpretation of ephemerality, but León-Portilla's reluctance to view the concept of ephemerality within the context of actual Nahua religion and philosophy is highly problematic.

León-Portilla argues that the tlamatinime (wise men) perceived earthly life and worldly things as transitory and continuously changing. From this perspective, they questioned the veracity of everything in the world, including their own existence. According to León-Portilla (1992a:163–68), this concern of the tlamatinime is evidence that they differed from the dominant militaristic, sanguinary culture. I would argue, however, that perceiving the world and life as transitory is not unique to the tlamatinime, but rather constitutes a belief common to all the Nahuas. They knew that they would be destroyed, just as the previous suns had been destroyed. For them life on earth was uncertain, brief, and transitory. The Nahua priests and rulers were certainly aware of the possible termination of the fifth sun. The Mexica ruler declared in his inauguration that his position was borrowed from the god. According to the *Florentine Codex*, a great nobleman or priest addressed the newly inaugurated king:

> Be especially welcomed. Pay special attention. Perhaps it is our desert, our merit, that we dream, that we see [only] in dreams that which our lord placeth upon thee, wisheth upon thee—fame, honor; that he

leaveth not that which he hath cherished; perhaps it is separated from thee; perhaps he seeketh a replacement for thee.... Perhaps just for a little while thou dreamest, thou seekest in dream. Perhaps he just passeth his glory, his honor before thy face. And perhaps he just causeth thee to smell—perhaps he just passeth before thy lips—his freshness, his tenderness, his sweetness, his fragrance, his heat, his warmth, which come from him, the wealth of him by whom we live. (*Florentine Codex* 1950–1982, 6:51–52)

The Mexica chronicler Alvarado Tezozomoc also records how the Mexica rulers perceived their role as stewards in the service of god. When the Mexica king Tizoc was crowned, Nezahualcoyotl and Totoquihuaztli advised the king: "Dijéronle: mirad que no es vuestro asiento ni silla, sino de ellos, que de prestado es, y será vuelto a cuyo es, que no habeis de permanecer para siempre jamás, y esta la teneis como arrendada" (They told him: consider that it is not your seat nor throne, but theirs, which is borrowed and will be returned to its owner, and that you will never stay forever, and you only rented it) (1987:439). The Mexica rulers who, according to León-Portilla, promoted the politics of militarism are no different from the tlamatinime. Just as the tlamatinime perceived life as transitory, the Mexica rulers surely understood that their position was to be equally fleeting.

As León-Portilla correctly points out, ephemerality is one of the most notable themes in the songs. He discusses several other poets who treat topics very similar to those of the songs attributed to Nezahualcoyotl: Tecayehuatzin and Ayocuan of Huexotzinco, Totoquihuaztli of Tlacopan, and Tochihuitzin of Tenochtitlan (1996:120).[2] León-Portilla presents all of these poets as tlamatinime whose view of life as brief and transitory contrasted sharply with the dominant Mexica philosophy. This contrast, however, is not consistent with the historical and political context in which each of these rulers lived. As explained before, Totoquihuaztli maintained a close political relationship with the Mexica and conquered many neighboring cities in alliance with them. According to Fray Diego Durán (1994:191), this Tlacopaneca king even participated in human sacrifice with the Mexica king. Thus, to separate him from the Mexica in terms of his political and religious perspectives is misleading.[3]

In addition, there is no evidence to suggest that the Mexica noble Tochihuitzin maintained different philosophical beliefs from his fellow Mexica. León-Portilla's interpretation of the poem attributed to Tochihuitzin may be influenced by the fact that in the original documents it was incorporated into a Huexotzinca piece.[4] The Mexica Tochihuitzin, however, seems to have subscribed to the practices and beliefs of the dominant religion, politics, and culture of Tenochtitlan. Even according to the biographical information provided by León-Portilla (1992b:150–52), Tochihuitzin made a contribution to the expansion of the Mexica territory by participating in the conquests of neighboring cities as a son of the great conqueror Itzcoatl and a nephew and son-in-law of Tlacaelel. Thus, Tochihuitzin cannot truly be distinguished from any other Mexica leader, including Nezahualcoyotl, who was his cousin as well as a political ally of his father, Itzcoatl. In this context, the following song attributed to Tochihuitzin by León-Portilla naturally conveys the same concept of ephemerality presented in Nezahualcoyotl's poems:

> We only rise from sleep,
> We come only to dream,
> it is not true, it is not true,
> that we come on earth to live.
> As an herb in springtime,
> so is our nature.
> Our hearts give birth, make sprout,
> the flowers of our flesh.
> Some open their corollas,
> then they become dry. (*Cantares* 1985:f.14v, in León-Portilla
>   1992b:153)

I would argue that the theme of ephemerality in Nahua poetry is not limited to a particular area or to particular poets, but rather is common to all indigenous compositions regardless of the political affiliation in central Mexico of their alleged authors. One of the anonymous Huexotzinca songs expresses the same concept of ephemerality and uses the same metaphors that appear in the poems attributed to Nezahualcoyotl by Garibay and León-Portilla: "Create them, you princes, you Huexotzincans! And though they're jades, and though they're gold, they'll pass away to the place where all are shorn, the Place Unknown. None will be left" (*Cantares* 1985, 18, 37). Even the Mexica songs that are not attributed to Tochihuitzin show their ephemeral sensibility toward earthly life. Their metaphors are different from those of the previous songs, but they convey the same concept:

> In but a day we're gone, in but a night we're shorn on earth. And as for having come to know each other, this we merely borrow here on earth. (*Cantares* 1985, 42, 7)

> Let them all be borrowed! Gold drums are roaring, pealing, in this mixcoacalli! Not forever on earth can a man be a lord. Lordship, honor, and nobility are not forever, O princes. Briefly, briefly do we live on earth. (*Cantares* 1985, 39, 2)

One of the Tepechpan songs that Garibay and León-Portilla attribute to Cuacuauhtzin also describes the ephemerality of life on earth.[5] And here again, the metaphors the poet uses are the same as those that appear in the poems inspired by Nezahualcoyotl:

> Where would we go
> That we never have to die?
> Though I be precious stone,
> Though I be gold,
> I will be dissolved,
> There in the crucible melted down,
> I have only my life,
> I, Cuacuahtzin, I am dispossessed. (*Romances* 1993:ff. 26–27v,
>   in León-Portilla 1992b:109)

This same song is also collected in the other song text, *Cantares*, but is classified as a Chalca piece (*Cantares* 1985, 62, 25). Again, this phenomenon cannot be explained by some sectarian or partisan relationship between the Chalca and the Tepechpan ruler Cuacuauhtzin, but rather by the common and popular cultural background that manifests itself in the shared notion of ephemerality expressed through poetry among the city-states in central Mexico. The awareness of the ephemerality of earthly life is found not only in the songs attributed to Nezahualcoyotl and those of the Huexotzinca and Chalca, but also in the songs of the Mexica. Singing the brevity of life was a popular practice among the city-states in central Mexico, and it further supports the argument that they shared a common cultural heritage.

War and Sacrifice in In xochitl in cuicatl

Rather than peace and beauty, war and sacrifice are the major topics in Nahua poetry. As stated before, war was an essential means for the indigenous rulers in central Mexico to obtain captives. They would then nourish the gods with the blood and hearts of the captives so that the universe could continue. Nahua songs reflect this worldview in various ways. They praise war, battles, conquests, and their conquerors.[6] They praise *yaomiquiliztli* (war death), *xochimiquiliztli* (flower death), and *itzmiquiliztli* (obsidian-knife death), and they describe the soldiers who die in these deaths as precious *xochitl* (flowers). All these religious-militaristic activities have been associated primarily with the Mexica imperialist tradition. However, Nahua songs, regardless of their regional origin, clearly contain all these militaristic ideas.

The following stanza from Chalco perfectly reflects this religious-militaristic theme:

> Look south and east! Rouse yourself where flood and blazes are spreading, where sovereignty, empire, pure flowers, are won. A plume tassel is

not obtained without cause. With sword and shield, on the battlefields of earth, you earn the pure flowers that you covet, that you want, my friends, that He enables you to earn, that He bestows on you: He, the Ever Present, the Ever Near. (*Cantares* 1985, 6, 4)

The poet introduces the war not only as a most important political endeavor that allows the expansion of territory, but also as a religious activity that enables the natives to acquire captives to sacrifice to their god. Thus, the poet eagerly encourages his friends to participate in war in order to gain captives, or pure flowers, with the help of their god. However, obtaining captives requires not only the help of god but also their own efforts: "Vainly do you covet what you seek, my friend: how can you win the pure flowers if you do not give yourself to war? With your shoulders and your sweat you earn the pure flowers: the tearful war-wailing He enables you to earn: He the Ever present, the Ever near" (*Cantares* 1985, 6, 5). In addition, this stanza reveals a rather surprising dimension to the concept of captivity: if one wishes to catch a captive, he throws himself into the war, which means that he may acquire a pure flower, but at the same time he may become the pure flower of others. Thus, the battlefield is a joyful place for both captors and captives. The next stanza from Tenochtitlan also describes this idea in detail:

> There! The blaze is seething, stirring. Honor is won, shield fame is won. Lords are strewn at the place of the bells.
> They'll never tire, these war flowers. They're massing ah! At the flood's edge.
> These jaguar flowers, these shields flowers, are blossoming. Lords are strewn at the place of the bells.
> There! Jaguar cacao flowers are massed at the place of the sprinkling down, the field! They are diffusing fragrance in our mist. Who does not desire them? They're praise. They're honor.
> Restless are the flowers. Restless ones are pleasures. Heart flowers are created.
> There! On the field of battle princes are born. Ah! They're praise. They're honor. (*Cantares* 1985, 24, 3–6)

The stanzas praise the tireless and restless efforts of warriors in the battlefield. The warriors who are represented by war flowers (*yaoxochitl*), jaguar flowers (*oceloxochitl*), and shield flowers (*chimalxochitl*) are spread over the battlefield as if it were a field in bloom. There, these warriors disperse like flowers, diffuse their fragrance, and finally they are converted into heart flowers (*yolloxochitl*), which actually represent captives who die on the battlefield or who will be dedicated to the gods by having their hearts opened in a sacrificial death ceremony. The captives are blissful and fortunate because they are "praise" and "honor" for the god. For the Mexica, the battlefield is an earthly paradise where pleasure and happiness are acquired.

The people of central Mexico considered participating in war and acquiring captives admirable, but the question of how to die was also a serious matter for them. They had seemingly contradictory desires: they wanted either to gain war captives to sacrifice or become war captives to be sacrificed to the gods. The next stanza from Huexotzinco, for example, promotes both *yaoxochimiquiliztli* (war-flower death) and *itzmiquiliztli* (obsidian-knife death):

> There, in battle, where war begins, upon that field, lords are smoking, whirling, twisting due to flower war death, you lords and princes! And they're Chichimecs!
> Let my heart be not afraid upon that field. I crave knife death. Our hearts want war death. (*Cantares* 1985, 16, 4–5)

The songs from the city-states of the Aztec empire also extol sacrificial death:

> I grieve, I weep. What good is this? The shield flowers are carried away, they're sent aloft. Ah, where can I find what my heart desires?
> Incomparable war death! Incomparable flower death! Life Giver has blessed it. Ah, where can I find what my heart desires? (*Cantares* 1985, 31, 5)

Similar to many other songs, those attributed to Nezahualcoyotl also promote war and flower death. The following song, for example, reflects the image of this king as a great warrior:[7]

> ¡Esmeraldas, oro
> tus flores, oh dios!
>
> Sólo tu riqueza,
> oh por quien se vive,
> la muerte al filo de obsidiana,
> la muerte en guerra.
>
> Con muerte en guerra
> os daréis a conocer.
>
> Al borde de la guerra, cerca de la hoguera
> os dais a conocer.
>
> Polvo de escudo se tiende,
> niebla de dardos se tiende.

¿Acaso en verdad
es lugar a darse a conocer
el sitio del misterio?

Sólo el renombre.
el señorío
muere en la guerra:
un poco se lleva hacia
el sitio de los descorporizados. (*Romances* 1993, 1, 54)

Emeralds, gold
your flowers, oh God!

Only your wealth,
oh Life Giver,
the death by the edge of obsidian knife,
the death in war.

With death in war
you will come to know.

At the edge of the war, near the fire
you bring yourselves to light.

Dust from a shield spreads itself,
fog from darts spreads itself.

Perhaps truly
It is an opportunity to come to know
the place of the mystery?

Only the fame.
The power
dies in war:
A little is carried toward
the place of the disembodied. (author's translation)

This song synthesizes all the ideas of the Nahuas regarding war and sacrifice. The poet begins to describe warriors as the flowers of god and praises their death, which is the only richness or sustenance of god. The death, here, is not a normal death but rather itzmiquiliztli (obsidian-knife death) and yaomiquiliztli (war death). The first refers to death in religious ceremonies in which Nahua priests take out the heart of the sacrificed and offer it to the sun as nourishment. The second refers to death on the battlefield. The poet asserts that only with these deaths are the victims able to know the gods and to go to the land of the gods.

To better understand the exaltation of war and sacrificial death in Nahua poetry, we must examine the "promised war," that is, the *xochiyaoyotl* (flower war), which was conducted among the city-states in the Basin of Mexico and the Valley of Puebla-Tlaxcala. León-Portilla insists that the practice of conducting wars such as the xochiyaoyotl was introduced by Tlacaelel to provide captives to Huitzilopochtli. Don Domingo de San Antón Muñón Chimalpahin Cuauhtlehuanitzin (1998, 2:65) records, however, that there occurred various flower wars between the Chalca and the Mexica even much earlier than Tlacaelel's era.[8] In the beginning, both sides released their captives after the war, but from 1415 on they began to sacrifice the captives. This flower war was not exclusive to the Mexica or Chalca, however. It appears to have been a very important and popular practice among the city-states in central Mexico. Chimalpahin (1998, 2:37) records that even the cities within the Chalca area practiced the flower war. According to him, one of the Chalca ethnic groups, the Tlacochcalca, conducted such wars against the other Chalca group, the Acxoteca, in 1324. The flower war between the three main allies of the Aztec empire (Tenochtitlan, Texcoco, and Tlacopan) and other city-states (primarily, Huexotzinco, Tlaxcala, and Cholula) was conducted by mutual agreement of these nations for their mutual benefit. They designated the time and place for the war, and each side needed to take captives for sacrifices to their respective gods—Huitzilopochtli, for instance, for the Aztec allies, and Camaxtli for the Tlaxcalteca.[9] The most precious captives for the Aztecs, Huexotzinca, Tlaxcalteca, and Cholulteca were those obtained from this war. By mutual consent this flower war seems to have turned into real war by the end of the fifteenth century (Isaac 1983:427), but the religious purpose still continued despite the intensified hostility among these city-states.

The Mexica chronicler Alvarado Tezozomoc records that the Mexica ruler Ahuitzotl invited the enemy nobles of Huexotzinco, Cholula, and Tlaxcala to his coronation ceremony.[10] The nobles of Huexotzinco and Cholula gladly came to attend, and they enjoyed dancing with the Mexica nobles (Alvarado Tezozomoc 1987:476–78). Alvarado Tezozomoc also records that Moctezuma Xocoyotl sent his messengers to neighboring enemy city-states in order to invite them to a religious ceremony in Tenochtitlan. The messengers were told to invite neighboring nobles in the following way:

> Dijeron los mexicanos: señor nuestro, nuestra embajada es, que el rey nuevo de México, y todos los demás principales, os envían muchos saludos, y os ruegan, que para que vean la manera de que se hace la coronación, fiesta, alegrías y sacrificios á los dioses, se vayan á holgar algunos días, dejando aparte enemistades y guerras civiles entre nosotros, como

> es el *Xuchiyaoyotl*, que eso es con esfuerzo y valiente de los unos y los otros, salvo estas fiestas y convite. (Alvarado Tezozomoc 1987:591)

> The Mexica said: our lord, our embassy is, that the new king of Mexico-Tenochtitlan and all the other nobles, send you many greetings, and they beg you to come to see the way that the coronation, feast, joys and sacrifices to the gods are conducted, and to come to enjoy yourselves for several days, leaving aside enmities and civil wars between us such as the Xochiyaoyotl, which is with the effort and bravery of each side, except in these feasts and banquets. (author's translation)

All the invited enemy nobles came to Tenochtitlan and enjoyed performing "el areito y mitote con mucha vocería" (the song and dance with much clamor) (Alvarado Tezozomoc 1987:592). The Tlaxcalteca chronicler don Diego Muñoz Camargo records enmity and flower wars between the Mexica and the Tlaxcalteca, but at the same time he states that the Mexica and Tlaxcalteca nobles maintained a respectful political relationship:

> Sin embargo de esto [guerra florida], los señores mexicanos y tezcucanos, en tiempos que ponían treguas por algunas temporadas, enviaban a los señores de Tlaxcalla grandes presentes y dádivas de oro, ropa, cacao, sal y de todas las cosas de que carecían, sin que la gente plebeya lo entendiese, y se saludaban secretamente, guardándose el decoro que se debían. Mas con todos estos trabajos, la orden de su República jamás se dejaba de gobernar con la rectitud de sus costumbres, guardando inviolablemente el culto de sus dioses. (Muñoz Camargo 1986:140)

> In spite of this [flower war], during times of truce the Mexica and Texcoca kings sent the Tlaxcalteca nobles grand presents and gifts of gold, clothes, cocoa, salt, and all the things that they lacked, without the commoners understanding it, and they greeted each other secretly, keeping the decorum that they owed each other. Despite all these relations, the order of their Republic was never left ungoverned by the rectitude of their customs, and maintaining inviolably the worship of their gods. (author's translation)

The participation of the Tlaxcalteca, Huexotzinca, and Cholulteca nobles in the ceremonies of Tenochtitlan also means that they witnessed the Mexica priests sacrifice their people—the Tlaxcalteca, the Huexotzinca, and the Cholulteca. These Mexica enemies willingly came to see their own people die at the hand of their enemy. This does not seem to make much sense from a Western perspective, but it would be completely natural to the Nahuas. It was an honor, because the enemies as well as the hosts blessed the captives for their sacrifice to the gods. Here, we must remember that Nahua poets belonged to the noble class, which in many ways transcended political boundaries. Thus, as the product of the noble class, Nahua poetry promotes sacrificial death and reflects the ideology of sacrifice ascribed to the Mexica and their enemies.

The in xochitl in cuicatl was an artistic activity neither distanced from nor contradicted by the dominant political and religious system in central Mexico. Moreover, the producers of this poetry are indistinguishable in terms of their religious and philosophical perspectives. Rather, Nahua poetry was created and enjoyed by the elite social groups who inherited the religious and cultural traditions of Nahua society. In fact, the groups that belonged to the highest social class of rulers, captains, and priests used Nahua poems as a means of reproducing the existing social order through the educational system. The Aztec noble youth in Tenochtitlan learned Nahua songs from tlamatinime, who according to León-Portilla were sages and poets, at the calmecac where at the same time they learned the martial skills necessary to become warriors. The Nahua noble class also used songs to consolidate their own ideology, which was facilitated by a brotherhood of close friendships established among themselves.

The Texcoca chroniclers Pomar and Alva Ixtlilxochitl represent Nezahualcoyotl as a peaceful poet in order to show that their Texcoca tradition was different from that of the "bloodthirsty" Mexica and similar to that of the European invaders. Later historians and literary critics have uncritically accepted this interpretation. In the nineteenth century, Prescott (n.d.:99–100) interpreted Nezahualcoyotl's ephemerality as an anticipation of the destruction of the "barbarous" Mexica world so that he could justify the European conquest of Mexico. In the twentieth century, Garibay and León-Portilla polished and elaborated the image of Nezahualcoyotl as a peaceful poet in order to highlight the highly civilized and peace-loving nature of Nahua culture and demonstrate that it had not been extinguished by the barbarous and warlike Mexica. But to distinguish between songs composed by Nezahualcoyotl and those of other poets based on differing worldviews is impossible because Nezahualcoyotl supported and participated in the same religious and political institutions as the other poets: Mexica, Huexotzinca, Chalca, Tlaxcalteca, and others. Contrary to much contemporary scholarship, the songs attributed to Nezahualcoyotl confirm that he was a conqueror and warrior who shared the same cultural tradition as other Mexica and indigenous leaders recalled in so many other Nahua songs.

part four

Revising the Study of Nahua Religion

FROM THE BEGINNING OF THE ENCOUNTER BETWEEN EUROPE AND THE Americas, Spanish conquistadores and chroniclers insisted that the main reason they came to the New World was either to convert the barbarous natives to Christianity or to destroy their evil world. In this scheme, a special place is reserved for Nezahualcoyotl, who allegedly distrusted the bloodthirsty gods of the Mexica and somehow intuited a peaceful, unknown or true god, thus prefiguring the arrival of Christianity. The story of Nezahualcoyotl's unknown god first appeared in the chronicles of Spanish writers in the first half of the sixteenth century and was further developed by the Texcoca chroniclers Juan Bautista Pomar in the second half of the same century and don Fernando de Alva Ixtlilxochitl in the beginning of the seventeenth century. Starting in the seventeenth century, Creole patriots began using Nezahualcoyotl's unknown god in conjunction with the Quetzalcoatl–Saint Thomas myth as evidence of apostolic evangelization before the conquest. Even today, many scholars examine Nezahualcoyotl's intuition of the unknown or true god as an essential part of Aztec religion, and some of them present this intuition as a possible alternative to the practice of human sacrifice in Nahua religion. I would argue, however, that European and Europeanized chroniclers invented Nezahualcoyotl's unknown or true god by viewing the pre-Hispanic period from a Judeo-Christian perspective. Contrary to the argument of these scholars, Nezahualcoyotl was a great practitioner and philosopher of Nahua religion.

CHAPTER EIGHT

THE WESTERNIZATION OF NAHUA RELIGION
Nezahualcoyotl's Unknown God

The image of Nezahualcoyotl as a civilized and peaceful king is particularly conspicuous in descriptions of his religious ideas and practice. Some early chroniclers such as the Franciscan missionary Fray Andrés de Olmos describe Nezahualcoyotl as a religious skeptic, and later Spanish chroniclers such as Fray Gerónimo de Mendieta, Fray Juan de Torquemada, and Alonso de Zorita reproduce the same image. Developing this image of Nezahualcoyotl, Texcoca chroniclers such as Juan Bautista Pomar and don Fernando de Alva Ixtlilxochitl argue that Nezahualcoyotl intuited the existence of an unknown, true god, and he prohibited the practice of human sacrifice in his city. These Texcoca chroniclers interpret Nezahualcoyotl's intuition of this god and his peaceful religious practice not only as a clear contrast to the Mexica who, according to the chroniclers, dedicated themselves to war and human sacrifice, but also as a precursor to Christianity even before the conquest. The image of Nezahualcoyotl as a Christian-like civilized and peaceful king has predominated in both literary and historical texts from the colonial times to the present. Among them, worth mentioning are the seventeenth-century chronicles of don Carlos de Sigüenza y Góngora (1995), the histories of don Mariano Fernández de Echeverría y Veytia (1944) and Father Francisco Javier Clavijero (1991) in the eighteenth century, the work of William H. Prescott (n.d.) in the nineteenth century, and the writings of Francis Gillmor (1983), José María Vigil (1957), Miguel León-Portilla (1972, 1992a:184), and José Luis Martínez (1996) in the twentieth century. However, the religious system that Nezahualcoyotl instituted in his city of Texcoco and the historical context in which Nezahualcoyotl allegedly intuited the unknown god and built a temple to worship him do not corroborate the image of Nezahualcoyotl as a revolutionary opposed to the traditional practices of indigenous religion. In addition, the Nahua songs attributed to Nezahualcoyotl that Pomar and Alva Ixtlilxochitl present as clear evidence of his intuition of the unknown god do not support the idea that he was a revolutionary religious skeptic. On the contrary, they indicate that he was a symbolic figure of traditional indigenous religion.

The Foundation of Nezahualcoyotl's Unknown or True God

The complete story of the peaceful poet-king Nezahualcoyotl appears mostly in Texcoca sources: an anonymous text titled "La guerra de Chalco y sucesos posteriores hasta la muerte de Nezahualcoyotzin" (Anonymous 1997), Juan Bautista Pomar's *Relación geográfica de Texcoco* (1993), and Alva Ixtlilxochitl's works (1997). As mentioned earlier, the first chronicler to record the story, however, was a Franciscan, Fray Andrés de Olmos. Mendieta (1971:83) and Torquemada (1975, 2:80) both use Olmos as a source and include almost identical versions of the story. The following passage is from Mendieta's version entitled

> **De lo que un señor de Tezcuco sintió acerca de sus dioses, con otras cosas:**
> De lo que arriba se ha tratado, bien se colige que diversos pueblos, y provincias, personas, tenian diversas opiniones cerca de sus dioses, y que algunos dudaban de ellos y aun los blasfemaban cuando no se hacian las cosas á su contento, ni les sucedian como ellos deseaban y querian. Y esto no es tanto de admirar en personas viles y bajas, ó puestas en extremas necesidades, cuanto es de notar en personas calificadas y en grandes señores, como en su tiempo lo eran los reyes de Tezcuco Nezahualcoyotzin y Nezahualpiltzintli, el último de los cuales no solo con el corazon dudó ser dioses los que adoraban, mas aun de palabra lo dio á entender, diciendo que no le cuadraban ni estaba satisfecho de que eran dioses, por las razones que su viveza y buen natural le mostraban. (Mendieta 1971:83)

> **Of What a King of Texcoco Felt about His Gods, with Other Things:**
> About what has been dealt with above, it is well inferred that diverse towns, provinces, and people had diverse opinions about their gods, and that some of them distrusted and even blasphemed the gods when things were not done to their satisfaction or did not happen to them as they desired and wanted. And this is not so much admirable among vile and lowly people, or those in extreme need, as it is notable among noble people and great kings, as the kings of Texcoco Nezahualcoyotl and Nezahualpilli were in their time, the last one of whom not only doubted in his heart that those that they worshipped were gods, but beyond that he also made it understood with words,

saying that he did not agree nor was he satisfied that they were gods based on reasons that his intelligence and natural law showed him. (author's translation)

The Spanish friars noticed that some natives distrusted their gods, and they present Nezahualcoyotl and his son Nezahualpilli as examples. Mendieta here focuses on Nezahualpilli (Nezahualpiltzintli in the text), but later when he discusses Nezahualcoyotl, he presents one of the two kings as the most representative skeptic of indigenous gods. Torquemada (1975, 2:80) and Zorita (1999:152–53) do not help clarify matters: the former identifies Nezahualpilli as the conspicuous religious skeptic while the latter records that either Nezahualcoyotl or Nezahualpilli was the one who most doubted his god. I argue that the king about whose religious skepticism the Spanish friars provide the most information must be Nezahualcoyotl, because later chroniclers predominantly focus on this king's religious practices rather than those of his son, Nezahualpilli. For the Spanish priests, however, identifying the most skeptical king was not an important issue. More significant for them was the fact that there existed an indigenous leader who detested his own religion. They repeatedly reproduce this image in order to convince their readers that there were some "good," reasonable natives who would embrace Christianity willingly and desert their old beliefs. The following episode into which Mendieta inserted the same story of Nezahualcoyotl and his son's skepticism about the indigenous gods illustrates how he took advantage of those good, reasonable natives in order to justify the arrival of Christianity:

> Y así, se cuentan muchas virtudes de algunos señores y principales del tiempo de la infidelidad, en especial de un Nezahualpiltzintli, y de otro Nezahualcoyotzin, reyes de Tezcuco, el uno de los cuales no solo con el corazon dubdó ser dioses los que adoraban, mas aun lo decia á otros que no le cuadraban ni tenia para sí que aquellos eran dioses. Y entre los otros vicios, como mas feo, dicen que aborrecia al pecado nefando, y que hacia matar á los que lo cometian. Y así habria otros á quien Dios alumbraria para vivir conforme á la ley de naturaleza y dictámen de la razon. Y al propósito de esto hace lo que uno de primeros evangelizadores de esta nueva Iglesia dejó escripto en un su libro, que cuando ya los españoles venian por la mar para entrar en esta Nueva España, entre otros indios que tenian para sacrificar en la ciudad de México en el barrio llamado Tlatelulco, estaba un indio, el cual debia de ser hombre simple y que vivia en ley de naturaleza sin ofensa de nadie (porque de estos hubo y hay entre ellos algunos que no saben sino obedecer á lo que les mandan, y estarse al rincón, y vivir sin algun perjuicio): este indio, sabiendo que lo habian de sacrificar presto, llamaba en su corazon á Dios, y vino á él un mensajero de cielo

porque lo habian de sacrificar presto, llamaba en su corazon á Dios, y vino á él un mensajero del cielo, que los indios llamaron ave del cielo porque traia alas y diadema, y despuse que han visto cómo pintamos los ángeles, dicen que era de aquella manera. Este ángel dijo á aquel indio: ((Ten esfuerzo y confianza, no temas, que Dios del cielo habrá de ti misericordia; y dí á estos que ahora sacrifican y derraman sangre, que muy presto cesará el sacrificar y el derramar sangre humana, y que ya vienen los que han de mandar y enseñorearse en esta tierra.)) Este indio fue sacrificado adonde ahora está la horca en el Tlatelulco, y murió llamando á Dios del cielo. (Mendieta 1971:181–82)

And thus, many virtues of some kings and nobles during the time of infidelity are told, especially those of Nezahualpilli and of Nezahualcoyotzin, kings of Texcoco, one of whom not only doubted with his heart that those that he worshipped were gods, but he even said to the others that he did not agree with them nor considered them as gods. And among the other vices, they say that he detested sodomy as the ugliest and that he had those who committed it killed. And thus there would be others whom God would illuminate to live according to the law of nature and the judgment of reason. And for this purpose he does what one of the first evangelists of this new Church wrote in his book; when the Spaniards already were coming by sea to enter this New Spain, there was one Indian among those who were being held for sacrifice in the neighborhood of Tlatelolco in Mexico City who must have been a simple man who lived by the law of nature without offending anybody (because there were some of these and among them there are those who do not know but to obey what they are ordered, and to be in the corner, and to live without causing any harm): this Indian, knowing that he would be sacrificed soon, called to God in his heart and a messenger came to him from the sky. The Indians called the messenger a bird of the sky because it had wings and a crown. After they have seen how we paint the angels, they say that the bird was in that shape. This angel said to that Indian: ((Have courage and confidence, do not fear, God of the heavens will have mercy on you; and tell these people, who now sacrifice and spill blood, that very soon the sacrificing and the spilling human blood will cease and that those who will govern and take over this land already come.)) This Indian was sacrificed in Tlatelolco where the gallows now is and he died calling to God of the heavens. (author's translation)

Along with Nezahualcoyotl and Nezahualpilli, Mendieta presents here another incredulous native who was about to be sacrificed and whom an angel told that the god would show him mercy and that a certain group of people would abolish human sacrifice. But unlike Nezahualcoyotl and Nezahualpilli, this man seems to belong to a lower social class because he was one of "those who do not know but to obey what they are ordered." With this episode, Mendieta attempts to establish that there were indigenous people of all social classes who detested the predominant indigenous religious practices and that they would welcome the more reasonable Christian god, because they were already using their reason and following natural law before the conquest. With the two stories of the incredulous natives, Mendieta justifies the conquest, which would save those "good, reasonable" Indians from the barbarous indigenous gods. According to this logic, Nezahualcoyotl and his son, Nezahualpilli, would have willingly submitted to the Spaniards and accepted Christianity. Mendieta's use of Nezahualcoyotl in order to justify the conquest is even clearer when the original source of this second story is examined. Mendieta (1971:172) acknowledged Fray Martín de Valencia and his fellow Franciscans as primary sources for Book 3 in which the second episode was included. Its original source, however, was not Valencia's work but rather Fray Toribio de Benavente's (Motolinia's) *Memoriales*.[1] In chapter 55 of Book I in the *Memoriales*, Motolinia records exactly the same episode of an Indian who was going to be sacrificed. Nowhere, however, does Motolinia connect the episode with Nezahualcoyotl's religious ideas. The difference between Motolinia's version of this story from the 1540s and Mendieta's version of the 1580s demonstrates the way in which a colonial ideology invented the image of Nezahualcoyotl as a religious skeptic.

The Texcoca chroniclers such as Pomar, Alva Ixtlilxochitl, and the anonymous author of "La guerra de Chalco" took advantage of the description of Nezahualcoyotl as a religious skeptic in order to Christianize the entire history of pre-Hispanic Texcoco. They incorporated this idea into almost every aspect of Nezahualcoyotl's life in an attempt to expound on how this king rejected the indigenous gods and worshipped an unknown god that, according to the chroniclers, was a pre-Hispanic version of the Christian god. Pomar states that Nezahualcoyotl searched for this god in the polytheistic religious environment of Texcoco. Although Nezahualcoyotl practiced human sacrifice as required by the official religion, Pomar insists that he searched for a true or supreme deity like the Christian god who created everything in the world. Pomar (1993:174–75) also provides the god's indigenous name, Tloque Nahuaque (Owner of the Near and the Close).

"La guerra de Chalco" describes in detail the historical context of Nezahualcoyotl's skepticism about the indigenous gods, his search for a new god, and his new religious practices. This text focuses on the war of the Texcoca against the Chalca as the primary historical context in which Nezahualcoyotl began to doubt indigenous gods. The Chalca king rebelled against Nezahualcoyotl, which caused a war between the two city-states. The Texcoca were not able to conquer Chalco easily, and many of them were captured and sacrificed in this city. In this desperate situation, Nezahualcoyotl made sacrifices dedicated to indigenous gods following his priests' recommendation, but they changed nothing. Disappointed, Nezahualcoyotl became skeptical about the power of those gods and began to search for a true god:

> "Verdaderamente los dioses que yo adoro, que son ídolos de piedra que no hablan, ni sienten, no pudieron hacer ni formar la hermosura del cielo, el sol, luna y estrellas que lo hermosean y dan luz a la tierra; ríos, aguas y fuentes, árboles y plantas que la hermosean; las gentes que la poseen y todo los creado. A algún dios muy poderoso, oculto y no conocido es el creador de todo el universo. El sólo es el que puede consolarme en mi aflicción y socorrerme en tan grande angustia como mi corazón siente; a él quiero por mi ayudador y amparo." Y para mejor alcanzar y conseguir lo que pretendía acordó de retirarse, como se retiró a su bosque de Tezcutzingo, y allí, recogido y apartado de los negocios y cosas que le pudieran perturbar, ayunó cuarenta días al dios todopoderoso, creador de todas las cosas, oculto y no conocido, y ofreciéndole, en lugar de sacrificio, incienso y copal al salir del sol y al mediodía y a puesta del sol y a la media noche. (Anonymous 1997:556–57)

> "Truly the gods, which I worship, are idols of stone that do not speak nor feel, and could not make nor create the beauty of the sky such as the sun, the moon and the stars that beautify the sky and give light to the earth; and such as rivers, water and fountains, trees and plants that beautify the earth; nor the people who possess it and everything created. Some very powerful, hidden, and unknown god is the creator of the entire universe. He is the only one that can console me in my affliction and help me in such great anguish as my heart feels; I want him to be my helper and protection." And in order to better reach and to obtain what he intended, he decided to isolate himself as he retired to his forest of Tetzcotzinco, and there isolated and retired from the works and things that could disturb him, he fasted forty days for the omnipotent God, hidden and unknown creator of everything, offering him, instead of sacrifice, incense and resin at sunrise, noon, sunset, and midnight. (author's translation)

Here, Nezahualcoyotl's unknown god is described as a god of gods, that is, the true god, and Nezahualcoyotl's religious ceremony was practiced in a peaceful way. He fasted and offered only incense to his god instead of human sacrifice. Finally, the Texcoca defeated the Chalca with the mysterious valor of Nezahualcoyotl's seventeen-year-old son, Axoquentzin. Nezahualcoyotl, who had fasted and prayed for the victory, believed that his unknown god was responsible for it. He then decided to construct a splendid temple in honor of this new god and prohibited human sacrifice in his city:

Muchas gracias te doy, dios todopoderoso y hacedor de todas las cosas, como causa que eres de todas las causas, que bien y verdaderamente creo que estás en los cielos claros y hermosos que alumbran la tierra, y desde allá gobiernas, socorres y haces mercedes a los que te llaman y piden tu favor, como conmigo lo has hecho, y te prometo reconocerte por mi señor y creador, y de en agradecimiento del bien recibido, de hacerte un templo donde seas reverenciado y se haga ofrenda toda la vida, hasta que tu, señor, te dignes de mostrarte a éste tu esclavo y a los demás de mi reino, y de hoy en adelante ordenaré que no se sacrifique en todo él, gente humana, porque tengo para mí te ofendes de ello. (Anonymous 1997:558–59)

I give many thanks to you, omnipotent god and creator of all the things, as the cause of all the causes. I well and truly believe that you are in the clear and beautiful heavens that light the earth and that from there you govern, help and grant favors to those who call you and they ask your favor, just like you have done with me. And I promise you to recognize you as my lord and creator, and for gratitude of good reception, I build you a temple where you will be venerated and offerings will be made lifelong, until you, lord, deign to show to this your slave and to the others of my kingdom, and henceforth I will order that human beings not be sacrificed in the entire temple because I believe that you are offended by it. (author's translation)

As O'Gorman (1997:67) observes, Alva Ixtlilxochitl used this text as a major source in writing his works. Whenever he deals with Nezahualcoyotl, he describes the king's unknown god in detail and develops the idea in the broader history of Texcoco. In Alva Ixtlilxochitl's chronicles (1997), Nezahualcoyotl appears as a force of opposition to the traditional indigenous gods—especially the Mexica god Huitzilopochtli—and as a peaceful counterpart of the bloody Mexica who were conducting human sacrifices. Alva Ixtlilxochitl (1997, 1:502) even identifies Nezahualcoyotl's unknown god with the Christian god. According to him, Nezahualcoyotl seems to play the role of an apostle who tried to transform the barbarous indigenous into a civilized and peaceful people exactly as the Christian friars would do for the indigenous people after the conquest:

Y también dijo [Nezahualcoyotl], que los ídolos eran demonios y no dioses como decían los mexicanos y culhuas, y que el sacrificio que se les hacía de hombres humanos, no era tanto por que se les debía hacer, sino para aplacarlos que no les hiciesen mal en sus personas y haciendas, porque si fueran dioses amarían sus criaturas, y no consintieran que sus sacerdotes los mataran y sacrificaran y así vedó a los mexicanos que no sacrificaran a sus hijos. (Alva Ixtlilxochitl 1997, 1:447)

> And he [Nezahualcoyotl] also said that the idols were devils and not gods as the Mexica and Colhuaque insisted, and that the sacrifice that was done of men was not so much because it must be done for them, but rather to appease the idols so that they do not harm them in their persons or their property, because if the idols were gods, they would love their creatures and would not allow their priests to kill and sacrifice them, and thus he prohibited the Mexica from sacrificing their children. (author's translation)

Alva Ixtlilxochitl's chronicles create an image of Nezahualcoyotl as a Christian-like apostle by combining the religious skepticism and the peaceful piety that appear in Pomar's *Relación* (1993) and the anonymous "La guerra de Chalco" (1997), respectively. The most important feature of this image of Nezahualcoyotl was his rejection of human sacrifice and his attempt to convert neighboring cities—especially Tenochtitlan—to his new peaceful religion.

After the conquest, the non-Mexica chroniclers attempt to distinguish themselves from the Mexica. They are very cautious when they deal with their own religious traditions. They try to justify their practice of human sacrifice by insisting that this barbaric ceremony was forced upon them by the Mexica and that, therefore, their people were innocent. They condemn the Mexica for instituting such cruelties as human sacrifice. The two Texcoca chroniclers, Pomar (1993) and Alva Ixtlilxochitl (1997), in particular stand out in this regard. Pomar insists that

> En lo que toca a sus *ceremonias y sacrificios*, lo que se ha podido sacar de raíz, investigando la verdad de ello es que el sacrificio de los hombres a estos ídolos, que fue invención de los mexicanos en esta manera: Que después que los señores de Azcapotzalco los dejaron asentar y poblar adonde ahora es la ciudad de México, con título de sus vasallos, andando con el tiempo, . . . se rebelaron contra sus señores y de tal manera que, tomando las armas contra ellos, en poco tiempo los sojuzgaron, y que por honrar más a sus ídolos, les hicieron sacrificios de hombres. (Pomar 1993:166)

> About their ceremonies and sacrifices, what has been able to be determined, investigating the truth of the matter, is that the sacrifice of humans to these idols was an invention of the Mexica in this way: that after the kings of Azcapotzalco allowed them to settle down and to populate where Mexico City is now, with title of their vassals, as time went on, . . . they rebelled against their kings, taking up weapons against them, and in short time they subdued their masters. And in order to better honor their idols, they conducted sacrifices of men. (author's translation)

Alva Ixtlilxochitl shares Pomar's perspective and develops it even further. According to Alva Ixtlilxochitl, Texcoco had better political, cultural, and religious traditions than those of the Mexica. The Texcoca religious system was peaceful and civilized, differing significantly from that of the bloodthirsty Mexica, who instituted human sacrifice and forced the other natives to practice it. For Alva Ixtlilxochitl and Pomar, Nezahualcoyotl is central to their argument, and the peaceful, benevolent, bloodless, unknown god serves to prove their religious difference from the bloodthirsty god of the Mexica, Huitzilopochtli. Furthermore, these Texcoca chroniclers insist that the monotheistic religious tradition established by Nezahualcoyotl was very similar to that of the invaders. According to them, the Texcoca welcomed the arrival of Christianity, helping the conquistadores conquer the home of the evil Mexica, Tenochtitlan, because they had been prepared by the traditions instituted by Nezahualcoyotl. Thus, just like the Spanish friars, the Texcoca chroniclers engaged in justifying the conquest by taking advantage of the image of Nezahualcoyotl as a religious skeptic. They asserted that they drew on indigenous sources such as songs, pictorial codices, and maps in their accounts, but these sources support neither the peaceful image of Nezahualcoyotl nor the existence of his god. Quite to the contrary, they demonstrate that he was a great protector and follower of indigenous religion and that his unknown god was an invention of later chroniclers and historians.

Texcoca Religion under Nezahualcoyotl

As examined in chapter 4, when Nezahualcoyotl gained control of Texcoco in 1433, he needed to reconstruct its political, religious, and artistic institutions, because Texcoco had almost been destroyed as a result of numerous wars over a short period of time. Before Nezahualcoyotl's reign and before the Tepanec-Acolhuacan war in Texcoco, there were six principal clans, each of whom had their own major god: the Tlailotlaca, for example, served Tezcatlipoca, and the Mexica served Huitzilopochtli. During the Tepanec war, most of the six clans fled to Tlaxcala and Huexotzinco, and some of them did not return to Texcoco even after Nezahualcoyotl restored the city. Thus, Nezahualcoyotl had a particular interest in rebuilding the temples and introducing the religious practices of the other states. Nezahualcoyotl accepted new immigrants from the Mexica and other conquered city-states, and he helped them establish themselves in Texcoco by distributing lands to them. His efforts to reestablish religious institutions in his city were recorded in many sources. Alva Ixtlilxochitl (1997, 1:379) recounts that when Nezahualcoyotl returned to Texcoco, he asked the Mexica king Itzcoatl to send him priests from Tenochtitlan.[2] The *Mapa Tlotzin* (Aubin 1886b) clearly records that Nezahualcoyotl gathered "*ídolos*," that is, the indigenous gods (see figure 4.4).[3] Pomar describes in detail Nezahualcoyotl's reconstruction of the religious system in Texcoco: Nezahualcoyotl was the one who placed Tezcatlipoca in the barrio of Huitznahuac, gathered other gods, and dedicated the temple of Tezcatlipoca to them:

> El cu de Tezcatlipoca, ídolo principal, estaba, como se ha dicho, en el barrio de Huitznáhuac; mucho mas pequeño, pero de la misma hechura, salvo que no tenía división en las gradas. Averiguóse que Nezahualcoyotzin dejó estar en este barrio a este ídolo a contemplación de los indios de él, a cuyo cargo era el guardarlo, porque sus antepasados lo habían traído al tiempo que a esta tierra vinieron, en la forma que adelante se dirá. Tenía también este templo encima de la casa de los ídolos, tres sobrados, adonde así mismo se guardaba de la munición que se ha dicho. Hallóse que Nezahualcoyotzin fue el primero que recogió a éste, ídolos de diversas partes de todos los barrios de esta ciudad, en donde estaban derramados en muy pequeños cúes y templos, y les hizo el grande (de) que se ha hecho relación, y otos muchos, dentro de un cercado muy grande. (Pomar 1993:163–64)

> The temple of Tezcatlipoca, the main idol, was, as it has been said, in the neighborhood of Huitznahuac; a lot smaller but of the same form, except that it did not have division in the steps. It was verified that Nezahualcoyotzin left this idol in this neighborhood in favor of the Indians of the neighborhood, whose charge was to take care of it, because their ancestors had brought the idol when they came to this land in the way that will be told later. This temple also had on top of the house of the idols, three lofts, where the said arms were kept. It was Nezahualcoyotl who was the first person to collect in this temple idols of diverse parts of all the neighborhoods of this city, where they were scattered in very small sanctuaries and temples, and he constructed for them the large temple, of which an account has been made, and many others, inside a very large compound. (author's translation)

Nezahualcoyotl was interested not only in restoring traditional gods and temples in Texcoco, but also in reforming and modifying the existing temples. The king, who was raised in the Mexica tradition and was familiar with the Mexica religious system, enthusiastically introduced it into his city. He constructed the temple dedicated to Huitzilopochtli, much bigger than Tezcatlipoca's, and made the Mexica god more prominent in Texcoco than Tezcatlipoca, who had been introduced much earlier.[4] This is depicted in the *Codex en Cruz* (1981), according to which Nezahualcoyotl finished the temple in 1 Reed (1467) (figure 8.1). Moreover, he built this temple in the Mexica style by placing the rain god, Tlaloc, alongside Huitzilopochtli. According to Mexica sources, the practice of putting Tlaloc together with Huitzilopochtli began with the Mexica when they arrived at Tenochtitlan looking for the promised land. The *Códice Aubin*

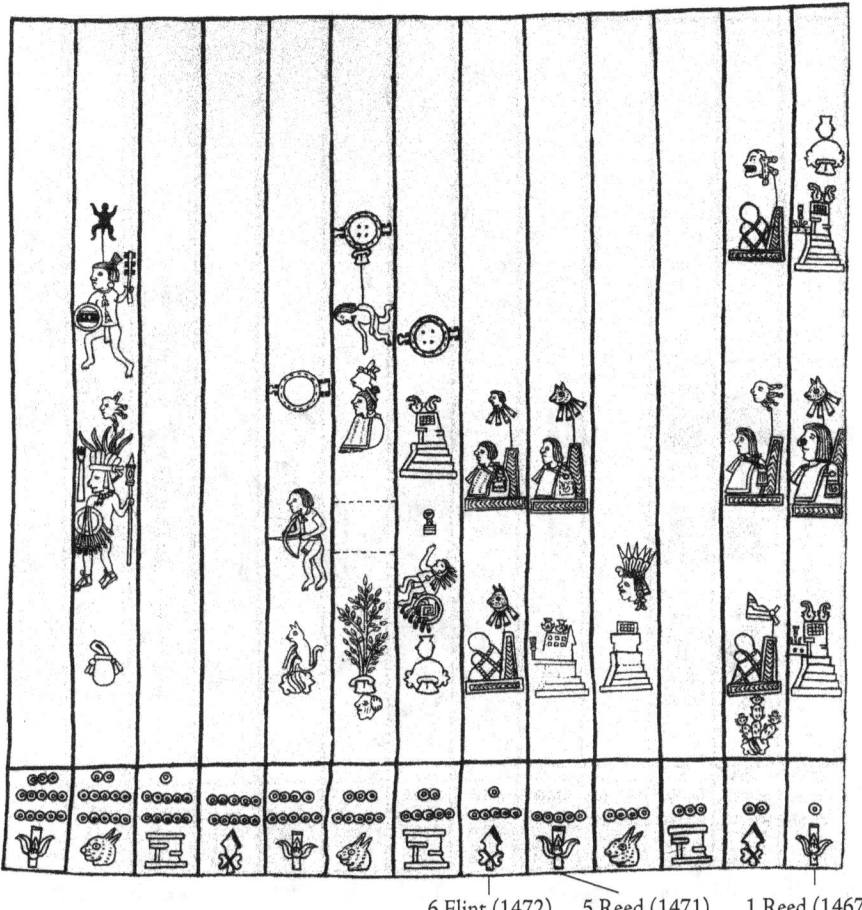

6 Flint (1472)   5 Reed (1471)   1 Reed (1467)

FIG. 8.1

Nezahualcoyotl's construction of the temple dedicated to Huitzilopochtli from the *Codex en Cruz* (1981). Reproduced with permission of the University of Utah Press.

In the middle of the column of the year 1 Reed (1467), Nezahualcoyotl (Fasted Coyote) appears seated on his authority mat (*icpalli*), and below him is a temple. According to Charles Dibble's interpretation (*Codex en Cruz* 1981, 1:20), the temple had recently been constructed for Huitzilopochtli: "From the cross-hatching on the roof and the decoration at the top and by comparison with other temple-pyramids in the Codex, this can be identified as the temple-pyramid of the god Huitzilopochtli. Protruding forward is a fire board with blackened holes and a fire drill in place; smoke erupts from the base of the fire drill. This fire drill in association with a temple-pyramid indicates the boring of the first fire in the newly constructed sanctuary and, by extension, signifies the dedication ceremony for the new structure." The content of the column shows that the temple of Huitzilopochtli was dedicated in Texcoco under Nezahualcoyotl's reign. In the column of the year 5 Reed (1471), Nezahualcoyotl also constructed a new temple that was probably dedicated to the rain god Tlaloc (*Codex en Cruz* 1981, 1:21–22). Nezahualcoyotl died in the year 6 Flint (1472), and above his mummy bundle, his son Nezahualpilli (Fasted Lord) is depicted as succeeding him.

THE WESTERNIZATION OF NAHUA RELIGION

FIG. 8.2

The primitive Templo Mayor in Tenochtitlan: Tlaloc with Huitzilopochtli from the *Códice Aubin* (1963:48). Reproduced with permission of José Porrúa Turanzas.

According to the Mexica sources, Huitzilopochtli told the Mexica to settle down where an eagle was devouring a snake on a cactus. They found the eagle near the lake in the Basin of Mexico and established themselves there.

The reed in the figure indicates their settlement near the lake. Immediately after establishing their settlement, they captured aquatic animals such as fish, frog, and water snake and sold them for wood, stone, and lime in order to construct a temple dedicated to Huitzilopochtli. The two primitive huts in the figure refer to the beginning stage of the Templo Mayor in Tenochtitlan.

(1963:40–41) records that one of the Mexica leaders, Axolohua, was drowned in water and Tlaloc spoke to him: "Ha llegado mi hijo Huitzilopochtli, pues aquí será su casa. Pues él la dedicará porque aquí viviremos unidos en la tierra" (My son Huitzilopochtli has arrived, for here will be his house. So, he will dedicate it because we will live here together on earth). The Mexica made an altar for this event: below the nopal, there are two huts dedicated to Huitzilopochtli and Tlaloc. This primitive altar was a basic model for Huitzilopochtli's future temple in Tenochtitlan (figure 8.2). Many colonial chronicles record that Tlaloc was placed together with Huitzilopochtli on the top of Huitzilopochtli's temple. According to Pomar (1993:166), Nezahualcoyotl introduced this system in Texcoco: "Dicen que Nezahualcoyotzin, por reverencia a este ídolo [Tlaloc] hizo el otro, de que se ha tratado, poniéndose en el cu y templo principal de esta ciudad, en compañía de Huitzilopochtli" (They say that Nezahualcoyotl, in reverence to this idol [Tlaloc] built the other, which has been discussed, placing it in the sanctuary and main temple of this city, in company with Huitzilopochtli). Alva Ixtlilxochitl also confirms Nezahualcoyotl's construction of the temple dedicated to the two gods and gives more detailed information:

> Los templos eran más de cuarenta; pero el principal y mayor que era Huitzilopuchtli y Tláloc [sic, por Tláloc] cuadrado y macizo, hechas de cal y canto las paredes de la parte afuera, y lo de adentro terraplenado de barro y piedra: tenía en cada cuadro ochenta brazas largas, y de alto este terraplén o cue veintisiete estados, y se subía por la parte de poniente por unas gradas que eran ciento y sesenta: comenzaba su edificio por el cimiento ancho, y como iba levantándose, iba disminuyendo y estrechando de todas partes en forma piramidal con sus grandes relieves, que como iba subiendo, asimismo le iban disminuyendo, y de trecho en trecho las gradas hacían un descanso, y encima estaba edificado un templo con dos capillas, la una mayor que otra: la mayor caía a la parte del sur en donde estaba el ídolo Huitzilopochtli: y la menor que estaba a la parte del norte, era del ídolo Tláloc, . . . y en medio de las puertas de las dos capillas estaba una piedra tumbada que llamaban téchate, en donde sacrificaban los cautivos en guerra; y tenía cada una de estas capillas tres sobrados que se mandaban por la parte de adentro por unas escaleras de madera movediza, y los sobrados estaban llenos de todo género de armas, como eran macanas, rodelas, arcos, flechas, lanzas y guijarros, y todo género de vestimentos, arreos y adornos de guerra. (Alva Ixtlilxochitl 1997, 2:98–99)

> The temples were more than forty in number; but the main and largest one that was Huitzilopochtli and Tlaloc [sic, by Tlaloc], was square and solid. The walls of the outside part were made of lime and stone and those of the inside filled with mud stone: this temple or embankment had in each square eighty long fathoms, and of height twenty-seven *estado*,[5] and it could be climbed on the west side with some steps that were one hundred and sixty: it began with the wide foundation, and as it went rising, it diminished and narrowed on all sides in the shape of a pyramid with its large reliefs. As it went up, it also diminished and the steps became gradually reduced, and on top there was built a temple with two chapels, one bigger than the other: the biggest was on the southern side where the idol Huitzilopochtli was placed:

and the smaller one that was on the northern side was of the idol Tlaloc, ... and in the middle of the doors of the two chapels there was an extended stone that they called techate, where they sacrificed the captives of war; and each one of these chapels had three lofts that were reached from inside by portable wooden ladders, and the lofts were full of every kind of weapons such as war clubs, round shields, bows, arrows, spears, and pebbles, and every kind of garments, adornments, and decorations of war. (author's translation)

This alphabetic description seems to be based on a vivid pictorial description of Huitzilopochtli's temple in Texcoco, which appears in the *Códice Ixtlilxochitl* (1996), a text that Alva Ixtlilxochitl himself produced (figure 8.3). After building the temple dedicated to Huitzilopochtli, Nezahualcoyotl willfully searched for victims for sacrifice just like the Mexica did after the construction of the Templo Mayor in Tenochtitlan.

The *Annals of Cuauhtitlan* (1992:110–11) record that upon constructing the temple dedicated to Huitzilopochtli in 1 Reed (1467), the same year mentioned above, Nezahualcoyotl made an effort to capture sacrificial victims: "It was the year 1 Reed that Nezahualcoyotzin's temple was built to the top. And when it was topped, he went to implore the elder Moteuczomatzin to grant some Tzompanca, some Xilotzinca, and some Citlaltepeca. These he requested [as sacrificial victims] for his dedication ceremony. And the Tenochtitlan ruler was obliging. He granted them, etc." Thus, Nezahualcoyotl provoked a war against the Tzompanca, the Xilotzinca, and the Citlaltepeca. In Citlaltepec, however, the Texcoca were defeated and driven out because the Citlaltepeca, including women and children, fought against them like jaguars and eagles.

Nezahualcoyotl's participation in human sacrifice even in Tenochtitlan was recorded by Alvarado Tezozomoc (1987) and Durán (1994). Durán (1994:191) records that Nezahualcoyotl himself participated in sacrificing the captives from the Mixtec area with the king Moctezuma Ilhuicamina, Tlacaelel, and the king of Tlacopan.[6] Mexica chronicler Alvarado Tezozomoc describes in detail the close relationship Nezahualcoyotl had with the Mexica in religion and politics. In Alvarado Tezozomoc's chronicle, for example, Nezahualcoyotl enthusiastically participated in the foundation of the Templo Mayor dedicated to Huitzilopochtli in Tenochtitlan. When the Mexica king Moctezuma Ilhuicamina calls on the rulers of his subject cities to ask them to furnish labor and materials for the construction of the temple, Nezahualcoyotl, in the manner of a Mexica leader, explains the justification of this construction to these rulers because, according to him, they had been receiving the favor and help of the great god Huitzilopochtli:

Señores y nuestro rey Moctezuma, hijo y nieto nuestro tan amado como querido y temido: y á vos, señor Cihuacoatl Tlacaeleltzin y todos

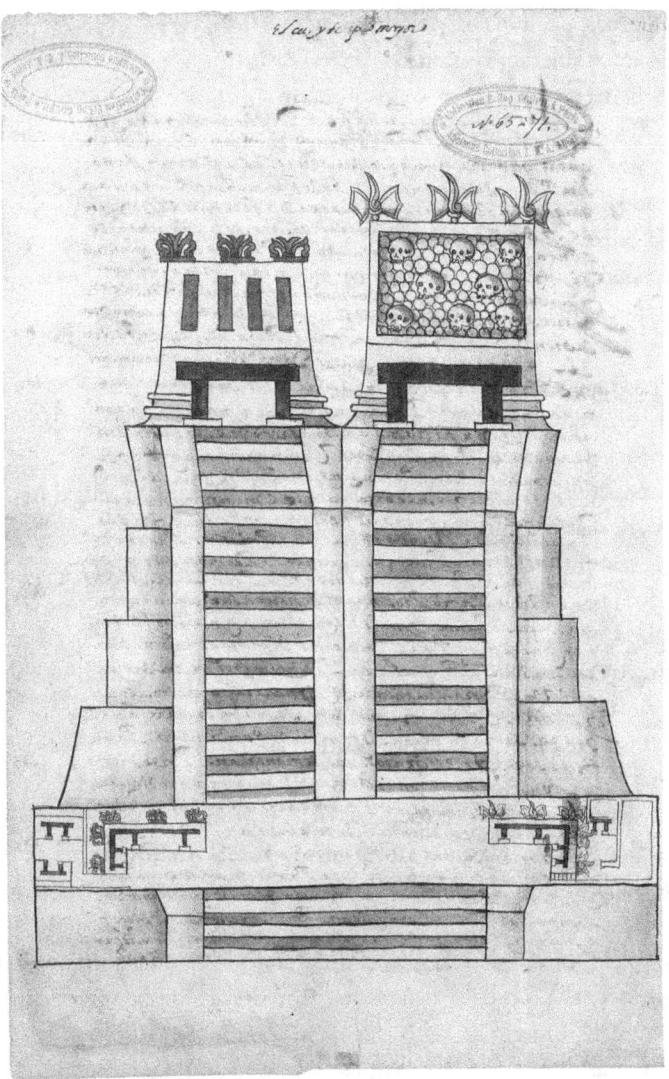

FIG. 8.3
Huitzilopochtli's temple in Texcoco from the *Códice Ixtlilxochitl* (1996:f. 112v). Reproduced with permission of the Bibliothèque nationale de France.

By comparing this illustration to Juan Bautista Pomar's alphabetic description of Huitzilopochtli's temple in Texcoco in *Relación geográfica de Texcoco*, several scholars (Chavero 1904:7–8; Robertson 1994:149–51; Anders, Jansen, and Reyes García in *Códice Ixtlilxochitl* 1996:18) argue that this illustration was originally attached to Pomar's *Relación*. This illustration demonstrates that the temple of Huitzilopochtli in Texcoco had the same structure as that of the Mexica temple in Tenochtitlan. In addition, the other illustrations of the *Códice Ixtlilxochitl* depict the eighteen monthly religious ceremonies, and these are the same ceremonies that the Mexica of Tenochtitlan practiced. The illustrations from the *Códice Ixtlilxochitl* that Alva Ixtlilxochitl himself collected suggest that Mexica and Texcoca religions were virtually identical.

los demás principales y mexicanos que aquí están todos ayuntados, recibimos singular contento y alegría de lo que se nos manda: y es bien, y es lícito que tan buen señor y tan gran Dios como es el Tetzahuitl Huitzilopochtli, que nos tiene abrigados con su favor y amparo, que estamos debajo de él, como recibiendo alegría á su sombra como árbol grande de Ceiba puchotl ó ciprés ancho ahuehuetl: habiéndonos recibido en su gracia y favor, es bien que se haga nos decís; pues estamos ociosos, nos ocuparemos en esto: pero sepamos, señores, qué es menester para ello. (Alvarado Tezozomoc 1987:288–89)

Our lords and our king Moctezuma, our son and grandson as much beloved as esteemed and feared: and we receive the most exceptional comfort and happiness that you are sent to us, Lord Cihuacoatl Tlacaeleltzin and all the other nobles and the Mexica joined here: and it is good and right that we be under such a good lord and great god as Tetzahuitl Huitzilopochtli, who protects us with his favor and protection, receiving happiness in his shadow like the large tree of Ceiba puchotl or wide cypress ahuehuetl. Because he has received us with his favor and grace, it is good that what he tells us should be fulfilled; for we are idle, so we dedicate ourselves to this: but let us know, lords, what is necessary for it. (author's translation)

The religious system that Nezahualcoyotl instituted in Texcoco was the same as that of the Mexica. Both cities, Texcoco and Tenochtitlan, served Huitzilopochtli and Tezcatlipoca as their major gods and constructed the largest and the most beautiful temples dedicated to these gods (Alvarado Tezozomoc 1987:93, 109; Durán 1971:70, 109; Pomar 1993:159). In addition, just like the Mexica kings, the Texcoca rulers "celebrated their feasts and sacrifices with the same order and ritual, with the same ceremonies and sacrifices, and with the death of as many men as took place in Tenochtitlan" (Durán 1994:458). As Chavero pointed out,

De familia mexicana y educado en México, había estado en esta ciudad todavía cuatro años más, del 1427 al 1431, después de que recobró su señorío. Natural fue que llevarse a Tetzcuco la misma organización civil y religiosa de los mexicanos. Por eso su templo mayor, como el de México, estaba dedicado a Tlaloc y a Huitzilopochtli dios esencialmente mexicano. Así la antigua sociológica chichimeca que poco a poco se había ido modificando con la inmigración de pueblos extraños, desapareció por completo bajo Nezahualcoyotl, y se sustituyó por la cultura y costumbres de México. (Chavero cited in Alva Ixtlilxochitl 1997, 2:99)

Of Mexica family and educated in Mexico, he had been in this city for four more years, from 1427 to 1431, after he recovered his kingdom. It was natural for him to import the same civil and religious organization of the Mexica to Texcoco. Therefore its main temple, like that of Mexico, was dedicated to Tlaloc and to Huitzilopochtli, the essentially Mexica God. Thus the old sociological aspects of Chichimec culture, which little by little had been modified with the immigration of foreign groups, completely disappeared under Nezahualcoyotl, and was substituted by the culture and customs of Mexico-Tenochtitlan. (author's translation)

Thus, the Texcoca religion under Nezahualcoyotl was the result of a Mexicanization that assimilated the civil and religious organizations of Tenochtitlan. The image of Nezahualcoyotl as one who rejected human sacrifice by intuiting an unknown Christian-like god is simply inconsistent both with the political and religious context of fifteenth-century Texcoco and with indigenous pictographic scripts.

The religious tradition reconstructed by Nezahualcoyotl continued with his successor, his son Nezahualpilli. His son expanded the temple dedicated to Huitzilopochtli and made a large sacrifice of captives (Alva Ixtlilxochitl 1997, 2:150). Moreover, he continued to participate in religious ceremonies in Tenochtitlan, and just like his father, he even took part in human sacrifice. When the Spaniards forced the natives to convert to Christianity, several records show that the Texcoca were one of the most tenacious groups who clung to their old religion. According to the *Crónica mexicana* (Alvarado Tezozomoc 1987:137), when the mother of Fernando Cortés Ixtlilxochitl, the son of Nezahualpilli, heard about the baptism of her son, she reacted negatively by saying that "debía de haber perdido el juicio, pues tan presto se había dejado vencer de unos pocos de bárbaros como eran los cristianos" (he must have lost the judgment, because he let himself be conquered so quickly by a few barbarians that the Christians were). Moreover, don Carlos Ometochtzin, son of Nezahualpilli and grandson of Nezahualcoyotl, rejected the invaders' religion by secretly worshiping indigenous gods and was finally burned, an act that will be addressed in detail later.

Nezahualcoyotl's Unknown God in Indigenous Songs

Pomar and Alva Ixtlilxochitl claim that indigenous songs contain evidence of Nezahualcoyotl's unknown god. Pomar (1993:175) explains, for example, that he found many names and epithets of Nezahualcoyotl's god in the fragments of old songs. Alva Ixtlilxochitl (1997, 1:546) briefly records that after the victory against the Chalca, Nezahualcoyotl dedicated himself to the unknown god and composed more than sixty songs to worship him. They both record that the terms

Tloque Nahuaque (Owner of the Near and the Close) and Ipalnemohuani (By Him People Live) are the Nahua names of Nezahualcoyotl's unknown god. We find these Nahua names in *Romances de los señores de la Nueva España* (1993), which Pomar attached to his chronicle, and also in *Cantares Mexicanos* (1985). In addition to these names, the songs also record other names such as Yohualli-Ehecatl (Night-Wind) and Moyocoyatzin (One Who Invents Himself). A literal reading of the songs may provide a clue as to why Pomar and Alva Ixtlilxochitl assimilate Nezahualcoyotl's unknown god to the Christian god. There are many songs that use these indigenous names indiscriminately along with Christian names, such as Dios, Jesucristo, and Santa María, or Nahua names translated directly from Spanish like Icelteotl (Only God), Tota (Our Father), and Tonan (Our Mother). The following stanza is one of these examples: "For this I weep. I grieve. I'm bereft in this company here on earth. What does your heart require, O Life Giver [Ipalnemohuani]? Be entertained! Let bereavement suppurate near you, O Spirit [Teotl]! O God [Dios], you want me dead!" (*Cantares* 1985, 18, 28). In this stanza, the Nahua name of the god, Ipalnemohuani, is not distinguished from Christian names, Dios or Icelteotl: all of these terms refer to the same god. One of the most famous songs attributed to Nezahualcoyotl does the same:

> In no place can be the house of He Who invents Himself
>   [Moyocoyatzin]
> But in all places He is invoked,
> In all places He is venerated,
> His glory, His fame are sought on the earth,
>
> It is He Who invents everything.
> He is Who invents Himself [Moyocoyatzin]: God [Teotl]
>
> In all places He is invoked,
> In all places He is venerated,
> His glory, His fame are sought on the earth.
>
> No one here is able,
> No one is able to be intimate
> With the Giver of Life [Ipalnemohuani]:
> Only He is invoked,
>
> At His side,
> Near to Him,
> One can live on the earth. (*Romances* 1993:ff. 4v–5v, in León-Portilla
>   1992b:85)

This song indiscriminately uses the various epithets for the indigenous and Christian gods: Ipalnemohuani, Moyocoyatzin, Teotl, and Dios. Based on this kind of song, Pomar and Alva Ixtlilxochitl seem to insist that Tloque Nahuaque and Ipalnemohuani were the Christian-like god. Whether these names in the songs refer exclusively to the Christian god as Pomar and Alva Ixtlilxochitl insist, however, remains to be determined.

In their attempt to convert the natives after the conquest of central Mexico, the Spanish priests were forced to either use Spanish words or find Nahua equivalents for Christian concepts.[7] Some of them adapted indigenous terms such as "Ipalnemohuani," "Tloque Nahuaque," and other names to designate the Christian god, but this caused a great deal of confusion in the meaning of the names because they already carried a very specific significance in the indigenous religion. The conversation between Spanish priests and Aztec priests in *Coloquios y doctrina cristiana* (Sahagún 1986) provides a clear example of this confusion. Both Nahua and Christian priests use "Ipalnemohuani" and "Tloque Nahuaque," but each understands the terms in different ways. The Christian priests use "Ipalnemohuani" or "Tloque Nahuaque" to speak of their god while Aztec priests clearly have their own gods in mind.[8] Thus, the Aztec priests react to this religious instruction by claiming not only that they already understood the gods, Tloque Nahuaque, but also that this understanding was correct:

> Vosotros dijisteis
> que nosotros no conocíamos
> al Dueño del cerca y del junto [Tloque Nahuaque],
> a aquél de quien son el cielo, la tierra.
> Habéis dicho
> que no son verdaderos dioses los nuestros.
> Nueva palabra es esta,
> la que habláis
> y por ella estamos perturbados,
> por ella estamos espantados.
> Porque nuestros progenitores,
> los que vinieron a ser, a vivir en la tierra,
> no hablaron así.
> En verdad ellos nos dieron
> su norma de vida,
> tenían por verdaderos,
> servían,
> reverenciaban a los dioses. Ellos nos enseñaron,
> todas sus formas de culto,
> sus modos de reverenciar [a los dioses]. (Sahagún 1986:148–51)

> You said,
> that we do not know,
> the Owner of the Near and the Close [Tloque Nahuaque],
> the Possessor of Heaven and Earth.
> You said,
> that our gods are not true gods.
> What you say
> is a new word,
> it makes us mad
> it makes us frightened.
> Because our ancestors,
> those who came to be, to live on the earth,
> did not speak in this way.
> Truly they gave us
> their rules of life,
> they considered them true
> they served,
> they honored the gods. They taught us
> all their forms of veneration,
> their ways of worshiping [the gods]. (author's translation)

Other indigenous sources also confirm that those names or epithets were clearly assigned to the Nahua gods. Sahagún's informants in Book Six of the *Florentine Codex* (1950–1982, 6:7–20) certify that the majority of the names were used to invoke Tezcatlipoca. In this book, there are twelve prayers to the gods, eleven of them to Tezcatlipoca, ruler of heaven and earth and all mankind. This supreme god is designated with a variety of names: Tloque Nahuaque (Owner of the Near and the Close), Ipalnemohuani (By Him People Live), Teyocoyani (One Who Creates People), Yohualli Ehecatl (Night-Wind), Moyocoyatzin (One Who Invents Himself), Monenequi (Tyrannical One), Titlacahuani (Our Master), and so on. In the dialogue between Aztecs and Spaniards, a clear conceptual difference in religious understanding can be detected. The Christian priests stress the doctrine of one true god. Whenever they use "Ipalnemohuani" or "Tloque Nahuaque," they tend to add epithets like *nelli teotl* (true god) or *iceltzin teotl* (the only god), by which they mean the Christian god. In contrast, whenever the Aztec priests use these names, it is an unambiguous reference to their gods in the plural, not to a single god.

The conceptual ambiguity, however, deepened because Catholic priests started to use alternately "Tloque Nahuaque" and "Ipalnemohuani" with and without their qualifiers nelli teotl or iceltzin teotl. This phenomenon is notable in their explanation of religious theory in the latter part of the conversation. They begin to contradict the polytheism of Aztec religion by insisting that there were not many gods but a "nelli zan iceltzin teotl" (true and only

God). The priests argue that the god is invisible—"amo vualneci amo uel toconitta" (he is not visible, we cannot see him) (Sahagún 1986:168)—and that he is the owner of heaven and earth ("in ilhuicahua in tlaltipacque"). The priests explain how Ipalnemohuani created the world: "in iehoatzin ypalnemoanj, / in oqujmochivili / ixqujch ittonj yoa in amo ittoni" (he, Ipalnemohuani, / created everything visible and invisible) (Sahagún 1986:188). Thus, he, Ipalnemohuani or Tloque Nahuaque, is the true god who created the sun, the moon, the stars, the fire, the wind, the water, and all kinds of animals and fish. Here, the names of indigenous gods are clearly used by Christian priests to represent the Christian god. In the priest's sermon, the gods of the Aztecs, such as the sun, the moon, and the stars, are not gods but rather creations of the Christian god. According to Arthur J. O. Anderson (1993:xx), Fray Bernardino de Sahagún, who collected this conversation, also argues that all the indigenous gods, the sun, the moon, and the ocean, were *diablome, tzitzimime,* and *coleleti.*

Fray Diego Valadés, who began his missionary work in the 1550s, continued to use the same understanding of the Christian god and indigenous gods to preach to the natives (Palomera 1989:x–xi). In his *Retórica cristiana* (1989), Valadés included a chapter entitled "Ejemplo de una exhortación a los indios para que abandonaran sus ritos y costumbres y para que abrazasen nuestra fe católica" (Example of a sermon to the Indians so that they would abandon their rites and customs and so that they would embrace our Catholic faith). He first defined the Christian god as "Señor del cielo y de la tierra" (King of heaven and earth) when he and his fellow friars came to New Spain to make known this true god to the natives, and thus save their souls from idolatry:

> Así que hemos venido a vosotros para conduciros a una vida nueva y a la verdadera libertad, y para que conozcáis cuán grande es la diferencia entre el verdadero Dios, a quien nosotros adoramos, y esas seudodivinidades, a quienes rendís culto. El dios verdadero, que nosotros conocemos, es el creador de todas las cosas visibles e invisibles; todas le obedecen y El mismo de ninguna depende; pues El es la mente directora del universo y su principio, y El a su vez no tiene principio ni fin. El todo lo estima por nada en comparación del alma racional, a la que ama sobre todas las cosas, puesto que ha sido creada a su imagen y semejanza, y a quien ha descubierto algunos vestigios de su divinidad, por los que puede venir a conocerle. (Valadés 1989:397)

> So we have come to you in order to lead you to a new life and to the true liberty, so that you recognize how great is the difference between the true God, whom we worship, and those false gods, whom you worship. The true God, whom we know, is the creator of all the visible and invisible things; everything obeys him and he himself depends on nothing; because He is the directing intellect of the universe and its principle, and

consequently He does not have a beginning nor an end. He esteems everything as nothing in comparison to the rational soul, which he loves over all the things, because it has been created in his image and semblance, and to whom he has revealed some traces of his divinity through which the rational soul can come to know him. (author's translation)

Valadés presents the Christian god as the true and omnipotent universal god, and then he compares this Christian god to the indigenous gods:

> Vuestros dioses no son dioses, sino criaturas destituidas por completo del poder de producir algo; más aún, ni siquiera son capaces de producir las más pequeña y miserable cosa que se encuentra en el universo; lo cual podéis comprobar por vosotros mismos. Vosotros adoráis las rocas, barro, leños, árboles, el Sol, la Luna, las estrellas, a más de otras cosas ciertamente indignas, como son los topos, las culebras y los brutos; lo cual está en pugna con la razón más que otra cosa alguna, pues todo eso ha sido, en parte, creado por el poder divino, en parte también fabricado por vosotros mismos. (Valadés 1989:397)

> Your gods are not gods, but creatures completely destitute of the power to produce anything; moreover they are not even capable of producing the smallest and miserable thing that is found in the universe; which you can verify for yourselves. You worship the rocks, clay, logs, trees, the Sun, the Moon, the stars, in addition to other assuredly unworthy things such as moles, snakes, and beasts; which is opposed to the reason more than any other thing because all of it has been, in part, created by the divine power, in part also fabricated by yourselves. (author's translation)

Valadés argues that none of the gods that the natives worship are the real gods: they are the creatures produced by the Christian god and also partially the natives themselves. Thus, indigenous gods do not have any capacity to create even insignificant and worthless things.

I would argue that Pomar, who was asked to write a relación for the Spanish king, and Alva Ixtlilxochitl, who worked as a bilingual interpreter in the colonial court system, were well familiar with the Christian teachings of the Spanish friars and willfully misinterpreted indigenous songs in order to make their ancestor Nezahualcoyotl a precursor of Christianity. Based on the songs attributed to Nezahualcoyotl, Pomar describes Nezahualcoyotl's unknown god as follows:

> Y de eso dan testimonios muchos cantos antiguos que hoy se saben a pedazos, porque en ellos hay muchos nombres y epítetos honrosos

de Dios, como es el decir que había uno solo y que éste era el hacedor del cielo y de la tierra y sustentaba todo lo hecho y lo criado por él, y que estaba donde no tenía segundo lugar de nueve andanzas, y que no se había visto jamás en forma ni cuerpo humano ni en otra figura. (Pomar 1993:175)

And many old songs that today are known only partially give testimony of that, because in them there are many honorable names and epithets of God, such as the reference to there being only one and that he was the creator of the sky and of the earth and he supported all the things created and raised by himself, and that he was where he did not have second place in nine spheres, and that his form had never been seen, neither in a human body nor in any other image. (author's translation)

Pomar (1993:175) gives "in Tloque in Nahuaque" as the Nahua name of Nezahualcoyotl's unknown god, which he translates as "el señor del cielo y de la tierra" (the king of heaven and earth). Alva Ixtlilxochitl identifies the same name as referring to this god in a fragmented poem by Nezahualcoyotl, which also uses other names such as Ipalnemohuani and Teyocoyani:

Ipan Yn chahconauhtla manpan meztica intlatoque nahuaque ipalnemohuani teyocoyani ic el teotl oquiyocox yinxquex quexquix mita ynamota, que bien interpretado quiere decir: "después de nueve andanas está el criador del cielo y de la tierra, por quien viven las criaturas, y un solo dios que crió las cosas visibles y e invisibles." (Alva Ixtlilxochitl 1997, 1:404–5)

Ipan Yn chahconauhtla manpan meztica intlatoque nahuaque ipalnemohuani teyocoyani ic the teotl oquiyocox yinxquex quexquix put ynamota, which well translated means: "After nine spheres is the creator of the sky and of the earth, by whom the creatures live, and a single God that created the visible and invisible things." (author's translation)

The two Texcoca chroniclers present almost the same description of Nezahualcoyotl's unknown god as a single god who created heaven and earth and all visible and invisible things. This concept is exactly the same as that of the Christian god that the Catholic priests preached to the natives. In this context, Pomar and Alva Ixtlilxochitl clearly follow the Christian rather than the indigenous tradition in interpreting the old songs.

Rather than following the religion imposed by the invaders, the natives tried to preserve their religious practices and their gods, Ipalnemohuani and Tloque Nahuaque. Many colonial sources record the rejection of European religion by the natives. The Tlaxcalteca chronicler Diego Muñoz Camargo (1986) records what is probably the natives' first rejection of Christianity. According to this chronicler, like the twelve priests in the *Coloquios y doctrina cristiana* (Sahagún 1986), Cortés tried to convert the indigenous leaders to Christianity by explaining to them his "santísimo ley y fe verdadera, que es la del verdadero Dios Jesucristo nuestro señor Unigénito, Hijo de Dios y Salvador del Mundo" (most holy law and true faith, which is that of the true God Jesus Christ, our only-begotten lord, Son of God and Savior of the World) (Muñoz Camargo 1986:200). The Tlaxcalteca leaders refused to accept the Catholic religion and defended their own:

> Ante todas cosas hemos de consentir que nos derribes y desbarates nuestros ídolos, que son semejanza de nuestros dioses, a los cuales adoramos y reverenciamos de tantos siglos atrás nosotros y nuestros antepasados, que con tanta religión observaron y guardaron en el culto de ellos. ¿Cómo quieres tú que con tanta facilidad los dejemos y consintamos que con tus violentas y sacrílegas manos te dejemos profanar los dioses que en tanto tenemos y estimamos? (Muñoz Camargo 1986:203)

> Before everything we should allow you to knock down and destroy our idols, which are semblances of our gods, to whom for so many centuries we and our ancestors, who with so much piety observed and maintained their cult, have worshipped and venerated for so many centuries before us and our ancestors. How is it that you want us to abandon them so easily and to permit you with your violent and sacrilegious hands to desecrate the gods that we hold in such regard and esteem? (author's translation)

The Tlaxcalteca leaders clearly stated that they had not just one god but many gods and that they did not want to abandon their gods, because "el sol y la luna y demás estrellas relumbrantes se enfadarían contra nosotros y ya no nos mostrarían más su luz ni claridad" (the sun and the moon and other shining stars would get angry with us and they would no longer show us their light nor brightness) (Muñoz Camargo 1986:203). Here again, the indigenous leaders not only emphasized their polytheism, but also manifested their intention to maintain their religion.

According to León-Portilla (1974) and Klor de Alva (1982), even after several decades of evangelization by the Catholic friars, most of the natives still worshipped their old gods in the guise of Christianity. Many friars in the middle and end of the sixteenth century such as Sahagún, Durán, and Torquemada were aware of the incomplete conversion of the natives. Sahagún describes this situation poignantly:

Hallóse después de pocos años muy evidentemente la falta que de la prudencia serpentina hubo en la fundación de esta nueva Iglesia, porque se ignoraba la conspiración que habían hecho entre sí los principales y sátrapas de recibir a Jesucristo entre sus dioses como uno de ellos, y honrarle como los mismos españoles le honran, conforme a la costumbre antigua que tenían, que cuando venía alguna gente forastera a poblar cerca de los que estaban ya poblados, cuando les parecía, tomaban por dios al dios que traían los recién llegados, y de esta manera dicen que Tezcatlipoca es el dios de los de Tlamanalco, porque le trajeron consigo, y Huitzilopochtli es el dios de mexicanos, porque le trajeron consigo. . . .

De esta manera se inclinaron con facilidad a tomar por dios al Dios de los españoles, pero no para que dejasen los suyos antiguos, y esto ocultaron en el catecismo cuando se bautizaron, y al tiempo del catecismo, preguntados si creían en Dios Padre, Hijo y Espíritu Santo, con los demás artículos de la fe, respondían *quemachca*, que sí, conforme a la conspiración y costumbre que tenían; preguntados si renegaban de todos los otros dioses que habían adorado, respondían también *quemachca*, que sí, pálidamente y mentirosamente. (Sahagún cited in León-Portilla 1974:15)

After a few years there was very clearly defect caused by the malicious shrewdness exercised in the foundation of this new Church, because people did not know about the conspiracy which the main nobles and satraps had devised to receive Jesus as one of their gods and to honor him just like the Spaniards themselves honor him; according to the old habit that they had, when some foreign people came to settle down close to those who were already settled, when the latter felt it convenient, they took as god the god that the recent arrivals had brought, and in this manner they say that Tezcatlipoca is the god of those of Tlamanalco, because they brought him with them, and Huitzilopochtli is the god of the Mexica, because they brought him with them. . . .

In this manner they were easily inclined to take as god the God of the Spaniards, but to the point of abandoning their old ones; and this they hid in the catechism when they were baptized. During the catechism, when they were asked if they believed in Father God, Son, and Holy Spirit, with the other articles of the faith, they responded *quemachca*, that they did, following the conspiracy and custom that they had; when they were asked if they denied all the other gods that they had worshipped, they responded also *quemachca*, that they did, timidly and falsely. (author's translation)

In the middle of the sixteenth century, Sahagún notes that the natives were still not fully converted to Christianity. They accepted and understood the Christian god, but from an indigenous polytheistic perspective. Sahagún points out that the indigenous leaders, "los principales y sátrapas," were responsible for the incomplete conversion.

Mestizo chroniclers also describe this same phenomenon. Muñoz Camargo recorded how strongly ancient religious tradition survived in Tlaxcala when he wrote his chronicle in 1566:

> Y ansí fue que luego callaron y comenzaron a ocultar y esconder secretamente muchos ídolos y estatuas, como después adelante andando el tiempo se vio y ha visto, donde secretamente muchos de ellos los servían y adoraban como de antes, aconsejándoles el demonio que no desmayasen, ni los hombres advenedizos los engañasen, lo cual les decían en sueños y otras apariencias, mayormente cuando tomaban y bebían cosas provocativas a ver visiones, que para semejantes casos las tenían y tomaban, por cuya causa muchos de ellos estuvieron endurecidos, rebeldes y obstinados para su conversión. Y ansí, agora en nuestros tiempos, que fue el año de mil quinientos sesenta y seis, muchos principales viejos pidieron agua del Bautismo, porque de vergüenza y empaño no se habían querido bautizar, los cuales habían quedado en aquellos que habían sido duros y pertinaces en dejar los ídolos. (Muñoz Camargo 1986:206–7)

> And this is why later they silenced and began to secretly hide and conceal many idols and statues, as later as time went on it was seen and has been seen, where secretly many of them served and worshipped the idols like before, with the devil advising them not to be dismayed nor to be deceived by the foreigners, which things he told them in dreams and in other ways, especially when they took and drank things that provoke visions, which they had and drank for similar situations, because of which many of them were resistant, rebellious, and stubborn in their conversion. And thus in our times, which was the year 1566, many noble elders who because of shame and blemish had not wanted to be baptized, remaining among those who had been hard and obstinate in abandoning the idols, asked to be baptized. (author's translation)

This is important for the understanding of indigenous communities in the middle of the sixteenth century because it reveals that the natives had not been assimilated into the European religion but rather that they were practicing and conserving their old religion in secret ways. And as Sahagún pointed out, the indigenous leaders played a major role in this practice.

The rejection of European religion by the natives is also evident in the accusations of indigenous leaders by the Inquisition. Among the inquisitional trials, I will focus here on the two indigenous leaders, Martín Ocelotl and don Carlos Ometochtzin Chichimecatecuhtli, because they belonged the highest nobility of Texcoco and its neighboring cities, and their reactions to Christianity may be representative of the native aristocracy in general. According to Klor de Alva (1981:128–40) and Kobayashi (1996:536–37), Martín Ocelotl was trained as a priest before the conquest and was baptized in 1526 in Texcoco.[9] He made many friends among indigenous local rulers and secretly practiced old rites with them. He even predicted the demise of Spanish colonialism by arguing that the Spanish priests would turn into the tzitzimime, a kind of evil creature, who would devour people at the end of the present epoch (Klor de Alva 1981:135). In 1537 he was found guilty and sentenced to confinement for life in Seville.

The case of the other leader, don Carlos Ometochtzin Chichimecatecuhtli, is more important, because he once served as the ruler of Texcoco and was Nezahualcoyotl's grandson. He was accused of keeping pagan pictorial books, secret altars, and idols. According to the testimony of witnesses, he said, "pues oye hermano que de verdad te digo que eso que se enseña en el colegio, todo es burla" (thus, listen brother, for truly I tell you that which is taught in the school, everything is mockery) (*Proceso inquisitorial* 1980:40). Ometochtzin even insisted that the natives should follow the gods of his ancestors:

> Pues oye hermano, que nuestros padres y agüelos dixieron, cuando murieron, que de verdad se dixo que los dioses que ellos tenían y amaban fueron hechos en el cielo y en la tierra, por tanto hermano sólo aquello sigamos que nuestros agüelos y nuestros padres tuvieron y dixieron cuando murieron. (*Proceso inquisitorial* 1980:40–41)

> Thus, listen brother, our parents and grandfathers said, when they died, that it was truly told that the gods that they had and loved were created in the sky and in the earth, therefore brother let's follow only that which our grandfathers and our parents believed and said when they died. (author's translation)

Ometochtzin was found guilty and was burned in 1539. The case of Ometochtzin reveals the attitude of many Nahua intellectuals toward European religion in the middle of the sixteenth century. Even though he received a monastic education as he himself states—"Yo me crié en la iglesia y casa de Dios como tú" (I grew up in the church and house of God like you) (*Proceso inquisitorial* 1980:42)—don Carlos Ometochtzin maintained the same polytheistic religious ideas as his ancestors.

As these examples show, the supplanting of indigenous gods by the Christian notion of god was not quite successful even in the mid-sixteenth century when the Nahua songs of *Romances* (1993) and *Cantares* (1985) were collected. The case of Martín Ocelotl and don Carlos Ometochtzin and the examples of the "principales y satrápas" and "antiguos principales" recorded in Sahagún's and Muñoz Camargo's chronicles demonstrate that the natives were only superficially converted. According to Klor de Alva (1982:353), "Without changing their religious conviction, they simply borrowed from Christianity whatever elements were necessary to appear Christian. Most of the documents I have studied intimate that this was indeed commonly the case among Aztecs of both privileged and non privileged classes, and was especially true for the latter." One of the many examples of borrowing "from Christianity whatever elements were necessary to appear Christian" occurred in the singing of religious songs, which was widely practiced for Christian conversion in the native communities. Sahagún sees this indigenous singing of songs as a great threat to native conversion, and he himself wrote Christian psalms in Nahuatl to replace the old songs:

> Since the time they were baptized efforts have been made to force them to abandon those old canticles of praise to their false gods and to sing only in praise of God and His saints, and to do so in the daytime in the festival seasons, on Sundays, and on the saints' days of their churches. And for this purpose in many places they have been given canticles, and they have accepted and sung them, and still sing them in some places. But in other places—in most places—they persist in going back to singing their old canticles in their houses or their palaces (a circumstances that arouses a good deal of suspicion as to the sincerity of their Christian Faith); for in the old canticles mostly idolatrous things are sung in a style so obscure that none can understand them well except they themselves. And they use other canticles to persuade the population to what they want, or about war or other matters that are not good; for they have canticles composed for these [purposes] that they refuse to abandon. In order easily to counteract this mischief, in this year 1583, in this volume, called *Christian Psalmody*, these canticles have been printed in the Nahuatl language so that they will completely abandon the old canticles, a penalty being imposed applicable to any who go back to singing the old canticles. (Sahagún 1993:7)

Sahagún published the book *Psalmodia christiana* in 1583, but he started to write the psalms in Nahuatl twenty or thirty years prior to that time. A manuscript copy of the book began circulating among the Indians around 1564 (Anderson 1993:xxxii–xxxiii; Burkhart 1996:67). This year falls in the middle of the period between 1550 and 1570, during which most of the songs in *Cantares* and the

Romances were originally collected (Bierhorst 1985:9). The information that Sahagún records provides an important clue for how to understand the Nahua songs of the two collections. Until the publication of the *Psalmodia* in 1583, pre-Hispanic song practice maintained its original form without much radical change. Even though the natives sang Christian songs, they sang them mostly in the church. Outside the church, they were singing songs dedicated to their gods in their houses and palaces. As the main hosts of these song performances, the indigenous leaders were able to preserve their old traditions among the plebeians by controlling the content and context of the performance. Thus, except for several overtly Christian songs in *Cantares* and *Romances*, the indigenous terms used in these poems refer to the original indigenous concept of gods rather than the Christian god.[10]

Reyes García (1993:90) insists that many of these songs should be understood "within a specific historical context: the exploitation and ideological repression that native Mexicans suffered as a result of the Spanish invasion. Faced with pain, death and wholesale erasure of their own values, the Indians of the sixteenth century exclaimed bitterly: 'before our eyes and in our time the ancient words [about the brevity of life] have come to be fulfilled.'" As shown in the mode of icnocuicatl (bereavement song or orphan song) in *Cantares*, the song composers and singers, who belonged to the same upper class of indigenous society as Martín Ocelotl and don Carlos Ometochtzin, the "principales y satrápas" of Sahagún, and the "antiguos principales" of Muñoz Camargo, express a longing for their old gods:

> where is the dios
> for whom we live [Ipalnemohuani]?
> where are you?
> your sad friends await you
> with songs they are grieving
> with flowers they seek you
> they feel pain
> searching for your soul
> strength, honor, ay! (*Cantares* 1985:f. 12r, in Reyes García 1993:93)

This stanza reflects the anguish of the indigenous leaders who lost their god under the invaders. Even though they were forced to worship the god of the invaders, they still continued to search for their own god with longing and pain. At the same time, this stanza maintains the pre-Hispanic political, cultural, and religious tradition involving a unified search for their god's spiritual aid.

One of the most famous songs attributed to Nezahualcoyotl and presented as evidence of his nonbelief in indigenous gods can be better understood in the colonial context:

> Are You real, are You rooted?
> Is it only as to come inebriated?
> The Giver of Life [Ipalnemohuani]:
> is this true?
> Perhaps, as they say, it is not true?
> May our hearts
> Be not tormented!
>
> All that is real,
> All that is rooted,
> They say that it is not real,
> It is not rooted.
> The Giver of Life [Ipalnemohuani]
> Only appears absolute.
> May our hearts
> Be not tormented,
> Because He is the Giver of Life. (*Romances* 1993:ff. 19v–20r, in León-Portilla 1992b:84)

These stanzas come from the song entitled "To the Kind God" ("A lo divino gentílico") in *Romances*. If we read Garibay's complete translation of the song (*Romances* 1993), it seems to have a pre-Hispanic origin because it expresses awe and fear of the god and the brevity of earthly life as discussed in chapter 6. According to Pomar (1993), Alva Ixtlilxochitl (1997), and modern scholars such as León-Portilla (1972:37–38), this poem clearly conveys skepticism about the existence of indigenous gods. The image of Nezahualcoyotl presented in this poem supports both this argument and the peaceful and philosophical image of Nezahualcoyotl proposed by those chroniclers and scholars. But this interpretation isolates the poem fragment from both its larger literary and historical contexts. If we also read the other stanzas that accompany this poem fragment and place them in the colonial context in which they were produced, then the poem not only expresses a completely different attitude toward indigenous gods, but also conveys a vastly different image of Nezahualcoyotl.

The song "A lo divino gentílico" (To the Kind God) consists of eleven stanzas. Here again are the two stanzas reproduced above along with two additional stanzas that follow:

> Are You real, are You rooted?
> Is it only as to come inebriated?
> The Giver of Life [Ipalnemohuani]:
> is this true?
> Perhaps, as they say, it is not true?
> May our hearts
> Be not tormented!

All that is real,
All that is rooted,
They say that it is not real,
It is not rooted.
The Giver of Life [Ipalnemohuani]
Only appears absolute.
May our hearts
Be not tormented,
Because He is the Giver of Life. (*Romances* 1993:ff. 19v–20r, in León-
   Portilla 1992b:84)

Only he: [God] Life Giver [Ipalnemohuani] ...
I was without knowing correctly ...
Who perhaps never? Who perhaps never?
I did not have pleasure among the men.

But You kindly cause it rain,
From you your wealth and destiny come,
Oh Life Giver [Ipalnemohuani] ...
Fragrant flowers, valuable flowers:
I desired them anxiously!
I was without knowing correctly. (author's translation)

Sólo él: [dios] por quien todo vive [Ipalnemohuani] ...
Yo estaba sin saber rectamente ...
¿Quién acaso nunca? ¿Quién acaso nunca?
No tenía yo deleite entre los hombres.

Pero Tú amablemente la haces llover,
De ti procede tu riqueza y dicha,
Oh por quien todo vive [Ipalnemohuani] ...
Flores perfumadas, flores valiosas:
¡yo las deseaba ansioso!
Yo estaba sin saber rectamente. (*Romances* 1993, 53)

The first two stanzas are merely introductory phrases to what follows. In the introductory stanzas, the poet wonders if the god is true by asking himself, "Are you real," and then he himself answers that nothing, including the god, is true. Even the god is arbitrary. Because of this uncertainty, the poet prays not to suffer, not to "be tormented." In the next two stanzas, however, he asserts that he knows the god exists and that he is the creator of earthly things such as perfumed flowers, referring metaphorically to the divine words of songs or to the sacrificial warriors. In the first two stanzas, the poet employs the present tense, which refers to the song-present, the colonial period, and asks if the indigenous god is true or not. But in the next two stanzas, he realizes that the god is true, laments the loss of his former desire for the flowers created by the indigenous god, and regrets that he did not appreciate them adequately in the past. By comparing his understanding of the god in the colonial period with that of the precolonial period, the poet stresses how much he misses his lost god. The poet selected Nezahualcoyotl as his muse because he felt better able to explain his feelings about colonial society through the voice of Nezahualcoyotl, who was a religious and philosophical symbol in the indigenous tradition.

The Conquest of Chalco, Nezahualcoyotl's Unknown God, and Tetzcotzinco

According to "La guerra de Chalco" (Anonymous 1997) and Alva Ixtlilxochitl's writings (1997), Nezahualcoyotl and his Mexica allies were badly defeated by the Chalca at the beginning of the war. Even the sons of Nezahualcoyotl and Axayacatl were captured and killed by the Chalca. The human sacrifice and other religious rites recommended by the priests did not improve the situation, so Nezahualcoyotl retired to Tetzcotzinco, the most sacred place of Texcoco. There, while he was praying and fasting for forty days in honor of his unknown god, a mysterious, angelic messenger from the unknown god spoke with one of his servants and revealed to him that Nezahualcoyotl's son, Axoquentzin, would conquer Chalco. The king did not believe the servant and imprisoned him, but this revelation turned out to be true. The seventeen-year-old son of Nezahualcoyotl, Axoquentzin, happened upon the battlefield where his brothers were fighting against the Chalca. One of his brothers reproached him because he should not have been there due to his young age. Ashamed and angry, Axoquentzin armed himself and unexpectedly defeated the formidable Chalca by capturing the Chalca king. Later the story reveals that the angelic messenger also appeared to Axoquentzin, told him to go to the battlefield, and assured him that the messenger would protect him.

According to the Texcoca sources, the unknown god first appears in this account of Texcoca victory in the Chalca war. The codices, chronicles, and songs of Tenochtitlan and of Chalco about the Chalca war, however, present a very different picture. Chalco was one of the most ancient regions in the Basin of Mexico, certainly older than Texcoco and Tenochtitlan. According to the *Códice Xolotl* (1996:map 1), when the first ruler of Texcoco, Xolotl, arrived at the lake of the basin, Chalco had already been inhabited by the Tolteca. According to the *Codex Mendoza* (1992:ff. 4r–5r), Chalco was conquered several times by the Mexica even before the alliance of the three cities. The Chalca, however, continuously rebelled and constantly defied Aztec authority. Chalco was so powerful that even many Aztec-allied cities could not conquer it easily.

The Mexica chronicler Alvarado Tezozomoc's record (1987) of the conquest of Chalco differs clearly from the Texcoca version. According to Alvarado Tezozomoc, the conquest was carried out by the forces of Tenochtitlan rather than by only one prince of Texcoco. The Mexica had difficulty dominating their enemy; indeed, they were defeated at the very start of the war. Three brothers of Moctezuma Ilhuicamina were captured and sacrificed by the Chalca. This historical event is also painted on plate XVIII of the *Codex Azcatitlan* (1995). A dead person appears connected to Chalco by a dotted line (*Codex Azcatitlan* 1995:figure 4.6). Barlow identifies him as one of the Chalca lords who died in the conquest. I would argue, however, that he represents an important Mexica lord, maybe one of the three sacrificed in Chalco, not only because his costume and hairstyle are the same as those of other Mexica lords in the plate, but also because the indigenous tlacuilo (painter-scribe) would normally only include information relevant to his own city, not the enemy's. In Alvarado Tezozomoc's version, the Texcoca play no role in the conquest of Chalco, a feat that was accomplished solely by the Mexica.

On the other hand, the sources of the defeated Chalca describe the conquest from a different perspective. Some Chalca songs in *Cantares Mexicanos* (1985) narrate that the military expedition was conducted neither by the Texcoca Axoquentzin nor by the Mexica alone, but rather by the all the Aztec allied forces. The following passage identifies the leaders of the Mexica and the Texcoca as participants in the war: "Among the rushes you sing, O Montezuma, O Nezahualcoyotl, Alas! You destroy the realm: you ruin Chalco here on earth. Alas, may your hearts be grieving!" (*Cantares* 185, 51, 10). Another stanza of the same song also records that "Multiple eagles and jaguars, multiple Mexicans, Acolhuans, and Tepanecs, do the Chalcans become" (*Cantares* 1985, 51, 36). This Chalca song states that the Mexica, the Texcoca (Acolhuaque), and Tlacopaneca (Tepaneca) conquered Chalco. In addition, the Chalca indigenous annalist Chimalpahin (1998, 2:255–65) describes the war between the invaders and the Chalca. According to his version, the war began in 11 Reed (1451) and ended in 12 House (1465). The conflict lasted more than fifteen years, and the Mexica played a crucial role. Like Alvarado Tezozomoc, Chimalpahin narrates the sacrifice of the three Mexica *pipiltzin* or "precious nobles": Tlacahuepan, Chahuecue, and Quetzalcuauh. Chimalpahin concludes that Chalco was defeated by the courage of Moctezuma Ilhuicamina and his companion Cihuacoatl Tlacaelel. Neither the Mexica nor the Chalca version indicates any contribution of Axoquentzin to this conquest. Thus, these texts call into question the Texcoca chroniclers' insistence that Axoquentzin played a decisive role in the conquest of Chalco.

According to "La guerra de Chalco" (Anonymous 1997) and Alva Ixtlilxochitl's chronicles (1997), Tetzcotzinco appears as the most sacred place in the story of Nezahualcoyotl's unknown god because Nezahualcoyotl intuited and worshiped his unknown god there. After his intuition of this god, Nezahualcoyotl prohibited human sacrifice in his city-state Texcoco and constructed a temple dedicated to him. Alva Ixtlilxochitl (1997, 1:546) records that Nezahualcoyotl built the temple in one of his palaces, and he later states that the king built it directly in front of Huitzilopochtli's temple as an expression of his opposition to this Mexica god (1997, 2:126–27). However, Clavijero (1991:540) claims that Nezahualcoyotl built the temple in Tetzcotzinco. Whether the temple was constructed in Tetzcotzinco or not, both sources agree that it was a peaceful place where Nezahualcoyotl intuited the unknown god and where human sacrifice was not practiced. Tetzcotzinco was, in fact, one of the most sacred places in the Texcoca region, not because it was associated with Nezahualcoyotl's unknown god, but rather for its association with the rain god, Tlaloc. According to Townsend (1992:132–44), Nezahualcoyotl's Tetzcotzinco project was inspired by the Tlaloc temple located at the base of Mount Tlaloc where the Mexica rulers performed rites to "bring forth the life-giving water" (1992:132). Since water was so important for fertility in Aztec society, these rain-making rites were one of the most important ceremonies in Tenochtitlan, and the Mexica rulers had to go to the mountain with sacrificial offerings. By examining archaeological monuments, Townsend demonstrates that three shrines dedicated to Tlaloc, maize goddesses, and water goddesses, respectively, were constructed in Tetzcotzinco and that human sacrifices dedicated to these gods were regular occurrences. Some Spanish friars in the sixteenth century such as Fray Diego Valadés describe Tetzcotzinco as the most idolatrous place where massive human sacrifices were carried out:

> Yo mismo supe. De boca de ciertos indios ancianos, que en el templo de Tetzcutzingo, que dista media milla de Texcoco, se habían inmolados años atrás, en un solemne sacrificio, sesenta y seis mil hombres, hechos prisioneros en la guerra contra los tlaxcaltecas (espectáculo que ciertamente es digno de lamentarse y deplorarse); el cual templo era más famoso de todos, cuyas ruinas aún pueden verse en el presente. Mas esta ferocidad, propia de animales, ha sido ya trocada en mejor condición por la bondad divina, gracias a fray Martín de Valencia y a once padres que le acompañan, los cuales como doce lumbreras, a semejanza de los doce apóstoles, fueron los primeros de nuestra Orden franciscana que marcharon a ese nuevo Mundo para establecer la nueva Iglesia. (Valadés 1989:395)

> I myself found out from the mouth of some elderly Indians that in the temple of Tetzcotzingo, which is a half mile from Texcoco, sixty-six thousand men captured in the war against the Tlaxcalteca had been sacrificed years ago in a solemn sacrifice (a spectacle that must be certainly regretted and be deplored). The temple was the most famous of all, whose ruins still can be seen in the present. But this ferocity, typical

of animals, already has been replaced with the best condition through divine kindness, thanks to fray Martin of Valencia and to eleven priests who accompany him, who like twelve luminaries, similar to the twelve apostles, were the pioneers of our Franciscan Order who went to the New World to establish the new Church. (author's translation)

For Valadés, Tetzcotzinco was the most important indigenous temple, and he contrasts the violent practice of human sacrifice in that temple with the civilized condition of the Indians after being converted to Christianity. According to Patrick Lesbre (2001:336), this condemnation of Tetzcotzinco by the Spanish missionary chroniclers in the sixteenth century prompted Alva Ixtlilxochitl to transform Tetzcotzinco into a totally nonviolent place with flower gardens and zoos of exotic animals.[11] However, the archaeological monuments in Tetzcotzinco do not corroborate Alva Ixtlilxochitl's claim, and the Spanish priests clearly verify that Tetzcotzinco was one of the most sacred places for pre-Hispanic Texcoca religion where human sacrifice was regularly conducted.

According to the story of Axoquentzin represented in "La guerra de Chalco" (Anonymous 1997) and Alva Ixtlilxochitl's works (1997), a young man appears as an angelic messenger of Nezahualcoyotl's unknown god and reveals to the king the victory that his son Axoquentzin would bring over the Chalca. In the religious or mythological tradition of central Mexico, however, the indigenous gods did not send messengers but rather communicated directly with their religious leaders. The god Huitzilopochtli guided the Mexica from Aztlan to Tenochtitlan by verbally communicating with his priests. Pomar (1993:164) also records that the god Tezcatlipoca guided the Colhuaque to Texcoco by talking directly to his believers. Moreover, the god of the Tlaxcalteca, Camaxtli, brought his people to Tlaxcala by talking with his followers: "Y les decía y revelaba lo que había de suceder y lo que habían de hacer, en qué partes y lugares habían de poblar y permanecer" (And he told them and revealed what would happen and what they would do, in what parts and places they would populate and settle down) (Muñoz Camargo 1986:89). These texts demonstrate that the notion of an angelic messenger sent from a god is not consistent with the indigenous religious tradition. This image was most likely adopted from the European biblical tradition. Furthermore, the entire episode closely resembles the story of David and Goliath: young David, who visited his brothers in the war, killed the formidable Goliath. Just like David, the young Axoquentzin arrives on the battlefield as a visitor and suddenly kills the Chalca king whose seemingly invincible, Goliath-like power even the combined forces of the Aztec troops could not defeat.

The Spanish priests began to present Nezahualcoyotl as a religious skeptic and identified him as a precursor of Christianity before the conquest. Texcoca chroniclers such as Pomar and Alva Ixtlilxochitl graciously embraced this idea and further embellished it in their (mis)interpretation of their sources in order to bring their nation's religious tradition in line with that of the European invaders. These Texcoca chroniclers transformed Nezahualcoyotl into a Christian-like figure who conceived of the peaceful unknown god in clear contrast to the Spanish image of the bloodthirsty Mexica. Later historians and literary critics relied on the image of Nezahualcoyotl provided by the European and Europeanized chroniclers without challenging their interpretation of the indigenous sources or cross-checking these sources with those of other regions. However, Nezahualcoyotl was in fact a crucial religious symbol in Texcoco, not because he had begun worshiping an unknown god as typically depicted in alphabetic texts, but rather because he reconstructed his city and participated actively in the practice of Nahua religion.

CHAPTER NINE

Conclusion

The European invasion of the Americas involved not only the expropriation of land, labor, and material from the natives, but also the occidentalization of their history, arts, and religion. The native elites in New Spain strived to defend their land and to maintain their old traditions under colonial rule, in some cases to the point of sacrificing their lives. In this process of colonization, however, some of those who were fully Europeanized viewed their own society and traditions from the colonizers' perspective. In many cases, they even transformed the reality of their own society and traditions in order to make them fit the colonizers' expectations. As the title indicates, this book is dedicated to revising the pre-Hispanic history, poetry, and religion that colonial chroniclers manipulated and misinterpreted. In this revision, I have focused on the canonical images of the Texcoca king Nezahualcoyotl, and I have demonstrated how these canonical images were invented and propagated from the conquest to the present. In doing so, this book proposes several new directions in Nahua studies.

I suggest that a critical approach needs to reconsider the works of Spanish friars and mestizo chroniclers. Most scholars who study Nezahualcoyotl rely on works by Toribio de Benavente or Motolinia, Juan de Torquemada, Juan Bautista Pomar, and don Fernando Alva Ixtlilxochitl as their primary sources without taking into account the colonial context in which these works were produced. I think that a consideration of this context is extremely important, however, because colonial chroniclers had a prefabricated ideological mindset that influenced the way they dealt with pre-Hispanic traditions. As colonizers, the first Spanish friars such as Motolinia and Andrés de Olmos introduced a Judeo-Christian perspective into their accounts of pre-Hispanic history. As soon as their chronicles appeared, they were read as authoritative histories.

In the composition of their works, later Spanish chroniclers such as Fray Bartolomé de Las Casas, Alonso de Zorita, Fray Gerónimo de Mendieta, Fray Juan de Torquemada, and Fray Agustín de Vetancurt often copied directly, in many cases verbatim, from these earlier texts. Other Europeanized chroniclers such as Juan Bautista Pomar, don Fernando de Alva Ixtlilxochitl, and don Diego Muñoz Camargo acquired a similar Judeo-Christian perspective from the Spanish friars. This Europeanized version of pre-Hispanic indigenous history was reinforced in the later colonial period and has continued through the present. Innumerable historians and Nahua scholars from the colonial period to the present draw from the many colonial chronicles and modern studies, but they overlook the fact that most of their sources are infused with the colonizer's perspective. The canonical images of Nezahualcoyotl are a clear example of the way this perspective shaped the construction of indigenous history in the colonial period. The colonial influence has been largely ignored in current studies of Nezahualcoyotl, and often in the study of general Nahua history and culture as well.

I propose that Nahua scholars recognize the importance of indigenous pictorial and Nahuatl-language texts and use them as the most valuable sources for the study of the pre-Hispanic period in Mexico. Among the colonial sources, indigenous pictorial and Nahuatl texts are the sources least affected by colonial ideologies. Unlike the European and Europeanized chroniclers' Spanish texts based on the European model of historiography, the authors of most indigenous pictorial and Nahuatl texts were natives, and they recorded their histories according to the conventions of pre-Hispanic indigenous historiography. These indigenous texts may have been adjusted to the colonial situation, but they provide a richer and more reliable indigenous history than the European alphabetic texts that rewrote and interpreted the indigenous past according to European historiographical criteria. As some scholars have argued (Boone 2000; Boone and Mignolo 1994; Brotherston 1992, 1995, 2005; Wood 2003), pictorial texts, as the original medium of indigenous historiography, must be recognized as one of the most important sources of information for pre-Hispanic and colonial studies. Most modern scholars, however, have relied on European alphabetic texts as their primary sources, largely ignoring the pictorial texts from which these very same alphabetic texts drew when they were composed in the colonial period. One of the main reasons that the colonial depictions of Nezahualcoyotl have continued to be popular until today is that most scholars who study Nezahualcoyotl have been reluctant to use pictorial sources such as the *Codex Xolotl*, the *Mapa Quinatzin*, the *Mapa Tlotzin*, the *Codex Azcatitlan*, the *Codex Mendoza*, the *Codex en Cruz*, and many others. Ignorance of pictorial texts, however, is not limited to studies of Nezahualcoyotl; it also characterizes many other studies of pre-Hispanic history and culture. As shown in this book, the study of pictorial texts should form an integral part of Nahua studies.

Returning to original indigenous sources in Nahua studies is even more urgent and critical when leading scholars cite these sources but interpret them based on accounts contained in colonial chronicles. Most studies of Nezahualcoyotl after the 1960s tend to simply accept uncritically the work of Angel María Garibay K., Miguel León-Portilla, and Jerome Offner without recognizing the problematic nature of the colonial sources upon which their work is based. Garibay's and León-Portilla's works have been extremely influential in the study of Nahua literature and culture. Their translations and interpretations of Nahua songs made Nahua literature more accessible to students and scholars. It would not be an exaggeration to say that interest in Nahua poetry was revived by the efforts of these great scholars. Offner's contribution is also significant. He conducted the first and most comprehensive study of pre-Hispanic legal practices by focusing on Nezahualcoyotl's legal system. Garibay, León-Portilla, and Offner base their studies on indigenous sources such as pictorial codices and Nahua annals and songs, and to this extent they were pioneers in recognizing the importance of these sources. However, they also uncritically accept the interpretation of the pictorial texts found in colonial chronicles such as those of Alva Ixtlilxochitl. By doing so, they ironically reproduce the same highly biased colonial ideology that informed these colonial texts.

In addition to emphasizing the significance of indigenous sources, I suggest that an interdisciplinary approach is critical for the study of pre-Hispanic Mexico. To better understand pre-Hispanic indigenous literature, in particular, scholars must study the political, historical, religious, and cultural context, because pre-Hispanic indigenous society maintained unique literary representations that were far different from those of the colonized society after the conquest. The reconstruction of pre-Hispanic indigenous society always requires the broadest possible framework and an interdisciplinary approach that takes into account indigenous literary and historiographic representations and practices. Evaluating the pre-Hispanic literary tradition based solely on colonial alphabetic texts leads to the misinterpretation of indigenous poetic images and ideas. This interdisciplinary approach is important as well for other studies, such as the study of pre-Hispanic history. Most historians neglect literary texts such as Nahua songs because they assume that these texts do not convey much information about pre-Hispanic history. However, as shown in this study, the Nahua songs were one of the most important indigenous media for recording their history during the precolonial period. Thus, an interdisciplinary approach is a significant way of enriching our understanding of pre-Hispanic Mexico.

Finally, most scholars who examine pre-Hispanic indigenous figures such as Quetzalcoatl, Moctezuma, Huitzilopochtli, and others focus on their religious or political roles during the pre-Hispanic period. A few researchers study the differences and modifications in the roles of pre-Hispanic figures before and after the conquest. However, little has been done to present comprehensive research on the portrayal of a pre-Hispanic indigenous figure and the way in which the descriptions of this figure change from the colonial period to the present. This study's focus on Nezahualcoyotl fills this gap while attempting to inspire similar studies in Nahua history, religion, and literature.

Epilogue

Nezahualcoyotl and the Irony of Colonialism in Ernesto Cardenal's Poetry

Nezahualcoyotl has been an important source of artistic inspiration for many creative writers. Most of them write biographical novels about Nezahualcoyotl, but some of them take advantage of Nezahualcoyotl's peace-loving ideology in order to criticize current political practice.[1] The Nicaraguan priest, poet, and political activist Ernesto Cardenal re-creates Nezahualcoyotl as a universal symbol of peace and presents him in opposition to forms of political injustice such as colonialism, capitalism, and dictatorships. However, Cardenal contradicts himself by basing his representation of Nezahualcoyotl on the peaceful and civilized images created and propagated by colonial ideologies.

Ernesto Cardenal is well known for incorporating indigenous themes into his poetry. In *Homenaje a los indios americanos* (1972) and later its expanded version, *Los ovnis de oro* (1992), indigenous cultural, religious, economic, and political systems appear frequently as major sources of poetic inspiration. In these poems, Cardenal deals with various indigenous civilizations that include the Aztecs, the Maya-Quiche, the Incas, the Guarani, the Cunas, and those of the North American Indians. Among these indigenous peoples, Cardenal pays special attention to the Aztecs not only by focusing on specific historical figures such as Quetzalcoatl and Nezahualcoyotl, but also by applying Nahua poetics in his own poetry. In *Los ovnis de oro* (1992), there are eleven poems that treat pre-Hispanic indigenous society in Mexico, and most of them deal with Quetzalcoatl and Nezahualcoyotl. Two of the longest are even entitled "Quetzalcoatl" and "Nezahualcoyotl." In addition, Cardenal employs the major themes of Nahua poetry such as brotherhood, and he inserts some fragments of actual Nahua poems within his own. Moreover, he named seven of these eleven poems "Cantares mexicanos" following the title of the Nahua song collection of the same name.

As Eduardo F. Elias (1982) and Robert Pring-Mill (1992) point out, the presence of past indigenous cultures in Cardenal's poetry serves as a subtext to denounce the oppressive and unjust situation of contemporary Latin America: Cardenal finds good and evil in the indigenous past, and he represents the victory of the prior over the latter, by which he implies the inevitable end of evil in the present dominated by colonialism, imperialism, capitalism, and contemporary military dictators. Cardenal focuses on Quetzalcoatl and his disciple Nezahualcoyotl, who have long been symbols of pre-Hispanic indigenous civilization, appearing in numerous historical and literary texts. Cardenal presents these two indigenous heroes as symbolic of the good in pre-Hispanic Mexico because of their peaceful religious, political, and cultural practices. Against the ideology of Quetzalcoatl and Nezahualcoyotl, Cardenal introduces the Aztecs and their main god Huitzilopochtli as the symbols of evil because of their practice of human sacrifice and their imperialistic political and economic system.[2] The poetry extends this struggle between good and evil from the past into the present by establishing a connection between the barbarous practices of the Aztecs and the military and economic oppression carried out by modern dictators and imperialists. This connection implies that as the Aztecs were destroyed by the Spaniards, so too will modern dictators and imperialists meet their end.

The poetic battle between good and evil and the inescapable demise of the latter that Cardenal reconstructs in his poetry seem very compelling because he draws on historical texts such as Juan Bautista Pomar's *Relación geográfica de Texcoco* (1993), Fray Bernardino de Sahagún's works, and literary texts such as *Cantares Mexicanos* (1985). In addition, Cardenal utilizes major contemporary historical, archaeological, and literary scholarly research on pre-Hispanic Mexico such as the works of Angel María Garibay K., Miguel León-Portilla, and Davíd Carrasco. Cardenal, however, "can often rely disappointingly on secondary sources and push favorable readings of his own too hard" (Brotherston 1975:12). Thus, by simply following the secondary sources without comparing them to their original sources, Cardenal engages in a colonization of indigenous culture that distorts the images of Quetzalcoatl, Nezahualcoyotl, and the Aztecs, the very kind of injustice he criticizes so severely.

Following his colonial and modern sources, Cardenal describes Quetzalcoatl as a precursor of Nezahualcoyotl. He was an ideal god and ruler who established peace, liberty, social harmony, and devotion to pacific religious values in Toltec society. Just as the Spanish friars first did in the sixteenth century, Cardenal identifies Quetzalcoatl with the biblical figure of Saint Thomas. This Christian-like Quetzalcoatl, however, was forced by the other indigenous gods to leave his city of Tula because of his rejection of human sacrifice. Thereafter, Tula was transformed into a barbarous place where human sacrifice and militarism dominated, and this continued in Tenochtitlan:

> Now Huitzilopochtli,
> Lord of war:
> supreme god.
> Alter the defeat of the worshippers of Quetzalcóatl
> Human sacrifices.
>
> ...
>
> In the center of Tenochtitlan
> The Main Temple
> Sanctifying the conquests. (Cardenal 1992:305)[3]

Quetzalcoatl, as a patron god of peace and love, was replaced by Huitzilopochtli, a god of war and human sacrifice. In Tenochtitlan, militaristic imperialism was introduced to obtain captives for the ritual human sacrifice to Huitzilopochtli.

In Cardenal's poetry, Nezahualcoyotl appears as a follower of Quetzalcoatl's ideology and thus as another symbol of good: "The tradition of the Toltecs blossomed there in Texcoco 'followers of the old doctrine' (of Quetzalcóatl)" (Cardenal 1992:239). He was the religious sage who rejected human sacrifice by worshiping a Quetzalcoatl- or Christian-like unknown god, the prophet who anticipated the destruction of the Aztecs, and the pacific poet-king who dedicated himself to composing beautiful songs rather than military campaigns. With these civilized and peaceful images, Cardenal also establishes a series of contrasts between Nezahualcoyotl and the Aztecs. The Aztecs construct a splendid temple dedicated to their god Huitzilopochtli, and in front of this structure Nezahualcoyotl constructs an even larger temple dedicated to his unknown god:

> A pyramid for *Tloque Nahuaque*
> Master of Presence and Inwardness
> Invisible as night and impalpable as wind.
> With 9 flights
> Above, on the outside, only black with stars
> And no idol inside
> Here across from the pyramid of the Fierce God
> And taller than *it*.
> Precisely across from the pyramid of Huitzilopochtli-Nazi
> The pyramid of the Unknown God, with neither
> Image nor sacrificial stone in it . . .
> Coyote with Not, Fasting Coyote
> Prayed alone in there (Cardenal 1992:219)

The Aztecs offer "human hearts" to their god Huitzilopochtli, while Nezahualcoyotl, "Coyote with Not," "Fasting Coyote," which describes his pictorial representation in the codices, merely prayed and fasted. The famous Aztec leader

Tlacaelel increases the number of human sacrifices for his god, while, "My ideology is Non-Violence, Nezahualcoyotl said" (Cardenal 1992:239). Nezahualcoyotl promotes brotherhood while the Aztecs frequently provoke wars. In addition, the Aztecs oppress their commoners while Nezahualcoyotl treats his just like himself. The Aztec leaders changed or burned the historical pictorial books while Nezahualcoyotl established the death penalty for those who deliberately altered history. As a great philosopher and sage, Nezahualcoyotl detested Aztec barbarism and predicted the downfall of the Aztec world using the motif of disillusionment: that everything in the world, even though it is precious gold or jade, is brief and transitory (Cardenal 1992:186–88).

Cardenal (1992:244–53) describes some pre-Hispanic sages (tlamatinime) like Nezahualcoyotl who rejected the dominant ideology of Huitzilopochtli. These tlamatinime as "opponents of the Aztec regime" (1992:251) faithfully followed the peaceful ideology of Quetzalcoatl (1992:244–53). They pursued poetry, rather than war or human sacrifice, as a way to access a peace-loving god such as Quetzalcoatl. Cardenal's interpretation of Nahua poetry, in xochitl in cuicatl (flower and song), and Nahua philosophy is clearly indebted to León-Portilla's study of Nahua poetry and philosophy. More specifically, León-Portilla's contrast between the horrible Aztecs and the peaceful figures of Quetzalcoatl and Nezahualcoyotl and his analysis of Nahua poetry as a reaction against human sacrifice figures prominently in Cardenal's conception of Aztec philosophy. And León-Portilla presents Nezahualcoyotl as the paragon of tlamatinime. In Cardenal's poetry, these tlamatinime frequently met in Nezahualcoyotl's palace to promote their peaceful god and engage in the composition of songs:

> They gather in the Poetry Room.
> The Giver of Life paints things with Beauty
> Colors with Flower-Song
>   Things are his Codex
> Those colors of the lake, ruby silver of flowers
> Are his *flowers and songs*, his poems
>   We live only in his painting
> We come near him with poems, with paintings.
> We make songs in honor of the One who invents himself
>   And is the inventor of things
> And he is in the songs
>   Not in the "blossoming wars" but in FLOWER-SONG
>   And gives the poems
> While we smoke. (Cardenal 1992:225)

The god that is represented by "the Giver of Life" and "One who invents himself" is described as a lover of beautiful things like flowers, poems/songs, and pictorial books. In Cardenal's poems, this god appears in contrast to the flower war conducted by the Aztecs and their neighboring cities to obtain captives to sacrifice to their gods. The divinity that Cardenal describes refers to a peaceful god—such as the Christianized Quetzalcoatl or the unknown god that Nezahualcoyotl worshiped—who requires peaceful songs rather than human blood.

Cardenal focuses on the concepts of friendship or brotherhood that the sage-poets, tlamatinime, promote in their songs. For Cardenal, brotherhood is an exemplary ideology of the peace-loving indigenous sage-poets who rejected human sacrifice. In the following poem, via the voice of the poet Cuacuauhtzin, Cardenal demonstrates how the ideals of brotherhood contrast with the sanguinary Aztec practice:

> And Cuacuauhtzin sings:
> "let us all be friends!
> Let us know each other through songs.
> We are leaving but the songs will remain.
> I hear a song and I become sad ...
> The rains arrived, and yet I cry.
> I shall leave rain, flowers and songs behind.
> That is why I cry, that is why I sing."
> —"You are friends of the Brotherhood, of the Society."
> Lake Texcoco full of canoes.
> Canoes and chinampas, with girls.
> Smoke of human sacrifices
> Far away, over Tenochtitlan.
> And white against the sky, the Sleeping Woman.
> "The society, the Brotherhood of poets
> Will not disappear because of me" (Cardenal 1992:225)

Cuacuauhtzin invites his fellows to get to know each other with songs and illuminates the ephemeral life on earth by comparing the shortness of life with the durability of the songs. The transitory nature of life makes the poet sad, but he finds consolation in the company of his friends. Then, the voice of Cardenal contrasts this brotherhood with human sacrifice. The lake of Texcoco, the hometown of the most representative peaceful poet, Nezahualcoyotl, appears as a symbol of civilization and peace, a place filled with canoes and floating gardens (*chinampas*) where the tlamatinime entertained themselves with songs and with women. Meanwhile, the capital city of the Aztecs, Tenochtitlan, is busy burning the bodies of the sacrificed. Again, Cuacuauhtzin appears and asserts that the society and the brotherhood of poets will not cease because of him, which means that they and their civilized actions, not Aztec human sacrifice, will preserve the universe.

Just as in his treatment of Quetzalcoatl, Cardenal establishes many contrasts between Nezahualcoyotl and both the Aztecs and modern dictators and imperialists. The following stanzas from "Nezahualcoyotl" show a contrast by presenting the king as a symbol of the ideal political leader who rejects military actions and the accumulation of wealth and focuses on poetry:

> I have not come to make wars on earth
> But to pick flowers
> I am the singer-king who looks for flowers
>   I, Nezahualcoyotl
> My palace is full of singers
>   Not of soldiers.
>
> Picker of cacao flowers . . .
> Not Cacaos (the coins
> For buying and selling in markets, and not for drinking)
>   But the flower.
> Let millionaires treasure their Cacaos, let dictators
>   Treasure their xiquiplies of Cacaos
>   And I the flowers.
> My valuable flowers.
> Gentlemen,
> The cacao flower is more valuable than the cacao.
>
> I pick the flowers of friendship. Flowers
> Of love, Dictators!
>   Flowers of song. (Cardenal 1992:193)

In the first stanza, Cardenal presents Nezahualcoyotl as a peaceful ruler who is only interested in composing or singing poems, not in wars through which his contemporaries, the Aztecs, are trying to obtain captives. Thus, his palace is filled with singers rather than warriors. This stanza focuses on the past and contrasts Nezahualcoyotl with the Aztecs. The second stanza opposes Nezahualcoyotl's peaceful act to the greed of modern dictators or imperialists. Cardenal shows that Nezahualcoyotl is interested only in the flowers of cacao, rather than cacao beans, which were used as money in Aztec society and which symbolize the wealth that the Aztec imperialists and modern dictators obtain through oppression and exploitation. In the final stanza, Cardenal denounces any type of dictator by presenting Nezahualcoyotl as an ideal leader who searches for flowers or poems, friendship, and love.[4]

Many critics assert that Cardenal is one of the most important poets in contemporary Latin American literature (Borgeson 1984:17–18). As a revolutionary priest, his tireless fight against injustices related to dictatorship, militarism, colonialism, and capitalism is carried out in his personal life as well as in his poetic works. His special interest in indigenous culture is not surprising considering the fact that indigenous peoples have suffered the most in Latin America. By adopting the colonizers' interpretation of pre-Hispanic indigenous history, however, Cardenal condemns the Aztecs, who suffered the conquest and subsequent colonialism just as much as other indigenous groups. This condemnation ignores the voice of these indigenous people and perpetuates the same misconceptions that have dominated since the colonial period.

To blame Cardenal for his misrepresentations may be unfair; although his Catholic ideology influences his views, he is also a victim of the shoddy yet prominent scholarship upon which he relies. Furthermore, the "history" in Cardenal's poetry should not be read as "true." Rather, it is a fictional history created by the poet. But the drawing of historical contrasts and parallels should carry with it a certain responsibility to those represented, and this responsibility is even more important in political poetry such as Cardenal's, which pursues justice through artistic activity. In Cardenal's poetry, the parallel between the Aztecs and contemporary dictators on the one hand and the contrast between the Aztecs and Quetzalcoatl and Nezahualcoyotl on the other are inaccurate and misleading. Most literary critics examine Cardenal's indigenous poetry without questioning the historical validity of Cardenal's interpretation of Aztec figures and poetry, and thus repeat this colonial interpretation of Aztec history and culture. As Pring-Mill (1992:53) argues, Cardenal is the most socially committed poet since Pablo Neruda: "His determination to change the world around him, and to motivate his readers to contribute to its improvement, is always uppermost." Ironically, however, by perpetuating the colonial images of Quetzalcoatl, Nezahualcoyotl, and the Aztecs, Cardenal is complicit in the very colonialism that he so much abhors.

NOTES

INTRODUCTION

1. With the term "Aztec," I refer to the allied political organization between Tenochtitlan and other city-states such as Texcoco, Tlacopan, Xochimilco, Chalco, and many others in the Basin of Mexico. If a distinction is necessary among them, a regional or ethnic-based term such as "Mexica" or "Texcoca" is used.
2. Cortés (1993) and Díaz del Castillo (1992) argue that the Spaniards arrived to impose peaceful Christianity and civilization on the bloodthirsty Mexica, and so avenge those who had been subjected to Tenochtitlan.
3. Ricard (1995:84–87) provides a brief history of the other religious orders such as the Dominicans and the Augustinians.
4. For more detailed information on Franciscan millennialism, see Baudot (1995:76–89) and Lafaye (1976:32–37).
5. I am borrowing here the term "diffusionist" from Carrasco (2000:55–62) who classifies the major studies about the origin of the Toltecs and their god and ruler Quetzalcoatl into three categories: diffusionist, symbolic, and historical design. According to him, the diffusionists have sought the origin of Indian culture outside of the New World. They argue that some foreign, Christian-like genius came to the New World and taught the Indians religion and other cultural artifacts.
6. López Austín (1973) and Gillespie (1989:183–84) also study the similarities between the indigenous god Quetzalcoatl and the Christian apostle Saint Thomas.
7. Nicholson's study (2001) is essential to understanding the role of Quetzalcoatl before and after the conquest. He summarizes and studies almost all the colonial pictorial and alphabetic sources on Quetzalcoatl in Mesoamerica.
8. From the beginning of the conquest, the origin of the Indians was a serious issue for Spanish intellectuals and friars in the sixteenth century. All of them agreed that the Indians were descendants of Adam and Eve, but there were various hypotheses on how and when they came to the New World. At the beginning of the seventeenth century, a Dominican friar, Gregorio García, summarized the debate on indigenous origin. See also Brading (1991:196–200) for the historical context in which García's book appeared.

9. Baudot (1996:163–245) examines how most of Olmos's study remains in fragmented form, inserted in the works of other Spanish chroniclers such as Mendieta and Torquemada.
10. Baudot (1996:141–42, 337, 347) demonstrates that Las Casas's work on the indigenous history of New Spain borrows liberally from Olmos and Motolinia.
11. Alva Ixtlilxochitl played an important role in the propagation of the tradition of the Virgin of Guadalupe. He possessed the most important document, *Nican mopohua* (Here It Begins) and was assumed to be its author (Brading 2001:117–18).
12. Other scholars such as Nicholson (2001:125–29), Lockhart (1991), and Velazco (2003: 44–46) also noticed a strong colonial influence in Alva Ixtlilxochitl's chronicles.
13. Brading (2001) examines how the Creoles searched for their own native Mary, the Virgin of Guadalupe. Brading argues that the Virgin of Guadalupe was actually created by the Creoles who wanted to have their own native American Virgin in order to promote their native land.
14. See also Keen (1971:260–309) and Brading (1991:422–46) for Enlightened philosophers' attacks on the Americas.
15. Phelan (1960), who studies the Creole interest in the indigenous past in the eighteenth century, calls this Creole interest "Neo-Aztecism" and argues that the Neo-Aztecism served as an origin of Mexican nationalism.
16. For more detailed information on the political groups in nineteenth-century Mexico, see Bushnell and Macaulay (1988:61–71), Hale (1968:290–305), and Brading (1985:70–81, 1991:648–50).
17. Jara (1989:366–75) provides more detailed study on Mier and his political use of the Virgin of Guadalupe.
18. This edition does not provide a publication date.
19. In this context, I challenge the specific aspects of previous and current scholars' work on Nezahualcoyotl.
20. Keen (1971:464) studies the impact of the Mexican Revolution on Aztec studies: "The Mexican revolution of 1910 to 1920 contributed immeasurably to the second discovery of ancient Mexico. What distinguished that revolution from previous efforts at social and political reconstruction of Mexico was the intervention of the Indian and Mestizo masses." He briefly mentions the achievements of most representative scholars in this period in Mexico (1971:463–508).

CHAPTER ONE

1. Archaeological evidence confirms that the native historiographical tradition, tlacuilolli, had developed by the first millennium BC. It is still being practiced in some regions of Mexico (Brotherston 1992:52–53).
2. For census and classification of the pictorial texts, see Glass (1975:3–80) and Glass and Robertson (1975:81–252).
3. According to Baudot (1995:170–72, 340–45), Olmos and Motolinia started writing their ethnographic works during the 1530s.
4. For a comprehensive inventory of colonial alphabetic texts in Nahuatl and Spanish, see Gibson (1975:311–21) and Gibson and Glass (1975:322–400).
5. Torquemada (1975, 2:80), Mendieta (1971:181), and Zorita (1999:152–53) present Nezahualcoyotl and his son Nezahualpilli as religious skeptics who doubted their indigenous gods.
6. For general characteristics of the mestizo chronicles, see Lienhard (1983).
7. René Acuña published the 113 surviving relaciones, except the 54 relaciones from Yucatán, with a brief prologue for each one. In this publication, he included several versions of the questionnaire titled *Memoria de las cosas que se ha de responder, y de*

que se han de hacer las relaciones. Mundy (2000) conducted a comprehensive study of indigenous pictorial tradition in the relaciones and included an English translation of the questionnaire (2000:227–30).

8. Pomar's original text is now lost. Only a seventeenth-century copy has survived, and it shows some indications of the illustrations contained in the original text. The illustrations in the *Códice Ixtlilxochitl* are believed to be either Pomar's originals or copies of them. (See figure 8.3.)

9. Pomar does not mention any non-Texcoca elderly informants in his work. Of course, there would have been no reason for him to consult non-Texcoca sources because he was assigned to write the history of Texcoco. The history of other cities was another's task.

10. Alva Ixtlilxochitl (1997, 1:285–88) even wrote a detailed chapter about how he obtained his sources. Some of the informants mentioned in this chapter also appear as sources of information about Nezahualcoyotl.

11. In the preface of his book *Monarquía indiana* (1975), Torquemada mentions that he drew from the works of Motolinia, Sahagún, Mendieta, and many others. For this reason, León-Portilla (1986a:vii) calls the *Monarquía indiana* the chronicle of the chronicles.

12. If we take into consideration the family history of Alva Ixtlilxochitl, his reason for writing the chronicles can be explained more easily. As a great-grandson of don Fernando Cortés Ixtlilxochitl, who was a grandson of Nezahualcoyotl and ally to Hernán Cortés, Alva Ixtlilxochitl and his family had maintained hereditary rights over San Juan Teotihuacan since the conquest. However, these rights were challenged at the beginning of the seventeenth century by some of the townspeople and there occurred a series of lawsuits (Schwaller 1999:4–5). In this situation, Alva Ixtlilxochitl naturally documented the contribution of his ancestors to the conquest and evangelization in order to insist that his family deserved royal favor.

13. Of course, there are many other pictorial scripts from Texcoco and other neighboring cities, such as Tenochtitlan, that depict some of Nezahualcoyotl's achievements. Castillo Farreras (1972) reconstructs the life of Nezahualcoyotl from his birth to his death by collecting all the pictorial descriptions available in the codices. Because of its early publication, this book does not contain recently published codices, but it is a seminal study that provides access to almost every pictographic source on Nezahualcoyotl and his times.

14. Boone (2000:64–86) takes a different approach to the study of Aztec pictorial scripts. She divides them into three groups according to their narrative structure: annals, *regestae* (or event-oriented) histories, and cartographic histories.

15. One of the most impressive examples may be don Carlos Ometochtzin, who was a cacique of Texcoco and a descendant of Nezahualcoyotl. According to the records of an inquisition trial, he was burned in 1539 because he secretly kept religious idols and practiced religious rituals. This inquisitorial case will be examined in later chapters.

16. Mundy (2000:215–16), who studies the maps of the *Relaciones geográficas*, defines this colonial situation in which indigenous tlacuiloque find themselves as "double consciousness."

17. Glass (1975:11–19) categorizes the pictorial codices that survived or were produced under Spanish rule into four groups according to their origin. First, there survived a few pre-Hispanic codices and maps that generally deal with religious and historical books from the Maya and Mixtec area. Second, some pictorial codices were drawn under Spanish patronage. They were painted for Spanish readers such as the Spanish king and priests who had interest in the indigenous history and customs of the new colony. The *Codex Mendoza*, for example, falls into this category. Some of these codices, such as the *Codex Telleriano-Remensis* and the *Códice Ixtlilxochitl*, were produced for the church, which was faced with problems of converting a whole population and destroying a highly organized religion in New Spain (1975:14). Third, the native

noble class made copies of preexisting genealogical dynastic histories or repainted new books by combining pre- and post-Hispanic pictorial materials in an attempt to establish or maintain legitimacy and social status after the conquest. This group includes the majority of the native codices, including almost all of the Texcoca maps and annals and the Mexica codices. The final category of pictorial texts is concerned with such colonial institutions as *encomienda* tribute or the proof of land titles before Spanish courts (1975:17). This group includes the *Códice de Tepetlaoztoc*.

18. Due to the importance of Sahagún in Nahua studies, there have been many works published about him. Among them, *Sixteenth-Century Mexico: The Work of Sahagún* (Edmonson 1974), *The Work of Bernardino de Sahagún: Pioneer Ethnographer of Sixteenth-Century Aztec Mexico* (Klor de Alva, Nicholson, and Quiñones Keber 1988), and *Representing Aztec Ritual Performance, Text, and Image in the Work of Sahagún* (Quiñones Keber 2002) are particularly useful.

19. The *Crónica mexicana* belongs to the group of the *Crónica X*, which, now missing, served as a historical basis for numerous chronicles. According to Barlow (1945), an anonymous author wrote the *Crónica X* in Nahuatl shortly after the conquest, and it was a popular source for later chronicles such as Durán's *The History of the Indies of New Spain* (1994), Alvarado Tezozomoc's *Crónica mexicana* (1987), and the *Codex Ramírez*. Barlow argues that Durán and Alvarado Tezozomoc based their accounts on the *Crónica X* and that the *Codex Ramírez* relied on both the *Crónica X* and Durán's chronicle.

CHAPTER TWO

1. My reading of the figures from the pictorial codices relies primarily on the interpretation of the editors of the codices from which the figures are taken and on Francis Berdan's translation (1992:163–238) of the glyphs from the *Codex Mendoza*. But, I add my own more detailed interpretation when it is relevant to my argument. In some cases, however, I argue for a completely different interpretation. I have included these segments of the pictorial texts because they provide much more information than alphabetic texts, and they illustrate the possibility of more diverse interpretations according to the perspective of the reader. In cases where I had difficulty interpreting the glyphs in the figures, I follow the interpretation of the editor of the codex in which the glyph appears. For a morphological interpretation of the personal names and Nahuatl toponyms, see the glossary.

2. Davies (1980:62–63) also points out that Chichimec leaders such as Huetzin, Tochintecuhtli, Yacanex, and Ocotochtli were contemporaries of Xolotl and his son Nopaltzin. Thus, Quinatzin, who was the great-grandson of Xolotl and grandson of Nopaltzin, cannot be their contemporary. As recorded in the *Annals of Cuauhtitlan* (1998:45, 47–55), there exists more than one Quinatzin in Chichimec history in the Basin of Mexico. The Quinatzin depicted as a contemporary of Xolotl in the *Códice Xolotl* (1996) was probably a great conqueror and seems to appear as Huehue Quinatzin in the *Annals of Cuauhtitlan*. Davies (1980:62–63) argues that this Quinatzin should be distinguished from the Texcoca Quinatzin, who founded Texcoco much later.

3. O'Gorman's list (1997:88–116) of Texcoca historical events based on Alva Ixtlilxochitl's chronicles is the most significant source for understanding the historical development of Texcoco and its relationship with other city-states in the Basin of Mexico.

4. For the Texcoca chronology, I use Alfonso Caso's study (1966) as follows: Xolotl (1172–1232), Nopaltzin (1232–1263), Tlotzin (1263–1298), Quinatzin (1298–1357), Techotlalatzin (1357–1409), Huehue Ixtlilxochitl (1409–1418), Nezahualcoyotl (1431–1472), Nezahualpilli (1472–1515), and Cacamatzin (1515–1520). The successor of Nopaltzin, however, should be Tlotzin's half brother Tenacacaltzin, as will be explained later in this chapter. For the correlation between the indigenous and Julian calendars, I rely upon Munro S. Edmonson's study (1988:12–13).

5. Based on the *Memorial breve* (Chimalpahin 1991) and the *Annals of Cuauhtitlan* (1992), Davies (1980:53–56) argues that Xolotl and Tochintecuhtli, the ruler of Huexotla, were the same person, because both sources often confuse the two and record extensive conquests of these two Chichimec leaders. Furthermore, in the *Memorial breve*, Tochintecuhtli comes from Tenayuca and his spouse's name is the same as that of Xolotl, Tomiyauh.
6. The *Códice Xolotl* (1996) records that they arrived in the same year 1 Flint, that is, forty-seven years after the settlement of Xolotl in Tenayuca (see figure 2.6, this volume). As Jiménez Moreno argues (1954–1955:229), however, they came to the basin separately and at different times. According to him, the Tepaneca of Azcapotzalco arrived first in 1230, and later the Otomíes settled in Xaltocan in 1250. Finally, the Acolhuaque arrived at Coatlichan in 1260. However, I believe that Tzontecomatl and Chiconcuauh arrived at the basin almost at the same time as Xolotl or slightly thereafter since the *Anales de Tlatelolco* (1948: 21) record that Xolotl (Tecuanitzin in this version) in Tenayuca, Tzontecomatl in Coatlichan, and Chiconcuauh (Opantzin in this version) in Xaltocan were contemporaries.
7. Davies (1980:68–69) argues that Quinatzin's voluntary renunciation of Tenayuca seems apocryphal. He also argues that the Texcoca sources invented Quinatzin's heroism in order to convert their founder into a great conqueror like Tochintecuhtli of Huexotla.
8. The marriage between the Toltec princes and the Chichimec rulers was sometimes forced. See the interpretation of figure 2.9, this volume.
9. Gillespie (1989) examines in detail the Mexica kings' marriages with Colhuacan princesses and their political significance in the Mexica dynasty. According to her, this kind of marriage tradition continued until Moctezuma Xocoyotl.
10. With the exception of this quote from note 76 at the end of the *tercera relación*, I use Tena's translation of Chimalpahin's *Relaciones* throughout this book (Chimalpahin 1998). Here I am using Rendon's translation (Chimalpahin 1965) because it seems to be more logical and contextualized. Either translation, however, indicates a close connection between Topiltzin and Moctezuma Xocoyotzin.

CHAPTER THREE

1. Gibson (1971:384) argues that Texcoco was the strongest city-state in the basin until Nezahualcoyotl's reign, which will be examined in detail in the next chapter.
2. The *Anales de Tlatelolco* (1948:31) show that Azcapotzalco was founded even earlier than Tenayuca by recording the arrival of Matlaccohuatl, grandfather of Aculhua or Acolnahuactl. See also Offner (1983:24).
3. As examined in chapter 2, Yacanex was a later Chichimec immigrant who wanted to ally himself to the Toltecs through marriage, just like previous Chichimec leaders had done. But Huetzin of Coatlichan also wanted the same Colhuacan princess for his wife, and war broke out between these two Chichimec groups.
4. The *Códice de Tepetlaoztoc* (1992), which shows the version of the defeated people of Tepetlaoztoc, records neither this war nor their subjection to Coatlichan.
5. Davies (1980:63) argues that Huetzin, rather than Nopaltzin, conquered Colhuacan, and Calnek (1973:426) maintains that Huetzin was the ruler of Coatlichan and Colhuacan.
6. According to Offner (1979:232), Coxcox was actually the ruler of Coatlichan and Colhuacan.
7. Texcoco seems to have inherited the name "Acolhuacan" during Nezahualcoyotl's reign in the fifteenth century when it displaced Coatlichan to assume the leading role in the eastern basin. Many Texcoca sources and those of other regions use "Acolhuacan" to refer to Texcoco starting around 1431 when Nezahualcoyotl began ruling Texcoco.

8. Alva Ixtlilxochitl (1997, 1:533) also records that Quinatzin's brother Tochintecuhtli was the ruler of Huexotzinco, and that his other brother Xiuhquetzaltecuhtli was the ruler of Tepeticpac, a major province of Tlaxcala. This information seems dubious. I believe that Alva Ixtlilxochitl's text confuses Huexotla with Huexotzinco. Other surviving Tlaxcalteca sources such as don Diego Muñoz Camargo's *Historia de Tlaxcala* (1986) do not corroborate Alva Ixtlilxochitl's version.

9. Alva Ixtlilxochitl (1997, 2:29) records that Tozquentzin's brothers, Coxcox and Mozocomatzin, inherited Coatlichan and Colhuacan, respectively.

10. Offner (1979, 1983:38) also notes that Alva Ixtlilxochitl and Juan de Torquemada misinterpreted the events of Techotlalatzin's reign depicted in the *Códice Xolotl*. Offner argues that Techotlalatzin was not the supreme ruler of the Basin of Mexico but rather that he had a very small empire concentrated in the eastern basin.

11. For a more detailed description of this war, see Davies (1980:293–99) and Brundage (1972:62–65).

12. Alva Ixtlilxochitl's interpretation is still accepted by many leading scholars. See Dibble (*Códice Xolotl* 1996:92) and Offner (1983:41).

13. León-Portilla (1967a) examines in detail this Toltecization of the Chichimec Texcoca in the Texcoca pictorial sources, the *Códice Xolotl*, the *Mapa Quinatzin*, and the *Mapa Tlotzin*. See also Jiménez Moreno, Miranda, and Fernández (1970:111).

14. Offner (1979:234–36) examines the impact of these immigrant groups during Techotlalatzin's reign. He also examines how Torquemada misinterpreted this historical event.

CHAPTER FOUR

1. The real reason Tezozomoc and his son Maxtla wanted to kill Nezahualcoyotl was probably that Nezahualcoyotl refused to recognize Tezozomoc's authority in the basin. On the other hand, the only way Nezahualcoyotl could claim the throne of Texcoco was to overthrow Tezozomoc's empire, because he did not have any genealogical connection to Tezozomoc. Nonohualcatzin, the husband of Nezahualcoyotl's half sister, Tozquentzin, whom Tezozomoc appointed as the ruler of Texcoco, had a certain connection with this Tepanec king.

2. These two sources narrate almost the same story of Nezahualcoyotl. Some scholars (Gibson 1956:5) have noticed that Alva Ixtlilxochitl was aware of the *Annals of Cuauhtitlan* (1992). Thus, he probably used these annals to reconstruct Nezahualcoyotl's life.

3. The Mexica school system was well organized and included several types of schools such as calmecac, *telpochcalli*, and *cuicacalli*. Students received training in military, religious, and artistic skills (Carrasco 1998:109–15).

4. See map 7 of the *Códice Xolotl* (1996). All the leaders of Acolhuacan fled to Huexotzinco and Tlaxcala, and most of them did not come back until the end of the Tepanec-Mexica war, which destroyed the Tepanec imperial system in Acolhuacan. During their exile, many rulers of this region were replaced by Tezozomoc. The ruler of the leading city in Acolhuacan, Coatlichan, was replaced by Tezozomoc's grandson, Quetzalmacaztli.

5. The contribution of Nezahualcoyotl to the Tepanec-Mexica war is still in debate. Major scholars of Nahua history, such as Hassig (1988:143–45), recognize Nezahualcoyotl's military as well as diplomatic efforts as a decisive factor in the defeat of Maxtla's Tepanec allies.

6. Almost the same situation arises at the beginning of the sixteenth century when Nezahualpilli died without appointing his successor. The Mexica king, Moctezuma, supported his nephew Cacamatzin and made him the ruler of Texcoco, which caused a civil war in Texcoco. Cacamatzin's half brother, Fernando Cortés Ixtlilxochitl,

proclaimed himself the legitimate ruler of Texcoco and occupied the northern part of the Texcoca domain. This political division expedited the fall of the Aztec empire because Fernando Cortés Ixtlilxochitl allied with Cortés and helped him conquer the capital of his Mexica enemy, Tenochtitlan.

7. The Mexicas' selection of Tlacopan as the regional center in the western basin should also be understood in the same context. When the Mexica overthrew the Tepaneca and adopted the Azcapotzalca political and tributary system, they selected Tlacopan, instead of other major cities such as Coyoacan, as their primary partner in the western Basin of Mexico.

8. From the moment when Nezahualcoyotl allied with the Mexica, Texcoco became the most dominant city in the eastern Basin of Mexico and assumed the role previously played by Coatlichan. Texcoco also took on Coatlichan's designation as Acolhuacan, which had been used to refer to Coatlichan during its period of political dominance.

9. According to Brotherston (1995:67), this event is also recorded from the point of view of the conquered of Tepetlaoztoc. By focusing on the abrupt change of Cocopin's clothing and authority mat depicted in the *Códice de Tepetlaoztoc*, Brotherston explains Nezahualcoyotl's influence in this region. See also the *Códice de Tepetlaoztoc* (1992).

10. Offner (1983:97–104) and Carrasco (1999:161–66) examine in detail the tribute role of the fourteen cities by comparing them with the Texcoca tributary list of Motolinia, Alva Ixtlilxochitl, Torquemada, and the *Annals of Cuauhtitlan*. Most of these texts, however, appear to be based on Texcoca sources.

11. Folio 19 of the *Codex Mendoza* (1992) and folio 5 of the *Matrícula de tributos* (1997) describe the tribute collected in the Acolhuacan region. The two sources record different head towns for the region; that is to say, the *Codex Mendoza* lists Acolhuacan while the *Matrícula de tributos* identifies Acolman as the head town. Barlow (1949b:68) argues that "Acolhuacan" refers to Coatlichan, but I would argue that Acolman should be the head town because most of the cities listed under Acolman in the *Matrícula de tributos* or Acolhuacan in the *Codex Mendoza*, such as Tepechpan, Tepetlaoztoc, and Tezoyucan, were subject to Acolman even before the Tepanec-Acolhuacan war. See the detailed debate on this issue in Berdan and Anawalt (1992:38).

12. Many scholars, such as Gibson (1971:383–84) and Berdan (2005:44–45), have accepted the 2:2:1 distribution rate following Texcoca tradition.

13. Carrasco (1950:116–19, 268–72, 1984) studies the tribute system and the territorial structure of the Tepanec empire as an immediate precursor of the Aztec empire, and the latter inherited several imperial structures from the former.

14. There has been significant research on this topic. Barlow (1994) discovered and commented on leaf 3 of the *Mapa Quinatzin*. Offner (1983) conducted comprehensive and detailed research on the Texcoca legal system based on Texcoca sources. Offner's work, however, is misleading because his uncritical reliance on Texcoca sources such as Alva Ixtlilxochitl leads him to start with the argument that the Texcoca legal system was the most civilized among indigenous people in pre-Hispanic Mexico, very different from that of Tenochtitlan. More recently, Mohar B. (2000:227–42) demonstrates similarities between the Mexica and Texcoca legal systems by comparing leaf 3 of the *Mapa Quinatzin* and the behavior chapter of the *Codex Mendoza*.

15. Mohar B. (2004) recently published the *Mapa Quinatzin* with a computerized technology. With this edition, students and scholars now can interact with the map and its easy to access, clear images.

16. See also Vetancurt (1971:89–92).

17. Robert Barlow's modern interpretation of this figure was ambiguous and incorrect. See his errors in Offner (1983:73–74).

CHAPTER FIVE

1. Here, I am employing the term that Garibay coined in the 1960s. Garibay (1992:18–19, 67) examined a unique structure in Nahuatl that conveys a single idea with two similar words. He called it *difrasismo*, and "in xochitl in cuicatl" is an example of this difrasismo that refers to Nahua poetry.
2. As discussed in chapter 1, Alva Ixtlilxochitl (1997, 2:137) explains that Pomar's chronicle was one of his sources.
3. Bierhorst (1985:110–22) aptly summarizes the study of Aztec poetry by briefly reviewing the chronicles of Sahagún and Durán from the colonial period and the works of Garibay, León-Portilla, and many others to the present. Martínez (1972:154–57) presents a brief history of the poems attributed to Nezahualcoyotl from Alva Ixtlilxochitl to the twentieth century.
4. Martínez (1972:139–69) provides a brief summary of the translation of Nezahualcoyotl's poems. Also see Brotherston (1972) and Bierhorst (1985:103–5).
5. Leander (1976:29–37) lists thirty-three poets identified by Garibay.
6. For instance, Martínez (1972) also published a book on Nezahualcoyotl by combining all the songs that Garibay (1993) and León-Portilla (1972) had identified as authored by Nezahualcoyotl. According to him, "Nezahualcoyotl es el que tiene un número mayor de poemas atribuidos: treinta y seis del conjunto total de cerca de doscientos cantos" (Nezahualcoyotl is the one who has a greater number of attributed poems: thirty-six of the total group of near two hundred songs) (1972:103).
7. Brotherston (1972:400) and Segala (1990:211–16, 265–68) also notice this pattern of performance by the singers.
8. See illustrations of Nahua musicians and their instruments in *Florentine Codex* (1950–1982), Book Four and Book Eight.
9. For more information on Nahua song performance and other musical elements of Nahua songs, see Bierhorst (1985:70–82) and Karttunen and Lockhart (1980:22–33).
10. Here, I use the translations of Bierhorst (1985) for the songs of *Cantares* with reference to each song and stanza in the translator's numbering. For the songs from *Romances*, Garibay's translations (1993) are used with his numbering of each song and stanza. However, for the individual songs whose composer is identified by Garibay and León-Portilla, the translations of these scholars are used regardless of the collection to which they originally belonged, and the reference to these translations is indicated by page numbers, not song and stanza numbers, on which they appear.
11. See *Poesía nahuatl* (1993, 2:lxx–lxxi) for Garibay's argument. León-Portilla includes these songs in *Nezahualcoyotl* (1972:58–59, 66–67) and *Quince poetas* (1994:110–11).
12. Tamoanchan and other places like Tlalocan that appear in *Cantares* and in *Romances* refer to paradise in the pre-Hispanic indigenous tradition: "algo similar al Jardín del Edén de otras culturas" (something similar to the Garden of the Eden of other cultures) (Garibay 1993, 1:104). López-Austín (1994) examines the concept of Tamoanchan in the Mesoamerican world from the pre-Hispanic period to the present.
13. The first religious school was founded by Fray Pedro de Gante in Texcoco in 1523 even before the arrival of the Twelve Fathers, and later schools were quickly founded in other regions (Ricard 1995:321–24).
14. For the names of the Nahua scholars and their Spanish teachers, see Ricard (1995: 340–42) and Burkhart (1996:55–71).
15. Burkhart (1989:195–202) lists thirteen important catechistic books and manuscripts, most of which were published or written in the 1550s and 1560s.
16. Burkhart (1996:71) explains that the Spanish friars did not credit their indigenous collaborators for three reasons: (1) they believed that their words could be translated into Nahuatl without significant modification; (2) they needed to gain legitimacy for

their writings as priests and Nahuatl speakers, which would help them get permission to publish their doctrinal works in Nahuatl; and (3) they wished to protect their Nahua informants from possible accusations from ecclesiastical and civil authorities who might have protested native collaboration.

CHAPTER SIX

1. Itzcoatl's burning of the previous history is recorded in the *Florentine Codex*. Like Garibay and León-Portilla, many scholars tend to view this action as a symbol of Mexica barbarity and as evidence that the Mexica rewrote the history of pre-Hispanic Mexico. It might be an important issue in the study of pre-Hispanic Mexican history, but it did not suppress other indigenous versions of the past. There are many other surviving sources from other city-states such as Texcoco, Chalco, Cuauhtitlan, and Tlaxcala.
2. See *Nezahualcoyotl: Poesía y pensamiento* (León-Portilla 1972:17–20).
3. In support of his argument, Martínez quotes the phrase "destruyen nuestros libros los jefes guerreros" (the warlords destroy our books) directly from Garibay's translation of a song attributed to Nezahualcoyotl. Garibay's translation of the original Nahuatl text, however, is very misleading. Garibay (1993, 3:10–11) presents the original sentence in Nahuatl that included the translated phrase as follows: "Zanio cuicatl tonequimilol, quipoloa, aya, in totlacuilolli tepilhuan, oo." He translates the whole sentence as "Sólo los cantos son nuestros atavío: destruyen nuestros libros los jefes guerreros" (Only the songs are our adornment: the warlords destroy our books). Here, the translation of *tepilhuan*, however, is inconsistent with the way he translates the same term in other poems. Here, he translates "tepilhuan" as "warriors" (*guerreros*), but he translates it in many other songs as "lords" ("señores" and "reyes"). For instance, in the latter part of the same song, which Garibay entitles the "Monólogo de Nezahualcóyotl," he translates the same word, "tepilhuan," as "princes" and "kings": "xochineneliuhtiaz noyollo, yehuan tepilhuan on teteuctin in," for example, is translated as "con flores mi corazón ha de ser entrelazado: ¡son los príncipes, los reyes!" (with flowers my heart will be intertwined: they are the princes, the kings!). Garibay does not explain why he translated the word "tepilhuan" as "warriors" in the first phrase and as "princes" and "kings" in the stanzas attributed to Nezahualcoyotl, but he seems clearly predisposed to translate the songs attributed to Nezahualcoyotl in a particular way. For a more detailed study on Garibay's and León-Portilla's translation of Nahuatl song texts, see Payas (2004).
4. Segala also challenges the contrast between Quetzalcoatl and Huitzilopochtli that León-Portilla has established in his study of Nahua history and literature. Segala (1990:32–35, 191–200) argues that there are no significant differences between the beliefs and practices of Nezahualcoyotl, who worshipped Quetzalcoatl, and the Mexica, who revered Huitzilopochtli.
5. Motolinia (Benavente 1971:70–71, 75–81) also notes that the Mexica and Tlaxcala practiced the same religious ceremonies such as human sacrifice.
6. These texts are major sources for the cosmogony of pre-Hispanic times. Nicholson (1971:397–403) aptly summarizes all three. See also *Myths of Ancient Mexico* by Graulich (1997), which explains in detail the concept of the suns in ancient Mexico.
7. Although all of the sources mentioned here are from Tenochtitlan, the legend is not exclusively Mexica but is shared by all the people of Mesoamerica. Brotherston (1992:238–45) shows that the story of the four suns described in Mexica sources such as the *Legend of the Suns* and the *Sun Stone* is a schematic summary of the *Popol Vuh*.
8. According to the *Primeros memoriales* (Sahagún 1997b:74), the Aztecs feed the gods as follows: "The feeding [of the gods] was done in this manner: When they cut open the breast of a slave or a captive, then they collected the blood in a bowl and perhaps cast a paper into the bowl, which absorbed the blood. Then they carried [the blood] in the bowl and on the lips of all devils they smeared the blood, all the blood, of the sacrificial victim."

9. There is a debate regarding the historicity of the conversation recorded in the *Coloquios* (Sahagún 1986). Some scholars consider the conversation a pure creation of Sahagún or Franciscan friars while others consider it a reconstruction of an actual historical event (Díaz Balsera 2005:20–21). I include some parts of the conversation in this book because as Lockhart (1992:206–6) points out, "whatever their degree of factual authenticity, the speeches presented correspond to our general understanding of religious interaction between the two peoples."

10. Garibay (1992:84–91) first classifies Nahua songs according to the type of dance associated with them or the mode of the songs. According to him, icnocuicatl is understood as follows: "La tristeza y la melancolía de la vida ha pasado como niebla en este poema de regocijo. Hay otros en que es el tema fundamental y casi único. Se le da en el Ms. El nombre de *Icnocuicatl*. Literalmente, 'Canto de desolación, de orfandad.' Ideológicamente tiene parentesco con las elegías, o cantos líricos, de los poetas de Occidentes, en que se canta la amargura del vivir" (The sadness and the melancholy of life have passed as fog in this joyful poem. There are others in which this theme is fundamental and almost unique. It is given the name of *Icnocuicatl* in the Ms. Literally, "Song of desolation, of orphanhood." Ideologically it is similar to the elegies, or lyrical songs, of the poets of the West, in which the bitterness of life is sung). Bierhorst (1985:92–96) also classifies the existing songs into several groups according to stylistics and instrumental accompaniment, national origin, and thematic content.

11. According to Alvarado Tezozomoc (1987:62), when Tlacaelel called a meeting to elect a new king after Itzcoatl's death, this Mexica leader described the death of the king as the demise of the sun: "Y a la luz que nos alumbraba es apagada, la voz á cuyo aliento se movia todo este Reyno está enmudecida y soterrada, y el espejo en que todos se miraban esta obscurecido. Por tanto, ilustres varones, no conviene que el Reyno esté mas en tinieblas; salga otro nuevo sol que lo alumbre, echad los ojos á nuestros príncipes y caballeros que han procedido de nosotros y de nuestro Rey muerto; bien teneis en que escoger, ¿quién os parece que será, oh Mexicanos, aquel que seguirá bien las pisadas de nuestro buen Rey pasado? ¿Quién conservará lo que él nos dejo ganado, imitándole en ser amparo del huérfano, de la viuda, de los pobres y pequeños? Decid lo que os parece según lo que habeis notado y visto en los príncipes que tenemos" (And the light that illuminated us is extinguished, the voice in response to whose breath this whole kingdom moved is silenced and buried, and the mirror in which everyone watched themselves is darkened. Therefore, illuminated lords, it is not advisable that the kingdom continue in darkness; let there appear another new sun to illuminate it, cast your eyes on our princes and nobles who have descended from us and from our dead King; you have good options from which to choose, who seems to you that he will be, O Mexica, the one who will follow well the steps of our good King of the past? Who will conserve what he left us, imitating him in being the protection of the orphan, of the widow, of the poor and the young? Say what you think according to what you have noticed and seen in the princes whom we have).

12. Chavero (1958:595–98), Saville (1925:76–77), and Nicholson and Quiñones Keber (1983:146–47) study the images of the huehuetl. My interpretation of these images is based primarily on the study of these scholars, but the relationship posited here between the Nahua cosmology depicted in the huehuetl images and song practice is my own.

13. See different versions and translations of the song in the *Florentine Codex* (1950–1982, 2:210) and Sullivan (2003:178–79).

CHAPTER SEVEN

1. Even though the versions of the songs that Alva Ixtlilxochitl and Torquemada attributed to Nezahualcoyotl constitute a serious distortion of Nahua poetics, they have been published repeatedly since the colonial period, and the particular notion of

ephemerality expressed in them has been presented as the most representative theme of Nahua poetry. Brotherston (1972) demonstrates how and in what context all the poems traditionally attributed to Nezahualcoyotl were forged by comparing them to what appears to be the original text upon which they are based from *Cantares*. Brotherston points out that these forged poems attributed to Nezahualcoyotl have been published repeatedly, as if they were originals, even after the discovery of the authentic Nahuatl poems.

2. León-Portilla (1992a:167, 173) describes Huexotzinco as Tochihuitzin's home city, but later he changes it to Tenochtitlan (1992b:150–52).

3. León-Portilla does not present any song attributed to Totoquihuaztli that shows ephemerality.

4. According to León-Portilla (1992b:150), Tochihuitzin's full name is Tochihuitzin Coyolchiuhqui.

5. León-Portilla (1992b:99–106) identifies Cuacuauhtzin, the Tepechpan king, as the author of this song based on Alva Ixtlilxochitl's chronicle and the glossator's notes in *Romances*. According to Alva Ixtlilxochitl, Nezahualcoyotl, who was so attracted to the wife of Cuacuauhtzin, sent this king to a war against Tlaxcala so that he might be killed. Cuacuauhtzin was aware of Nezahualcoyotl's nefarious intentions and sang the song before he went to die. This Texcoca version of the episode of David and Urias in the Old Testament, however, is not evidence for attributing authorship to Cuacuauhtzin because this song was collected in *Cantares* (1985, 62, 17–24) as a part of a bereavement song without any note indicating authorship. In addition, the song commemorates many Mexica princes such as Tlacahuepan. More plausible is that the Cuacuauhtzin commemorated in the song should be identified as Cuacuauhtzin or Cuacuauhpitzahuac, the first ruler of Tlatelolco (*Anales de Tlatelolco* 1948: 22; Garibay 1992:389).

6. Garibay (1992:207) classifies this kind of song of war as Yaocuicatl and argues that an understanding of it requires a profound knowledge of indigenous traditions: "Resulta muy difícil, si no imposible, comprender una literatura sin el conocimiento de las ideas e instituciones del pueblo de donde procede. Nadie llegará a la médula de Homero, o de los Salmos, si no capta lo esencial de la cultura, o helénica o hebrea. Por lo tanto, antes de tratar el último género de los poemas que hemos clasificado entre los líricos, tenemos que hacer aquí un resumen de lo que constantemente estará pasando a los ojos de quien los lea. De los nombres que esta clase de cantos llevan son fáciles de entender el de *Yaocuicatl*, 'canto de guerra,' porque a ella alude, o la celebra y rememora; el de *Tecucuicatl*, *Teuccuicatl*, o sea, 'canto de príncipes,' porque o los celebra, o ellos privativamente los cantaban" (It turns out to be very difficult, if not impossible, to understand a literature without the knowledge of the ideas and institutions of the people from which it comes. Nobody will reach the substance of Homer, or of the Psalms, if he does not understand the essence of the Hellenic or Hebrew culture. Therefore, before dealing with the last genre of the poems that we have classified among the lyrics, we must summarize here what those who read them will constantly find. Among the names that this kind of song carries it is easy to understand that of Yaocuicatl, "song of war," because it alludes or celebrates and commemorates war; that of Tecucuicatl, Teuccuicatl, that is to say, "song of princes," because it either celebrates them or they sang them privately).

7. Garibay and Martínez attribute this song to Nezahualcoyotl in the introduction to *Poesía nahuatl* (1993, 1:88–99) and *Nezahualcoyotl, vida y obra* (1996:212), respectively.

8. This flower war seems to have been a Mesoamerican tradition. According to Davies (1987:237), "it could even be derived from Teotihuacan times, and the figures in certain murals, richly caparisoned and yet armed with darts or arrows, are rather suggestive of such forms of warfare. Ritual or semi-ritual encounters are a common feature among tribal peoples throughout the Americas; the Mexica may have differed only in seeking to preserve the practice at a stage in their development when they no longer ruled a village but an empire."

9. According to Alva Ixtlilxochitl, Nezahualcoyotl introduced the flower war between the Triple Alliance, Huexotzinco, and Tlaxcala so that each nation could regularly acquire captives to sacrifice to its gods. Alva Ixtlilxochitl (1997, 2:111–13) argues that the real reason Nezahualcoyotl introduced this war was to reduce human sacrifice by limiting the sacrificial victims to war captives. His argument, however, is not convincing, because war captives constituted the majority of sacrificial victims, and Nahua city-states believed that the most precious captives were those who were obtained in the flower war. Thus, if Nezahualcoyotl really proposed this kind of war, then his action confirms, contrary to Alva Ixtlilxochitl's argument, that the king must have been a very religious person who supported the most important ceremony of the Nahua religion, human sacrifice.

10. According to Pomar (1993:196–97), Texcoca rulers and their Huexotzinca and Tlaxcalteca enemies also maintained a friendship by exchanging gifts.

CHAPTER EIGHT

1. See Icazbalceta (1971:xxxviii) and O'Gorman (1971:lxi–lxii) for Motolinia's influence on Mendieta's chronicle.
2. In the chronicles of Alva Ixtlilxochitl (1997) and Pomar (1993) there exist many contradictory descriptions of their native land. The inconsistency may be due to their attempts to bring indigenous history into line with a European ideology. Thus, a comparison must be made between their story and those of the chroniclers of other regions in order to better understand the historical, religious, and cultural context of central Mexico in pre-Hispanic times.
3. For the whole sentence in Nahuatl and its translation in the map, see figure 4.4. in chapter 4.
4. As shown in chapter 3, the worship of Tezcatlipoca was introduced to Texcoco by the Tlailotlaca at the beginning of the fourteenth century during Nezahualcoyotl's great-grandfather Quinatzin's reign. Meanwhile Huitzilopochtli was introduced in the second half of the fourteenth century during the reign of Quinatzin's son, Techotlalatzin.
5. Each *estado* had forty-nine square feet according to the dictionary of Real Academia Española.
6. According to Barlow, plate XVIII of the *Codex Azcatitlan* (1995) provides another example of Nezahualcoyotl's participation in human sacrifice in the Mexica temple. Barlow identifies Nezahualcoyotl as the warrior who is driving two captives from Chalco (see figure 4.6, this volume). This scene appears directly below Huitzilopochtli's temple in Tlatelolco, indicating that he was transporting captives for sacrifice. The identity of this warrior, however, is somewhat ambiguous. The name-glyph that identifies the warrior is a coyote head (*coyotl*) with no collar (a symbol of fasting). The head of the coyote signifies the name Coyotl, but the absence of a collar suggests that this may not be the "fasted coyote" or Nezahualcoyotl. Furthermore, Nezahualcoyotl's complete name-glyph, a fasted coyote with a collar, appears earlier on the same plate in the conquest of Tulantzinco. Nevertheless, there is no record of any other historical figure contemporary with Nezahualcoyotl who had the name Coyotl. This ambiguity remains to be resolved.
7. In preaching Christianity to the indigenous cultures of the Americas, the Spanish friars debated for several decades about whether they should use Spanish words for religious terms or find equivalents in the indigenous languages (Ricard 1995:127–37).
8. Lockhart (1999:98–99) calls this mutual misunderstanding "Double Mistaken Identity, in which each side of the cultural exchange presumes that a given form or concept is functioning in the way familiar within its own tradition and is unaware of or unimpressed by the other side's interpretation."
9. For more discussion of the case of Martín Ocelotl, see Lafaye (1976:20–22).

10. Burkhart (1992:340–41) argues that even in Sahagún's Nahuatl psalms the influence of indigenous religion is evident, even though their main content and themes are Christian and, as the Spanish friars directed, they must have been reformulated by the native Nahua translators: "However, the Nahua interpreters did not always have priests dictating precisely what they should say, for some devotional texts are clearly of indigenous composition. The choice of subjects, the sophisticated literary style, the metaphorical language, and the extent to which Christian teachings are reformulated indicate that, within the bounds of what the priests who sponsored and preserved their work would tolerate, Nahua scholars are exercising their own creative genius. The amanuenses have become authors and have appropriated the discourse of Christian devotion to articulate their own view of the Christian order and their place within it. These texts are important records of colonial Nahua religion; they are also testaments of cultural survival and masterworks of Native American literature."
11. Lesbre (2001:336–39) includes more descriptions of Tetzcotzinco by the Spanish friars in the sixteenth century such as Antonio de Ciudad Real and Agustín Dávila Padilla. All of them equally record Tetzcotzinco as an important religious place where human sacrifice was actively conducted.

EPILOGUE

1. To cite only a few of the many novels or novelistic histories of Nezahualcoyotl: Gillmor (1968), Selva (1972), List Arzubide (1975), Campos (1994), Elisondo (1996), Lugo Pérez (1996), Martínez Chimal (1997), Fuente (1999), and Mena (2003).
2. Throughout this book, I have used the term "Aztecs" to indicate the people of Tenochtitlan and their allies such as Texcoco and Tlacopan (Tacuba). In his poetry, however, Cardenal uses it only to refer to the people of Tenochtitlan. In this epilogue, the term "Aztecs" will be used strictly in this sense, following Cardenal's usage.
3. All of Cardenal's poems quoted here come from *Ovnis de oro* (1992)!
4. Borgeson (1984) examines Cardenal's trans-temporal usage of popular and colloquial language such as "*moneda*" in the discussed poem. According to Borgeson (1984:94), this linguistic application creates a special effect in Cardenal's poetry: "Como consecuencia, la misma contemporaneidad del lenguaje, con suma ironía, manifiesta la paralización social y moral de nuestros días. Igualmente, el lenguaje muy del día también pone en manifiesto la vitalidad con que la humanidad busca resolver sus problemas más persistentes; el vocabulario, puede cambiar, pero las preocupaciones son de siempre" (Consequently, the same contemporaneity of the language, with maximum irony, manifests the social and moral paralysis of our days. Likewise, the language very much of the period also exhibits the vitality with which humanity seeks to resolve its more persistent problems; the vocabulary may change, but the worries are perpetual).

GLOSSARY

This glossary translates all the personal and place-name glyphs that appear in the figures. I would like to draw a conceptual distinction here between the linguistic morphology of the Nahua names and the pictographic morphology of their glyphs. In most cases, the pictographic elements of a glyph correspond to the meaning of the linguistic morphemes they are intended to signify. For instance, the personal name Chimalli means "shield," and its glyph consists of a shield connected to the person to whose name it corresponds. In many cases, however, glyphs do not contain pictographic morphemes for all of the linguistic morphemes of the names they represent, and thus the reader needs substantial cultural knowledge in order to read the glyph due to the conventional relationship between the pictographic representation and its linguistic meaning (Dibble 1971; Prem 1992). In such cases, the analysis of the glyph must fill in the missing linguistic morphemes. In cases where a linguistic morpheme is not easily represented pictographically, the scribe employs a rebus, a pictographic pun in which the mimetic image is intended to represent its phonetic articulation rather than its pictographic meaning. For instance, the linguistic morphology of the place-name Cuauhtitlan breaks down as *cuahu*(-*itl*) (tree) + -*ti*- (ligature) + -*tlan* (locative) and is translated as "Place near Trees" or "Place near the Forest." In creating a pictographic glyph for this toponym, the "tree" morpheme is unproblematic, but the locative element "tlan" is not so easily represented pictographically. In order to solve this problem, the scribe uses the image of teeth, which is *tlantli* in Nahuatl. The teeth then function as a pun to signify the locative "tlan," which has a similar phonetic value. Thus, the pictographic morphology of this toponym is made up of *cuahuitl* (tree) + *tlantli* (teeth). The "ti" ligature must be supplied by the reader. In such cases, I provide both the pictographic and linguistic morphologies of each personal and place-name and its respective glyph. The linguistic and pictographic analysis of the names and their translations in the glossary are limited to the codices cited in this book. There are cases in which the obscurity of the linguistic or pictographic morphology supports other interpretations.

Aacatl [*a*(-*tl*) (water) + *acatl* (reed)]. "Water Reed"; a Mexica priest.
Acamapichtli [*aca*(-*tl*) (reed) + *mapichtli* (fist)]. "Reed Fist"; a Mexica ruler of Tenochtitlan.
Achitometl [*a*(-*tl*) (water) + *chi*(-*yantli*) (chia) + *metl* (maguey)]. "Water Maguey"; a Colhuacan ruler.

Acolhuacan [Linguistic morphology: *a(-tl)* (water) + *col(-li)* (bent) + *-hua* (possessive) + *-can* (locative)]. "Place of Those Who Live near Bent Water."*
[Pictographic morphology: *a(-tl)* (water) + (*col[-li]* [bent] + *ma[-itl]* [arm]) (arm bent at the elbow = bent)].

Acolhuaque [Linguistic morphology: *a(-tl)* (water) + *col(-li)* (bent) + *-hua* (possessive) + *-que* (people)]. "People Who Live near Bent Water."
[Pictographic morphology: *a(-tl)* (water) + (*col[-li]* [bent] + *ma[-itl]* [arm]) (arm bent at the elbow = bent)].

Acolman [Linguistic morphology: *a(-tl)* (water) + *col(-li)* (bent) + *-man* (locative)]. "Place of Bent Water."
[Pictographic morphology: *a(-tl)* (water) + (*col[-li]* [bent] + *ma[-itl]* [arm]) (arm bent at the elbow = bent)].

Aculhua [Linguistic morphology: *a(-tl)* (water) + *col(-li)* (bent) + *-hua* (possessive)]. "One Who Lives near Bent Water."
[Pictographic morphology: *a(-tl)* (water) + (*col[-li]* [bent] + *ma[-itl]* [arm]) (arm bent at the elbow = bent)]. Founder of Azcapotzalco.

Amacui [*ama(-tl)* (paper) + *-cui* (take)]. "Paper Grasper"; a Chichimec leader.

Apanecatl [Linguistic morphology: *apan(-tli)* (river) + *-e-* (ligature) + *-catl* (person)]. "Someone from River."
[Pictographic morphology: *apan(-tli)* (river)]. A Mexica priest.

Atotoztli [*a(-tl)* (water) + *tototl* (bird)]. "Water-Bird"; Colhuacan princess, a daughter of Achitometl.

Azcapotzalco [*azca(-tl)* (ant) + *potzal(-li)* (mound) + *-co* (locative)]. "Place of Ant Mound."

Azcaxochitl [*azca(-tl)* (ant) + *xochitl* (flower)]. "Ant Flower"; wife of Nopaltzin.

Cexiuhtlacuilolli [*ce* (one or each) + *xiuh(-itl)* (year) + *tlacuilolli* (something written)]. "Something written each year"; annals.

Chalca [*chal(-chihuitl)* (precious stone) + *-ca* (people)]. "People of Chalco."

Chalco [Linguistic morphology: *chal(-chihuitl)* (precious stone) + *-co* (locative)]. "Place of Precious Stone."
[Pictographic morphology: *chal(-chihuitl)* (precious stone) + *co(-mitl)* (pot)].

---

* In the linguistic morphology of "Acolhuacan," the last two morphemes appear to be unambiguous: the "can" is a locative indicating place, and the "hua" is a possessive, which in place names refers to "residents of" the place in question. The first portion of this name ("Acol") is more problematic. One might be tempted to argue that Acolhuacan may be analyzed as [*ahcol(-li)* (shoulder) + *-hua* (possessive suffix) + *-can* (locative)], which means "Place of Those Who Have Shoulders," that is to say, "Place of Strong People." However, as Prem (1992:61–62) points out, in "ahcolli," the initial "a" is short, followed by a glottal stop, while in "Acolhuacan" it is long with no glottal stop. I would suggest that the linguistic morphology of "acol" is actually reflected in the glyph for "Acolhuacan," which consists of two elements: water and an arm bent at the elbow. The term for water in Nahuatl is "atl," with a long initial vowel and no glottal stop. If the stem of "atl" constitutes the initial vowel of "Acolhuacan," that leaves "col," which would appear to be the stem of the patientive noun "colli," referring to "something curved or bent," and metonymically, "grandfather." In at least one version of the glyph, the water is issuing from the top of the arm, which may indicate the shoulder joint. But another possibility is that the referent of this glyph is not the arm itself but rather its condition of being bent. So Acolhuacan may break down as: [*a(-tl)* (water) + *col(-li)* (bent) + *-hua* (possessive) + *-can* (locative)], which gives a meaning of "Place of Those Who Have Bent Water," or "Place of Those Who Live near Bent Water." Although I can find no attestations of "acolli" in other contexts, it could refer to a bend in a river, an inlet, or something similar. In her edition of the *Codex Mendoza*, Berdan (1992:169) identifies the morphology of "Acolhuacan" in this way, but I am indebted to Galen Brokaw for the analysis presented here.

Chiauhtla(n) [Linguistic morphology: *chiyahu* (greasy) + *-tla(-n)* (locative)]. "Greasy Place." [Pictographic morphology: *chiyahu(-ac)* (greasy) + *-tla(-n)* (teeth)].

Chichimecatecuhtli [*Chichimeca* (people of Chichimec) + *tecuhtli* (lord)]. "Chichimec lord."

Chichiquil [*chichiquil(-li)* (guiding feathers on a spear)]. "Guiding Feather"; a Tlailotlaca who collected the dead body of Huehue Ixtlilxochitl and burned it.

Chicometecpatl [*chicome* (seven) + *tecpatl* (flint)]. "Seven Flint"; a ruler of Xicotepec.

Chicomoztoc [*chicom(-e)* (seven) + *ozto(-tl)* (cave) + *-c* (locative)]. "Seven Caves."

Chiconauhtla(n) [Linguistic morphology: *chiconahui* (nine) + *-tlan* (locative)]. "Place of Nine." [Pictographic morphology: *chiconahui* (nine) + *-tlan* (teeth; locative)].

Chiconcuauh [*chicome* (seven) + *cuauh(-tli)* (eagle)]. "Seven Eagle"; founder of Xaltocan.

Chimalli [*chimalli* (shield)]. "Shield."

Chimalma [*chimal(-li)* (shield) + *ma(-itl)* (hand)]. "Shield-Hand"; Mexica female priest.

Chimalpaneca [*chimal(-li)* (shield) + *-pan* (locative) + *-e-* (ligature) + *-ca* (people)]. "People of Shield Place."

Chimalpopoca [*chimal(-li)* (shield) + *popoca* (smoke)]. "Smoking Shield"; a Mexica ruler of Tenochtitlan.

Cipactli [*cipactli* (crocodile)]. "Crocodile"; son of Nezahualcoyotl, a ruler of Xicotepec.

Coacuech [*coa(-tl)* (snake) + *cuech(-tli)* (bell or snail)]. "Snake Bell"; a Chichimec leader, a vassal of Yacanex.

Coatlichan [*coatl* (snake) + *i* (its) + *-chan* (home)]. "Snake Home."

Cocopin [*co(-mitl)* (pot) + *copin(-a)* (remove)]. "Removing Pot"; a ruler of Tepetlaoztoc.

Colhuacan [*col(-li)* (grandfather or ancestor) + *-hua* (possessive suffix) + *-can* (locative)]. "Place of Ancestors."

Colhuaque [*col(-li)* (grandfather or ancestor) + *-hua* (possessive suffix) + *-que* (people)]. "People of Colhuacan."

Coyoacan [*coyo(-tl)* (coyote) + *-hua* (possessive suffix) + *-can* (locative)]. "Place of One Who Has Coyotes."

Cozcaque [*cozca(-tl)* (necklace) + *-que* (possessive suffix)]. "One Who Has Necklace"; Chichimec leader, Yacanex's vassal.

Cuauhcihuatl [*cuauh(-tli)* (eagle) + *cihuatl* (woman)]. "Eagle Woman"; Quinatzin's wife.

Cuauhcoatl [*cuauh(-tli)* (eagle) + *coatl* (snake)]. "Eagle Snake"; a Mexica priest.

Cuauhnahuac [Linguistic morphology: *cuahu(-itl)* (tree) + *nahuac* (near)]. "Place near Trees." [Pictographic morphology: *cuahu(-itl)* (tree) + *nahua(-tl)* (agreeable sound)].

Cuauhtitlan [Linguistic morphology: *cuahu(-itl)* (tree) + *-ti-* (ligature) + *-tlan* (locative)]. "Place near Trees."
[Pictographic morphology: *cuahu(-itl)* (tree) + *-tlan(-tli)* (teeth)].

Cuauhtli [*cuauhtli* (eagle)]. "Eagle"; eagle warriors.

Cuauhyacac [Linguistic morphology: *cuauh(-itl)* (tree) + *yaca(-tl)* (peak) + *-c* (locative)]. "Peak on a Tree."
[Pictographic morphology: *cuauh(-itl)* (tree) + *yaca(-tl)* (nose)].

Cuicacalli [*cuica(-tl)* (song) + *calli* (house)]. "Song House."

Cuicatlan [*cuicatl* (song) + *-tlan* (locative)]. "Place of Song."

Huehuetzin [*huehue* (old man) + *-tzin* (honorific suffix)]. "Old man."

Huetzin [*huehuetl* (drum)]. "Upright Drum"; Coatlichan or Acolhuacan ruler.

Huexotla [*huexo(-tl)* (willow) + *-tlan* (locative)]. "Place of Willow."

Huexotzinca [*huexo(-tl)* (willow) + *-tzin(-tli)* (diminutive suffix) + *-ca* (people)]. "People of Huexotzinco (Little Willow)."

Huexotzinco [Linguistic morphology: *huexo(-tl)* (willow) + *-tzin(-tli)* (diminutive suffix) + *-co* (locative)]. "Place of Little Willow."
 [Pictographic morphology: *huexo(-tl)* (willow) + *-tzin(-tli)* (buttocks)].
Huitzilopochtli [*huitzil(-lin)* (hummingbird) + *opochtli* (left)]. "Hummingbird Left"; Mexica main god.
Huitznahuaque [*huitz(-tli)* (thorn) + *nahua(-c)* (near) + *-que* (people)]. "People of Huitznahuac" (People of the Place near Thorns).
Icpacxochitl [Linguistic morphology: *icpacxochitl*]. "Chaplets."
 [Pictographic morphology: *icpac* (on the head of) + *xochitl* (flower)]. "Flower on the Head"; wife of Tlotzin.
Ilamatzin [*ilama(-tl)* (old woman) + *-tzin* (honorific)]. "Old woman."
Ilancueitl [Linguistic morphology: *ilam(-atl)* (old woman) + *cueitl* (skirt)]. "Old Woman Skirt"; Colhuacan princess, a daughter of Achitometl and wife of the Mexica ruler Acamapichtli. [Pictographic morphology: illegible but *cueitl* (skirt) can be seen].
Itzcoatl [*itz(-tli)* (obsidian) + *coatl* (snake)]. "Obsidian Snake"; a Mexica ruler of Tenochtitlan.
Itzmitl [*itz(-tli)* (obsidian) + *mitl* (arrow)]. "Obsidian Arrow"; a Coatlichan ruler, father of Huetzin.
Ixtlilxochitl [*ix(-tli)* (eye) + *tlil(-li)* (black) + *xochitl* (flower)]. "Black Eyes Flower"; a ruler of Texcoco, father of Nezahualcoyotl.
Maccuahuitl [*ma(-itl)* (hand) + *c(-o)* (locative) + *cuahuitl* (stick)]. "Stick on hand" or "club."
Malinalca [*malinal(-li)* (something twisted) + *-ca* (people)]. "People of Malinalco (Twisted Place)."
Malinalxochitl [*malinal(-li)* (twisted) + *xochitl* (flower)]. "Twisted Flower"; wife of Amacui.
Matlatzinca [*matla(-tl)* (net) + *tzin(-co)* (locative) + *-ca* (people)]. "People of Matlatzinco (Net People)."
Mexitzin [*me(-tl)* (maguey) + *-tzin* (plural maker)]. "People of Mexitl"; Mexitl refers to a leader of the Mexica.
Moctezuma Ilhuicamina (more exactly in Nahuatl, Motecuhzoma) [*mo* (reflexive) + *tecuh(-tli)* (lord) + *zoma* (angry)] [*Ihuica(-tl)* (sky) + *mina* (shoot arrows)]. "Angry Lord," "Sky Shooter"; a Mexica ruler of Tenochtitlan.
Nauhyotl [(*nahui*) (four) + *-yotl* (-ness)]. "Essence of Four"; a leader of the Colhuaque.
Nezahualcoyotl [*nezahual(-li)* (fasted) + *coyotl* (coyote)]. "Fasted Coyote"; a ruler of Texcoco.
Nopaltzin [*nopal* (cactus) + *-tzin* (honorific)]. "Cactus"; a ruler of Tenayuca, son of Xolotl.
Ocotochtli [Linguistic morphology: *ocotochtli*]. "Bobcat."
 [Pictographic morphology: *oco(-tl)* (pine tree) + *tochtli* (rabbit)]. A Chichimec leader, a vassal of Yacanex.
Ollin [*ollin* (movement)]. "Movement" or "earthquake."
Opantecuhtli [*o(-tli)* (road) + *pan(-tli)* (flag) + *tecuhtli* (lord)]. "Lord of the Road Flag"; a Coatlichan ruler.
Otompan [*otom(-itl)* + *-pan* (locative)]. "Place of Otomíes."
Quinatzin [Linguistic morphology: unknown].
 [Pictographic morphology: a head of deer that growls (*quiquinaca*)]; founder of Texcoco.
Techotlalatzin [*tech* from *tetl* (stone) + *tlala(-catetl)* (dove) + *-tzin* (honorific)]. "Stone Dove"; a ruler of Texcoco and father of Huehue Ixtlilxochitl.
Tenacacaltzin [*tena(-mitl)* (wall)]. "Wall," probably City-Wall; a ruler of Tenayuca, a son of Nopaltzin and half brother of Tlotzin.

Tennahuacatl [Linguistic morphology: *Tennahua(-c)* + *-catl* (person)]. "Someone from Tennahuac."
[Pictographic morphology: *te(-tl)* (stone) + *(te)-n(-tli)* (lip) + *nahuacatl* (speaking)]. A leader of the Mexica.

Tenochtitlan [*te(-tl)* (stone) + *noch(-tli)* (cactus fruit) + *-titlan* (locative)]. "Place of the Cactus Fruit on the Stone"; capital of the Aztec empire.

Teocalli [*teo(-tl)* (sacred) + *calli* (house)]. "Temple."

Tepaneca [Linguistic morphology: *tepan* (place name) + *-ca* (people)]. "People from Tepan." [Pictographic morphology: *te(-tl)* (stone) + *pan(-tli)* (flag)].

Tepechpan [*te(-tl)* (stone) + *pech(-tli)* (mat) + *-pan* (locative)]. "Place of the Stone Mat."

Tepetlaoztoc [*te(-tl)* (stone) + *petla(-tl)* (reed mat) + *ozto(-tl)* (cave) + *-c* (locative)]. "Cave of the Stone Mat."

Texcoco [Linguistic morphology: unknown].
[Pictographic morphology: *tex(-calli)* (craggy mountain) + *co(-mitl)* (olla)]. "Place of Craggy Mountain."

Teyolcohuatzin [*te(-tl)* (stone) + *yol(-li)* (heart) + *-coatl* (snake) + *-tzin* (honorific)]. "Stone Heart Snake"; a ruler of Acolman, son of Tezozomoc.

Tezcacoatl [*tezca(-tl)* (mirror) + *coatl* (snake)]. "Mirror Snake"; a Mexica priest.

Tezoyucan [*te(-tl)* (stone) or *te(-zontli)* (volcanic stone) + *zo* (pierced) + *-yucan* (locative)]. "Place of Pierced Stone."

Tezozomoc [*te(-tl)* (stone) + *zozoma* (very angry)]. "Angry Stone"; a ruler of Azcapotzalco.

Tlacateotzin [*tlaca(-tl)* (person) + *teo(-tl)* (god)]. "Human Sun."

Tlacopan [Linguistic morphology: *tlaco(-tl)* (stick) + *-pan* (locative)]. "Place of Sticks." [Pictographic morphology: *tlacotl* (stick) + *co(-mitl)* (pot)].

Tlacotzin [*tlacotli* (slave) + *-tzin* (honorific)]. "Slave"; a ruler of Huexotla.

Tlahuica [*tlahui(-tolli)* (something bent, arch) + *-ca* (people)]. "People of Arch."

Tlailotlaca [*tlailo(-a)* (returning) + *tlaca* (people)]. "Returning People."

Tlalnahuacatzin [*tlal(-li)* (earth) + *nahua* (speaking) + *-tzin* (honorific)]. "Speaking Earth."

Tlaltecatzin [*tlal(-li)* (earth) + *teca(-tl)* (resident of) + *-tzin* (honorific)]. "Resident on the Earth."

Tlamina [Linguistic morphology: *tla* (something) + *-mina* (shoot arrows)]. "Shooter."
[Pictographic morphology: *tlan(-tli)* (tooth) + *mina* (shoot arrows)]. A leader of Huitznahuaque.

Tlatelolco [*tlatel(-li)* (earth mound) + *ol(-tic)* (round) + *-co* (locative)]. "Place of the Round Earth Mound."

Tlatocatlatzacuilotzin [*tlatoca(-yotl)* (kingship) + *tlatzacuilo* (something closed)]. "Lord Kingship"; a ruler of Acolman.

Tliltotocuauhtepahzolli [*tlil(-li)* (black) + *toto(-tl)* (bird) + *cuahu(-itl)* (wood) + *tepahzolli* (nest)]. "Black Bird on a Wood Nest"; a ruler of Xicotepec.

Tlotzin or **Tlotzin Pochotl** [*tlo(-tli)* (falcon) + *-tzin* (honorific)] [*pochotl* (silk-cotton tree)]. "Falcon"; a ruler of Texcoco, father of Huehue Ixtlilxochitl.

Tochmiltzin [*toch(-tli)* (rabbit) + *mil(-li)* (field) + *-tzin* (honorific)]. "Rabbit Field"; a ruler of Chiconahuatla.

Tolteca [*tol(-li)* (reed) + *-teca(-tli)* (residents of)]. "People of Tula or Tollan"; Toltecs.

Tomiyauh [Linguistic morphology: *to* (our) + *miyahua(-tl)* (tassel and flower of maize)]. "Our Maize Flower."
[Pictographic morphology: *to(-totl)* (bird) + *miyahua(-tl)* (tassel and flower of maize). Wife of Xolotl.

Tozatzin [*toza(-n)* (gopher) + *-tzin* (honorific)]. "Lord of the Gopher"; a priest of Huexotla.

Tulantzinco [Linguistic morphology: *tol*(-*lin*) (reed) + -*tlan* (locative) + -*tzin* (diminutive suffix) + -*co* (locative)]. "Place of Little Reeds."
 [Pictographic morphology: *tol*(-*lin*) (reed) + *tzin* (-*tli*) (buttocks)].
Tzompantli [Linguistic morphology: *tzon*(-*tli*) (head) + *pantli* (row)]. "Skull Rack."
 [Pictographic morphology: *tzon*(-*tli*) (hair) + *pantli* (flag)]. A ruler of Xaltocan.
Tzontecomatl [Linguistic morphology: *tzontecomatl*]. "Head."
 [Pictographic morphology: *tzon*(-*tli*) (hair) + *tecomitl* (gourd)]. A Chichimec leader, founder of Acolhuacan or Coatlichan.
Xaltocan [*xal*(-*li*) (sand) + *toca*(-*tl*) (spider) + -*n* (locative)]. "Place of the Sand Spider."
Xicotepec [*xico*(-*tl*) (bumblebee) + *tepe*(-*tl*) (hill) + -*c* (locative)]. "Bumblebee Hill."
Xihutlapohualli [*xihu*(-*itl*) + *tlapohualli* (counting)]. "Year counting."
Xipetecuhtli [*xipe* (shape of the indigenous god Xipe) + *tecuhtli* (ruler)]. "Lord Xipe"; a Chichimec leader, a vassal of Yacanex.
Xochimilca [*xochi*(-*tl*) (flower) + *mil*(-*li*) (field) + -*ca* (people)]. "People of Xochimilco."
Xochimilco [*xochi*(-*tl*) (flower) + *mil*(-*li*) (field) + -*co* (locative)]. "Place of Flower Field."
Xometzin [*xome*(-*tl*) (elder tree)]. "Elder Tree"; a ruler of Tepechpan.
Yacanex [*yaca*(-*tl*) (nose) + *nex*(-*tli*) (ash)]. "Ash Nose"; a Chichimec leader, a ruler of Tepetlaoztoc.
Zayollin [*zayolin* (fly)]. "Fly"; a ruler or nobleman of Tenayuca, companion of Tenacacaltzin.

REFERENCES

Adorno, Rolena. 1986. Literary Production and Suppression: Reading and Writing about Amerindians in Colonial Spanish America. *Dispositio* 11:1–25.

———. 1989a. Arms, Letters, and the Native Historian in Early Colonial Mexico. In *1492–1992: Re/Discovering Colonial Writing*, ed. René Jara and Nicholas Spadaccini, 201–24. Minneapolis, MN: Prisma Institute.

———. 1989b. The Warrior and the War Community: Constructions of the Civil Order in Mexican Conquest History. *Dispositio* 14:225–46.

Alcina Franch, José. 1957. *Floresta literaria de la América indígena*. Madrid: Aguilar.

———. 1968. *Poesía americana precolombina*. Madrid: Editorial Prensa Española.

———. 1992. *Azteca Mexica*. Barcelona: Lunwerg Editores.

Alva Ixtlilxochitl, Fernando de. 1997. *Obras históricas*. 2 vols. Ed. Edmundo O'Gorman. Mexico City: UNAM.

Alvarado Tezozomoc, Fernando. 1987. *Crónica mexicana/Códice Ramírez*. Ed. Manuel Orozco y Berra. Mexico City: Porrúa.

———. 1992. *Crónica mexicayotl*. Trans. Adrián León. Mexico City: UNAM.

Anales de Tlatelolco. 1948. Ed. Heinrich Berlin-Neubart. Mexico City: Antigua Librería Robredo.

Anderson, Arthur J. O. 1993. Introduction. In *Bernardino de Sahagún's Psalmodia Christiana (Christian Psalmody)*, xv–xxxix. Trans. Arthur J. O. Anderson. Salt Lake City: University of Utah Press.

Annals of Cuauhtitlan. 1992. In *History and Mythology of the Aztecs: The Codex Chimalpopoca*, 17–138. Trans. John Bierhorst. Tucson: University of Arizona Press.

Anonymous. 1997. "La guerra de Chalco y sucesos posteriores hasta la muerte de Nezahualcoyotzin." In *Obras históricas*, vol. 1, by Fernando de Alva Ixtlilxochitl, 553–62. Mexico City: Fondo de Cultura Económica.

Aubin, M. 1886a. Mapa Quinatzin. *Anales del Museo Nacional de México* 3:321–68.

———. 1886b. Mapa Tlotzin. *Anales del Museo Nacional de México* 3:304–20.

Barlow, R. H. 1945. La Crónica X: Versiones coloniales de la historia de los Mexica tenochca. *Revista Mexicana de Estudios Antropológicos* 7:65–87.

———. 1949a. Fundación de la Triple Alianza. *Anales del Instituto Nacional de Antropología e Historia* 3:147–57.

———. 1949b. *The Extent of the Empire of the Culhua Mexica*. Berkeley: University of California Press.

———. 1994. *Fuentes y estudios sobre el México indígena*. Vol. 5. Ed. Jesús Monjarás-Ruiz, Elena Limón, and María de la Cruz Paillés. Mexico City: Instituto Nacional de Antropología e Historia.

Baudot, Georges. 1979. *Las letras precolombinas*. Trans. Xavier Massimi. Mexico City: Siglo Veintiuno.

———. 1995. *Utopia and History in Mexico: The First Chroniclers of Mexican Civilization (1520–1569)*. Trans. Bernard R. Ortiz de Montellano and Thelma Ortiz de Montellano. Niwot: University Press of Colorado.

Benavente (Motolinia), Toribio de. 1971. *Memoriales o Libro de las cosas de la Nueva España y de los naturales de ella*. Mexico City: UNAM.

Berdan, F. Frances. 1992. The Place-Name, Personal Name, and Title Glyphs of the *Codex Mendoza*: Translations and Comments. In *The Codex Mendoza*, vol. 4, ed. Francis F. Berdan and Patricia Rieff Anawalt, 163–238. Berkeley: University of California Press.

———. 2005. *The Aztecs of Central Mexico: An Imperial Society*. 2nd ed. Belmont, CA: Thomson Wadsworth.

———, and Patricia Rieff Anawalt. 1992. *Description of Codex Mendoza*. Vol. 2 of *The Codex Mendoza*, ed. Francis F. Berdan and Patricia Rieff Anawalt. Berkeley: University of California Press.

Bierhorst, John. 1985. General Introduction and Commentary. In *Cantares Mexicanos: Songs of the Aztecs*, trans. John Bierhorst, 7–130. Stanford, CA: Stanford University Press.

———. 1992. Introduction. In *The Codex Chimalpopoca*, trans. John Bierhorst, 1–16. Tucson: University of Arizona Press.

Boone, Elizabeth Hill. 2000. *Stories in Red and Black: Pictorial Histories of the Aztecs and Mixtecs*. Austin: University of Texas Press.

———, and Walter D. Mignolo, eds. 1994. *Writing without Words: Alternative Literacies in Mesoamerica and the Andes*. Durham, NC: Duke University Press.

Borgeson, Paul W. 1984. *Hacia el hombre nuevo: Poesía y el pensamiento de Ernesto Cardenal*. London: Tamesis Books.

Boturini Benaducci, Lorenzo. 1990. *Historia general de la América septentrional*. Mexico City: UNAM.

Brading, David A. 1985. *The Origin of Mexican Nationalism*. Cambridge: Cambridge University Press.

———. 1991. *The First America: The Spanish Monarchy, Creole Patriots, and the Liberal State, 1492–1867*. Cambridge: Cambridge University Press.

———. 2001. *Mexican Phoenix. Our Lady of Guadalupe: Image and Tradition across Five Centuries*. Cambridge: Cambridge University Press.

Brinton, Daniel G. 1887. *Ancient Nahuatl Poetry*. New York: AMS.

Brotherston, Gordon. 1972. Nezahualcoyotl's "Lamentaciones" and Their Nahuatl Origins: The Westernization of Ephemerality. *Estudios de Cultura Náhuatl* 10:393–408.

———. 1975. *Latin American Poetry*. New York: Cambridge University Press.

———. 1979. *Image of the New World*. London and New York: Thames and Hudson.

———. 1992. *Book of the Fourth World. Reading the Native Americas through Their Literature*. London and New York: Cambridge University Press.

———. 1995. *Painted Books from Mexico*. London: British Museum.

———. 2005. *Feather Crown: The Eighteen Feasts of the Mexica Year*. London: British Museum.

Brumfiel, Elizabeth M. 1983. Aztec State Making: Ecology, Structure, and the Origin of the State. *American Anthropologist* 85 (2): 261–84.

———. 2001. Aztec Hearths and Mind: Religion and the State in the Aztec Empire. In *Empires: Perspectives from Archaeology and History*, ed. Susan E. Alcock et al., 283–310. Cambridge: Cambridge University Press.

Brundage, Burr Cartwright. 1972. *A Rain of Darts: The Mexica Aztecs*. Austin: University of Texas Press.

———. 1979. *The Fifth Sun*. Austin: University of Texas Press.

Burkhart, Louise. 1988. Doctrinal Aspects of Sahagún's *Coloquios*. In *The Works of Bernardino de Sahagún: Pioneer Ethnographer of Sixteenth-Century Aztec Mexico*, ed. J. Jorge de Alva, H. B. Nicholson, and Eloise Quiñones Keber, 65–82. Albany, NY: Institute for Mesoamerican Studies.

———. 1989. *The Slippery Earth: Nahua-Christian Moral Dialogue in Sixteenth-Century Mexico*. Tucson: University of Arizona Press.

———. 1992. The Amanuenses Have Appropriated the Text. In *On the Translation of Native American Literatures*, ed. Brian Swann, 339–55. Washington, D.C.: Smithsonian Institution Press.

———. 1996. *Holy Wednesday*. Philadelphia: University of Pennsylvania Press.

Bushnell, David, and Neill Macaulay. 1988. *The Emergence of Latin America in the Nineteenth Century*. New York: Oxford University Press.

Bustamante, Carlos María de. 1970. *Tezcoco en los últimos tiempos de sus antiguos reyes*. Ed. Ernesto Lemoine. Mexico City: Biblioteca Enciclopédica del Estado de México.

Calnek, Edward E. 1973. The Historical Validity of the Codex Xolotl. *American Antiquity* 38 (4): 423–27.

Campos, Marco Antonio. 1994. *En recuerdo de Nezahualcoyotl*. Mexico City: Editorial Diana.

———. 1998. Prólogo. In *Las Aztecas*, by José Joaquín Pesado. Mexico City: Factoría Ediciones, S de R L.

Campos, Rubén M. 1936. *La producción literaria de los Aztecas: Compilación de cantos y discursos de los antiguos mexicanos, tomados de viva voz por los conquistadores y dispersos en varios textos de la historia antigua de México*. Mexico City: Talleres Gráficos del Museo Nacional de Arqueología, Historia y Etnografía.

Cantares Mexicanos: Songs of the Aztecs. 1985. Trans. John Bierhorst. Stanford, CA: Stanford University Press.

Cardenal, Ernesto. 1972. *Homenaje a los indios americanos*. Buenos Aires: Ediciones Carlos Lohlé.

———. 1992. *Los ovnis de oro*. Bloomington: Indiana University Press.

Carochi, Horacio. 1982. *Arte de la lengua mexicana*. Mexico City: Museo Nacional.

Carrasco, Davíd. 1998. *Daily Life of the Aztecs: People of the Sun and Earth*. Westport, CT: Greenwood Press.

———. 2000. *Quetzalcoatl and the Irony of Empire: Myth and Prophecies in the Aztec Tradition*. Boulder: University Press of Colorado.

———. 2003. Toward the Splendid City: Knowing the Worlds of Moctezuma. In *Moctezuma's Mexico: Visions of the Aztec World*, ed. David Carrasco and Eduardo Matos Moctezuma, 99–148. Boulder: University Press of Colorado.

Carrasco, Pedro. 1950. *Los Otomíes: Cultura e historia prehispánicas de los pueblos mesoamericanos de habla otomiana*. Mexico City: UNAM.

———. 1976. La sociedad mexicana antes de la conquista. In *Historia general de México*, vol 1, 165–288. Mexico City: El Colegio de México.

———. 1984. The Extent of the Tepanec Empire. In *The Native Sources and the History of the Valley of Mexico: Proceedings of International Congress of Americanists, Manchester 1982*, ed. J. de Durand-Forest, 73–79. Oxford: BAR.

———. 1999. *The Tenochca Empire of Ancient Mexico: The Triple Alliance of Tenochtitlan, Tetzcoco, and Tlacopan*. Norman: University of Oklahoma Press.

Caso, Alfonso. 1966. La época de los señores independientes. *Revista Mexicana de Estudios Antropológicos* 20:147–52.
———. 1967. *Los calendarios prehispánicos*. Mexico City: UNAM.
Castillo Farreras, Víctor. 1972. *Nezahualcoyotl: Crónica y pinturas de su tiempo*. Texcoco: Gobierno del Estado de México.
Chavero, Alfredo. 1904. *El monolito de Coatlichan*. Mexico City: Mexico Imprenta del Museo Nacional.
———. 1958. *México a través de los siglos*. Mexico City: Editorial Cumbre, S. A.
Chimalpahin Cuauhtlehuanitzin, Domingo Francisco de San Antón Muñón. 1965. *Relaciones originales de Chalco Amaquemecan*. Trans. S. Rendón. Mexico City: Fondo de Cultura.
———. 1991. *Memorial breve*. Mexico City: UNAM.
———. 1998. *Las ocho relaciones y el memorial de Colhuacan*. 2 vols. Trans. Rafael Tena. Mexico City: Consejo Nacional para la Cultura y las Letras.
Clavijero, Francisco Javier. 1991. *Historia antigua de México*. Ed. Mariano Cuevas. Mexico City: Porrúa.
Clezio, Le. 1993. *The Mexican Dream, or, The Interrupted Thought of Amerindian Civilizations*. Trans. Teresa Lavender Fagan. Chicago: University of Chicago Press.
Codex Azcatitlan. 1995. Ed. Robert H. Barlow. Paris: Bibliothèque Nationale de France.
Codex Chimalpahin. 1997. Trans. Arthur J. O. Anderson and Susan Schroeder. 2 vols. Norman: University of Oklahoma Press.
Codex en Cruz. 1981. Ed. Charles Dibble. Salt Lake City: University of Utah Press.
Codex Mendoza. 1992. Ed. Francis F. Berdan and Patricia Rieff Anawalt. 4 vols. Berkeley: University of California Press.
Codex Mexicanus. See Menguin 1952.
Codex Telleriano-Remensis. 1995. Ed. Eloise Quiñones Keber. Austin: University of Texas Press.
Códice Aubin (Historia de la nación mexicana). 1963. Ed. Charles Dibble. Madrid: José Porrúa Turanzas.
Códice de Tepetlaoztoc. 1992. Ed. Perla Valle. Mexico City: Instituto Nacional de Antropología e Historia.
Códice de Xicotepec. 1995. Ed. Guy Stresser-Pean, trans. Araceli Méndez. Mexico City: Fondo de Cultura Económica.
Códice Ixtlilxochitl. 1996. Ed. Ferdinand Anders, Maarten Jansen, and Luis Reyes García. Mexico: Fondo de Cultura Económica.
Códice Techialoyan García Granados. 1992. Toluca: El Colegio Mexiquense a.c.
Códice Xolotl. 1996. Ed. Charles Dibble. Mexico City: Instituto de Investigaciones Históricas.
Códices y documentos sobre México: Primer simposio. 1994. Ed. Constanza Vega Sosa. Mexico City: Instituto Nacional de Antropología e Historia.
Coe, Michael D., and Rex Koontz. 2002. *Mexico from the Olmecs to the Aztecs*. London: Thames and Hudson.
Coloquio de documentos pictográficos de tradición nahuatl. 1989. Ed. Carlos Martínez Marín. Mexico City: UNAM.
Cortés, Hernán. 1993. *Cartas de relación*. Ed. Angel Delgado Gómez. Madrid: Clásicos Castalia.
Dakin, Karen. 1986. A Nahuatl-English Dictionary and Concordance to the *Cantares Mexicanos*: With an Analytic Transcription and Grammatical Notes. *Linguistic Anthropology* 88:1015–16.
Damrosch, David. 1993. The Aesthetics of Conquest: Aztec Poetry. In *New World Encounters*, ed. Stephen Greenblatt, 139–58. Berkeley and Los Angeles: University of California Press.

Davies, Nigel. 1980. *The Toltec Heritage: From the Fall of Tula to the Rise of Tenochtitlán*. Norman: University of Oklahoma Press.

———. 1987. *The Aztec Empire: The Toltec Resurgence*. Norman: University of Oklahoma Press.

Díaz Balsera, Viviana. 2005. *The Pyramid under the Cross: Franciscan Discourses of Evangelization and the Nahua Christian Subject in Sixteenth-Century Mexico*. Tucson: University of Arizona Press.

Díaz del Castillo, Bernal. 1992. *Historia de la conquista de Nueva España*. Mexico City: Editorial Porrúa.

Dibble, Charles. 1954–1955. Los Chichmecas de Xolotl. *Revista Mexicana de Estudios Antropológicos* 14:285–88.

———. 1971. Writing in Central Mexico. In *The Handbook of Middle American Indians*. Vol. 10, *The Archaeology of Northern Mesoamerica*, ed. Gordon F. Ekholm and Ignacio Bernal, 322–32. Austin: University of Texas Press.

———. 1990. The Boban Calendar Wheel. *Estudios de Cultura Náhuatl* 20:173–82.

———. 1996. Prefacio. In *Códice de Xicotepec*, ed. Guy Stresser-Pean, trans. Araceli Méndez, 7–8. Mexico City: Fondo de Cultura Económica.

Douglas, Eduardo de. 2003. Figures of Speech: Pictorial History in the *Quinatzin Map* of about 1542. *Art Bulletin* 85:281–309.

Durán, Diego. 1971. *Book of the Gods and Rites and the Ancient Calendar*. Trans. and ed. Fernando Horcasitas and Doris Heyden. Norman: University of Oklahoma Press.

———. 1994. *The History of the Indies of New Spain*. Trans. Doris Heyden. Norman: University of Oklahoma Press.

Edmonson, Munro S., ed. 1974. *Sixteenth-Century Mexico: The Work of Sahagún*. Albuquerque: University of New Mexico Press.

———. 1988. *The Book of the Year: Middle American Calendrical System*. Salt Lake City: University of Utah Press.

Eguiara y Eguren, Juan José de. 1944. *Prólogos a la biblioteca mexicana*. Mexico City: Fondo de Cultura Económica.

Elias, Eduardo F. 1982. Homenaje a los indios americanos de Ernesto Cardenal. Lecciones del pasado. *Chasqui* 12 (1): 45–60.

Elisondo, Carlos. 1996. *Vida y grandeza del gran señor Nezahualcóyotl*. Toluca: Instituto Mexiquense de Cultura.

Epistolario de Nueva España, 1505–1818. 1940. Collected by Paso y Troncoso. Vol. 14. Mexico City: Antigua Librería Robredo.

Evans, Susan Toby. 2001. Aztec-Period Political Organization in the Teotihuacan Valley. *Ancient Mesoamerica* 12 (1): 89–100.

Florentine Codex. 1950–1982. 12 vols. Trans. Arthur J. O. Anderson and Charles Dibble. Salt Lake City: University of Utah Press.

Florescano, Enrique. 1994. *Memory, Myth, and Time in Mexico from the Aztecs to Independence*. Trans. Albert G. Bork. Austin: University of Texas Press.

———. 1999. *The Myth of Quetzalcoatl*. Trans. Raúl Velázquez. Baltimore: Johns Hopkins University Press.

Fuente, Carmen de la. 1999. *Nezahualcóyotl, brazo de león: (Pieza épica)*. Toluca: Instituto Mexiquense de Cultura.

García, Gregorio. 1981. *Origen de los indios del Nuevo Mundo*. Mexico: Fondo de Cultura Económica.

Garibay K., Angel María. 1961. *Llave del nahuatl: Colección de trozos clásicos con gramática y vocabulario para utilidad de los principiantes*. Mexico City: Porrúa.

———. 1992. *Historia de la literatura nahuatl*. Mexico City: Porrúa.

———, ed. and trans. 1993. *Poesía náhuatl*. 3 vols. Mexico City: UNAM.

Gibson, Charles. 1956. Llamamiento General, Repartimiento, and the Empire of Acolhuacan. *Hispanic American Historical Review* 36:1–27.

———. 1964. *The Aztecs under Spanish Rule: A History of the Indians of the Valley of Mexico, 1519–1810.* Stanford, CA: Stanford University Press.

———. 1971. Structure of the Aztec Empire. In *The Handbook of Middle American Indians.* Vol. 10, *The Archaeology of Northern Mesoamerica*, ed. Gordon F. Ekholm and Ignacio Bernal, 376–94. Austin: University of Texas Press.

———. 1975. Prose Sources in the Native Historical Tradition. In *The Handbook of Middle American Indians.* Vol. 15, *Guide to Ethnohistorical Sources*, ed. Howard F. Cline, 311–21. Austin: University of Texas Press.

———, and John B. Glass. 1975. A Census of Native Middle American Pictorial Manuscripts. In *The Handbook of Middle American Indians.* Vol. 14, *Guide to Ethnohistorical Sources*, ed. Howard F. Cline, 81–252. Austin: University of Texas Press.

Gillespie, Susan D. 1989. *The Aztec Kings: The Construction of Rulership in Mexica History.* Tucson: University of Arizona Press.

———. 1998. The Aztec Triple Alliance: A Postconquest Tradition. In *Native Traditions in the Postconquest World*, ed. Elizabeth Hill Boone and Tom Cummins, 233–63. Washington, D.C.: Dumbarton Oaks.

Gillmor, Frances. 1983. *Flute of the Smoking Mirror, A Portrait of Nezahualcoyotl, Poet-King of the Aztecs.* Albuquerque: University of New Mexico Press.

Glass, John B. 1975. A Survey of Native Middle American Pictorial Manuscripts. In *The Handbook of Middle American Indians.* Vol. 14, *Guide to Ethnohistorical Sources*, ed. Howard F. Cline, 3–80. Austin: University of Texas Press.

———, and Donald Robertson. 1975. A Census of Native Middle American Pictorial Manuscripts. In *The Handbook of Middle American Indians.* Vol. 14, *Guide to Ethnohistorical Sources*, ed. Howard F. Cline, 81–252. Austin: University of Texas Press.

Granados y Gálvez, Joseph Joaquín. 1987. *Tardes americanas: Gobierno gentil y católico: Breve y particular noticia de toda la historia indiana: Sucesos, casos notables, y cosas ignoradas, desde la entrada de la gran nación tulteca á esta tierra de Anahuac, hasta los presentes tiempos.* Mexico City: M. A. Porrúa.

Graulich, Michel. 1997. *Myths of Ancient Mexico.* Trans. Bernard R. Ortiz de Montellano and Thelma Ortiza de Montellano. Norman: University of Oklahoma Press.

Hale, Charles A. 1968. *Mexican Liberalism in the Age of Mora, 1821–1853.* New Haven, CT, and London: Yale University Press.

Haly, Richard. 1986. Poetics of the Aztecs. *New Scholar: An Americanist Review* 10:85–133.

Hassig, Ross. 1988. *Aztec Warfare: Imperial Expansion and Political Control.* Norman and London: University of Oklahoma Press.

Hicks, Frederic. 1979. Flowery War in Aztec History. *American Ethnologist* 6:87–92.

Histoire du Mechique. 1965. In *Teogonía e historia de los mexicanos*, ed. and trans. Angel María Garibay K., 69–120. Mexico City: Editorial Porrúa.

Historia de los mexicanos por sus pinturas. 1941. In *Nueva colección de documentos para la Historia de México*, vol. 3, ed. Joaquín García Icazbalceta, 209–40. Mexico City: Editorial Chávez Hayhoe.

Historia Tolteca-Chichimeca. 1989. Ed. Paul Kirchhoff et al. Mexico City: Fondo de Cultura Económica.

Hodge, Mary G. 1984. *Aztec City-States.* Studies in Latin American Ethnohistory and Archeology 3. Memoirs of the Museum of Anthropology 18. Ann Arbor: University of Michigan.

———. 1996. Political Organization of the Central Provinces. In *Aztec Imperial Strategies*, by Frances F. Berdan et al., 17–45. Washington, D.C.: Dumbarton Oaks Research Library and Collection.

Icazbalceta, Joaquín García. 1971. Noticias del autor y de la obra. In *Historia eclesiástica indiana*, by Fray Jerónimo de Mendieta, xvii–xxxvi. Mexico: Antigua Librería.
Isaac, Barry L. 1983. The Aztec "Flowery War": A Geopolitical Explanation. *Journal of Anthropological Research* 39:415–32.
Jara, René. 1989. The Inscription of Creole Consciousness: Fray Servando de Mier. In *1492–1992: Re/Discovering Colonial Writing*, ed. René Jara and Nicholas Spadaccini, 349–79. Minneapolis: University of Minnesota Press.
Jiménez Moreno, Wigberto. 1954–1955. Síntesis de la historia precolonial del Valle de México. *Revista Mexicana de Estudios Antropológicos* 14:219–36.
———. 1961. Diferente principio del año entre diversos pueblos y sus consecuencias para la cronología prehispánica. *El México Antiguo* 9:137–50.
———, José Miranda, and María Teresa Fernández. 1970. *Historia de México*. Mexico City: Editorial E.C.L.A.L.S.A. Constitución, 18.
Karttunen, Frances. 1992. *An Analytical Dictionary of Nahuatl*. Norman: University of Oklahoma Press.
———, and James Lockhart. 1980. La estructura de la poesía nahuatl vista por sus variantes. *Estudios de Cultura Náhuatl* 14:15–64.
Keen, Benjamin. 1971. *The Aztec Image in Western Thought*. New Brunswick, NJ: Rutgers University Press.
Kirchhoff, Paul. 1948. Civilizing the Chichimecs: A Charter in the Culture History of Ancient Mexico. *Latin American Studies* 5:80–85.
Klor de Alva, Juan José. 1981. Martín Ocelotl: Clandestine Cult Leader. In *Struggle and Survival in Colonial America*, ed. David G. Sweet and Gary B. Nash, 128–41. Berkeley: University of California Press.
———. 1982. Spiritual Conflict and Accommodation in New Spain: Toward a Typology of Aztec Response to Christianity. In *The Inca and Aztec States, 1400–1800: Anthropology and History*, ed. George A. Collier, Renato I. Rosaldo, and John D. Wirth, 345–66. New York: Academic Press.
———. 1989. Language, Politics, and Translation: Colonial Discourse and Classical Nahuatl in New Spain. In *The Art of Translation: Voices from the Field*, ed. Rosanna Warren, 143–62. Boston: Northeastern University Press.
———, H. B. Nicholson, and Eloise Quiñones Keber, eds. 1988. *The Work of Bernardino de Sahagun: Pioneer Ethnographer of Sixteenth-Century Aztec Mexico*. Albany, NY: Institute for Mesoamerica Studies.
Kobayasi, José María. 1974. *La educación como conquista (empresa franciscana en México)*. Mexico City: El Colegio de México.
Kobayasi, Munehiro. 1996. De la manera en que nuestros antepasados vivieron, vivamo. Procesos inquisitoriales de tres indios texcocanos en 1530. In *Mesoamerica y los Andes*, ed. Mayán Cervantes, 533–55. Mexico City: Ediciones de la Casa Chata.
Krickerberg, Walter. 1995. *Las antiguas culturas mexicanas*. Mexico City: Fondo de Cultura Económica.
Lafaye, Jacques. 1976. *Quetzalcóatl and Guadalupe: The Formation of Mexican National Consciousness, 1531–1813*. Trans. Benjamin Keen. Chicago: University of Chicago Press.
Las Casas, Bartolomé de. 1967. *Apologética historia sumaria*. 2 vols. Ed. Edmundo O'Gorman. Mexico City: UNAM.
Leander, Birgitta. 1976. *In xochitl in cuicatl. Flor y canto: La poesía de los aztecas*. Mexico City: Instituto de Investigaciones.
Legend of the Suns. 1992. In *History and Mythology of the Aztecs: The Codex Chimalpopoca*, trans. John Bierhorst. Tucson: University of Arizona Press.
Lesbre, Patrick. 2001. El Tetzcutzinco en la obra de Fernando de Alva Ixtlilxochitl: Realeza, religión prehispánica y cronistas coloniales. *Estudios de Cultura Náhuatl* 32:323–40.

León-Portilla, Miguel. 1963. *Aztec Thought and Culture*. Trans. Jack Emory Davis. Norman: University of Oklahoma Press.

———. 1966. *La filosofía nahuatl estudiada en sus fuentes*. Mexico City: UNAM.

———. 1967a. El proceso de aculturación de los Chichimecas de Xolotl. *Estudios de Cultura Nahuatl* 7:59–86.

———. 1967b. *Trece poetas del mundo azteca*. Mexico City: UNAM.

———. 1972. *Nezahualcoyotl: Poesía y pensamiento*. Texcoco: Gobierno del Estado de Mexico.

———. 1974. Testimonios náhuas sobre la conquista espiritual. *Estudios de Cultura Náhuatl* 11:11–36.

———. 1980. *Toltecayotl, aspectos de la cultura nahuatl*. Mexico City: Fondo de Cultura Económica.

———. 1986a. Introducción. In *Juan de Torquemada, monarquía indiana*, vii–xxxi. Mexico City: Editorial Porrúa, S. A.

———. 1986b. Review of *Cantares Mexicanos, Songs of the Aztecs* by John Bierhorst. *Mexican Studies/Estudios Mexicanos* 2 (1): 129–44.

———. 1992a. *The Aztec Image of Self and Society*. Ed. and trans. Jorge Klor de Alva. Salt Lake City: University of Utah Press.

———. 1992b. *Fifteen Poets of the Aztec World*. Norman: University of Oklahoma Press.

———. 1994. *Quince poetas del mundo nahuatl*. Mexico City: Diana.

———. 1995. *Toltecayotl: Aspectos de la cultura náhuatl*. Mexico City: Fondo de Cultura Económica.

———. 1996. *Los antiguos mexicanos a través de sus crónicas y cantares*. Mexico City: Fondo de Cultura Económica.

Lienhard, Martín. 1983. La crónica mestiza en México y el Perú hasta 1620: Apuntes para su estudio histórico-literario. *Revista de Crítica Literaria Latinoamericana* 17:105–15.

List Arzubide, Germán. 1975. *Tlatoani: Vida del gran señor Nezahualcoyotl*. Mexico City: Librería de M. Porrúa.

Lockhart, James. 1991. Care, Ingenuity and Irresponsibility: The Bierhorst Edition of the *Cantares Mexicanos*. *Review in Anthropology* 16 (1–4): 119–32.

———. 1992. *The Nahuas after the Conquest*. Stanford, CA: Stanford University Press.

———. 1999. Double Mistaken Identity: Some Nahua Concepts in Postconquest Guise. In *Of Things of the Indies: Essays Old and New in Early Latin American History*, 98–119. Stanford, CA: Stanford University Press.

López-Austín, Alfredo. 1973. *Hombre-Dios: Religión y política en el mundo náhuatl*. Mexico City: UNAM.

———. 1994. *Tamoanchan y Tlalocan*. Mexico City: Fondo de Cultura Económica.

Lugo Pérez, Roque. 1996. *Nezahualcóyotl, el hacedor de todas las cosas*. Toluca: Instituto Mexiquense de Cultura.

Mapa Quinatzin. See Aubin 1886a.

Mapa Tlotzin. See Aubin 1886b.

Martínez, José Luis. 1996. *Nezahualcoyotl. Vida y Obra*. Mexico City: Fondo de Cultura Económica.

Martínez Chimal, Mauricio Alberto. 1997. *El rey bajo el florido*. Toluca: Instituto Mexiquense de Cultura.

Mascaró y Sosa, Pedro. 1972. *El emperador Nezahualcoyotl: Considerado como poeta elegiaco*. Mexico City: Gobierno del Estado de México.

Matrícula de tributos. 1997. Ed. Víctor Castillo Farreras. Mexico City: Secretaría de Hacienda y Crédito Público.

Mena, Tania. 2003. *Nezahualcóyotl*. Spain: Dastin, S. L.

Mendieta, Gerónimo de. 1971. *Historia eclesiástica indiana*. Mexico City: Editorial Porrúa.

Menguin, Ernst. 1952. Commentaire de *Codex Mexicanus*. *Journal de la Société des Americanistes* 41:387–498.

Mier, Servando Teresa de. 1946. *Memorias*. Ed. Antonio Castro Leal. Mexico City: Editorial Porrúa.

———. 1990. *Historia de la revolución de Nueva España*. Paris: Publications de la Sorbonne.

Mignolo, Walter. 1986. La lengua, la letra, el territorio o La crisis de los estudios literarios coloniales. *Dispositio* 11:137–60.

———.1989a. Colonial Situations, Geographical Discourses and Territorial Representations: Toward a Diatopical Understanding of Colonial Semiosis. *Dispositio* 14:93–140.

———. 1989b. Literacy and Colonization: The New World Experience. In *1492–1992: Re/Discovering Colonial Writing*, ed. René Jara and Nicholas Spadaccini, 51–96. Minneapolis, MN: Prisma Institute.

———. 1993a. Colonial and Postcolonial Discourse: Cultural Critique or Academic Colonialism. *Latin American Research Review* 28 (3): 120–34.

———. 1993b. Misunderstanding and Colonization: The Reconfiguration of Memory and Space. *South Atlantic Quarterly* 92 (2): 209–60.

Mohar B., Luz María. 2000. Los delitos y castigos entre Acolhuas y Mexicas. Comparación de dos documentos. In *Códices y documentos sobre México: Tercer Simposio Internacional*, coordinated by Constanza Vega Sosa, 227–42. Mexico City: Instituto Nacional de Antropología e Historia.

———. 2004. *Códice Mapa Quinatzin: Justicia y derechos humanos en el México antiguo*. Mexico City: Comisión Nacional de Derechos Humanos México.

Motolinia. *See* Benavente 1971.

Mundy, Barbara E. 2000. *The Mapping of New Spain: Indigenous Cartography and the Maps of the Relaciones Geográficas*. Chicago: University of Chicago Press.

Muñoz Camargo, Diego. 1986. *Historia de Tlaxcala*. Madrid: Historia 16.

Nicholson, Henry B. 1971. Religion in Pre-Hispanic Central Mexico. In *Handbook of Middle American Indians*. Vol. 10, *Archaeology of Northern Mesoamerica*, ed. Gordon F. Ekholm and Ignacio Bernal, 395–446. Austin: University of Texas Press.

———. 2001. *Topiltzin Quetzalcoatl: The Once and Future Lord of the Toltecs*. Boulder: University Press of Colorado.

———, and Eloise Quiñones Keber. 1983. *Art of Aztec Mexico: Treasures of Tenochtitlan*. Washington, D.C.: National Gallery of Art.

Offner, Jerome A. 1979. A Representation of the Extent and Structuring of the Empire of Techotlalatzin, Fourteenth Century Ruler of Texcoco. *Ethnohistory* 26 (3): 231–41.

———. 1983. *Law and Politics in Aztec Texcoco*. Cambridge: Cambridge University Press.

O'Gorman, Edmundo. 1971. Estudio analítico de los escritos históricos de Motolinía. In *Memoriales: Libro de las cosas de la Nueva España y de los naturales de ella*, by Toribio de Benavente. Mexico City: UNAM.

———. 1997. Estudio introductorio. In *Obras históricas*, by Alva Ixtlilxochitl. Ed. Edmundo O'Gorman. Mexico City: UNAM.

Orozco y Berra, Manuel. 1960. *Historia antigua y de la conquista de México*. 3 vols. Mexico City: Editorial Porrúa, S. A.

Pacheco, José Emilio. 1973. *Iras y no volverás*. Mexico City: Fondo de Cultura Económica.

Palomera, Esteban J. 1989. Introducción. In *Retórica cristiana*, by Diego Valadés. Mexico City: Fondo de Cultura Económica.

Parsons, Jeffrey. 1970. An Archeological Evaluation of the *Códice Xolotl*. *American Antiquity* 35:431–40.

———. 1971. *Prehistoric Settlement Patterns in the Texcoco Region, Mexico*. Memoirs of the Museum of Anthropology 3. Ann Arbor: University of Michigan.

Payas, Gertrudis. 2004. Translation in Historiography: The Garibay/León-Portilla Complex and the Making of a Pre-Hispanic Past. *Meta* 49 (3): 544–61.

Pesado, Joaquín. 1998. *Las Aztecas: Poesías tomadas de los antiguos cantares mexicanos*. Mexico City: Factoría Ediciones.

Phelan, J. L. 1960. Neo-Aztecism in the Eighteenth Century and the Genesis of Mexican Nationalism. In *Culture in History*, ed. Stanley Diamond, 760–70. New York: Columbia University Press.

Pomar, Juan Bautista. 1993. *Relación geográfica de Texcoco*. In *Poesía nahuatl*, vol. 1, ed. Angel María Garibay K., 149–219. Mexico City: UNAM.

Prem, Hanns J. 1992. Aztec Writing. In *The Handbook of Middle American Indians*. Supplement, vol. 5, *Epigraphy*, ed. Victoria Reifler Bricker, 53–69. Austin: University of Texas Press.

Prescott, William H. n.d. *History of the Conquest of Mexico*. Philadelphia, PA: J. B. Lippincott.

Pring-Mill, Robert. 1992. Cardenal's Treatment of Amerindian Cultures in Homenaje a los Indios Americanos. *Renaissance and Modern Studies* 35:52–74.

Proceso inquisitorial del cacique de Tetzcoco, don Carlos Ometochtzin, Chichimecatecotl. 1980. Ed. Miguel León-Portilla. Mexico City: Biblioteca Enciclopédica del Estado de México.

Quiñones Keber, Eloise. 1988. The Aztec Image of Topiltzin Quetzalcoatl. In *Smoke and Mist: Mesoamerican Studies in Memory of Thelma D. Sullivan*, ed. Kathryn Josser and Karin Dakin, 329–43. Oxford: BAR.

———, ed. 2002. *Representing Aztec Ritual Performance, Text, and Image in the Work of Sahagún*. Boulder: University Press of Colorado.

Rabasa, José. 1993. Writing and Evangelization in Sixteenth-Century Mexico. In *Early Images of the Americas: Transfer and Invention*, ed. Williams Jerry M. and Robert Earl Lewis, 65–92. Tucson: University of Arizona Press.

Ramírez, José Fernando. 2001. *Obras históricas*. Mexico City: UNAM.

Relaciones geográficas del siglo XVI: México. 1982–1988. Ed. René Acuña. 10 vols. Mexico City: UNAM.

Reyes García, Luis. 1993. Cantares Mexicanos: Approaching the Nahuatl Text. *Indiana Journal of Hispanic Literatures* 1 (2): 89–100.

Ricard, Robert. 1995. *La conquista espiritual de Mexico*. Mexico City: Fondo de Cultura Económica.

Robertson, Donald. 1994. *Mexican Manuscript Painting of the Early Colonial Period: The Metropolitan Schools*. Norman: University of Oklahoma Press.

Romances de los señores de la Nueva España. 1993. In *Poesía nahuatl*, vol. 1, ed. and trans. Angel María Garibay K., 1–101. Mexico City: UNAM.

Sahagún, Bernardino de. 1986. *Coloquios y doctrina cristiana*. Ed. and trans. Miguel León-Portilla. Mexico City: UNAM.

———. 1993. *Bernardino de Sahagún's Psalmodia Christiana (Christian Psalmody)*. Trans. Arthur J. O. Anderson. Salt Lake City: University of Utah Press.

———. 1997a. *Historia general de las cosas de Nueva España*. Ed. Angel María Garibay K. Mexico City: Editorial Porrúa.

———. 1997b. *Primeros memoriales*. Trans. Thelma D. Sullivan. Norman: University of Oklahoma Press.

Salville, Marshall H. 1925. *The Wood-Carver's Art in Ancient Mexico*. New York: Museum of the American Indian Heye Foundation.

Schroeder, Susan. 1997. Introduction. In *Codex Chimalpahin: Society and Politics in Mexico Tenochtitlan, Tlatelolco, Texcoco, Culhuacan, and Other Nahua Altepetl in Central Mexico*, ed. and trans. Arthur J. O. Anderson and Susan Schroeder, 3–13. Norman: University of Oklahoma Press.

Schwaller, John Frederick. 1999. Don Bartolomé de Alva, Nahuatl Scholar of the Seventeenth Century. In *A Guide to Confession Large and Small in the Mexican language,1634*, by don Bartolomé de Alva, ed. Barry D. Sell and John Frederick Schwaller with Lu Ann Homza, 3–15. Norman: University of Oklahoma Press.

Segala, Amos. 1990. *Literatura náhuatl: Fuentes, identidades, representaciones.* Trans. Mónica Manssur. Mexico City: Grijalbo.

Selva, Salomón de la. 1972. *Acolmixtli Nezahualcoyotl: Poema en tres tiempos clásicos.* Mexico City: Gobierno del Estado de México.

Sigüenza y Góngora, Carlos de. 1995. *Paraíso occidental.* Mexico City: Consejo Nacional para la Cultura y las Letras.

Smith, Michael E. 2003. *The Aztecs.* Oxford: Blackwell.

———, and Frances F. Berdan. 1996. Introduction. In *Aztec Imperial Strategies*, by Frances Berdan et al., 1–9. Washington, D.C.: Dumbarton Oaks Research Library and Collection.

Spitler, Susan. 1998. The *Mapa Tlotzin*: Preconquest History in Colonial Mexico. *Journal de la Societe des Americanistas* 84:71–81.

———. 2000. El equilbrio entre la veracidad histórica y el propósito en los códices de Texcoco. In *Códices y documentos sobre México: Tercer Simposio Internacional*, coordinated by Constanza Vega Sosa, 617–31. Mexico City: Instituto Nacional de Antropología e Historia.

Stresser-Péan, Guy. 1995. *El códice de Xicotepec, Estudio e interpretación.* Mexico City: Fondo de Cultura Económica.

Sullivan, Thelma D. 2003. *A Scattering of Jades: Stories, Poems, and Prayers of the Aztecs.* Trans. Thelma D. Sullivan, ed. T. J. Knab. Tucson: University of Arizona Press.

Thomas, Hugh. 1993. *Conquest: Montezuma, Cortés, and the Fall of Old Mexico.* New York: Touchstone.

Tira de la peregrinación. 1964. In *Antigüedades de México de México basadas en la recopilación de Lord Kingsborough*, vol. 2, 7–29. Mexico City: Secretaria de Hacienda y Crédito Público.

Tira de Tepechpan. 1978. Ed. Xavier Noguez. Mexico City: Biblioteca Enciclopédica del Estado de México.

Torquemada, Juan de. 1975. *Monarquía indiana.* 3 vols. Ed. Miguel León-Portilla. Mexico City: Porrúa.

Townsend, Richard F. 1992. *The Aztecs.* London: Thames and Hudson.

Vaillant, George C. 1953. *Aztecs of Mexico: Origin, Rise and Fall of the Aztec Nation.* New York: Doubleday.

Valadés, Diego. 1989. *Retórica cristiana.* Mexico City: Fondo de Cultura Económica.

Velazco, Salvador. 2003. *Visiones de Anáhuac: Reconstrucciones historiografías y etnicidades emergentes en el México colonial: Fernando de Alva Ixtlilxóchitl, Diego Muñoz Camargo y Hernando Alvarado Tezozomoc.* Guadalajara: Universidad de Guadalajara.

Vetancurt, Agustín de. 1971. *Teatro mexicano.* Mexico City: Editorial Porrúa.

Veytia, Mariano Fernández de Echeverría. 1944. *Historia antigua de México.* 2 vols. Mexico City: Editorial Leyenda. S. A.

Vigil, José María. 1957. *Nezahualcoyotl, el rey poeta.* Mexico City: Ediciones de Andrea.

Wood, Stephanie. 2003. *Transcending Conquest: Nahua Views of Spanish Colonial Mexico.* Norman: University of Oklahoma Press.

Zantwijk, Rudolph van. 1985. *The Aztec Arrangement.* Norman: University of Oklahoma Press.

Zorita, Alonso de. 1999. *Relación de la Nueva España.* Ed. Ethelia Ruiz Medrano, Wiebke Ahrndt, and José Mariano Leyva. Mexico City: Conaculta.

INDEX

Page numbers in italics indicate illustrations.

Acolhuacan. *See* Coatlichan
Acolman, 83–86, *85*
Alva Ixtlilxochitl, don Fernando de: Bierhorst on Triple Alliance mistranslations of, 106; Chavero on work of, 15; on Christianity in Texcoco, 65; *Códice Xolotl* misinterpreted by, 62–63, 80–81, 87, *88*; data collection sources of, 29–31, 243; family history of, 243; on Ixtlilxochitl, Cortés, and Nezahualcoyotl, 33–34; on Ixtlilxochitl, Cortés, destroying temple of Huitzilopochtli, 33; on Mexica and Colhuaque connection, 71; on Mexican Creoles, 8; Mexica sources of information for, 31–32; Mexica view of Nezahualcoyotl misinterpreted by, 32; Nahua ephemerality, *Cantares* compared to chronicles of, 177–78; Nahua poetry's ephemerality and, 173; Nahua song's ephemerality, Nezahualcoyotl and, 174–75; on Nezahualcoyotl and politics, 4–5; on Nezahualcoyotl compared to King David, 5; Nezahualcoyotl's modern image created by, 96; on Nezahualcoyotl saving Mexica from Azcapotzalco, 100–101; on Nezahualcoyotl's civilized religious practices, 72; on Nezahualcoyotl's Huitzilopochtli, Tlaloc temple, 205–6, 207; on Nezahualcoyotl's laws, 125, 127; on Nezahualcoyotl's leadership in Triple Alliance, 105, 116–17; on Nezahualcoyotl's life, 29; on Nezahualcoyotl's Nahua poetry, 131–32, 133, 250–51; on Nezahualcoyotl's prophet status, 178–79; on Nezahualcoyotl's Texcoca subject cities, 115–16; on Nezahualcoyotl's Texcoco government, 113; on Nezahualcoyotl's unknown god, 215; on Nezahualcoyotl's unknown god and Christianity, 199–200; on Nezahualcoyotl, Texcoco, and help from Mexica, 103; on power struggles of Quinatzin, 81–82; Quetzalcoatl–Saint Thomas myth and, 65; Quinatzin, Xolotl and confusion in texts of, 54, 61–62; on Texcoca connection to Toltecs, 67; on Texcoca councils, 118; on Texcoca inheritance of Toltec, Chichimec traditions, 50; on Texcoca laws, 120–25, 127; on Texcoca religion compared to Mexica, 201; on Texcoca royal descendants and poverty, 34–36; Texcoca supremacy exaggerated by, 85–86; on Texcoco history, 6, 28–29; Texcoco history chronicling and motives of, 32–33, 36; on Texcoco, Huehue Ixtlilxochitl in Tepanec-Acolhuacan war, 86–87; Texcoco sources of information for, 31; on Tezozomoc's distribution of Texcoco, 87, 90; on Topiltzin Quetzalcoatl and

Quetzalcoatl, 65–67; on Topiltzin Quetzalcoatl, Toltec relation to Texcoco, 64–65; Torquemada, Spanish sources of information for, 31; Torquemada's views compared to, 6; the Virgin of Guadalupe and, 242

Alvarado Tezozomoc, Fernando: on Mexica service to god, 181; on Mexica tribute distribution, 117–18; on Nezahualcoyotl, 43; on Nezahualcoyotl's relationship to Mexica politics, religion, 206, 208; on Texcoco, Mexica, and Chalco conquest, 225

Ancient Nahuatl Poetry (Brinton), 11

Annals of Cuauhtitlan (anonymous), 43; Nezahualcoyotl and human sacrifice in, 206

Axayacatzin, 146–47

Axoquentzin: Chalco defeated by, 224; Nezahualcoyotl's unknown god revealing victory of, 227

Azcapotzalco: Alva Ixtlilxochitl on Nezahualcoyotl saving Mexica from, 100–101; expansion of, 86; history of, 75–76

Aztec(s): *Cantares*, traditional religious longing of, 221; Cardenal on Nezahualcoyotl compared to, 235–39; Cardenal's portrayal of, 234; Christianity rejected by, 215–17; Christian priest's terminology confusion with, 211–13; Franciscans' view of, 2–3; Mexican revolution's impact on studies of, 242; Muñoz Camargo on Christianity rejected by, 216; Muñoz Camargo on Christianity, survival of tradition of, 218; sacrificial death in songs from, 185; Sahagún on Christianity rejected by, 216–17; Spanish friars' historical view of, 2; term of, 241, 253; Topiltzin Quetzalcoatl in texts of, 63; Valadés on Christianity for, 213–14; Valadés on gods of, 214. *See also* Mexica

Benaducci, Lorenzo Boturini, 8

Benavente, Toribio de, Fray, 2; data collected by, 20; on Mexica pictorial script types, 21–22; on Nahua song performance, 140; Nezahualcoyotl compared to King David by, 24; on Nezahualcoyotl's legal system, 24, 96, 122–23; pictorial scripts and indigenous informants aiding, 22–23; regional influence on sources of, 23–24; Texaca postconquest rulers and relations with, 24

bereavement song. *See* icnocuicatl

Berra, Manuel Orozco y, 10

Bierhorst, John, 15; on Alva Ixtlilxochitl's mistranslations of Triple Alliance, 106; on Nahua poetry authorship, 134–35, 148–49

Brinton, Daniel G., 11; Nahua poetry of Nezahualcoyotl, translations by Vigil and, 132

Brotherston, Gordon, 15; on legal system before Nezahualcoyotl, 124–25; on Nezahualcoyotl and icnocuicatl, 144–45; on Xolotl's empire, 57, 59

Brundage, Burr Cartwright, 13

Burkhart, Louise: on power relationship of Spanish friars and indigenous people, 21, 248–49; on Spanish friars' data collection methods, 20–21

Bustamante, Carlos María de, 10

cabecera-sujeto system: Spanish colonizers adopting, 38–39; Spanish colonizers in Tenochtitlan, Texcoca, Tlacopan and, 39

Campos, Rubén, 11–12

Cantares, 138–39; authorship, glossator's notes in, 147–48; Aztecs' traditional religious longing in, 221; Nahua ephemerality, chronicles of Alva Ixtlilxochitl, Torquemada and, 177–78; Nahua songs and ephemerality in, 176–77; Nahua songs and religious-militaristic themes in, 183–85

Cantares Mexicanos, 44

Cardenal, Ernesto, 16, 154; Aztecs portrayed as evil by, 234; on Cuacuauhtzin, 237; legacy of, 238–39; León-Portilla influencing, 236; Nahua poetry in work of, 233–44; on Nezahualcoyotl compared to Aztecs, 235–39; Nezahualcoyotl, Quetzalcoatl displayed as good by, 234; Nezahualcoyotl's misrepresentation by, 233; on Quetzalcoatl's peace and love, 234–35

Carrasco, Davíd, 70

Casas, Las, 3–4

Chalco: Alvarado Tezozomoc on Texcoco, Mexica and conquest of,

225; Axoquentzin defeating, 224; Chimalpahin on conquest of, 225; history of, 224–25; "La guerra de Chalco" on Nezahualcoyotl's defeat by, 224; Texcoco war with, 197–98. *See also* "La guerra de Chalco"

Chavero, Alfredo: on Alva Ixtlilxochitl's work, 15; on Mexica religious system compared to Texcoco, 208–9

Chichimec(s): Alva Ixtlilxochitl on Texcoco inheriting traditions from Toltecs and, 50; *Códice Xolotl*, battles over Colhuaque princesses of, 67, 68, 69; *Códice Xolotl* depicting Xolotl and leaders of, 59, 60; Texcoca historians, Toltec heritage, and favoring, 64; Toltec culture influencing, 91; Toltec history with, 49–50; Toltec marriages to, 67, 245

chichimecayaoyotl, 79, 81

Chimalpahin, 43–44; on Chalco conquest, 225

Christianity: Alva Ixtlilxochitl on Nezahualcoyotl's unknown god and, 199–200; Alva Ixtlilxochitl, Texcoco and, 65; Aztec priests' terminology confusion with, 211–13; Aztec rejection of, 215–17; Keber on Topiltzin Quetzalcoatl and, 64; Mendieta on Nezahualcoyotl, Nezahualpilli and arrival of, 195–97; Mexican Creoles' symbolism in, 8; Muñoz Camargo on Aztec rejection of, 216; Muñoz Camargo on Aztec tradition surviving, 218; Nahua song, Nezahualcoyotl's unknown god and god in, 210–11; Nahua song used by Spanish friars teaching, 149–50; Nezahualcoyotl and arrival of, 191; Nezahualcoyotl's image in, 193, 227–28; Ocelotl rejecting, 219; Ometochtzin Chichimecatecuhtli rejecting, 219; Sahagún on Aztec rejection of, 216–17; Sahagún on Nahua song threatening, 220; Spanish colonizers beliefs in, 2; Spanish friars comparing Quetzalcoatl to, 3; Texcoco and imposition of, 209; Texcoco, Nezahualcoyotl's religious skepticism, spread of, 197; Topiltzin Quetzalcoatl and, 72; Valadés on Aztecs and teaching of, 213–14

Clavijero, Francisco Javier, Father, 97

Coatlichan: history of, 76, 78; power of, 78, 80; Tepanec-Acolhuacan war and role of, 87; Texcoca power shifted from, 247; Texcoco and influence of, 82; Tezozomoc's control of, 90. *See also* Tepanec-Acolhuacan war

Codex Azcatitlan, 42–43

Codex Boturini, 42

Codex en Cruz, 202, 203

Codex Mendoza, 42; Mexica examples of misconduct and punishment in, 124–25; Mexica youth in school in, 99, 100

Codex Mexicanus, 42–43

Codex Telleriano-Remensis, 42–43

Códice Aubin, 42

Códice de Tepetlaoztoc, 57, 59

Códice Techialoyan García Granados, 59, 61

Códice Xolotl: Acolman during reign of Tezozomoc and Huehue Ixtlilxochitl in, 83–86, *85*; Alva Ixtlilxochitl misinterpreting, 62–63, 80–81, 87, *88*; Chichimec battles over Colhuaque princesses in, 67, 68, 69; importance of, 37–38; Nezahualcoyotl as heir to Huehue Ixtlilxochitl in, 87, *88*; Nezahualcoyotl seeing murder of Huehue Ixtlilxochitl in, 144; postcolonial issues addressed in, 39; Quinatzin welcoming Tlailotlaca in, 91, *93*; Quinatzin, Xolotl depicted in, *53*; Techotlalatzin welcoming immigrants in, 91, *94*; Tenacacaltzin's succession to Nopaltzin in, 62; Texcoca pictorial scripts, confusion, *Mapa Tlotzin*, *Mapa Quinatzin* and, 56; Texcoca supremacy depicted in, 40, 82; Tezozomoc's distribution of cities after Tepanec-Acolhuacan war in, 87, *89*; Xolotl and Chichimec leaders in, 59, *60*; Xolotl's arrival depicted in, *58*; Xolotl's empires according to, 56–57; Xolotl's reign in Tenayuca in, 75; Yacanex tribute to Huetzin in, 76, *77*; Yacanex warring with Huetzin in, 76, *78*, 79

Colhuaque: Alva Ixtlilxochitl on Mexica connection to, 71; *Códice Xolotl*, Chichimec battles over princesses of, 67, 68, 69; history of, 75; Huetzin conquering, 78; Topiltzin Quetzalcoatl and Mexica marriage to princesses of, 69

Coloquios y doctria cristiana (Sahagún), 211–12

Cortés, Hernán, 2

Crónica mexicana (Alvarado Tezozomoc), 43; on Mexica legal system, 123
Cuacuahpitzahuac, 76
Cuacuauhtzin, 237
Cuauhtitlan, 108, *109*
cuicani (singer-composer), 136
"Cuicapeuhcayotl": *Florentine Codex* and, 163; Nahua cosmogony in, 162–63; world of god promoted in, 168–69
cuicapicqui. *See* cuicani
cuicatl. *See* Nahua song
cuicatlan (song place), 136, 137

David (King): Alva Ixtlilxochitl comparing Nezahualcoyotl to, 5; Benavente comparing Nezahualcoyotl to, 24; Prescott comparing Nezahualcoyotl to, 97
Davies, Nigel: on Texcoca power and Quinatzin, 74; on Texcoco history, 15
del Castillo, Bernal Díaz, 2
Dibble, Charles, 57
Durán, Diego, Fray, 2; on Mexica social/political system, 119; on Mexica tribute distribution, 117–18; on Nahua poetry composition, 136; on Nahua song patronage, 145; on Nezahualcoyotl, 108; on Nezahualcoyotl and human sacrifice, 206; Quetzalcoatl interpreted by, 3

Florentine Codex (Sahagún): "Cuicapeuhcayotl" in, 163; ephemerality in, 180–81; Nezahualcoyotl depicted in, 42; Sahagún preparing, 41
Florescano, Enrique, 4
flower war. *See* xochiyaoyotl
Franciscan(s): Aztecs viewed by, 2–3; indigenous religion studied by, 27; Nezahualcoyotl's representation and motives of, 36–37

Garibay K., Angel María: on Itzcoatl, Mexica warlike tradition, 151–52, 249; Nahua studies of, 11–12, 248; on Nezahualcoyotl's authorship of Nahua poetry, 133–34; *Romances de los señores de la Nueva España* translated by León-Portilla and, 132–33
Gibson, Charles, 73–74, 245
Gillespie, Susan, 106
Glass, John B., 243–44

Haly, Richard, 137–38
historiography: Spanish friars impacting Mexico and, 20
History of the Conquest of Mexico (Prescott), 10
Huehue Ixtlilxochitl, 6; Alva Ixtlilxochitl on Tepanec-Acolhuacan war, Texcoco and, 86–87; *Códice Xolotl*, Acolman during reign of Tezozomoc and, 83–86, *85*; *Códice Xolotl*, Nezahualcoyotl as heir to, 87, *88*; *Códice Xolotl*, Nezahualcoyotl witnessing murder of, 144
huehuetl (upright drum), *169*; Nahua song and, 169–71
Huetzin: *Códice Xolotl*, tribute of Yacanex to, 76, *77*; *Códice Xolotl*, war of Yacanex with, 76, 78, *79*; Colhuaque conquered by, 78
Huitzilopochtli: Alva Ixtlilxochitl on Ixtlilxochitl, Cortés destroying temple of, 33; Alva Ixtlilxochitl on Nezahualcoyotl's temple to Tlaloc and, 205–6, *207*; *Codex en Cruz*, Nezahualcoyotl building temple to, 202, *203*; Pomar on Nezahualcoyotl's temple to Tlaloc and, 205; Tenochtitlan temple, Mexica style for, 202, 204, *204–5*

icnocuicatl: Brotherston on Nezahualcoyotl and, 144–45; Nahua poetry's function in, 165
in xochitl in cuicatl (Nahua song-poetry), 131; León-Portilla on, 163–64, 180; mission of, 164–65; purpose of, 172; war and sacrifice in, 183–89
Itzcoatl: Garibay K. on Mexica warlike tradition and, 151–52, 249; Nezahualcoyotl crowned by Texcoco and, *101*, 102
Ixtlilxochitl, Cortés: Alva Ixtlilxochitl on Nezahualcoyotl and, 33–34; Alva Ixtlilxochitl on temple of Huitzilopochtli destruction by, 33

Karttunen, Frances, 141
Keber, Eloise Quiñones: on Christianity and Topiltzin Quetzalcoatl, 64; on Mexica as heirs of Topiltzin Quetzalcoatl, 69
Krickerberg, Walter, 13

Lafaye, Jacques, 3
"La guerra de Chalco": on Nezahualcoyotl's defeat by Chalco, 224; Nezahualcoyotl's religious skepticism in, 197–98; Nezahualcoyotl's unknown god in, 198–99
Las Aztecas (Pesado), 10
Las Casas, Bartolomé de, Fray, 2
law(s): Alva Ixtlilxochitl on Nezahualcoyotl and, 125, 127; Alva Ixtlilxochitl on Texcoco and, 120–25, 127; *Mapa Quinatzin* on Texcoco and adultery in, 120, 121; *Mapa Quinatzin* on Texcoco and nobleman misconduct in, 121, 123; *Mapa Quinatzin* on Texcoco and robbery in, 120–21, 122
Leander, Birgitta, 154
legal system: Benavente on Nezahualcoyotl and, 24, 96, 122–23; Brotherston on Nezahualcoyotl and prior, 124–25; *Crónica mexicana* on Mexica and, 123; Pomar on Nezahualcoyotl and, 120; of Tenochtitlan, 123–24; Tenochtitlan compared to Texcoco on, 124–25, 127; Torquemada on Texcoco and, 123. *See also* law(s)
León-Portilla, Miguel: Cardenal influenced by, 236; Mexica, views of philosophers studied by, 154; on Nahua poetry, 13–14; on Nahua poetry origins, 133; on Nahua poetry's divine origin, 163; on Nahua poetry's ephemerality, 180–83; Nezahualcoyotl in books of, 14; on Nezahualcoyotl's authorship of Nahua poetry, 134; *Romances de los señores de la Nueva España* translated by Garibay K. and, 132–33; on Tlacaelel's reforms in Mexica, 152; on Tochihuitzin's philosophical differences with Mexica, 181–82; on Toltec heritage in Mexica, 152–53; on Toltecs, 70; on in xochitl in cuicatl, 163–64, 180
Lockhart, James, 141

Mapa Quinatzin: importance of, 37–38; Nezahualcoyotl's, Nezahualpilli's court and tributaries in, 114, 115; Nezahualcoyotl, Texcoco gathering artisans in, 103, 104; postcolonial issues addressed in, 39; Quinatzin depicted in, 51; Texcoca laws on adultery in, 120, 121; Texcoca laws on nobleman misconduct in, 121, 123; Texcoca laws on robbery in, 120–21, 122; Texcoca pictorial scripts, confusion, *Mapa Tlotzin*, *Códice Xolotl* and, 56; Texcoca supremacy depicted in, 39–40
Mapa Tlotzin: importance of, 37–38; postcolonial issues addressed in, 39; Quinatzin's stature in, 55; Texcoca pictorial scripts, confusion, *Mapa Quinatzin*, *Códice Xolotl* and, 56; Texcoca supremacy depicted in, 40; Tlotzin and Quinatzin depicted in, 52; Tlotzin influenced by Toltecs in, 91, 92
Martínez, José Luis, 153–54
Mendieta, Gerónimo de: on Nezahualcoyotl and religious skepticism, 24–26, 194–95; on Nezahualcoyotl, Nezahualpilli, and arrival of Christianity, 195–97
Mexica: Alva Ixtlilxochitl and information sources from, 31–32; Alva Ixtlilxochitl misinterpreting Nezahualcoyotl as viewed by, 32; Alva Ixtlilxochitl on Azcapotzalca and Nezahualcoyotl saving, 100–101; Alva Ixtlilxochitl on Colhuaque connection to, 71; Alva Ixtlilxochitl on Nezahualcoyotl and Texcoco helped by, 103; Alva Ixtlilxochitl on Texcoca religion compared to, 201; Alvarado Tezozomoc on Chalco conquest, Texcoco and, 225; Alvarado Tezozomoc on Nezahualcoyotl and politics, religion in, 206, 208; Alvarado Tezozomoc on service to god of, 181; Alvarado Tezozomoc on tribute distribution in, 117–18; Benavente on pictorial script types of natives in, 21–22; Chavero on Texcoca religious system compared to, 208–9; Chimalpahin on, 44; *Codex Mendoza*, misconduct and punishment examples of, 124–25; *Codex Mendoza*, schooling of youth in, 99, 100; cosmogony of city-states and, 159–60; *Crónica mexicana* on legal system of, 123; Durán on social/political system in, 119; Durán on tribute distribution in, 117–18; ephemerality in songs of, 182–83; Garibay K. on warlike tradition of Itzcoatl and, 151–52, 249; immigration of ethnic groups of, 156, 157; Keber on Topiltzin Quetzalcoatl and, 69; León-Portilla on Tlacaelel's reforms in, 152; León-Portilla on Tochihuitzin

differing philosophically with, 181–82; León-Portilla on Toltec heritage in, 152–53; León-Portilla's study of philosophers on, 154; Martínez on Nezahualcoyotl's Nahua poetry v. militaristic practices of, 153–54; Nahua poetry, xochiyaoyotl, and sacrificial death in, 187–89; Nahua worldview compared to, 155–56; Nezahualcoyotl compared to warrior kings of, 108, 113; Nezahualcoyotl crowned by, 101; Nezahualcoyotl in alphabetical texts of, 43–45; Nezahualcoyotl in pictorial scripts of, 42–43; Nezahualcoyotl joining in conquests with, 107–8; Nezahualcoyotl's coronation and motives of, 103–4; Nezahualcoyotl's relationship with, 43; Nezahualcoyotl's status amongst nobility of, 118; Nezahualcoyotl's worldview compared to rulers of, 154; Nezahualcoyotl, Texcoco helped by, 102–3; Pomar on human sacrifice of, 200; school system of, 246; separation of ethnic groups from, 156, 158; Tenochtitlan temple to Huitzilopochtli, style of, 202, 204, 204–5; Tepaneca influence on ruling system of, 119; Tepaneca war, Nezahualcoyotl contributing to, 99–100; Texcoca religious system compared to, 208–9; Texcoco center for tribute collection, war preparation in, 107; Texcoco similarities found by Pomar for, 154–55; tlacuiloque recording history of, 19; Topiltzin Quetzalcoatl and Colhuaque princesses married to, 69; Topiltzin Quetzalcoatl's importance to, 70–71; tribute distribution in, 117; Triple Alliance and warfare practices of, 125, 126, 127; Triple Alliance instituted by, 107; war and pleasure of, 185. *See also* Aztec(s)

Mexican Creole(s): Alva Ixtlilxochitl on, 8; Christianity and symbolism of, 8; heritage defended by, 9; identity formation of, 7; Nezahualcoyotl praised by, 9–10; politics of, 9; Torquemada on, 7–8; the Virgin of Guadalupe and, 8, 242

Mexico: civil wars in, 10; indigenous history rediscovery in, 11; Nezahualcoyotl's fame in, 16; Spanish friars impacting historiography of, 20; Spanish friars teaching alphabetical literacy in, 19–20

Mier, 10

Monarquía indiana (Torquemada), 31

Moreno, Jiménez, 57

Motolinia. *See* Benavente, Toribio de, Fray

Muñoz Camargo, Diego, don: on Aztec rejection of Christianity, 216; on Aztec tradition surviving Christianity, 218

Nahua: Alva Ixtlilxochitl, Torquemada, compared to *Cantares*, ephemerality of, 177–78; Campos's studies of, 11–12; colonial context for studies of, 229–30; "Cuicapeuhcayotl" and cosmogony of, 162–63; ephemerality in, 173–74; flower and cosmology of, 171; Garibay K.'s studies of, 11–12, 248; historical distortion with, 1; human sacrifice according to, 161; Mexica worldview compared to, 155–56; Nahua poetry and noble class of, 189; Nahua poetry exalting brotherhood of, 165–67; Nezahualcoyotl and religion of, 191; pictorial scripts importance to studies of, 230; Spanish friars understanding cosmogony of, 160–61; studies on, 11; war and sacrifice ideas of, 186–87. *See also* in xochitl in cuicatl; Nahua poetry; Nahua song(s)

Nahua poetry: Alva Ixtlilxochitl on Nezahualcoyotl and, 131–32, 133, 250–51; Alva Ixtlilxochitl, Torquemada, ephemerality in, 173; authorship, postconquest in, 148–50; authorship, preconquest in, 147; Bierhorst on authorship of, 134–35, 148–49; Brinton, Vigil, translations of Nezahualcoyotl and, 132; Cardenal's work referencing, 233–34; conquest influence on, 135; divine origin of, 163–64; Durán on composition of, 136; ephemerality's theme and geography of, 182–83; Garibay K. on Nezahualcoyotl's authorship of, 133–34; historical reconsiderations for, 15–17; icnocuicatl and function of, 165; indigenous cosmology reflected in, 162; individual authors challenged in, 134–36; individual authors identified in, 132–34; León-Portilla on, 13–14; León-Portilla on divine origin of, 163; León-Portilla on ephemerality in, 180–83; León-

Portilla on Nezahualcoyotl's authorship of, 134; León-Portilla on origins of, 133; Martínez on Mexica militaristic practices v. Nezahualcoyotl and, 153–54; Nahua brotherhood found in, 165–67; Nahua noble class and, 189; Nahua song structure and confusion with authorship of, 140–42; of Nezahualcoyotl, 10–12; Nezahualcoyotl, authorship and glossator's notes in, 142–45; Nezahualcoyotl, ephemerality in, 173, 179–80; Nezahualcoyotl promoting divine origin for, 167–69; Nezahualcoyotl's authorship considerations for, 141–42, 151; Nezahualcoyotl's chroniclers exaggerations on, 129–30; performance of, 136; performances, independent singers, 138–40; Pomar on Nezahualcoyotl and, 131; Torquemada on Nezahualcoyotl and, 132, 250–51; translation issues of, 129–30; xochiyaoyotl, Mexica sacrificial death and, 187–89. See also Nahua song(s)

Nahua song(s): Alva Ixtlilxochitl, Nezahualcoyotl, ephemerality in, 174–75; Axayacatzin and, 146–47; Benavente on performance of, 140; *Cantares* and ephemerality in, 176–77; *Cantares*, religious-militaristic theme in, 183–85; cuicatlan and, 136, *137*; Durán on patronage for, 145; glossator's notes and ownership of, 145–47; Haly on singer compared to composer in, 137–38; historical importance of, 231; huehuetl in, 169–71; Nahua poetry authorship confusion, structure of, 140–42; Nezahualcoyotl, colonial interpretation of, 221–24; Nezahualcoyotl's unknown god and names in, 209–10; Nezahualcoyotl's unknown god, Christianity's god in, 210–11; Nezahualcoyotl, war and flower death in, 185–87, 189; performance of, 136–37; purpose of, 172; Sahagún on Christianity threatened by, 220; Sahagún on training in, 140; Spanish friars teaching Christianity through, 149–50; Torquemada, Nezahualcoyotl, ephemerality in, 175–76, 250–51; world of god promoted in, 168–69; Xochipilli and, 170–71. See also cuicani; cuicatlan; icnocuicatl

Nahua song-poetry. *See* in xochitl in cuicatl

Nezahualcoyotl: Alva Ixtlilxochitl creating modern image of, 96; Alva Ixtlilxochitl misinterpreting Mexica view of, 32; Alva Ixtlilxochitl, Nahua song's ephemerality, and, 174–75; Alva Ixtlilxochitl on Christianity and unknown god of, 199–200; Alva Ixtlilxochitl on civilized religious practices of, 72; Alva Ixtlilxochitl on Huitzilopochtli, Tlaloc temple built by, 205–6, *207*; Alva Ixtlilxochitl on Ixtlilxochitl, Cortés, and, 33–34; Alva Ixtlilxochitl on King David compared to, 5; Alva Ixtlilxochitl on laws created by, 125, 127; Alva Ixtlilxochitl on life of, 29; Alva Ixtlilxochitl on Mexica helping Texcoco and, 103; Alva Ixtlilxochitl on Mexica saved from Azcapotzalco by, 100–101; Alva Ixtlilxochitl on Nahua poetry of, 131–32, 133, 250–51; Alva Ixtlilxochitl on politics of, 4–5; Alva Ixtlilxochitl on Texcoca government of, 113; Alva Ixtlilxochitl on Texcoca subject cities and, 115–16; Alva Ixtlilxochitl on Triple Alliance, leadership of, 105, 116–17; Alva Ixtlilxochitl on unknown god of, 215; Alva Ixtlilxochitl, Torquemada, prophecy of, 178–79; Alvarado Tezozomoc on, 43; Alvarado Tezozomoc on Mexica politics, religion and, 206, 208; *Annals of Cuauhtitlan*, human sacrifice and, 206; Axoquentzin revealed victorious by unknown god of, 227; Benavente comparing King David to, 24; Benavente on legal system of, 24, 96, 122–23; birth of, 97, *98*; Brotherston on icnocuicatl and, 144–45; Brotherston on legal system before, 124–25; Cardenal comparing Aztecs to, 235–39; Cardenal focusing on Quetzalcoatl and, 234; Cardenal's misrepresentation of, 233; childhood of, 97, *99*; Christianity in image of, 193, 227–28; Christianity in Texcoco aided by religious skepticism of, 197; Christianity's arrival and, 191; *Codex en Cruz*, Huitzilopochtli temple built by, 202, *203*; *Códice Xolotl*, heir of Huehue Ixtlilxochitl as, *87, 88*; *Códice Xolotl*, Huehue Ixtlilxochitl's murder witnessed by, *144*; colonial influence in study of, 230; conquests of, 40; Cuauhtitlan conquest of, 108, *109*; Durán on, 108; Durán on human sacrifice and, 206; *Florentine Codex* depicting, 42; Franciscan's motives and representation of, 36–37; Garibay K. on Nahua poetry authorship of, 133–34; historical reconsiderations for, 15–17; Itzcoatl, Texcoco crowning, *101*, 102; Krickerberg on, 13; "La guerra de Chalco" and religious skepticism of, 197–98; "La guerra de Chalco" and unknown god of, 198–99; "La guerra de Chalco" on Chalco defeat of, 224; legacy of, 1; León-Portilla on Nahua poetry authorship of, 134; León-Portilla's books on, 14; *Mapa Quinatzin*, artisans gathered in Texcoco by, 103, *104*; *Mapa Quinatzin*, court and tributaries of Nezahualpilli and, *114*, 115; Martínez on Mexica militaristic practices v. Nahua poetry of, 153–54; Mendieta on Christianity's arrival and, 195–97; Mendieta on religious skepticism of, 24–26, 194–95; Mexica alphabetical texts on, 43–45; Mexica conquests with, 107–8; Mexica crowning, 101; Mexica helping Texcoco and, 102–3; Mexica motives for crowning, 103–4; Mexican Creoles praising, 9–10; Mexica nobility and status of, 118; Mexica pictorial scripts on, 42–43; Mexica's relationship with, 43; Mexica warrior kings compared to, 108, 113; Mexica worldview compared to, 154; Mexico and fame of, 16; modern study of, 11; Nahua poetry authorship considerations for, 141–42, 151; Nahua poetry, Brinton, Vigil translations attributed to, 132; Nahua poetry, chronicler's exaggerations on influence of, 129–30; Nahua poetry, ephemerality described by, 173, 179–80; Nahua poetry, glossator's notes and authorship of, 142–45; Nahua poetry of, 10–12; Nahua poetry's divine origin promoted by, 167–69; Nahua religion and, 191; Nahua song, Christianity's god, unknown god of, 210–11; Nahua song, colonial context and, 221–24; Nahua song, names of unknown god of, 209–10; Nahua songs promoting war and flower death by, 185–87, 189; Olmos on religious skepticism of, 24–26; Pomar on Huitzilopochtli, Tlaloc temple built by, 205; Pomar on legal system of, 120; Pomar on Nahua poetry of, 131; Pomar on Texcoca religious reconstruction of, 201–2; Pomar on unknown god of, 214–15; Pomar's view of, 4, 28; Prescott comparing King David to, 97; Quetzalcoatl, Saint Thomas and, 8; religious skepticism and, 193–96; song books on, 44; Spanish friars' views of, 3–4; Tenochtitlan life of, 99; Tepaneca war with Mexica and help from, 99–100; Tetzcotzinco and worship of unknown god by, 225–26; Texcoca religion prior to, 201; Texcoco rebuilding and, 6; Texcoco, religious importance of, 228; Texcoco remodeled after Tenochtitlan by, 103; Torquemada, Nahua song's ephemerality and, 175–76, 250–51; Torquemada on, 5–6, 96–97; Torquemada on Nahua poetry of, 132, 250–51; Triple Alliance formed by, 105; Tulantzinco conquest of, 108, 110; Vaillant on legacy of, 12–13; Xicotepec conquest of, 108, 111–12

Nezahualpilli, 24; *Mapa Quinatzin*, court and tributaries of Nezahualcoyotl and, *114*, 115; Mendieta on Christianity's arrival and, 195–97; religious skepticism of, 195

Nopaltzin, 62

Ocelotl, Martín, 219

Offner, Jerome A., 13; on Texcoca power and Quinatzin, 73–74

O'Gorman, Edmundo, 29

Olmos, Andrés de, Fray, 2; data collected by, 20; data collection methods of, 25; on Nezahualcoyotl and religious skepticism, 24–26; Texcoca motives influencing information for, 26–27

Ometochtzin Chichimecatecuhtli, Carlos, don, 178–79; Christianity rejected by, 219

orphan song. *See* icnocuicatl

painter-scribes. *See* tlacuiloque
Parsons, Jeffrey, 82–83
Pesado, José Joaquín, 10
Phillip II (King), 27–28
pictorial scripts: Benavente aided by indigenous informants and, 22–23; Benavente on Mexica types of, 21–22; Glass on categorizing, 243–44; *Mapa Tlotzin, Mapa Quinatzin, Códice Xolotl*, Texcoco, confusion with,

56; Mexica and Nezahualcoyotl in, 42–43; Nahua studies, importance of, 230; Quinatzin depicted in Texcoco and, 50, 54; reliability for study of, 230; Texcoca cultural development in, 90–91; Texcoca power exaggerated in, 74; Texcoca royal descendants commissioning, 41; Texcoco and currently available, 37; Toltecs and, 49–50; types of, 38. See also *Codex Azcatitlan*; *Codex Boturini*; *Codex Mendoza*; *Codex Mexicanus*; *Codex Telleriano-Remensis*; *Códice Aubin*; *Códice Xolotl*; *Mapa Quinatzin*; *Mapa Tlotzin*; *Tira de peregrinación*

poetry. See Nahua poetry

Pomar, Juan Bautista: data collection sources of, 27–28, 243; on Mexica and human sacrifice, 200; on Nezahualcoyotl, 4, 28; on Nezahualcoyotl's Huitzilopochtli, Tlaloc temple, 205; on Nezahualcoyotl's legal system, 120; on Nezahualcoyotl's Nahua poetry, 131; on Nezahualcoyotl's religious reconstruction of Texcoco, 201–2; on Nezahualcoyotl's unknown god, 214–15; songs found by, 44; Texcoca and Mexica similarities found in, 154–55; on Texcoca councils, 118; on Tezozomoc's empire, 119

Prescott, William H., 10; on Nezahualcoyotl compared to King David, 97

Quetzalcoatl: Alva Ixtlilxochitl, myth of Saint Thomas and, 65; Alva Ixtlilxochitl on Topiltzin Quetzalcoatl and, 65–67; Cardenal focusing on Nezahualcoyotl and, 234; Cardenal on peace and love of, 234–35; Durán interpreting, 3; Nezahualcoyotl following Saint Thomas and, 8; Sigüenza y Góngora's work on Saint Thomas and, 8; Spanish friars comparing Christianity to, 3

Quinatzin: Alva Ixtlilxochitl on power struggles of, 81–82; Alva Ixtlilxochitl's textual discrepancy with Xolotl and, 54, 61–62; *Códice Xolotl* depicting Xolotl and, 53; *Códice Xolotl*, Tlailotlaca welcomed by, 91, 93; Davies on Texcoca power and, 74; Gibson on Texcoca power and, 73–74, 245; *Mapa Quinatzin* depicting, 51; *Mapa Tlotzin* and stature of, 55; *Mapa Tlotzin* depicting Tlotzin and, 52; Offner on Texcoca power and, 73–74; Texcoca pictorial scripts and, 50, 54

Quince poetas del mundo nahuatl (León-Portilla), 134

Relación geográfica de Texcoco (Pomar), 27

Romances de los señores de la Nueva España, 44; Garibay K., León-Portilla translations of, 132–33

Sahagún, Bernardino de, Fray, 2; on Aztec rejection of Christianity, 216–17; *Florentine Codex* prepared by, 41; on Nahua song's threat to Christianity, 220; on Nahua song training, 140; works on, 244

Sigüenza y Góngora, Carlos de, don, 8

singer-composer. See cuicani

song place. See cuicatlan

Sousa, Pedro Mascaró y, 11

Spanish colonizers: cabecera-sujeto system adopted by, 38–39; cabecera-sujeto system in Tenochtitlan, Texcoca, Tlacopan and, 39; Christianity and beliefs of, 2

Spanish friar(s): Aztec history viewed by, 2; Burkhart on data collection methods of, 20–21; Burkhart on power relationship of indigenous people and, 21, 248–49; historiography of Mexico impacted by, 20; on Indian origins, 241; indigenous religion eradication by, 27; Mexico taught alphabetical literacy by, 19–20; Nahua cosmogony understood by, 160–61; Nahua song, Christianity taught by, 149–50; Nezahualcoyotl and views of, 3–4; Quetzalcoatl compared to Christianity by, 3. See also Benavente, Toribio de, Fray; Durán, Diego, Fray; Franciscan(s); Las Casas, Bartolomé de, Fray; Olmos, Andrés de, Fray; Sahagún, Bernardino de, Fray

Techotlalatzin: *Códice Xolotl*, immigrants welcomed by, 91, 94; marriage of, 83; Texcoco and reign of, 74; Texcoco conquest of Xaltocan by, 83, 84

Tenacacaltzin, 62

Tenayuca, 75

Tenochtitlan: Huitzilopochtli temple, Mexica style, built in, 202, 204, 204–5; legal system of, 123–24; Nezahualcoyotl's life in, 99; Nezahualcoyotl's Texcoco remodeled after, 103; Spanish colonizers' version of cabecera-sujeto system in, 39; Texcoca legal system compared to, 124–25, 127; Texcoco compared to, 97, 118–19; Triple Alliance leadership of, 106

Tepaneca: Mexica ruling system origins in, 119; Nezahualcoyotl contributing to Mexica in war with, 99–100. *See also* Tepanec-Acolhuacan war

Tepanec-Acolhuacan war, *80*; Alva Ixtlilxochitl on Texcoco, Huehue Ixtlilxochitl and, 86–87; beginnings of, 86; Coatlichan role in, 87; *Códice Xolotl*, Tezozomoc's distribution of cities after, 87, *89*; Texcoco immigrants rebelling in, 95

Tetzcotzinco: human sacrifice in, 226–27; Nezahualcoyotl worshiping unknown god in, 225–26; Valadés on, 226–27

Texcoco: Acolhuacan terminology of, 245; Alva Ixtlilxochitl and information sources from, 31; Alva Ixtlilxochitl, Christianity in, 65; Alva Ixtlilxochitl, exaggerated supremacy of, 85–86; Alva Ixtlilxochitl on Chichimec, Toltec traditions inherited by, 50; Alva Ixtlilxochitl on councils in, 118; Alva Ixtlilxochitl on history of, 6, 28–29; Alva Ixtlilxochitl on laws in, 120–25, 127; Alva Ixtlilxochitl on Mexica helping Nezahualcoyotl and, 103; Alva Ixtlilxochitl on Mexica religion compared to, 201; Alva Ixtlilxochitl on Nezahualcoyotl's government in, 113; Alva Ixtlilxochitl on Nezahualcoyotl's subject cities of, 115–16; Alva Ixtlilxochitl on poverty of royal descendants in, 34–36; Alva Ixtlilxochitl on Tepanec-Acolhuacan war, Huehue Ixtlilxochitl and, 86–87; Alva Ixtlilxochitl on Tezozomoc's distribution of cities in, 87, 90; Alva Ixtlilxochitl on Toltec connection to, 67; Alva Ixtlilxochitl on Topiltzin Quetzalcoatl, Toltecs relation to, 64–65; Alva Ixtlilxochitl's motives for chronicling history of, 32–33, 36; Alvarado Tezozomoc on Chalco conquest, Mexica and, 225; Benavente's relations with post conquest rulers of, 24; Chalco war with, 197–98; Chavero on Mexica religious system compared to, 208–9; Chichimec heritage favored over Toltec for historians form, 64; Christianity forced upon, 209; Clavijero on, 97; Coatlichan influence on, 82; Coatlichan power shifted to, 247; *Códice Xolotl* depicting supremacy of, 40, 82; councils in, 118; Davies on history of, 15; Davies on Quinatzin and power of, 74; dynasty and history of, 6; Gibson on Quinatzin and power of, 73–74, 245; historical reconsiderations for, 15; immigration influencing, 91, 93, 95; late formation of, 82–83; legal system of Tenochtitlan compared to, 124–25, 127; *Mapa Quinatzin* depicting supremacy of, 39–40; *Mapa Quinatzin*, laws on adultery of, *120*, *121*; *Mapa Quinatzin*, laws on nobleman misconduct of, *121*, *123*; *Mapa Quinatzin*, laws on robbery of, 120–21, *122*; *Mapa Quinatzin*, Nezahualcoyotl gathering artisans in, 103, *104*; *Mapa Tlotzin* depicting supremacy of, 40; *Mapa Tlotzin*, *Mapa Quinatzin*, *Códice Xolotl*, confusion, pictorial scripts of, 56; Mexica empire, tribute collection, war preparation in, 107; Mexica helping Nezahualcoyotl and, 102–3; Mexica religious system compared to, 208–9; Mexica similarities found by Pomar on, 154–55; Nezahualcoyotl crowned by Itzcoatl and, *101*, *102*; Nezahualcoyotl, prior religion in, 201; Nezahualcoyotl rebuilding, 6; Nezahualcoyotl's religious importance to, 228; Nezahualcoyotl's religious skepticism, Christianity popularized in, 197; Offner on Quinatzin and power of, 73–74; Olmos's data and motives of citizens in, 26–27; pictorial scripts commissioned by royal descendants of, 41; pictorial scripts, cultural development of, 90–91; pictorial scripts depicting Quinatzin from, 50, 54; pictorial scripts exaggerating power of, 74; pictorial scripts from, 37; Pomar on councils in, 118; Pomar on Nezahualcoyotl's religious reconstruction of, 201–2; Spanish colonizers version of cabecera-sujeto system in, 39; Techotlalatzin's reign in, 74; Tenochtitlan compared to, 97, 118–19;

Tenochtitlan for Nezahualcoyotl's remodeling, 103; Tepanec-Acolhuacan war and rebellion of immigrants in, 95; Torquemada on history of, 6; Torquemada on legal system of, 123; Xaltocan conquest by Techotlalatzin and, 83, *84*; Xolotl's exclusivity to, 59, 73

Tezozomoc, 76; Alva Ixtlilxochitl on Texcoca city distribution by, 87, 90; Coatlichan taken over by, 90; *Códice Xolotl*, Acolman during reign of Huehue Ixtlilxochitl and, 83–86, *85*; *Códice Xolotl*, after Tepanec-Acolhuacan war, city distribution of, 87, *89*; Pomar on empire of, 119

Thomas (Saint): Alva Ixtlilxochitl, myth of Quetzalcoatl and, 65; Nezahualcoyotl following Quetzalcoatl and, 8; Sigüenza y Góngora's work on Quetzalcoatl and, 8

Tira de peregrinación, 42

Tlacaelel, 152

Tlacopan, 39

tlacuiloque (painter-scribes), 19

Tlailotlaca: *Códice Xolotl*, Quinatzin welcoming, 91, *93*; painting skills of, 91, *92*, *93*

Tlaloc: Alva Ixtlilxochitl on Nezahualcoyotl's temple to Huitzilopochtli and, 205–6, *207*; Pomar on Nezahualcoyotl's temple to Huitzilopochtli and, 205

Tlotzin: *Mapa Tlotzin* depicting Quinatzin and, 52; *Mapa Tlotzin*, Toltec influence on, 91, *92*

Tochihuitzin, 181–82

Toltec(s): Alva Ixtlilxochitl on Texcoca connection to, 67; Alva Ixtlilxochitl on Texcoco inheriting traditions from Chichimecs and, 50; Alva Ixtlilxochitl on Texcoco relation to Topiltzin Quetzalcoatl and, 64–65; Chichimec culture influenced by, 91; Chichimec history with, 49–50; Chichimec marriages to, 67, 245; León-Portilla on essence of, 70; León-Portilla on Mexica and heritage of, 152–53; *Mapa Tlotzin*, Tlotzin influenced by, 91, *92*; pictorial scripts of, 49–50; Texcoca historians, Chichimec heritage favored over, 64; Xolotl inherited by, 50

Topiltzin Quetzalcoatl: Alva Ixtlilxochitl on Quetzalcoatl and, 65–67; Alva Ixtlilxochitl on Texcoco relation to Toltecs and, 64–65; Aztec texts and, 63; Christianity and, 72; Keber on Christianity and, 64; Keber on Mexica as heirs to, 69; Mexica and importance of, 70–71; Mexica marriage to Colhuaque princesses, connecting, 69; names of, 64

Torquemada, Juan de: Alva Ixtlilxochitl's Spanish sources of information including, 31; Alva Ixtlilxochitl's views compared to, 6; on Mexican Creoles, 7–8; Nahua ephemerality, *Cantares* compared to chronicles of, 177–78; Nahua poetry's ephemerality and, 173; Nahua song's ephemerality, Nezahualcoyotl and, 175–76, 250–51; on Nezahualcoyotl, 5–6, 96–97; on Nezahualcoyotl's Nahua poetry, 132, 250–51; on Nezahualcoyotl's prophet status, 178–79; on Texcoca legal system, 123; on Texcoco history, 6

Trece poetas del mundo nahuatl (León-Portilla), 134

Triple Alliance: Alva Ixtlilxochitl on Nezahualcoyotl's leadership of, 105, 116–17; Bierhorst on Alva Ixtlilxochitl's mistranslations regarding, 106; Gillespie on timing of, 106; Mexica instituting, 107; Mexica warfare practices with, 125, 126, 127; Nezahualcoyotl forming, 105; Tenochtitlan leadership of, 106

Tulantzinco, 108, *110*

upright drum. See huehuetl

Vaillant, George C., 12–13

Valadés, Diego, Fray, 214; on Aztec gods, 214; on Christianity for Aztecs, 213–14; on Tetzcotzinco, 226–27

Vigil, José María, 10; Nahua poetry of Nezahualcoyotl, translations by Brinton and, 132

Virgin of Guadalupe: Alva Ixtlilxochitl and, 242; Mexican Creoles and, 8, 242; Mier developing tradition of, 10

Xaltocan, 83, *84*

Xicotepec, 108, *111–12*

Xochipilli, 170–71

xochiyaoyotl (flower war), 187–89
Xolotl, 6; Alva Ixtlilxochitl's textual discrepancy with Quinatzin and, 54, 61–62; Brotherston on empire of, 57, 59; city-state founder claims on, 62–63; *Códice Techialoyan García Granados* depicting empire of, 59, 61; *Códice Xolotl* and empires of, 56–57; *Códice Xolotl* depicting arrival of, 58; *Códice Xolotl* depicting Chichimec leaders and, 59, 60; *Códice Xolotl* depicting Quinatzin and, 53; *Códice Xolotl*, Tenayuca during reign of, 75; Dibble on empire of, 57; Moreno on empire of, 57; Texcoca exclusivity to, 59, 73; Toltec inheritance of, 50

Yacanex: *Códice Xolotl*, Huetzin and tribute of, 76, 77; *Códice Xolotl*, Huetzin and war with, 76, 78, 79